Basic Marketing

Basic Marketing

Principles and Practice

Second Edition

TOM CANNON

Professor of Business Studies, Stirling University

HOLT, RINEHART AND WINSTON
London · New York · Sydney · Toronto

Holt, Rinehart and Winston Ltd: 1 St Anne's Road,
Eastbourne, East Sussex BN21 3UN

First published 1980
Second edition 1986

Phototypesetting by Georgia Origination, Liverpool
Printed and bound in Great Britain by Mackays of Chatham Ltd

British Library Cataloguing in Publication Data
Cannon, Tom
    Basic marketing: principles and practice.—
    2nd ed.
    1. Marketing
    I. Title
    658.8   HF5415
ISBN 0-03-910603-9

Last digit is print no: 9 8 7 6 5 4 3 2 1

Contents

To Robin and Rowan

Preface to the Second Edition

Few events are more certain to bring those of us involved in the systematic study of marketing more forcibly face to face with the pace of change in today's markets than the act of revising a marketing text. The first edition was published as recently as 1980. In the short period since then, major transformations have occurred. Even the process of preparing and writing the book has been affected.

The first edition was prepared in the time-honoured way of writing by hand, long and complex plans and preparing numerous drafts. Perhaps the most onerous aspect of the entire exercise was the detailed cataloguing of references and indexation of material. New technologies have transformed this process. Instead of the notebooks there are floppy discs. Instead of the box files of reference material, there is a data base package. Instead of the trusty pen and note pads there are the IBM PC and word processing software. The process of change will continue once the manuscript has been accepted. The copy on disc can be used for setting the type. Proofs can be checked with virtually no recourse to hard copy. It would seem that the only piece of old technology left in the process is the author. Whether that remains the case will not emerge until the next edition.

In the conclusion to the last edition a number of developing trends were explored. Among these were the deepening recession in the industrial, developed world, and the impact of this on the developing world. The influence that this would have on the changing relationships between the North and South was discussed. It has become clear that the phenomena described have had a profound effect on marketing management's behaviour. There is already a discernible trend for forward-sighted firms to reject the allure of 'easy' savings through cutting budgets in order to reap longer term benefits instead. Those firms which sustained or increased their marketing commitment have overcome the worst effects of the recession. Many have sustained the levels of growth seen in generally happier times. Corporations such as ASEAN, CBS, IBM, Hewlett–Packard, Kodak, Michelin, Shell, P & G, Exxon and DuPont, among the multinationals, have sustained their success through continuing commitment to marketing. In the UK the same phenomenon has been seen in companies like Sainsbury's, Marks & Spencer, United Biscuits, Guinness, Coats-Patons and Vickers. In Britain and North America there have been vivid illustrations of ailing giants regaining some of their former strength through embracing the marketing concept in depth. In the car industry the clearest examples are perhaps Jaguar and Chrysler. Both were brought back from the brink by Chief Executives who convinced their workforces that marketing started on the shop floor. New challengers have achieved much of their growth through the same process of integrating marketing into the total corporate effort. All shared two characteristics:

1. A commitment to marketing.
2. A determination to sustain this despite difficult trading conditions.

Quoting from the final chapter of the previous edition, in a description of the success of Vickers during the 'Great Depression' of the 1880s, it is becoming increasingly apparent that those firms which have coped best with the recession of the 1980s have:

'innovated a way through it, exploiting rather than mislaying their technical strengths . . . (they have) turned about to face the ill winds, and, to beat through them [have] simply "created a new business" '.

Innovation, allied to a willingness to use new technologies to meet customers' needs, has proved (predictably) to be the best guarantee of success in harsh economic circumstances. Many firms are better geared to achieve sustained, healthy and profitable growth after the recession than they were after the sustained growth of the 1950s and 1960s.

The structural changes discussed in the earlier edition have continued. The move to an increasingly service-orientated economy in Britain and Europe has been maintained. This process has been fuelled in part by the employment crisis. However, a far more important factor has been the rapid increase in the added value per employee from the increasing application of new technologies in manufacturing, retailing and services.

The scale and pace of this was not predicted. It is remarkable that there is not a single reference to Information Technology in the first edition (an omission shared with all five major UK and US marketing textbooks published in the same year). Industrial robots, personal computers and viewdata systems are phenomena which have emerged over the last five years to transform key areas of industry and commerce. All are dedicated, at least in part, to increasing productivity, and from this increase sustain ever greater added value. Companies today can talk of doubling their total turnover with no increases in their workforce. These new technologies are extending their impact far beyond the traditionally 'automated' areas of primary industries and manufacturing. Automated warehousing, electronic point of sale, bar coding, etc., are transforming retailing. Electronic funds transfer and cash dispensers have led to more changes in the face of banking over the last half decade than have occurred over the last half century. The change potential of the emerging technologies for home shopping and/or banking are still not fully understood. The next generation, with its 'expert systems,' biotechnologies, etc., seems certain to see even more dramatic, discontinuous change.

The restructuring of the world economic order highlighted in the preface to the first edition has continued. New economic powers such as Korea and other 'Pacific Basin' nations are joining Japan and West Germany in their challenge to US dominance of the Western industrial world. However, the strength and resilience of the US economy has been demonstrated by the remarkable growth rates achieved during 1982, 1983, and 1984. Although it is being suggested that this cannot be sustained during the mid-to-late 1980s, it would be rash to underestimate the innovativeness and resilience of the North American industrial machine. Interestingly, part of this growth has been achieved because US industrialists have recognised the need to adapt their strategies to changing and varied economic circumstances.

The last few years have seen some progress in the emergence of European and other non-North American marketing ideas. This has been shown most vividly in work in five areas: industrial marketing, especially the study of networking; innovation; services; small business; and cultural aspects of marketing. The awareness of the need to re-examine ideas, assumptions and applications in the light of changed circumstances and different conditions has stimulated new approaches and creative thinking.

The central role of the state has continued to be a major feature of non-US economies. However, in Britain and elsewhere political changes have led to attempts to 'roll back' the direct involvement of government, at least through state-owned corporations. The sale of major state-owned corporations, such as British Telecom, is a deliberate attempt to restructure relationships in this field. Despite these individual programmes of action, other developments are prompting counter-balancing pressure. The increasing size and complexity of the European Community is a notable illustration of this.

Inter-European trade is providing the focus for the international development of many of Britain's leading firms. The current strength of the US dollar has had relatively little influence on the growing Europeanism of UK industry. However, it has done a great deal to worsen the endemic Balance of Payments deficits of the US. International and export trade continues to play a far more significant role in the corporate activities of European firms than their North American rivals. The institutional and organisational structures which have emerged to handle these activities continue to be a major asset. More recently there has been a recognition of the strength of alternative models for handling international trade. A number of countries especially in the Pacific Basin are building up their systems based on the Japanese 'trading house' approach. Experiments along similar lines are even occurring in the US and Europe.

The overall approach of the text has remained constant. The heterogeneous nature of domestic and international markets and marketing is highlighted. Traditional forms and approaches are re-examined in this context. The diversity of different trading situations—industrial/consumer, producer/intermediary/service marketing, as well as the non-profit organisation—is examined with the emphasis on integrating traditional ideas with specialist needs. These are reviewed in terms of the complex conditions facing firms; both large and small, in recession, in developing economies and markets and in state-controlled countries, as well as in the advanced, free trade markets of Western Europe, North America and the Pacific Basin.

It is in this context that more general global phenomena will be explored. These include consumerism and environmentalism in addition to more industry-specific factors such as new technologies, fashions and trading conditions. All take forms which owe as much to the culture and tradition of their home market as to any wider movements. This can be seen in the contrasting approach to consumerism in North America and the UK. In the former, the pressure has been for political and legislative action to enforce compliance. In the latter, the focus tends to be on administrative action to encourage voluntary agreements and consensus. It would be a mistake to understate the value of either approach in its own context.

The most significant changes in the content and structure reflect changes in markets and developments in thinking, which have gathered pace over the last few years. The profound impact of the new Information Technologies is examined in depth. This is explored both in terms of its impact on markets and on marketing management. The additional discussion on marketing information systems reflects the growing significance of effective information management and control systems on operational efficiency.

Perhaps even more important, in terms of its long term impact on marketing thought, is the new emphasis on marketing strategies and planning. The greatly expanded discussion of this area reflects the growing recognition of the central importance of strategy in modern marketing. A number of major research studies have pointed out the critical significance of sustained commitment to strategic marketing. In many of the most successful firms, strategic decisions are the foundation of all subsequent policies and actions. It is no exaggeration to say that the *reality* of marketing is increasingly synonymous with strategic marketing.

Throughout the text, further cases have been included and a large number of illustrations have been added to both new and existing sections. These are designed to highlight key areas besides drawing out the relevance of the material under discussion to marketing in the real world. The fundamental assumption of this text is that the interplay of academic and practical knowledge holds the key to understanding and applying marketing.

This book has been written to incorporate syllabus developments in the Institute of Marketing's Diploma in Marketing, the CAM certificate and the continued evolution of business education under the auspices of the Business and Technical Education Council (BTEC) in England and in Scotland through SCOT VEC (Vocational Education Council and SCOT VEC, post-1984). The growing importance of undergraduate education in marketing is reflected in the approach of the text. Marketing education has emerged as a powerful force in shaping the quality of marketing management. The contributions of those who participated in the survey I conducted in 1984 for ESRC have built up a picture of the nature and shape of education in this area.

Any book as wide-ranging as this depends on the support and encouragement of many people. Numerous colleagues have played a part, especially John Dawson, Sue Shaw, Bob Clarke and Mike Willis at Stirling. Particular thanks are due to colleagues at other institutions who have commented on the text: the many members of the Marketing Education Group who have advised and assisted me over the years have been of great help. One of the most valuable experiences for any academic is the open and frank discussion of ideas with friends at other universities and colleges. My role as external examiner at Sunderland, Sheffield, Thames and City of London Polytechnics, besides City, Lancaster and Strathclyde Universities and Glasgow College of Technology over the last five years, has given me access to a remarkable amount of expertise, experience and insight. My publishers continue to show patience above and beyond the call of duty. Their efforts—especially of the Publisher, Stephen White, my editor, Simon Lake; and their colleagues, notably in sales and marketing—continue to be enormously encouraging. Fran, my wife, has made the greatest individual contribution. Beyond these there are the many students and businessmen who have forced me to think, review and revise the ideas contained here. To all my thanks are due. Although they have played their part, the final responsibility for the book in its final form must lie solely with the author.

1

Marketing Today

The economic difficulties of the last decade have posed many challenges to modern management. The slowing-down of growth—allied to growing unemployment, high interest rates, rapid technological change and new aggressive rivals—has forced firms seeking to survive and prosper to find ways of achieving maximum effectiveness in the use of their resources. It has been a time when firms have been obliged to scrutinise every area of expenditure to minimise waste and maximise returns. Management practice has been under the microscope to an extent unmatched in the past. Out of this re-examination have emerged certain clear conclusions, and perhaps the clearest and most specific of these has been the recognition of the central role of marketing in determining the health of a firm and through this the entire economy.

In their book *In Search of Excellence*, Peters and Waterman[1] point out that the 60 most successful US firms over the last 25 years shared a dedication to marketing as the key strategic discipline in their firm. All these firms were dedicated to that most important of marketing propositions, that the key to success lies in 'keeping close to the customer'.

> IBM's marketing vice-President, Francis G. (Buck) Rodgers, says, 'It's a shame that, in so many companies, whenever you get good service it's an exception. Not so at the excellent companies. Everyone gets into the act. Many of the innovative companies got their best ideas from customers. That comes from listening intently and regularly.
>
> T. J. Peters & R. J. Waterman[1]

This notion of marketing as the powerhouse for industrial growth and the prime mechanism for sustaining growth and prosperity is not new. Sir Winston Churchill pointed out that:

> (Advertising) sets before man the goal of a better life, better clothing, better food for himself and his family. It spurs individual exertion and greater production.

It is a point of view increasingly adopted by firms of different types in many situations. A recent survey of Small Businessmen found that this was the area of greatest concern to owner managers and the field in which they felt they needed most help in developing skills. Anyone visiting the rapidly growing countries of the Pacific Basin, such as Korea, Hong Kong and Singapore, will find successful industrialists who see marketing as the foundation upon which their growth will be based.[2]

This 'beneficial' view of marketing is not held universally. Vance Packard[3] has claimed that:

> The people of the United States are in a sense becoming a nation on a tiger. They must learn to consume more and more, or, they are warned, their magnificent, economic machine may turn and devour them.

This debate on the benefits and costs of marketing continues with vigour today. Some critics have argued that marketing can lead to conspicuous, even unnecessary consumption, while others have argued that the commercial benefits are far less than claimed. Mant[4] suggested that many of the gains from marketing are less considerable than often suggested. However, it is clear that many of the most successful firms remain convinced that their commitment to marketing has been critical to their achievement. L. G. Morgan of Yardley has claimed that:

> The lack of real understanding in this country of the concept and techniques of modern marketing is very largely responsible for our present industry failures and low growth record.

Much of the debate would appear to be based on very different understandings of the marketing concept. There is the view adopted by Drucker[5] that:

> Marketing is so basic that it cannot be considered a separate function . . . It is the view of business seen from the point of view of its final result, that is, from the customer's point of view.

There is the alternative perspective which sees marketing as synonymous with selling. It is clear that the alternatives lie between the *reality* of marketing and its *appearance*. The former focuses on the comprehensive consumer perspective of the marketing-orientated firm, while the latter confuses certain of its techniques with the substance.[6] (Dixon, 1983).

DEFINITIONS

There are numerous alternative definitions of marketing. Frequently the particular form reflects the preoccupations of individual authors. Most have certain basic features in common, especially the notion of looking at the firm from the point of view of the customer or striving to ensure mutual profitability from the marketing exchange. Other definitions place their emphasis on the essentially managerial nature of marketing. This can be seen in the definition put forward by the Institute of Marketing (UK):

> Marketing is the management process which identifies, anticipates and supplies customer requirements efficiently and profitably.

A complementary but more directive approach is adopted by Stapleton;[7]

> (It is) fundamental policy-forming activity devoted to selecting and developing suitable products for sale—promoting and distributing these products in a manner providing the optimal return on capital employed.

Recently, increasing numbers of writers have emphasised this *process* perspective on marketing, i.e. defining it in terms of the process of moving goods from concept to consumption in the most effective way (from both the customer's and the supplier's point of view). Runyon[8] captured this nicely with his description of it as:

> The performance of business activities that direct the flow of goods and services from producers to consumers.

Even this falls short of the all-encompassing approach, increasingly used to bring out the wider applicability of marketing. Kotler[9] provides one of the widest definitions:

> Marketing is human activity directed at satisfying needs and wants through exchange processes.

This extends the approach to include many forms of non-commercial transaction, including education, community activities and most social and political processes. It is a perspective which has generated considerable controversy, not least because it has challenged many traditional assumptions about roles and responsibilities in a variety of exchange-based situations.

All these definitions share certain basic characteristics which can be seen as the major elements of modern marketing:

1. *It is operational.* Managers must take action to achieve results. Benefits will not emerge from a passive attitude to the exchange.
2. *It is customer-orientated.* It makes the firm look outside itself, focusing on the needs or requirements of the customer. Its effectiveness lies in finding solutions to the challenges posed by these demands.
3. *It emphasises mutuality of benefit.* The exchanges work and persist because it is in the best interests of both parties to continue. Through this, both prosper; i.e., needs are satisfied by goods and services which the supplier will continue to supply because he profits, and which are bought because the customer's benefits exceed his costs.

The long-term nature of most healthy marketing relationships is central to this approach. The satisfaction of both parties is dependent on the excess of return over investment. That encourages both to return. For the firm it will mean a good return on the prices charged. For the individual or organisational customer it means greater satisfaction than could be achieved by refraining from the exchange. In simple diagrammatic terms, it changes relationships from the supplier push view to the mutual support view.

The supplier push view of transactions:

Supplier $\longrightarrow$ *Customer*

This approach emphasises the directive role of the producer in determining the nature of the product and service, then persuading the customer to purchase.

The interaction view of transactions:

Supplier $\longleftrightarrow$ *Customer*

This approach highlights the importance of the customer as the originator. It brings out the importance of an exchange of ideas, and at the same time suggests the scope for increased profits to the firm in supplying potential purchasers with items they need/want.

The idea that production should be based on the goal of satisfying customer needs lies at the root of the 'marketing revolution' in management thinking. The impact of this has been world-wide. Even in eastern Europe it is now acknowledged that:

> It is the specific responsibility of . . . (identified industries) to use their entire scientific and technological potential to produce consumer goods which directly serve to satisfy the needs of the people.
>
> > Report of the Central Committee
> > of the 9th Congress of the
> > Socialist Unity Party of the
> > German Democratic Republic.

Similar statements have emerged over the last few years from leaders as diverse as Mrs Thatcher and Deng Xiaoping. The notion that it is both popular and effective to seek to give the customer what he or she wants is becoming generally recognised. It is a long way from the famous story of customer relations in eastern Europe:

> The traveller had lost his luggage on a flight to Sofia. Faced with no immediate prospect of its return he went to a giant department store. The process of purchasing goods involves choosing the item at the counter, paying at a separate till, returning with a ticket and obtaining the goods. Having completed this (laborious) process the traveller returned to where there were stacked piles of shorts behind the counter. There were 3 stacks of white—one half sold—then three stacks of blue.
>
> The assistant took his ticket, turned to the stack of white shorts and handed them over. The customer pointed out that he wanted blue shorts.

'When we have sold the white shorts...then we will sell the blue ones,' replied the assistant....

Production-dominated transactions can too easily produce this response to customer needs. Organisations adopting this approach are finding it increasingly difficult to survive and thrive in today's competitive marketplace. Hammarkvist and others have taken this notion further by exploring the notion of markets as networks.[10]

THE CONCEPT IN THE FIRM

The concept—that firms exist, first and foremost, to satisfy customers' needs—has not been accommodated easily into the operations of many organisations. The notions that, 'Firms exist to make profits', 'Firms exist to create/protect jobs' or simply that 'Firms exist to survive' have been put forward as equally plausible purposes.

The real power of the marketing concept lies in two areas:

1. The reality of the marketplace, i.e. the alternative purposes stated above can only be achieved healthily, in the long term, if the customer is satisfied with the offering.
2. The recognition that, restating the comments above, firms will achieve their targets most effectively if they see that the closer they are to understanding the customer, the more likely they are to gain maximum profits, hence save/create jobs and survive.

Marketing is not the philanthropic pursuit it is sometimes seen as in other areas of corporate activity: it is the formal recognition that a firm can adopt two routes to business development. It can produce something to fit its convenience, and in a competitive environment face the massive risk and uphill struggle of pushing this on an unwilling

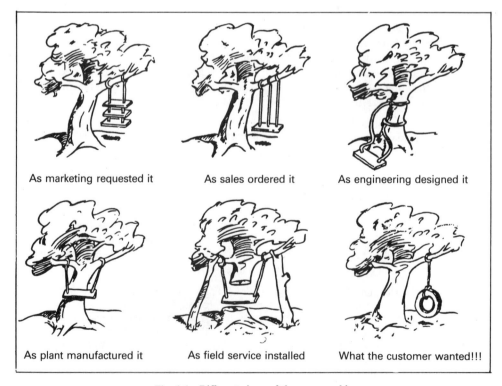

As marketing requested it   As sales ordered it   As engineering designed it

As plant manufactured it   As field service installed   What the customer wanted!!!

Fig. 1.1   Different views of the same problem.

public: or it can use its knowledge of buyer needs to design, develop or modify its offerings to meet those needs. Acceptance and returns will be earned in proportion to their understanding of these needs and ability to provide an offering to match them.

The power of marketing lies in linking the firm's capabilities to the needs of customers.

MARKETING THROUGHOUT THE FIRM

Effectiveness in marketing is something that affects everyone in a firm. The response of the marketplace will determine their prosperity. This means that marketing is not an activity that can be confined solely to those specialists working in the marketing function; everyone is involved. The shopfloor workers with their impact on quality; the first level supervisors who are of critical importance to output levels; the engineers who must design

Fig. 1.2 Stirling Futureworld.

quality and reliability into the product; receptionists and administrative staff who deal with customer queries, all are part of the marketing team. It's a point of view close to the heart of John Egan, the Chief Executive of Jaguar Cars. He has brought the firm 'back from the brink' by espousing and communicating this concept. Jaguar have come back from being a fading British marque to an international success story.

The notion of a total corporate commitment to marketing is extending beyond the private sector into public agencies. One of the most imaginative of these is the Stirling Futureworld programme. This was promoted as hard to the local authority's staff as it was to prospective visitors and investors.

> 'We recognised that if our own staff did not believe in it and work to make it a reality, we could not expect anyone else to support it.'
>
> Ian Wyles
> Convenor

THE EMERGENCE OF MARKETING

Although Stirling is one of the most ancient towns in Britain, marketing in some form pre-dates even its long history. Ancient Greece, Phoenicia, the Dravidian Thalassocracy of Southern India, the Mayan Empire of South America and, more recently, medieval Japan, Flanders and Venice, based their prosperity on their skill as traders. This turned on their success in understanding the needs of their customers and finding ways of supplying them. Even the Vikings were more traders than pirates. The lack of production skills and the limited output so limited trade that the primary area of activity was in luxury goods.

Fig. 1.3 'Sail the Flag'.

The most basic form of trade—barter—has existed ever since man was capable of generating a surplus of some crop or other. In agricultural societies it provided the scope for exchanging specific surpluses for other desired commodities. The market or fayre evolved to facilitate these exchanges. In fact the process of making the exchange system more efficient has characterised the progress of civilisation throughout the world.

Although the local market provided the venue for most barter trading, periods of stability saw the emergence of much wider networks of trade; primarily in luxuries, but occasionally in far more basic items. The trade in corn between Egypt and Italy in the time of the Roman Empire exemplifies this. Egypt was the breadbasket of the Empire during most of its later history. All the great empires provided an environment in which trade could prosper.

During the Middle Ages in Europe, traders, pedlars and hawkers provided not only goods but the only continuous form of communication available to most of the population. The most famous of these traders, Marco Polo, provided insights into cultures in countries far beyond his native Italy, besides dealing in the luxuries demanded from these places for his Florentine customers. Despite times during which this trade reached very large proportions, there were three major constraints, all directly associated with the exchange process itself:

1. The recurrent problem of obtaining acceptable currencies, hence the importance of imperial currencies and precious metals.
2. The limited production available in crafts-based industries.
3. The lack of a stable and secure environment.

The emergence of the great nations of Europe, their exploitation of the mineral and material resources of the New World and, most importantly, the Industrial Revolution—first in Britain, later in the USA, Germany, France and the other nations of Europe—solved these problems.

The impact of industrialisation

	Output *1785*	*Output* *1850*
Cotton	40 Mil. yds	2,025 Mil. yds
Coal	9 Mil. tons	49 Mil. tons
Iron	0.2 Mil. tons	2.25 Mil. tons

The figures above illustrate the dramatic growth in industrial output in the early part of the last century, a pattern of growth which continues to drive economies forward.

The internal national stability which occurred in the nation states provided an environment in which the merchant could trade and reasonably expect to benefit from his efforts in the long term. In Britain it led initially to the era of Mercantilism. Great trading companies such as the Muscovy, Levant, East India and Hudson Bay Companies grew up. A number of today's major trading organisations can trace their descent from these, such as Jardines (Hong Kong) Ltd, who have links with the East India Company. These companies were not a purely British phenomenon. The struggle between the merchants of the Hanseatic League from Germany and the Merchant Adventurers from England has many parallels today.

It was the Industrial Revolution, however, which provided the real breakthrough. The productive power of machines and industry could start to make headway against the shortages which had held back trade and economic progress.

Despite that, for much of the history of the post-industrial world, demand for most goods and commodities has far exceeded supply. Under these circumstances, the primary interest of manufacturers has been to increase their production efficiencies, normally striving to sell more at lower prices. This gives rise to what is generally described as *the production orientation*, i.e. the notion that customers will buy well-made products, produced in sufficient quantities to meet demand, with little or no marketing effort needed to achieve adequate sales.

The firm with this point of view focuses its attention on making a technically superior product, applying appropriate technologies to maximise output and operating efficiently. It is assumed that the customer will respond favourably to these actions. A comment by Sir George Harriman of BMC in 1959 epitomises this:

> 'We know what the customer wants; it's our job to make it at the right cost and then the public can be counted on to buy it.'

During periods of shortage and limited competition this *product orientation* can play a major role in corporate success. It provides the drive and commitment to achieve the increases in output necessary to sustain demand. However, a price has to be paid for success in this. Increases in output become linked to the emergence of competitors.

Many technical breakthroughs make it easier for competitors to enter markets. This leads to an excess of supply over (immediate) demand. A new perspective on business development is needed. The prime focus becomes the 'product push' or 'hard sell'. The overall corporate approach to the product remains virtually unchanged. Priority is still given to seeking increased efficiencies in manufacture or processing, generally with the aim of cutting prices. The firm still knows best; the problem now is to make sure the customer appreciates this.

This is the period in which a *sales orientation* dominates the firm. This is based on the notion that the volume needed to sustain the output generated by the new production efficiencies can only be achieved through heavyweight promotional efforts. It is even now the route taken by the firm which seeks to buy its way out of trouble. Often a decaying product, being overtaken by technology or consumer tastes, will be heavily promoted to extend its life. The most vivid recent example of this was in the 'price war' launched by British Leyland in the late 1970s to extend the life of its older models while waiting for the introduction of the new range of cars (such as the Metro and the Maestro). A similar phenomenon is seen when a new product which is falling short of its targets has large additional sums invested in its promotion in an attempt to make it 'lift off'. This pattern of behaviour can be seen in the numerous sales and discounting initiatives taken by manufacturers and retailers.

This approach can be seen in industrial markets equally often. A particular form occurs among the firms supplying a declining customer industry. Here a pattern can emerge where component and other suppliers fiercely compete on price to hold on to their share of a contracting 'cake'. Unfortunately this can lead to increasingly unprofitable business as the customers are frequently struggling to keep their costs down to stave off their own decline. The *declining market volume illusion* can mean that these suppliers meet the same fate as their customers, despite the fact that their own technology or process retains considerable potential for expansion. This was seen in the attempts of smaller firms supplying the shipbuilding industry who ignored the decline in that market. They persisted in spending increasing amounts on advertising sales and promotion as the market disappeared in front of them. There are signs that the same phenomenon is occurring in the automotive products industry. Ultimately, such firms find that the cost of the sustained uphill struggle against underlying market forces undermines the production process they are attempting to sustain. It drains scarce resources from research and development (R & D), quality control and process innovations, the cornerstones of the firm's future.

The strength of the *marketing approach* lies in the different view taken of the firm and its links with its customers and the wider market. Buyer need becomes the starting point for the production process. The firm defines its offering, products, services and the means of getting these to their actual and prospective customers on this basis. This approach has two unique and distinctive strengths:

1. It recognises that companies will only remain fit, healthy and competitive if they meet customer needs.

2.   It highlights the very real difference between the need and the means of satisfying it.

It is very easy for a firm, or even an industry, to convince itself that the products or services it offers are indispensable. In reality, all are just ways of meeting needs. As such they can be replaced by alternative offerings which meet these needs more effectively or are more suitable at a particular time or place. Among the best examples of this have been:

1.   The railway industry's failure to respond to the transport revolution of the 1940s and 1950s.
2.   The inability of any of the producers of duplicators or copiers to move into word processing successfully.
3.   The dismal showing of virtually all the traditional consumer electronics firms in the personal or home computer market.
4.   The failure of the movie industry to move into television.

In these and many other situations, established firms, even whole industries, with many apparent advantages have 'missed the boat' and seen their market disappear, contract or fail to grow while related or substitute products expand to meet customer needs.

This approach was the basis of one of the greatest marketing turn-arounds in the modern business environment. General Motors destroyed the overwhelming dominance of Ford. Their success highlights both the strength of the approach and the complex challenges it poses to management.

General Motors succeeded despite the (apparent) overwhelming strength of Ford in the US car market. In 1926 Ford sold 1 550 000 cars to General Motors' 750 000. The position was reversed within four years through two interrelated policies:*

1.   *The understanding of needs.* General Motors' analysis of the US car market showed that it was made up of many different customer groups. These had some needs in common but more importantly had many diverse requirements in a car. The basic common need identified and successfully exploited by Ford was the need to get from A to B. This was surrounded by many other needs which would determine purchase once the basic need was met. A simple extension was to get from A to B *in comfort*, even if this meant paying more.

   The success of General Motors did not lie merely in identifying this need or using a clever, related catchphrase in their advertising. The key to their success lay in the delivery of an augmented product which satisfied this need. Their production staff capitalised on a breakthrough in steel technology which helped them to stamp out steel into a body shell. The result was a car with real protection from the elements and dramatic improvements in comfort. Their efforts were complemented by promotional and distribution policies geared to fully realise the benefits of this total offering.

2.   *The match of need with total product proposition.* The firm realised that the product—the car itself—met only certain of the customers' needs. The name and the image had to be right if the customer was to be happy to show it to his family, friends and colleagues. The price had to be presented in ways which made it possible for the purchaser to afford it. This involved different models, trade-ins, financial services, etc. The customer needed the car to be available in the right place for him/her to view it, try it and once bought have it serviced. General Motors were among the first firms to draw together this *marketing mix*. This is the combination of *product, promotion, price* and *place*. It delivers to the customer the right product, with the right reputation, at the right price, in the right place.[11]

---

* Discussion in this section is based primarily on the description provided by Alfred P. Sloan in his detailed and insightful review of the events of the period in *My Years with General Motors*.[12]

Fig. 1.4   The 4 P's satisfy the 4 O's.

It is the fit of offering with the needs of the customer or customer group which determines success. Thomas[11] (1983) brings out the importance of linking this notion to marketing planning if it is to be effective.

Marketing highlights the extent to which products and services are bought by different groups to satisfy different needs. Different items can be purchased to meet the same need. For example, the need for esteem could be met through a prestigious car (Rolls-Royce)/type of credit card (American Express Platinum Card)/accounts in a particular store (Harrods)/holiday location (Ayers Rock).

Marketing demonstrates how immediate utility must be supplemented with information, image, price, physical distribution, availability, service and other facilities if customer satisfaction, repeat purchase and long-term market strength are to be achieved. For example, Fujitsu's personal computer might be able to match the IBM PC's ability to process data, but Fujitsu's lack of technical information, inability to match the quality image, shortage of outlets, lack of product availability, inadequate software and poor service support meant it failed to meet the total needs of customers and hence was uncompetitive, at least in 1985.

The emphasis on integrating these complex, dynamic and diverse forces takes the marketing concept beyond the traditional economic perspective of *supply and demand*. However, understanding the basics of this fundamental concept remains central to an appreciation of the underlying forces of the marketplace.

SUPPLY AND DEMAND*

For the economist the interplay between demand and supply underlies the entire concept of the market. Demand is the quantity of a product that people will buy at any one time for a given price. Supply is the quantity of a product that producers will provide at any one time for a given price. It is generally assumed that the demand curve is downward sloping: as prices go up, demand goes down. Similarly, it is assumed that the supply curve is upward sloping: as prices go up, supply goes up. From these two propositions the process by which prices and quantities are determined can be described graphically (Figure 1.5).

Given the assumptions mentioned above, equilibrium or balance will be achieved when the amount which customers are willing to purchase at a given price matches the amount producers are willing to sell at the same price. When there is excessive demand, prices will be forced up until there are fewer customers at the new price. When there is excessive supply, prices will drop until producers leave the market or curtail supplies until a new equilibrium is reached.

Like all theories, this is based on a series of assumptions:

1.   Perfect competition: a standard commodity is provided by numerous sellers to numerous buyers.

---

* For a full and lucid description of the basics of supply and demand read Dolan, *Basic Economics*, Chap. 3[13] or an equivalent economics text.

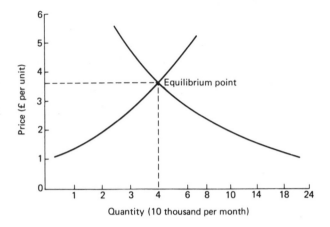

Fig. 1.5 How supply and demand determine price.

2. Perfect information: all buyers and sellers have at their disposal all the information that they need to judge the offers of other parties.
3. Ease of access and exit: buyers and sellers can enter the market at little cost and withdraw equally easily.
4. Economic man: prospective buyers actively seek to maximise the utility of each purchase.

Although this may describe the conditions which prevailed at the great commodity auctions such as the Liverpool Cotton Exchange, it bears relatively little resemblance to the real situation facing managers in the modern industrial environment.

Massive capital investments, the skills and expertise of buyers and sellers, the mass consumer markets and the highly specialised requirements of certain buyers have created a complex and highly differentiated market to contrast with the simple and undifferentiated market of perfect competition. It has been in the interest of both customers and suppliers to identify clearly their requirements and, on occasion, to use their market power to achieve them. For example, Marks and Spencer set high standards to their suppliers and use their buying power to ensure that their requirements are met; and Ford, Talbot and Leyland retain the power to withdraw their franchise from dealers who fail to maintain standards of service and business performance. At the same time the environment may be so complex that the time and effort involved in embarking on a full comparative evaluation of all alternatives would not be justified, even if the prospective buyer could fully evaluate the variables.

On a weekly shopping trip for a family over forty different lines may be purchased. Ideally, 'economic man' would consider: the alternative outlets, say five supermarkets; the alternative producers, perhaps four for each line; the alternative brands, perhaps three from each producer; and the five or six variables on which they are judged. This would involve analysing over 14000 pieces of information, a task well within the capacity of a mini-computer, but hardly the average shopper. Instead, most people build up a stock of experience, attitudes and loyalties, using these to simplify their buying (Figure 1.6).

Despite this, there are dangers in taking too complacent an attitude to the questions economists ask about the operating of the marketing system. Imperfections do exist, and it is in the interest of both producers and customers that the powerful analytical tools developed by economists are applied to this area. At the same time, the cross-fertilisation of ideas which has proved to be so fruitful in the past should not be hampered by entrenched positions.

TABLE 1 Mushroom light bulbs: 60 watt at 240 volts

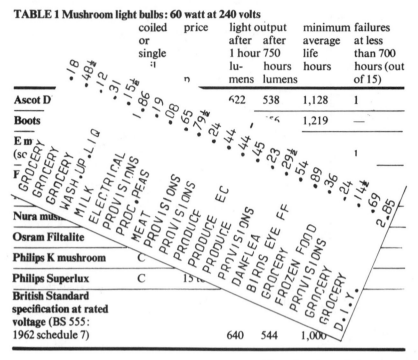

	coiled or single	price	light output after 1 hour lumens	after 750 hours lumens	minimum average life hours	failures at less than 700 hours (out of 15)
Ascot D			622	538	1,128	1
Boots					1,219	—
E m (sc						1
F						
Nura mus						
Osram Filtalite						
Philips K mushroom	C					
Philips Superlux	C	15				
British Standard specification at rated voltage (BS 555: 1962 schedule 7)			640	544	1,000	

Fig. 1.6   Data for decision? An illustration of the customer's problem of coping with the range of variables for each product (here light bulbs) and the number of items purchased on each shopping trip.

WHO ARE OUR CUSTOMERS?

The preceding discussion made a number of assumptions about the firm's knowledge of its customers, their location, nature and likely purchase behaviour. Often this level of awareness does not exist or there are fundamental misconceptions about key facts. Companies frequently assume that:

1. All customers are the same.
2. They are equally important.
3. They seek similar satisfactions from the product/service.
4. That customers and consumers are the same.

Often these are not true. The same product can be bought by a very wide range of people with nothing more in common than this particular action. This is sometimes reflected in the very different levels of relative importance. The 80:20 rule is central to much modern marketing thinking. It highlights the differences in relative importance between customers. Frequently, 80 per cent of the firm's output is purchased by 20 per cent of customers. These provided the bedrock for the firm's prosperity. Failure to recognise this can mean that the 80 per cent of customers who generate 20 per cent of demand can get vastly disproportionate attention. This is frequently to the disadvantage of key accounts. This phenomenon is called the *Pareto effect*. Reid (1985)[14] brings out the problems firms have in implementing strategies even when they are established.

   The same product can mean very different things to its many buyers. A car can be a means of getting from A to B, a status symbol, an employee perk, and many other things. Understanding this is vital if the design, its presentation, pricing and service support are to appeal to potential purchasers. Apparently minor slips can be fatal. A British firm launched its product into the market in Dubai with promotional material in Arabic, failing to realise that 90 per cent of the population originate from Pakistan, India, Iran or elsewhere. Simmons, the US bed manufacturer, made an even more basic error with the launch into the Japanese market. They failed to realise that most Japanese sleep on 'futons', a type of floor mat, and had no interest in Western type beds. Even the eight salesmen they recruited had never slept on a bed! Time also can have a profound effect as the tour operators Thomson's found when they were obliged to drop their 'Thomson's Gaytours' range of package holidays.[10]

Frequently, mistakes are made because the firm assumes that the individual making the purchase decision and the user are the same. The housewife may do most of the shopping but the tastes and wishes of the whole family will influence her. In industrial markets the 'buyer's' ability to exercise discretion varies considerably between firms and across different items.

Few illusions are more dangerous to the marketing-orientated firm than the illusion that it 'knows' its customers, unless that 'knowledge' is backed by hard evidence, regularly and systematically up-dated.

IN SEARCH OF EXCELLENCE

In their book, Peters and Waterman[1] give numerous illustrations of the commitment of the most successful US firms to understanding their customers and keeping close to their changing attitudes and tastes. There was the case of the Hewlett-Packard development engineer:

> Damn! Here was an HP engineer behaving as enthusiastically as any salesman you'd ever want to see.

The same phenomenon can be seen in the best European, Asian and Australasian companies.

Charles Forte constantly seeks for customer insights from his managers and staff. Bruce Putello of the Bank of Scotland regularly examines ways of building client feedback into the bank's operations. Bob Reid of Shell places customer feedback at the centre of the firm's operations.

The values they espouse can be illustrated by the following comment:

> Working with users will help us respond to their needs.
>
> An Wang
> Wang Laboratories

This notion of partnership is central to the success of virtually all the most successful firms. It is an approach that pays off. A study of the innovation process by E. Von Hipple and J. Utterback[15] found, in the words of Peters and Waterman:[1]

> Of eleven major innovations, ALL came from users. Of sixty-six major improvements 85% came from users and of eighty-three minor improvements 66% came from users.

THE KNOWLEDGE REVOLUTION

It is no coincidence that the list of sixty 'excellent' firms identified by Peters and Waterman was dominated by knowledge-based high-technology companies. There is growing consciousness that the changes in economic and industrial systems currently taking place are part of a far wider process of change. This has been described as the 'knowledge revolution', and is a change which could prove to be as profound as the Industrial Revolution of the last century. During this process of change, the successful application of *knowledge* through products, services and the full range of offerings will determine the success, even the survival of companies in all sectors of industry and commerce. Although the most overt symbol of the application of knowledge will lie in the use of scientific and engineering knowledge to produce novel solutions to product needs and services, the key to success will lie elsewhere. The programme of research conducted at the Science Policy Research Unit (SPRU) has clearly demonstrated that the key to commercial success lies in combining engineering or technical innovation with understanding of the marketplace and the customer. Piercy[16] takes this a step further by suggesting that 'information processing' is the newest marketing mix element.

ETHICS AND RELATED ISSUES

The history of marketing has been characterised by extensive discussion of the ethical and moral issues raised by the actions of firms seeking to understand and respond to the needs of customers. The market power which emerges from success in both these areas has been seen as conferring a potential for exploitation, a challenge to others without the resources (or will) to achieve this, even a threat to certain forms of freedom. These are issues which the marketing man must understand and answer in a responsible way. Traditionally, much of the discussion has been focused on the role of advertising; this is discussed at length in Chapter 19. More recently the actions of corporations operating in the less sophisticated developing countries have been challenged. The rise of consumerism is reviewed in Chapter 24. Debate on these issues has given rise to serious challenges to modern marketing thought and practice.

However, there is another side to the debate. Understanding leads far more often to positive action. This might be as clearly beneficial as the Volvo research into car safety. It might be very long term, such as the study of computer-assisted learning techniques of the physically and mentally disabled. It will frequently pose challenges to companies who fail to meet effectively the needs of their clients until obliged to by more responsive competitors. However, that is the key to progress. On the wider issue of freedom, market power does exist but critics should never lose sight of the fact that:

> The international trade which led to the disappearance of the feudal and signorial regimes, by replacing serfdom by individual liberty, opened the way to freedom of thought.
>
> Jacques Pirenne
> *Tides of*
> *History*[17]

This notion of responsibility is taking a number of forms today. In North America, two per cent Clubs exist, in which corporations pledge to give that proportion of their pre-tax profits to their community. In Britain 'Business in the Community' ('Scottish Business in the Community' in Scotland) is adopting a similar philosophy. Leading companies including Pilkingtons Glass, United Biscuits, Shell, Marks and Spencer, IBM, Barclays Bank and the Midland Bank are committing themselves to programmes of affirmative action to tackle the problems of their communities across the UK. Conscientious management is accepting the responsibilities that market power involves.

A GLOBAL CONCEPT

The underlying strength of the marketing approach to business can be seen in the way in which it has been adopted across much of the world. It has been most clearly adopted and perhaps most fully accepted in the US. Over the last two decades practitioners and academics in Europe and the Far East have taken up this orientation with such enthusiasm

US Firms		Non-US	
1.	Rockwells; B-1B Bomber	1.	Canon LBP-CX; Laser Printer
2.	Anheuser-Busch; LA Beer	2.	Boots; Ibuprofen
3.	IBM; PC AT	3.	Tonka; Gobots
4.	Apple; Macintosh	4.	USUAG-SSIH; Swatch
5.	Merrell Dow; Nicorette	5.	L'Oreal; Hold Styling Mousse

Fig. 1.7 The *Fortune* products of the year—1984.

and skill that the US position is now challenged. In the US market, an increasing proportion of the most successful new products are from overseas.

These products illustrate the extent of overseas success in the 'home' of marketing.

At the same time other developments, often emerging from the special and different market, social, cultural and physical conditions of these societies, have taken place. The importance of international trade, the role of the state, the relative importance of industrial marketing, different values, mores and religions and the dramatic differences in technology, climate, etc., all have to be incorporated into the overall perspective.

The basic dynamic of the marketing concept lies in its success in absorbing this diversity and adapting to these circumstances.

More recently the developing countries of the Pacific Basin, notably Taiwan, South Korea, Hong Kong and Singapore, have actively sought to integrate this approach into their international and domestic environments. The forms of this process have varied from the decision of the Government of Singapore to standardise all school and college tuition on English 'because it is the language of international trade', to the successful adoption of marketing by leading Korean firms such as Hyundai, Samsung and the Lucky Group.

Those OPEC countries which are trying to broaden their industrial base are showing the same commitment to expanding their marketing skills. It is now argued with increasing vigour and commitment that those developing countries eagerly seeking growth will benefit considerably from the adoption of a clearer marketing perspective. Agencies such as the World Bank, ILO and the International Trade Centre (Geneva) see this as central to their long-term strategies for economic development. The level of marketing skill in the West is seen by some as the most important 'non-tariff barrier' to trade facing developing countries. Increasingly, Third World leaders are abandoning their traditional hostility to marketing. They are recognising that this attitude frequently condemns their economy to low-price, low-added value competition in products, which does little to improve their long-term economic circumstances.[18]

> (Singapore's success) depends on a highly skilled and educated work force, which is willing to adapt to changing technology and changing markets.
>
> Lee Kwan Yew
> Prime Minister

It is the same trap out of which the countries of eastern Europe, members of the Council for Mutual Economic Assistance (CMEA, more commonly called ComeCon) are slowly emerging. Marketing is playing an increasing role in domestic trade in the Socialist countries. Goldman[19] points out the positive effect that branding and promotion have had on establishing and maintaining quality standards in production. In their overseas trade CMEA and other Socialist countries are working hard to understand the needs of buyers, despite being faced with the difficulties any country or industry with a traditionally production orientation inevitably faces. Approaches to price illustrate this:

The main reasons for using the cost-plus method are two. First, the state-owned enterprises under China's centralised planning economic system have been led to place their emphasis on the production side in the past. The cost-plus method is well suited to production-orientated enterprises and this is still utilised by the leaders of state-owned enterprises. Second, the cost-plus method is much easier to use than other pricing methods.

Mun Kin Chok[20]

Introducing a marketing approach has produced some major successes, particularly in dealings with the Third World. Especially noteworthy has been the introduction of novel and sophisticated forms of the oldest method of trade, barter.

_ Compensation trading, as it is more generally known, has emerged as an invaluable mechanism to cope with the serious shortages of foreign exchange faced by many Socialist and Third World countries.

> More than 60 large industrial projects are now under construction in the USSR under compensation agreements.
>
> V. Mordvinor
> Head of Dept.,
> USSR State Planning Committee

There are indications from other countries, notably those with large raw material surpluses, that this form of trade will play an increasing part in world trade.

Barter in action

Pepsi Cola agreed with the Soviet Union to build three major soft drink factories in the USSR. *Payment* came from sales of Russian vodka in the US, for which Pepsi Cola was the sole agent.

Marlboro broke into the Soviet market by agreeing to *payment* from sales of Soviet tobacco in the US.

A consortium of European firms provided the technology for a major oil and gas pipeline. *Payment* came in the form of revenue from sales of oil and gas in Western Europe.

Rank Xerox made major strides in Eastern Europe by accepting *payment* in a wide range of products.

The almost universal push towards growth and industrialisation is creating increasing opportunities for the introduction and adoption of a marketing perspective internationally and domestically, as firms and countries seek to realise the full commercial potential of their resources, skills and creativity.

W. W. Rostow[21] describes this process of economic development in terms of five stages: traditional society; transition; steady growth; drive to maturity; and mass consumption. At each stage the demands placed on the marketing-orientated firm change as the elements in the marketing system interact and adapt.

In the *traditional society* most economic activity is based around agriculture. There is little surplus, most of which is traded locally. The period of *transition* sees a growing efficiency in agriculture, as technology is used to boost agricultural productivity. There is a growing market for equipment, fertilisers and some consumer goods. The surpluses generated provide the resources for *steady growth*. This sees a growing emphasis on agricultural processing and infrastructure projects: schools, roads, etc. Markets now exist for a wide range of capital equipment and development services. The growing urbanisation of the population increases demands for entertainment and other facilities. This provides the framework for the *drive to maturity* during which there is a major shift to industrialisation. An increasing proportion of the population works in industry and commerce as the country becomes increasingly self-sufficient and starts to seek export

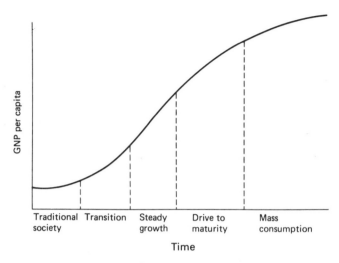

Fig. 1.8 The stages of economic growth.

opportunities. The era of *mass consumption* sees an affluent and sophisticated population seeking a variety of means to meet the various needs which their new affluence allows them to satisfy.

THE MARKETING SYSTEM

It is useful to think of the process of marketing as the links of a chain, which stretches from the raw materials suppliers to the end user.

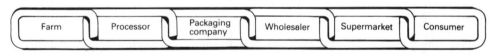

Fig. 1.9 The food chain.

No firm simply sells goods to specific unchanging customers. It may believe it does, like suppliers to the shipbuilding industry who failed to diversify when the industry contracted, but this is a dangerous, short-sighted fallacy. There may be intermediaries. There are probably suppliers. Few firms can avoid competitors. This network of relationships is continually interacting with the *cultural, technological, economic* and *political* forces surrounding it.

Figure 1.10 illustrates some of the numerous interacting forces which ultimately determine the future of a firm such as British Steel. The last five years have vividly illustrated the impact of these forces with:

1. The Steel Strike and the Miner's Strike affecting customer confidence and output.
2. Government policies, on cash limits and borrowing, influencing investment and development programmes.
3. Technological change stimulating new forms of competition.
4. The recession producing massive overcapacity.

Throughout the system, companies are involved in a constant process of converting the goods found in nature or provided by suppliers into offerings designed to meet the needs of industrial purchasers, intermediaries or final consumers.

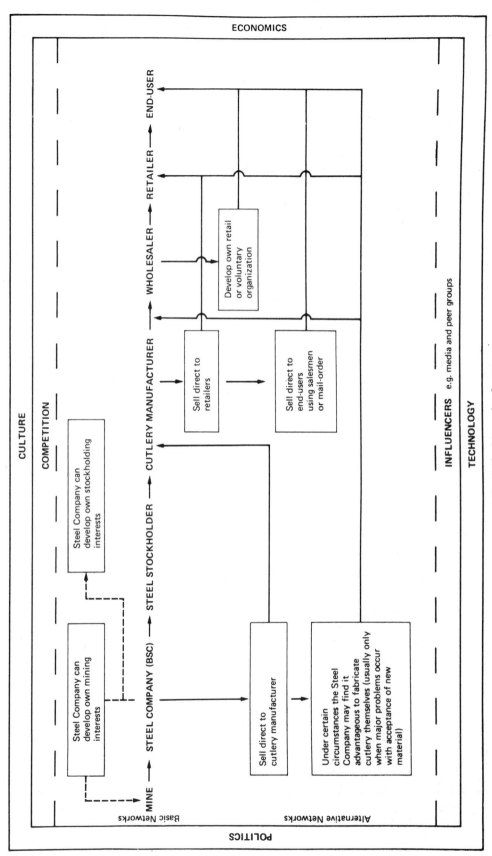

Fig. 1.10 Interacting forces.

The central role of marketing is to give direction to this process. Coordination of the other functions within the firm is as important as managing the specific aspects of the marketing mix under their control.

KEY POINTS

In this chapter it has been emphasised how effective marketing management is built on:

1. Understanding the exchange process and the environment in which it operates.
2. Insight into the people and institutions involved in the marketing system.
3. Recognition that effective management of the forces involved provides the returns to sustain company and national prosperity.

However, introducing a marketing perspective is neither easy nor automatic. It calls for understanding, commitment, sustained effort and effective management of the total effort.

Notes

1. Peters, T. J. & Waterman, R. H., *In Search of Excellence*. London: Harper and Row, 1982.
2. Beal, T., 'Domestic Consumer Demand and Japanese Global Marketing Strategy', Second World Marketing Congress, Stirling, 1985.
3. Packard, V., *The Waste Makers*. London: Penguin, 1960.
4. Mant, A., *The Rise and Fall of the British Manager*. London: Macmillan, 1977.
5. Drucker, P., *Management; Tasks, Responsibilities, Practices*. London: Harper and Row, 1973.
6. Dixon, D. F. and Blois, K. J., 'Some Limitations of the 4 P's as a Paradigm for Marketing', Marketing Education Group Annual Conference, Cranfield, 1983.
7. Stapleton, J., *Teach Yourself Marketing*. London: Teach Yourself Books, 1975.
8. Runyon, K. E., *The Practice of Marketing*. Columbus, Ohio: C. E. Merrill, 1982.
9. Kotler, P., *Marketing Management; Analysis, Planning and Control*. London: Prentice-Hall, 1984.
10. Hammarkvist, K. O., 'Markets as Networks', Marketing Education Group, Annual Conference, Cranfield, 1983.
11. Thomas, M., 'The Alpha and Omega of the 4 P's—Planning and Productivity', Marketing Education Group, Annual Conference, Cranfield, 1983.
12. Sloan, A. P., *My Years with General Motors*. London: Pan Books, 1963.
13. Dolan, E. G., *Basic Economics*. London: Holt, Rinehart and Winston, 1980.
14. Reid, D., 'Strategic Marketing Planning: Shortfalls and Implications', Second World Marketing Congress, Stirling, 1985.
15. Utterback, J. M., 'Patterns of Industrial Innovations', in *Technological Innovation and Corporate Strategy*. Cambridge, Massachusetts, Industrial Liaison Programme, 1978.
16. Piercy, N. & Evans, M., *Managing Marketing Information*. London: Croom Helm, 1985.
17. Pirenne, J., *Tides of History*. London: George Allen and Unwin, 1963.
18. Kaynak, E., *Marketing in the Third World*. New York: Praeger, 1982.
19. Goldman, M. I., *Soviet Marketing*. New York: Free Press, 1963.
20. Chok, M. K., 'Export Pricing of China's Industrial Goods', World Marketing Congress, Halifax, Nova Scotia, 1983.
21. Rostow, W. W., *Stages of Economic Growth*. Cambridge University Press, 1960.

Further Reading

Goldman, M. I., *Soviet Marketing*. Describes the impact of marketing on commercial activity in the USSR.

Kotler, P., *Marketing for Non-Profit Organisations*. London: Prentice Hall.

Levitt, T., 'Marketing Myopia', in Taylor, J. L., et al. (ed.) *Fundamentals of Marketing*. London: McGraw Hill. Brings out the importance of a marketing vision or perspective in looking beyond the current offering into new areas.

Peters, T. J. & Waterman, R. H., *In Search of Excellence*. Explores the key lessons for corporate success from the experiences of 60 of the most successful US corporations. Concludes that central to their achievements is a philosophy of 'keeping close to the customer'.

Weitz, B. A. & Wensley, R., *Strategic Marketing*. London: Kent Publishing, 1984. The introduction provides an excellent summation of the vital and central role of *strategy* in modern marketing thinking.

Glossary

Barter. Transactions which involve, in some form, the exchange of goods for goods, i.e. without the direct use of money. A number of forms exist today, notably

1. *Buy-back*: in development projects, where the supplier buys or gets some of the output from the project.
2. *Switch trading*: the supplier accepts the involvement of a third country which accepts goods from the customer and provides either money or goods which are much more acceptable to the supplier.

Barter trade is one of the most complex areas of international business today. Most firms are unwise to get involved without the involvement of outside specialists.

Consumer goods. Items provided primarily for purchase by, and the use of, individuals, as opposed to organisations or groups. Sometimes sub-divided into 'fast-moving consumer goods' (fmcg), i.e. the type of non-durable typically sold through supermarkets and similar outlets, and 'consumer durables', i.e. items designed to last a considerable time (e.g. televisions, cars, etc.).

Consumption. The pace at which a user consumes or uses up the items obtained. Economists sometimes use the phrase 'consumption function' to describe the means of measuring this.

Customer satisfaction. The degree to which the buyer finds the results of the transaction acceptable.

Developing Countries. Those nations of the world with low levels of industrialisation and generally poor standards of living, seeking industrialisation, urbanisation, increases in productivity and technological progress. Frequently split into 'underdeveloped' with $300–$500 per capita annual income; 'less developed', with $500–$1200; and 'newly industrialised', with over $1200.

Industrial Revolution. The period during the late 18th and early 19th centuries, when machines were first used on a wide scale to replace labour in the production process to dramatically increase output. Associated with the introduction, first of steam engines, then of other means of driving equipment and vehicles (ships, trains, etc.). The first industrial nation was Britain, followed by Germany, the US and France.

Innovation. The technical, industrial and commercial steps which lead to the marketing of new manufactured products or services and the commercial use of new technical processes, products or services.

Law of demand. The principle that the quantity of a product demanded by buyers tends to increase as the price of the product decreases, and tends to decrease as the price increases, all other things being equal.

Marketing. The management process responsible for identifying, anticipating and satisfying customer requirements profitably (Institute of Marketing's definition).

Marketing mix. The mixture of controllable marketing activities that are brought together to match the needs of a particular customer group. Normally seen in terms of combining the four utilities (benefits) of *price* (affordability), *product* (function), *promotion* (reputation and information) and *place* (availability).

Pacific Basin. The newly and rapidly industrialising countries of the Pacific region. A fully comprehensive list is impossible but should include; South Korea, Taiwan, Singapore, Hong Kong, and probably Indonesia, Malaysia and the Philippines.

Raw materials. Sometimes called 'primary products', as they exist in their 'raw' or untreated state and are traded as such, e.g. coal, iron ore, oil, wheat, timber.

CASE STUDY 1: BLACKTHORNE PUBLISHERS LTD

Introduction

In 1985 Blackthorne Publishers had established themselves as one of Britain's leading educational publishers. Sir Alexander Blackthorne had founded the company in the late nineteenth century and had dominated the firm until his death in 1952. His deep commitment, particularly to the sciences, still influenced the policies and approaches of the firm. Although the Blackthorne family retain a substantial investment in the firm, the management structure has been thoroughly 'professionalised', with no direct family involvement in the company. Although the traditions of demanding academic excellence and publishing 'important' works are seen as important to the firm's management, pressures on the firm are mounting, particularly from cutbacks in educational expenditure.

Background

In the past, Blackthorne books have been actively involved in the school sciences market, university-level science texts, particularly biology and molecular science, and their university paperback series, which covers a wide range of subjects. Other subjects have been included, as areas have developed either through editorial interest or the acceptance of academically important texts. This has extended their range into the social sciences, business and management and a number of arts subjects.

Although the educational publishing interests are the firm's primary area of activity, the firm does have a strong fiction imprint which has published a number of best-sellers over the past few years, and a paperback imprint handling a number of best-selling authors. For the sake of this analysis these will not be included in the case.

Organisation and structure

The educational publishing activities are organised around a group of commissioning editors, as shown in Figure 1.11. As the name suggests, the primary task of a commissioning editor is to identify likely areas for developing books, commission authors and manage the production of the text from manuscript to final production. All editors control a list of established texts, with responsibility to oversee their performance and authority to commission rewrites, order re-issues and delete texts from the series.

Although the commissioning editor has considerable authority over the development and production of material, the sales effort is handled through a sales manager with three full-time salesmen located in different parts of the country. Their activities are directed largely by the editorial board.

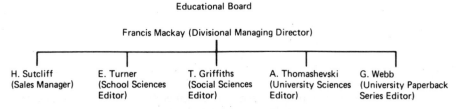

Educational Board

Francis Mackay (Divisional Managing Director)

| H. Sutcliff (Sales Manager) | E. Turner (School Sciences Editor) | T. Griffiths (Social Sciences Editor) | A. Thomashevski (University Sciences Editor) | G. Webb (University Paperback Series Editor) |

Fig. 1.11 Blackthorne Publishers (educational division).

The work of the commissioning editor

All the commissioning editors have some degree of subject expertise, although, clearly, this cannot encompass all the areas they deal with. It is seen as very important that the editors can converse with some authority with experts in the fields they cover. Their picture of the environment is supplemented by a series of academic advisory committees. These operate both on an established formal basis (all major series, e.g. the 'Frontiers of Biology' series, have a standing academic committee chaired by a prominent academic) and on an 'ad hoc' basis, any new developments being 'bounced off' such a group.

At the same time the editors see one of their primary tasks as establishing a broad network of contacts in educational circles to identify major developments and prospective authors.

The overwhelming majority of books published are commissioned by editors. Very few derive from unprompted manuscripts, although a large number of these are received.

Developments in the market

Although educational publishing has never been a particularly profitable area of business, the firm has historically managed to earn a good return for its efforts. However, the past five years have seen a significant decline in demand, largely because of the cutbacks in educational expenditure. This has had a particularly bad effect on the traditional educational publisher adopting a policy of: 'a very wide range of books published at relatively low prices (break-even not being achieved until years 2, 3 or 4). Marginal increases or reductions in sales have dramatic effects on profits. These lists reflect academic merit and importance.'

The effect has been felt at all levels: school expenditure per capita has actually declined in monetary terms; university libraries have been held back; and the 'book grant' element in a student grant has been held virtually static. The group's excellent profits for the last two years have been won largely through the success of the fiction imprint. The education division has contributed a declining share of the profits (Table 1.1).

To arrest this declining contribution is seen as a major task of the editorial group over the next three years.

Table 1.1   *Selected financial statistics 1979–1984 (£000)*

Year	Net profit (Education)	Net profit of group	Group net worth	Group assets	Common dividend paid
1984	514	746	7776	13 203	365
1983	497	701	7313	12 516	381
1982	485	614	6648	11 846	301
1981	551	656	6032	12 004	266
1980	605	748	5677	11 187	266
1979	638	751	5031	10 014	230

We cannot afford to bank on an annual best seller to keep us in business.

Charles Forthrop, Group Managing Director

Developments proposed

In mid-1985 an editorial conference agreed that each member would review the means by which their individual areas could contribute towards the achievement of this broad task. These could include comments on overall developments likely to contribute towards the target. At the December 1985 editorial conference the following proposals were put forward.

H. Sutcliff: 'The existing sales force is far too small to obtain any meaningful coverage of the market. At the moment they are chasing from school to school with little opportunity to sell properly and no opportunity to establish long-term relationships, particularly in the universities. The volume is in the schools, and that is where they must concentrate their efforts. Some increase in the sales force number is necessary, but I recognise that a significant increase is impossible at the moment. I would suggest that we recruit a number of part-time salesmen, perhaps retired schoolteachers, and pay them a small retainer, with most of their income deriving from commission. This would enable us to establish a strong presence in the market.'

E. Turner: 'There are a number of exciting developments occurring in my area which can make a great contribution to the future of the school sciences division. A Swedish publisher has been in touch about giving us the rights to their "Geography" series. This is directed towards the lower ability groups aged less than sixteen. My editorial advisers have pointed out that this group is very poorly served for reading material and the Swedish series looks relevant. I have been talking to the Schools Council and they are looking for a schools' mathematics project. I think we stand an excellent chance of winning the commission to develop this.'

T. Griffiths: 'I really think that the selection of books and texts that is on my list at the moment is adequate; if anything, there are too many. I believe that we need to work much harder at publicising and advertising our material. We seem to be poor at getting our material reviewed in the major journals, and even when it is reviewed there is often a problem with stocks. Last year there was a full-page review of one of my books in *Campaign*, the advertising magazine, but stocks had not been issued. Our publicity and promotion must be improved. We can steal some of the ideas and expertise of the fiction group.'

Ideas along these lines were reiterated by the other members of the editorial panel. At the end of the discussion, Francis Mackay concluded by saying:

> Although I have found everything that has been said here very interesting and relevant, I do not know whether we have really come to grips with the problem. I want to bounce these ideas off a few more people.

Tasks

1. Review the company's present position.
2. Highlight the problem areas as you see them.
3. Evaluate the suggestions put forward by the editorial team.
4. Put forward your ideas on the means of resolving their problems.

2

Managing the Marketing Effort

In Chapter 1 the marketing approach to business was defined and placed into a broad context. It was noted, in defining marketing, that one of its essential features is that it is operational. Management means facing up to the need to make decisions in the real world of business operations. These decisions can never be made in a vacuum. Their effects frequently go far beyond the firm, and they may have interactions throughout the marketing system. The following are some examples of decisions and their possible effects.

1. A car manufacturer may decide to reduce his distribution costs by cutting back drastically on the number of his direct dealerships. This can provide the perfect opportunity for a foreign competitor to pick up a substantial dealer network.
2. A small knitwear producer might decide to promote direct sales of her goods by mail order. This might alienate all her existing retail customers.
3. A utility such as gas or electricity can limit its service engineering apprenticeship intake, causing long-term problems of extended repair dates and alienated customers.
4. The trustees of an area of historical or natural interest can neglect the provision of support facilities, e.g. catering, creating a situation where visitors come only once and stay briefly.
5. A bank manager who tries to handle all his business accounts himself might neglect to pass on a small firm's request for specialist export advice to his international division, running the risk of providing inferior service to the client.

There are relatively few important decisions made in a company that do not have implications for the firm's marketing effort. The extent of this interaction is seldom fully recognised. At the same time the number of corporate personnel directly influencing the firm's marketing is frequently underestimated.

MARKETING MANAGEMENT

A casual glance at a newspaper almost any day will give the reader an idea of the range and depth of marketing management (Figure 2.1). Marketing directors, marketing executives, commercial strategy consultants, sales representatives, advertising managers, account executives, export sales managers, new product development managers, sales engineers, PR executives and many others are always being sought. The demands placed on them, the skills needed, the resources at their disposal and their backgrounds will be the primary interest of this chapter.

It must be emphasised that marketing is not an activity that can be conveniently compartmentalised and handed over to the man with marketing in his job description. It is a total corporate commitment in which everyone is involved. Appliance manufacturers may

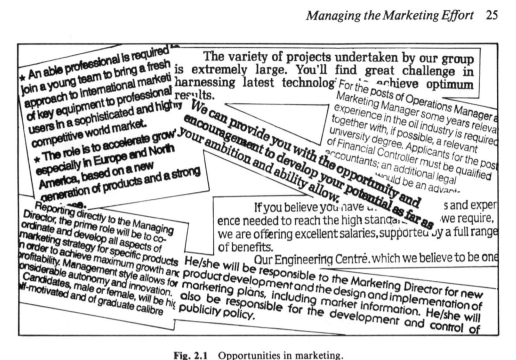

* An able professional is required to join a young team to bring a fresh approach to international marketi of key equipment to professional users in a sophisticated and high competitive world market.

* The role is to accelerate grow especially in Europe and North America, based on a new generation of products and a strong

Reporting directly to the Managing Director, the prime role will be to co-ordinate and develop all aspects of marketing strategy for specific products n order to achieve maximum growth and profitability. Management style allows for considerable autonomy and innovation. Candidates, male or female, will be hi lf-motivated and of graduate calibre

The variety of projects undertaken by our group is extremely large. You'll find great challenge in harnessing latest technolog results.

We can provide you with the opportunity and encouragement to develop your potential as far as your ambition and ability allow.

If you believe you have u. ence needed to reach the high standa we are offering excellent salaries, supported by a full range of benefits.

Our Engineering Centre. which we believe to be one He/she will be responsible to the Marketing Director for new product development and the design and implementation of marketing plans, including market information. He/she will also be responsible for the development and control of publicity policy.

For the posts of Operations Manager a Marketing Manager some years releva experience in the oil industry is require together with, if possible, a relevant university degree. Applicants for the post of Financial Controller must be qualified accountants; an additional legal would be an advan

Fig. 2.1 Opportunities in marketing.

Fig. 2.2 'Who sold you this then?' Reproduced with the permission of Video Arts Limited.

have a marketing department, but the service engineer probably has the most regular contact with customers. Banks may have a similar department, but the individual bank manager is in the front line of the selling effort. A university might have a public relations manager, but a lecturer's or professor's attitude to a journalist's questions is likely to be far more important in establishing the right climate of opinion. Video Arts Ltd, in an excellent series of short films, illustrated this clearly with the service engineer's comment, 'Who sold you this then?' (Figure 2.2).

Internal communication of this message of total company commitment can be as important in effective marketing as any advertising or promotional expenditure.

THE MARKETING MANAGER

The job advertisements listed above give some idea of the range of titles given to those involved in the marketing function. The precise names will vary among industries, firms and levels within companies. Despite that, there is a considerable degree of consistency in the functions and roles they perform.

The most basic task of those with a management responsibility within the marketing operation is to control, allocate and use responsibly the funds and other resources at their disposal. The product or brand manager of a consumer goods firm is likely to have a promotional budget. This can amount to many thousands, even millions of pounds. The manager's task is to understand the objectives set for his product or service, and to deploy his budget in the way most likely to achieve this goal.

In this work the product or brand manager is likely to work with other marketing managers with different titles. Some may be junior to him, such as assistant brand managers. Their role will be similar and supportive. However, the senior manager will have the additional responsibility of helping his junior to develop his management skills, besides ensuring that he understands the objectives of the firm for the products and services under their control. This process of communication is central to all marketing relationships. The product manager will need to work through and with colleagues in sales, advertising, research and development (R & D), production, distribution, services, etc. All of these can be described as members of marketing management. Some will be within the firm, e.g. sales and production; others will be outside the company, e.g. account executives with the company's advertising agency.

Piercy[1] describes the twin pressures being placed upon the marketing function. Growing awareness of the wider role of marketing throughout the firm is encouraging some writers and many firms to broaden the tasks given to marketing: it is intrinsic in all business policies. At the same time its activities are becoming more compartmentalised. Piercy[1] describes the 'disintegration' of the marketing department. This can take the form of giving specific functional areas considerable autonomy, hence 'diffusing' authority. In Britain this is seen most clearly in the freedom given to 'key account staff' in their negotiations with major clients. This was formalised first in fast-moving consumer goods (fmcgs). The major retailers achieved such a dominant market position that manufacturers were obliged to set up highly specialised units to deal directly with them.

In most marketing relationships the key to successful management lies in effective communication, understanding and persuasion, *not* authority and power. The product manager will need to build up relationships with the sales force, and must understand the problems they face; the same responsibility lies with each member of the sales force. The lynch-pin of their relationship is the common purpose they share, in working to achieve the firm's marketing objectives through an agreed strategy.[2]

The formulation of objectives and strategies is the central task of senior marketing management. Management are responsible for identifying opportunities in the market-place, relating these to the capabilities of the firm and developing solutions and strategies designed to convert these opportunities into profitable business. In this work management need to work continually to relate these *externalities* (opportunities, threats) to the *internal capabilities* (strengths, weaknesses) of the company.[3] This can only be done effectively through teamwork which goes beyond the immediate confines of the marketing function.

It has been said that marketing is a *total* company activity. This applies with particular strength to the responsibility of top management. It is their task to relate the marketing operations, especially the strategies, to the other functions in the firm and to the corporate plan.

Success in marketing management lies in using the special techniques and skills developed in this area to understand the environment in which the firm must operate. This understanding needs to be wedded to the creation of plans and strategies which make the best use of company resources to earn profits and gain differential advantage. Understanding the function of marketing in the firm's operations lies at the centre of this.

ROLE IN THE FIRM

In any company, large or small, manufacturing or service, those formally responsible for marketing must work with their colleagues. Even in the small, entrepreneurial firm where the marketing decision-maker may be also the owner, the external responsibilities for promotion, pricing, channel management and product management are matched with internal responsibilities.

Promotional activities must be geared to adequate stocks which in turn depend on the effectiveness of the forecasts. Production schedules are based on estimates of future demand. Inaccuracies soon show up in production dislocations, high costs and inadequate supplies of raw materials or components. Buying decisions in industrial concerns are greatly influenced by marketing or sales force estimates of the design or product needs of customers.

An effectively co-ordinated management team can achieve results that are beyond the scope of ill co-ordinated teams. Under certain circumstances a production manager will be able to produce small quantities profitably when generally only very large runs are feasible. Transport departments can occasionally cope with special packings and promotional offers far outside the scope of their normal operations. The ultimate responsibility for creating a climate in which the type of flexibility or responsiveness occasionally demanded by the market can be achieved lies with top management. All those directly responsible for the marketing effort have a special role to play. Relatively simple exercises in communication and involvement can earn massive pay-offs. For example, the brand manager who gives production management good notice of actions likely to affect them, discusses the objectives of special initiatives, e.g. requiring smaller quantities or new materials, and listens to their comments and advice is far more likely to earn real profits than those neglecting these activities. In many firms there is a hostile attitude to sales and marketing management, simply because of their failure to recognise the importance of effective internal communication and co-ordination. It appears to occur less frequently in smaller firms, where the tendency of top management to have a very intimate understanding of corporate capability is allied to easier and more frequent communication between areas.

A clear understanding of objectives and responsibilities is vital. Setting objectives and the entire planning process are discussed at length in Chapter 23. It must be recognised here that clear, actionable objectives geared to customer needs lie at the core of the operations of the marketing-orientated firm. In developing these, a clear view of total corporate capabilities must be wedded to a marketing audit.

The allocation of responsibilities within the marketing effort varies enormously between firms. Besides the differences at any particular point in time, the dynamic nature of the market-place has led to the emergence of new offices and areas of responsibility.

Product management emerged in firms like Procter and Gamble in the early part of the century. Its development and continuing popularity derive partly from the specific problems of the multi-product or multi-brand firm. In the inevitable debate about the allocation of corporate resources the product manager makes a major contribution by acting as the general manager responsible for his specific brand's sales and profitability. In this context he generally has responsibility for budgeting and planning, research and information systems, co-ordination, promotion and control:

> More than any other factor, it is his skill in working harmoniously with key people in the various disciplines that will heavily influence the success of the product and, of course, his own future work with the company.
>
> G. H. Evans

In the 1950s and 1960s firms were faced with an environment of apparently limitless opportunity if only the company could respond quickly and creatively. The response of firms like Westinghouse was to institute the concept of *venture management*. Special groups are set up to exploit opportunities, particularly of the new product type. The aim is to approximate the entrepreneur's willingness to become personally involved, committing large amounts of time and effort to achieve success. At a time of growth they could make progress where more conventional firms could not, particularly with marginal products.

In the adverse economic circumstances of the mid-1970s, success with this type of introduction became more difficult to achieve, while fully capitalising on the potential returns from existing products grew in importance. *Key account management* groups were set up by firms like Imperial Tobacco to handle their major customers. Their primary role is to earn the maximum returns over time from these key accounts.

Product management, venture management and key account management are only three of the many developments in the organisation of marketing that have emerged over the last half-century. At the same time functional groupings under marketing or sales directors have retained their popularity. Here the key marketing decision-maker operates through his own department structure. This can be illustrated by the type of company organisation chart familiar to most readers (Figure 2.3).

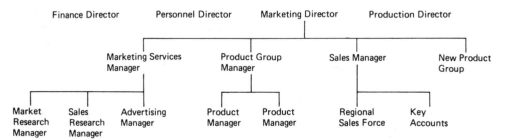

Fig. 2.3   Marketing organisational chart.

The optimum form of organisation is largely dependent on the environmental forces affecting the firm. When the needs of buyers can be grouped together into separate customer groups, market-based management systems have considerable merit. Two points need to be made about the type of chart in Figure 2.3:

1.   It is a highly simplified illustration of a complex system. The lines used for linkages are only a very small part of the network that will exist in a healthy firm. Communication, co-ordination and interaction will be operating horizontally as well as vertically. Equally important, the links will extend beyond the marketing department.

2. It reflects only the formal system. There will almost certainly be informal systems of great importance to the effective operation of the marketing function and the firm itself.

The optimum system will be the basis on which the firm will manage its exchanges with the market.

MARKETING AND ITS ENVIRONMENT

Effective control of the exchange process goes far beyond the continual stimulation of demand. Kotler suggests that marketing management is faced with very different tasks depending on the existing demand state (Table 2.1).

Table 2.1 *The different tasks of marketing management*

Demand state	Underlying buyer attitude	Marketing task	Formal name
Negative demand	Hostility	Disabuse demand	Conversional marketing
No demand	Indifference	Create demand	Stimulational marketing
Latent demand	Strong need but not gratified	Develop demand	Developmental marketing
Faltering demand	Declining interest	Revitalise demand	Remarketing
Irregular demand	Intermittent requirement	Synchronise demand	Syncromarketing
Full demand	Strong desire	Maintain demand	Maintenance marketing
Overfull demand	Excessive desire	Reduce demand	Demarketing
Unwholesome demand	Demand for undesirable product	Destroy demand	Countermarketing

Adapted from Kotler, P., *The Major Tasks of Marketing Management*

An understanding of the determinants of demand and the character of supply is vital to any manager attempting to carry out these tasks.

Demand

The patterns of demand existing in any market are determined by a wide range of forces. The demand curve shown in Figure 1.5 is made up of the demands of a number of individuals. Their specific social and economic circumstances, income or disposable funds, psychology, pressure from others (particularly in institutional or industrial buying), awareness and other factors influence the shape of the individual demand curve. For example, Mrs Brown may be forced to buy margarine as a low-priced substitute for butter because of her husband's low income. Mrs Jackson may buy margarine for cooking (Figure 2.4).

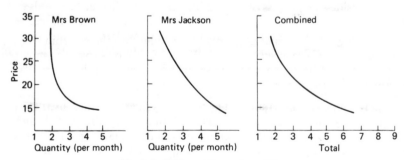

Fig. 2.4 Different demand conditions.

However, all these factors are subject to change. Mrs Brown's substitution of margarine for butter may be acceptable to her until her husband gets a new job with better wages, significantly increasing the family's disposable income. She switches to butter. However, his new position is far more sedentary than his previous post, and over time this leads to worries about his weight and desire for margarines higher in polyunsaturated fat.

Complex interrelationships exist between buyers, directly affecting a company's demand situation. This can even reverse the shape of the demand curve, for example when during a period of increasing prices people rush out to buy more. The expectation of continuing rising prices converts today's expenditure to investment in stocks. The effect of a combination of these phenomena was seen in the 'petrol panics' during the middle of 1979 in Britain and the US. Prices were going up and fears of shortages spread across both countries, resulting in long queues and worsened shortages.

Although demand is essentially a dynamic phenomenon a number of variables have a continuing impact.

Needs

To the marketeer, needs are the basis of the entire process of marketing. In its simplest form need is any lack or deficit within the person or organisation. Needs gain their special relevance to marketing when they are linked to the different phenomenon of drives:

> While need and drive are parallel, they are not the same.[4]

A drive is the internal pressure to satisfy a need. The interplay between needs and drives is determined by the motives of the individual or group:

> Motives initiate behaviour and direct it towards specific types of activity.[5]

The study of needs, drives and motives constitutes one of the main areas of study in both modern psychology and, more relevant to those involved in marketing, consumer behaviour and industrial buying. Needs are complex and varied. They range from physiological needs, such as hunger and thirst, through psychological needs, for example for love or esteem, to socially or culturally based needs such as self-fulfilment and ambition. Although these are discussed at length in Chapter 6, it is useful to note here a few of the basic approaches, particularly the effects of the choices associated with selecting: which needs to satisfy and the alternative means of satisfying them.

Physiological needs. The most basic needs are physiological. People must eat, drink and breathe in order to survive. There is also a need to minimise, by prudence or escape, risks to the person's safety. These provide only a basic insight. The individual may have a wide choice of ways of satisfying his hunger need, or may take actions, such as driving dangerously, which appear inconsistent with the basic needs.

Psychological needs. Individual and social psychology provide insights into a range of different needs besides the process of motivation, drive and choice. The needs can include affection, ego boosts, membership of groups or communities, ambition, and relief from anxiety. At any point in time these needs are interacting, with some achieving a degree of dominance which can lead to action. The nature of this interplay and the specific motives, drives and choices of individuals and groups have been studied from a number of perspectives within modern psychology.

Motivational research explores the interplay between needs and motives. Special emphasis has been placed on different kinds of needs, and a great deal of research in conscious and subconscious motivation has been carried out.

Attitude research has emphasised the state of mind which the individual takes into any social situation, e.g. a shopping expedition, creating a predisposition toward certain types of response or choice.

Cognitive research examines the ways in which the individual perceives, evaluates and structures his environment. Even a simple newspaper advertisement can be understood, viewed and responded to in widely different ways by apparently similar individuals.

Personality research has focused its attention on the individuality and consistency of response shown by people in social situations. The underlying proposition is that an individual's response to a situation is determined by a combination of specific traits that are particular to him. With this as the starting point, considerable effort has been invested in examining whether particular, general personality types can be spotted. Their response to offerings could then be predicted with a high degree of confidence.

In the broad area of psychological study two notions have emerged as particularly interesting over the last 25 years: cognitive dissonance[6] and lifestyle analysis.

The theory of cognitive dissonance proposes that in his cognitive system the individual constantly strives for balance or consistency. When imbalance, inconsistency or dissonance emerges there will be a need to reduce it by avoiding the situation, restructuring his perceptions, or gathering information to establish a new balance.

Lifestyle analysis has emerged from personality research. It is based on the proposition that study of the activities, interests, opinions and demographics of large numbers of respondents will highlight specific subgroups. These will respond to specific situations or offerings in broadly consistent ways. Lifestyle groups have been widely used in new product and promotional development.

Social and economic factors. It is important to recognise that the individual does not exist in isolation. He is a member of a particular society, community and family. For part of his time he works, studies or plays, generally in groups. This social and economic environment plays a major part in shaping his needs as well as the form of his motivation, drives and choice process. Five areas are particularly important to the marketing man: demography, location, income, socio-economic grouping and culture.

Demography is the study of populations. Its importance lies in the fact that all demand ultimately derives from people. Sheer numbers are only part of the picture. The structure of the population, i.e. the proportions in different age or sex groups, can have profound marketing implications. The different groups may have vastly different needs, motives and drives, with associated variations in their choice processes. Equally important are the patterns of change over time. This is illustrated by the increasing proportion of Britain's population aged over 55 years. This is matched in the Third World by disproportionate numbers of young people. Despite a considerable amount of research into population, long-term predictions have been characterised by significant error.

Location of population is important in both domestic and overseas markets (Figure 2.5). Even in Britain, which is relatively small, the population is unevenly spread, with concentrations in the South East, Midlands, North West and Strathclyde areas and relatively small numbers in the South West, East Anglia, parts of Wales and the Highlands. Apparently simple local phenomena such as hard or soft water can have major long-term implications for detergent companies. In larger countries, such as West Germany, the United States, Nigeria and Australia, climatic variations can have dramatic effects on wide ranges of consumer requirements. In some countries these locational forces are strengthened by federal constitutions.

Income provides the individual, family or firm with its primary means of exchange. It is closely related to the notion of wealth, which also takes into account assets which may be disposable under particular circumstances. The overall pattern of national income provides considerable insights into the range of opportunities in a market. This is particularly true when income rises sufficiently for considerable discretion to be exercised in its disposal. For this reason the concepts of disposable income and discretionary purchasing power are important. They both highlight the amounts left after certain deductions are made from gross income; in disposable income after taxes, superannuation

Fig. 2.5   Economic planning regions of England and Wales are used by marketing people as a basis of locational analysis.

and compulsory pension contributions, and in discretionary purchasing power after essential expenditure such as mortgage, rent, rates, lighting and heating. In international trade a picture of the pattern of per capita national income can be a powerful indicator of the types of needs that can be satisfied in different countries.

Socio-economic structure is determined partly by the income levels of specific sub-groups in the population. Basically it is the subdivision of the population into groups with broadly similar incomes, occupations, education levels and resources (Table 2.2).

Table 2.2   *Socio-economic divisions in marketing in Britain*

Registrar General	National Readership Survey	Occupations
I	A	Higher managerial, administrative or professional
II	B	Intermediate managerial, administrative or professional
III(n)	C_1	Supervisory, clerical, junior managerial or professional
III(m)	C_2	Skilled manual workers
IV	D	Semi-skilled and unskilled manual workers
V	E	State pensioners, widows, casual and lowest-grade earners

Members of different groups are likely to give different priorities to certain needs, and the upper socio-economic groupings are likely to be able to satisfy certain needs more easily than others. Similarly, expectations, values, usage and attitudes are likely to vary between groups. Media research has highlighted the different media habits and approaches to communication of different groups. All these have direct implications for the approach to motivation within groups and the choice process.

Culture is the basis of the entire social process, encompassing as it does knowledge, beliefs, art, morals, law and customs. It directly impinges on the values of every member of every society. It influences both the needs themselves and the means of satisfying them. In Britain, despite the overall cohesiveness of our society, certain products, forms of entertainment and types of service that are acceptable in one part of the country have only a limited popularity in others. For example, working men's clubs play a major part in the social life of those in the North of England, while in the South they are almost non-existent. Husbands in the South go shopping with their wives far more frequently than those in the North, and consequently have greater power to influence choice.

Institutional demand

In exploring the constituents of demand, attention has focused almost entirely on the consumer, with virtually no mention of industrial, commercial, intermediary, government or other demand. In fact the majority of companies are involved in servicing these markets, and the bulk of buying and selling is centred on this area.

One of the most critical features of demand in these markets is that it is primarily 'derived demand', i.e. it originates further down the marketing system. For example:

1. The industrial customer for specific raw materials or components will base the volume, timing, quality, type, and even price of his orders on his assumptions about his customers. Therefore the success of a product like stainless steel exhausts will depend on the car manufacturer's judgements about their appeal to car buyers.
2. The commercial customer's demands for specific products or services will be a function of his beliefs about how they will enhance his own offerings to his customers. For example, a bank might install outside automatic tills if it believes the extra customer service will have commercial benefits.
3. A retailer will base his purchasing policies on assumptions on throughput, 'stock turn rate' on goods. Therefore a new brand of chocolate will be ordered if the combination of manufacturer 'push' and customer 'pull' means real payoffs for the retailer.
4. A government department will base its requisitions on statutory obligations, specific regulations and on the benefits of the goods to the public or section of the public. For example, a hospital will invest in establishing self-contained cubicles for mental health patients rather than open wards if they are required to make provision for this type of patient, the funds are available, and it is judged that the patients will benefit.

Recent research has highlighted a powerful behavioural dimension to institutional demand. This brings out the degree to which many of the ideas mentioned earlier in exploring consumer demand can play a part in expanding our knowledge in this area.

All organisations have survival needs. These will range from the need for buildings and equipment, for power for lighting and heating, and for driving equipment, to the need for capital to establish and maintain the firm. As well as these basic needs, there may also be many less critical but often equally important needs, for example the need to present an image of social responsibility or to stay at the forefront of technology. These may play a part in contributing to overall corporate profitability but equally may reflect the values of company personnel.

Besides influencing the nature of the needs and the priority given to them, these behavioural factors directly affect the choice process. Source loyalty, innovativeness, and many similar phenomena have a major role in building up a picture of industrial demand. Location, prosperity, company resources, and technical background of personnel also play a part. Many large firms prefer to obtain supplies from firms in their immediate area. A firm with high profits or large resources may be able to invest heavily in new equipment or provide better facilities for its workers. In some industries it can be difficult to get engineers to experiment with new materials or applications because of their traditional training.

Although these behavioural dimensions are more important than used to be thought, institutional purchasing is still characterised by a high degree of professionalism, information collection and analysis. The buyer is likely to conduct a more extensive search, employ more objective criteria, have greater technical expertise and back-up, and have far greater power than the individual consumer. Also, institutional demand is more directly affected by coalition purchasing, involving managers from a number of areas. For example:

A marketing audit may highlight weaknesses in the firm's product array so a need for research into the market emerges. The research indicates an opportunity for a low-cost economy brand, and a need for new cheaper packaging may occur, to keep costs down. The new packaging may be incompatible with existing machinery, requiring the purchase of new equipment. The buying process will involve top management anxious to resolve the company's weakness, brand management keen to ensure customer acceptability, production management, and personnel, besides the purchasing staff who will generally be responsible for information gathering and sometimes testing, as well as finally placing the order.

Supply

As long as people or institutions have needs, thus creating demands, there will be opportunities to provide offerings to satisfy them. The means of satisfying needs are tangible products, perhaps to satisfy basic survival needs, and services, perhaps to meet more social needs.

These offerings can be directed both to the individual and to the institution; for example 'Coca Cola' satisfies the thirst of an individual, and the ICI Agriculture Division provides animal feedstuffs to farmers. They can encompass services as well as tangible products; for example Thames Television provides their audiences with programmes, and Securicor advise firms on how best to protect their property.

The suppliers of goods and services include private enterprise, non-profit-making organisations and the state. For example, farmers will meet some of their needs, e.g. tractors, from private enterprise, other needs, e.g. insurance, will be met by the National Farmers' Union, and yet other needs, e.g. advice and special grants, will be met by the Ministry of Agriculture and Fisheries.

Table 2.3   *Standard Industrial Classification*

Revised 1958	Revised 1968

Minimum
List
Heading

Order I
Agriculture, forestry, fishing
001 Agriculture and horticulture
002 Forestry
003 Fishing

Order II
Mining and quarrying
101 Coal mining
102 Stone and slate quarrying and mining
103 Chalk, clay, sand and gravel extraction

109 Other mining and quarrying

Order III
Food, drink and tobacco
211 Grain milling
212 Bread and flour confectionery
213 Biscuits
214 Bacon curing, meat and fish products
215 Milk products
216 Sugar
217 Cocoa, chocolate and sugar confectionery
218 Fruit and vegetable products
219 Animal and poultry foods

229 Food industries not elsewhere specified
231 Brewing and malting

239 Other drink industries
240 Tobacco

Order IV
Chemicals and allied industries
261 Coke ovens and manufactured fuel
262 Mineral oil refining
263 Lubricating oils and greases

271 Chemicals and dyes
272 Pharmaceutical and toilet preparations
273 Explosives and fireworks
274 Paint and printing ink
275 Vegetable and animal oils, fats, soap and detergents
276 Synthetic resins and plastics materials

277 Polishes, gelatine, adhesives, etc.

Order V
Metal manufacture
311 Iron and steel (general)
312 Steel tubes
313 Iron castings, etc.
321 Light metals
322 Copper, brass and other base metals

Minimum
List
Heading

Order I
Agriculture, forestry, fishing
001 Agriculture and horticulture
002 Forestry
003 Fishing

Order II
Mining and quarrying
101 Coal mining
102 Stone and slate quarrying and mining
103 Chalk, clay, sand and gravel extraction
104 Petroleum and natural gas
109 Other mining and quarrying

Order III
Food, drink and tobacco
211 Grain milling
212 Bread and flour confectionery
213 Biscuits
214 Bacon curing, meat and fish products
215 Milk and milk products
216 Sugar
217 Cocoa, chocolate and sugar confectionery
218 Fruit and vegetable products
219 Animal and poultry foods
221 Vegetable and animal oils and fats
229 Food industries not elsewhere specified
231 Brewing and malting
232 Soft drinks
239 Other drink industries
240 Tobacco

Order IV
Coal and petroleum products
261 Coke ovens and manufactured fuel
262 Mineral oil refining
263 Lubricating oils and greases

Order V
Chemicals and allied industries
271 General chemicals
272 Pharmaceutical chemicals and preparations
273 Toilet preparations
274 Paint
275 Soap and detergents

276 Synthetic resins and plastics materials and synthetic rubber
277 Dyestuffs and pigments
278 Fertilizers
279 Other chemical industries

Order VI
Metal manufacture
311 Iron and steel (general)
312 Steel tubes
313 Iron castings, etc.
321 Aluminium and aluminium alloys
322 Copper, brass and other copper alloys
323 Other base metals

Reproduced with the permission of the controller of HMSO.

All these goods and services, and the different organisations and types of enterprise are directly involved in the exchange process. In providing their offerings they are part of the marketing system. There are a number of ways of classifying these offerings.

The notion of a standard industrial classification is used throughout much of the world to classify economies into different industrial segments. All business activities are categorised into broad divisions, subdivided again, and then given a coding. Table 2.3 shows the Standard Industrialised Classifications used in the United Kingdom.

In international trade similar classification schemes exist in most countries. There is also the International Standard Industrial Classification (ISIC). Although there is not necessarily a relationship between the Standard Industrial Classification (SIC) and the International Standard Industrial Classification (ISIC), most agencies working in this area are attempting to build in maximum consistency.

These classifications are based largely on the production process, technology or product features. It is equally important for marketing management to categorise offerings from the user's perspective.

Consumer offerings

Convenience goods are frequently-bought items requiring limited search and no delays in supply—the typical items in the supermarket or corner shop.

Shopping goods are generally purchased less often. Search and analysis are involved, particularly of price, product features, service and availability. Many consumer-durables, e.g. washing machines and radios, fall into this category.

Speciality lines cater for the needs of special-interest goods. They include both subsets of more general areas, e.g. delicatessen lines, and autonomous groups, e.g. particular sports or hobbies.

Leisure services are those offerings geared to the non-domestic and non-work interests of people.

Domestic services are those services satisfying the home or work needs of individuals and families. Banks, building societies, certain local authority services and telephones are typical of these.

Although many organisations and companies are highly specialised, others cross a number of categories; for example, local authority parks and gardens are leisure services but the social services are generally domestic.

Industrial offerings

These are generally tied to the process of converting inputs into outputs which can be resold. They are thus related to three basic flows: information, goods and capital.

Information. Information services provide the basis for decision-making, resource allocation and communication. They include market research, advertising, and technical and consultancy services.

Goods. Raw materials are wholly unprocessed goods, e.g. grain and iron ore. Processed goods (fabricated materials) are items which have been converted from the raw material but are not usable unless combined with other items, e.g. plastic or aluminium mouldings and steel. Components are semi-finished goods which are brought together to make up the producer's offering, e.g. shock absorbers and cooker timers. Equipment includes items which are employed in the conversion processes but which are not transferred into the producer's goods, e.g. buildings, cement mixers and desks. Supplies are those items needed to sustain the production or commercial process but not directly incorporated in the product, e.g. gas and electricity.

Capital. Financial services are the services provided by those institutions which manage a firm's flow of funds out to its suppliers, through the organisation and in from customers, e.g. banks, credit agencies and factors.

Although a thorough understanding of the firm's offering, whether product or service, is important to effective marketing management, long-term success in the marketplace calls for a clear understanding that the buyer responds to a number of variables when making his purchase decision, and a recognition that it is the mix of these variables that determines the degree to which firms satisfy needs in the market.

The marketing mix

The variables are called the marketing mix (Figure 2.6). Individually they are the product or offering, price, physical distribution, intermediary or channel of distribution and promotion. This has been simplified to the four 'P's: product, price, place and promotion. It is the combination of these which constitutes the total product proposition. This provides the basic opportunity for satisfying customer needs.

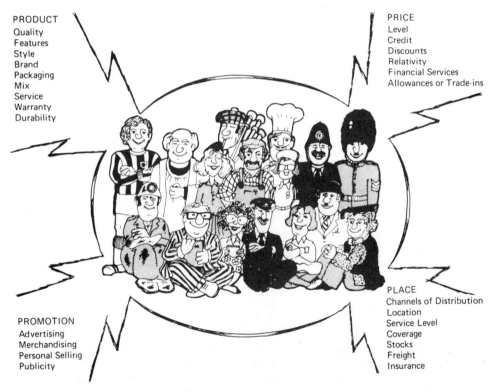

PRODUCT
Quality
Features
Style
Brand
Packaging
Mix
Service
Warranty
Durability

PRICE
Level
Credit
Discounts
Relativity
Financial Services
Allowances or Trade-ins

PLACE
Channels of Distribution
Location
Service Level
Coverage
Stocks
Freight
Insurance

PROMOTION
Advertising
Merchandising
Personal Selling
Publicity

Fig. 2.6 Different mixes will meet different needs and appeal to different subgroups.

Marketing calls for effective management of the individual mix elements and, perhaps even more important, their interaction. It is the right product, at the right time, in the right place, with the right price and presented in the right way that succeeds in satisfying buyer needs, as the following example shows:

British Leyland cut their distribution costs by reducing the numbers of their dealers, but their industrial troubles led to shortages of products at the remaining dealers, and lack of investment reduced the competitiveness of their products. These factors plus effective product development, successful promotion and competitive pricing were major elements in the successful foreign penetration of the UK market.

MARKETING POLICY

The creation of marketing policy is central to the integration of these themes. It involves:

1. Study of the likely future situations which the firm may face (scenario analysis).
2. Consideration of the different challenges which will be posed by these alternatives.
3. Careful examination of the company's ability to cope successfully with the challenges posed by changing conditions.
4. Review of the alternative *strategies* which the firm can adopt to make the best use of current or obtainable resources to achieve the best market position.
5. Taking the marketing management decisions, allocating resources and choosing the tactics which will convert these strategies to action in the marketplace.
6. Setting up procedures which will enable the firm to review progress and take action to adjust programmes of action in the light of changing circumstances and experience.

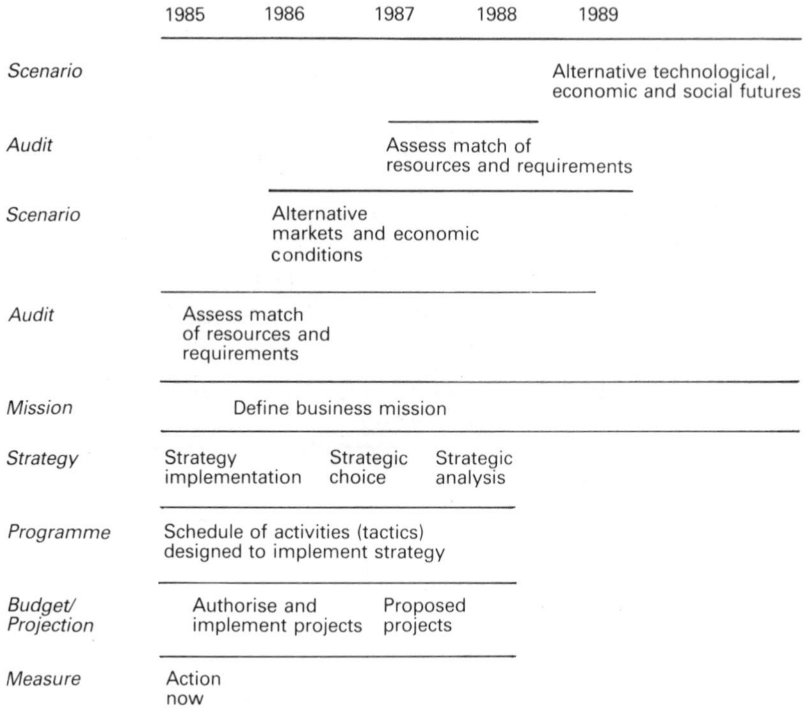

	1985	1986	1987	1988	1989
Scenario					Alternative technological, economic and social futures
Audit			Assess match of resources and requirements		
Scenario		Alternative markets and economic conditions			
Audit	Assess match of resources and requirements				
Mission	Define business mission				
Strategy	Strategy implementation		Strategic choice	Strategic analysis	
Programme	Schedule of activities (tactics) designed to implement strategy				
Budget/ Projection		Authorise and implement projects	Proposed projects		
Measure	Action now				

Fig. 2.7 Policies, programmes and scenarios. Adapted from R. E. Thomas, *Business Policy*.[7]

Figure 2.7 describes how the formulation of marketing policy is an on-going process. It involves looking into the future, considering how possible future situations (scenarios) will affect the firm. This examination will need to be much longer term in those areas in which 'lead times', i.e. the time it takes the firm to adapt, are longest — such as technological change. This will then need to be related to the company's ability to adapt.

An illustration of the need for flexibility is seen in a major manufacturer of filing cabinets. They saw that the impact of information technology and word processing could dramatically reduce the need for traditional forms of storage. A small plastic box for 'floppy discs' could hold the same volume of data as a conventional filing cabinet. An injection moulding machine could produce in two weeks the equivalent of their entire annual product of filing cabinets. In response, the firm has expanded its wider involvement in information technology-related products. It has used its good reputation, excellent distribution system and links with retailers and wholesalers to broaden its commercial base while developing new products and technologies. They are now geared to cope with the changes being ushered in by this technological future.

The process of regular *auditing* of skills and capabilities is central to strategy, and to the shorter term *'scenario analysis'*, which is related to changing market and economic conditions. Auditing is primarily designed to relate the firm's actions to short-to-medium term changes in trading conditions. These latter can include changes in demand and new competitors as well as proposed novel courses of action, e.g. new product launches. Relating capabilities to costs is the key to effectiveness. The earlier the firm starts adjusting to changing circumstances the more likely it is to adapt successfully.

At the core of the process of adjustment is an understanding of the *'business mission'*, i.e. the ability to answer the question *'What business are we in?'*. This is the most important question in marketing, as it requires that the firm look beyond its current offering and into the need it meets for its customers.

There are many examples of firms failing to appreciate the true nature of the business they are in. There was the failure of the railway companies to recognise that they were in the transport business (*not* railways), and of the motion picture companies to appreciate that they were in the entertainment business (*not* films). A very clear illustration of the benefits of this understanding may be seen in the realisation by Parker Pens of the business they are in.

Conventional analysis would see Parker as in the 'pens' or perhaps the 'writing implements' business. This would lead to policies being adopted in product development, distribution, pricing and promotion based on this business definition, e.g.:

1. People write all year, so advertising should be constant over the various months.
2. Distribution should be concentrated in specialist outlets, e.g. stationers.

However, careful analysis of the market brought out evidence which challenged this conventional belief. It became clear that the vast majority of quality pens (the type Parker produced) were not purchased by users. They were gifts! *Parker were in the gift business*.

The implications of this affected virtually all aspects of marketing activity:

1. Products were designed to enhance their 'presentation as gifts' as much as their functionality.
2. Gift packs and packaging were critical to success.
3. Advertising schedules reflected gift buying seasons, e.g. Christmas, more than use.
4. Distribution and production schedules were designed to reflect the same buyer and seasonal patterns.
5. Pricing became geared to competitive gifts not other pens.

In arriving at this definition of their 'mission', Parker managed to combine a definition which was broad enough to provide new avenues for development while not being so wide as to be meaningless.

The 'mission' describes the nature of the firm. The *'marketing strategy'* provides the firm with its sense of direction. Strategy involves 'the matching of the activities of an organisation with the environment in which it operates'.[8] It links the *conclusions* drawn from appreciation of the firm's current position in the environment with the *future* position the company seeks to occupy in the marketplace. Marketing strategies should also contain within them clear indications of the immediate policies and programmes of action to be adopted by the company.

The *marketing programmes* adopted by the firm focus on the two areas previously introduced under the titles 'target markets' and 'marketing mixes'. Central to thinking in this area is the notion that the more activities are focused around the needs of particular groups, the more likely they are to be successful. The company should attempt to define and describe the customer groups it wishes to reach as clearly as possible. These become the 'target' for the specific market-orientated actions it is taking. These actions are built from the resources under the company's control in the areas of *product*, *price*, *place* and *promotion*. Specific combinations will have a different degree of appeal to alternative target groups. Establishing the specific mix is only the first stage. The actions which emerge will need to be integrated and scheduled into a programme of action designed to achieve the desired results over time and in the most cost-effective way.

Budgeting is an integral part of this process. Establishing realistic funding levels is necessary at this stage. Often firms draw up marketing strategies far beyond their capacity to fund them. This is particularly true in overseas trade. Research[9] has indicated that underfunding is one of the most serious problems faced by exporters, regardless of whether they are concentrating on a few markets or attempting to skim a large number of different countries.

Effective management has been described as 'Doing the right things, *not* doing things right'. Critical to this notion is the process of *monitoring* and *measuring* performance against the firm's corporate and marketing objectives. Marketing success in the long term depends on learning from mistakes and continually striving for increased effectiveness and improved productivity. This can only be achieved if the company sets up systems to monitor and evaluate the returns from expenditures and actions.

Policy, strategy and structure

The earlier discussion of marketing's role in the firm indicates a number of alternative approaches to organising the marketing function in the firm. Two additional aspects of this must be included in any consideration of this area:

1. The relationship between the marketing function and the rest of the firm.
2. The fit between the strategies adopted and the organisational arrangements (structure) established to achieve them.

A number of distinctive organisational forms have been identified by researchers in Britain and the USA:[10,11]

The Entrepreneurial Firm. Controlled and managed by the owner-manager, who takes responsibility for most significant marketing decisions.

The Professionalised Company. The operations of the company are delegated to specific departments of functional areas managed and controlled by specialists, e.g. marketing, production, finance, etc.

The Divisionalised Firms. A head office exists which determines overall policy, but the divisions take most of the operational decisions. A firm such as Lucas, with its specialist divisions, illustrates this (see Figure 2.8).

The Holding Company. The centre exercises very loose control over the operating companies. They have considerable freedom, operating at times like 'independent' firms.

The organisation of the marketing operation, especially the responsibility for strategic decision-making, varies considerably between these different structures.

The best form of organisational arrangement is directly influenced by the environment faced by the company. Mintzberg[12] has put forward the following matrix to describe how

Environment

	Stable	Dynamic
Complex	*Banks* and other highly centralised firms	*Advanced Electronics* and other markets experiencing change
Simple	*Cars* and other established single product consumer goods	*Retailers* and other firms where the market requires freedom of action

Task

Fig. 2.8 Organisations and uncertainty. Adapted from G. Johnson and K. Scholes, *Exploring Corporate Strategy*.[8]

the nature of the business mission (in terms of complexity) and the character of the environment can be related, to suggest particular forms of organisational arrangement.

In the complex–stable situation, strategies can be centrally set and monitored, as the stability of the market enables the Head Office to use their greater resources while little is lost through central control. In the complex–dynamic case, any attempt to impose too much central direction may stifle creativity making it harder for the firm to adapt to changing circumstances. The simple–stable context gives considerable advantages to the firm that can mobilise its resources most efficiently against identified long term goals. The simple–dynamic situation gives the maximum benefit to strategies built on people-based responses to customer requests.

More recently authors such as Peters and Waterman[13] have emphasised the importance of establishing strategies first, then designing the organisation to achieve them. They suggest that this form of functionality in organisational design is the best defence against the inefficiencies which can emerge too easily in large and powerful corporations. The risk is that management may lose sight of the objectives and strategies while paying too much attention to company politics and personal position. A properly designed strategy, if matched with effective controls, should force the organisation to shape itself around the best means of achieving goals.

MARKETING CONTROLS

The excitement and challenge of deriving and implementing marketing strategies and programmes makes it very easy to lose sight of the equally important challenge of building systems of effective control into the firm's marketing procedures. Anyone familiar with Murphy's Laws—*If anything can go wrong, it will go wrong*, and *Of the things that can't go wrong, some will*—will recognise the importance of building in controls to ensure:

1. *That the firm making the mistakes is the first to be aware of them.* Some of the cheapest lessons to be learnt in marketing are those based on the mistakes of competitors who fail to build-in effective monitoring systems. However, this pattern works both ways.
2. *That adjustments and adaptations are made to programmes before errors become fatal.* Customers are surprisingly supportive of suppliers who realise their mistakes and try sincerely to correct them. The same client will have very little patience with the firm that is unaware of its failings.

Marketing controls exist to help management monitor and direct their actions in the field. It is intimately linked with supervision and surveillance. The controls set up by the firm should provide a basis for measuring performance against established and agreed criteria. The issue is discussed at length in Chapter 22. Here it is important to recognise that the primary aim of marketing control is to ensure that actions taken and their consequences conform to the policies and strategies established by the firm.

KEY POINTS

In this chapter a number of issues were raised which are central to marketing practice today:

1. Marketing policy can only be effective if it is based on an understanding of the market, the firm's place within it and an understanding of the likely consequence of actions.
2. Establishing 'what business we are in' is the cornerstone of the marketing approach.
3. The marketing strategy provides the firm with its sense of direction, besides providing the basis for the formulation of programmes of action and mechanisms of control.
4. Those involved in marketing management perform a wide range of tasks and hold a diverse array of job titles.
5. Marketing management is most effective when it operates in harmony with the rest of the firm's operational areas.

Throughout the rest of the text, these issues will be central to discussion of the areas of management action.

Notes

1. Piercy, N., *Marketing Organisation*. London: George Allen & Unwin, 1985.
2. Brownlie, D., 'The Anatomy of Strategic Marketing Planning', *Journal of Marketing Management*, 1, No.1, Summer 1985.
3. Clarkeson, A.H. & Stone, M.A., 'Strategic Marketing Planning Within a Medium Sized Scottish Company', Second World Marketing Congress, Stirling, 1985.
4. Kotler, P., 'The Major Tasks of Marketing Management', *Journal of Marketing*, October 1973.
5. Hilgard, E.R., Atkinson, R.C., & Atkinson, R.L. *Introduction to Psychology*. New York: Harcourt Brace, 1965.
6. Festinger, L., *A Theory of Cognitive Dissonance*. Stanford University Press, 1957.
7. Thomas, R.E., *Business Policy*. London: Philip Allan, 1983.
8. Johnson, G. & Scholes, K., *Exploring Corporate Strategy*. London: Prentice-Hall, 1984.
9. Piercy, N., *Export Strategy; Markets and Competition*. London: George Allen and Unwin, 1982.
10. Channon, D., *The Strategy and Structure of British Enterprise*. London: Macmillan, 1973.
11. Chandler, A.D., *Strategy and Structure*. Massachusetts Institute of Technology Press, 1962.
12. Mintzberg, H., *The Structure of Organisations*. Englewood Cliffs: Prentice-Hall, 1979.
13. Peters, T.J. & Waterman, R.H., *In Search of Excellence*. London: Harper and Row, 1982.

Glossary

Account. (1) In sales, an invoice. (2) In advertising, a client of an advertising, or other agency. Now being used far more widely to describe customers and customer groups. Key Account management is a term gaining increasing currency, which describes selling arrangements made to deal with major customers.

Audit. The assessment of the assets and liabilities of the firm. SWOT analysis (Strengths, Weaknesses, Opportunities, Threats) is frequently used as the basis of the marketing audit.

Budget. Statement of income and expenditure over time, usually linked to a timetable of events and actions for which monies have been allocated.

Communication. This is the process of transmitting information from one human being to another, whether directly and personally or indirectly and impersonally. Effective communication is a function of the reception of messages, not their transmission.

Control. This consists of directing and monitoring the actions taken by the firm and its members to ensure that the use of company resources contributes to the achievement of company goals.

Drive. An internal pressure to satisfy a need.

Mission. The statement of the nature of the firm in terms of the business it is in and the need(s) it meets.

Motives. The psychological state which affects the readiness of a person or organisation to adopt a course of action or continue with an existing pattern.

Needs. Any lack or deficit within an individual or organisation.

Objectives. The purposes and tasks set for the firm or a particular area of company activity, e.g. marketing.

Product/Brand Manager. The executive with overall responsibility for a specific product or brand within a multi-product (or brand) firm. Typically he or she has specific responsibility for promotional expenditures, with joint authority in other areas. The degree of profit responsibility varies between firms.

Programme. The schedule or sequence of events which draws together the specific actions or activities of the firm in a concerted way.

Scenario analysis. This is a strategic planning technique which involves identification of a range of alternative future environments which the firm is likely to face. On the basis of these the company examines its ability to cope with the challenges which they will pose. The extent to which different strategies strengthen the company's position can then be related to these scenarios.

Strategy. The process of matching the company's resources to the wider environment to produce a statement (or statements) which summarise the overall route the firm will take to achieve its objectives.

Tactic. The specific action taken to take the firm in the direction of achieving its overall strategy.

Venture management. The approach to new product development which involves bringing together teams of specialists to develop an offering from concept to launch.

CASE STUDY 2: CALEDONIA PLAIN CHOCOLATE

Introduction

In late 1983 the marketing audit conducted by Booker-Greer Limited's confectionery division highlighted a number of weaknesses in their marketing position. The two main weaknesses were:

1. Their strength in milk chocolate count lines was matched by poor performance in plain chocolate. This situation was made more serious because of the growing importance of plain chocolate in the market.
2. In a number of parts of the UK their market share was significantly worse than in the country as a whole. Among these Scotland stood out as particularly important because of its high per capita chocolate consumption and the unusually high sales of plain chocolate in that area.

Competitive history

Both these factors could be explained in part by a series of decisions made in the past. In the early 1950s the company had been the first major confectionery manufacturer to spot the trend away from toffees and boiled sweets.

For over thirty years the firm had sustained its position as one of the three largest confectionery manufacturers through a small number of major milk chocolate count lines backed by heavy advertising and extensive distribution. These traditional favourites had been supplemented by a number of new product launches. During the late 1970s and early 1980s a very high rate of new brand introduction by themselves and their competitors had occurred. Overall, Booker-Greer had come out of this period worse off than before. Unlike their two competitors they had not established a major new large-volume count-line on the market. (Although the two competitors had established only one new major product each, the long-term contribution of these was likely to be substantial.)

The current situation

Faced with the ever-escalating cost of introducing a new brand, the new product group embarked on a wide-ranging study of alternative strategies. In the light of the weaknesses in plain chocolate and in Scotland, it was recommended that the firm explore the scope for a brand geared to the specific needs of the Scottish market. It was hoped that this brand would take up some of the spare capacity then existing in the firm's manufacturing plant in Edinburgh.

In the past the firm had always worked very closely with their existing advertising agencies on new product development projects. In this case it was decided that extra insight into the market in Scotland could be achieved through a local Scottish agency. Four Scottish agencies, two based in Glasgow and two in Edinburgh, were asked to compete for the business, as was the Edinburgh office of one of their London agencies.

Of the competing agencies Alexander Gooch and Co. stood out as most committed to a distinctively Scottish offering. They were briefed to develop and research a new brand for possible launch in late 1985 or early 1986. Clear volume targets were set, amounting to 25 per cent of plain chocolate count lines (10 per cent total chocolate count line sales) in Scotland. This would minimise the impact on current sales of Booker-Greer products while biting into their competitors' market.

A number of names, packs and related advertising themes emerged, notably 'Stuart', 'Saltire', 'Caledonia' and 'Stirling' brand chocolates. These were researched in conjunction with a brand name and proposition, 'Silhouette', that had performed reasonably well in national research studies among both adults and children.

The research indicated considerable interest in the concept of a Scottish brand. The Caledonia brand and campaign (emphasising Scottish links, made in Scotland etc) did consistenly well, out-performing all other propositions including Silhouette. Unfortunately, two major problems emerged:

1.   Consumer preferences were for a milk chocolate Scottish brand.
2.   The results, although promising, suggested a market of less than 18 per cent of the plain chocolate market (for the plain brand) and 9 per cent of total chocolate count sales (if a milk chocolate brand was launched).

These results created a major debate within the firm about further actions. The brand group and advertising agency favoured progressing with the launch, initially with the plain brand but with a view to introducing a milk brand later. Both pointed to the overall appeal of the basic concept and suggested that the results might easily be an understatement, given the newness of the proposition. They also pointed to growing nationalist feeling in

Scotland and the brand manager in charge saw the national soccer squad's progress in the World Cup as a potential boost to sales.

The firm's research department recommended abandonment. In this they were supported by the corporate planning department, who pointed out the harsh reality that the offering had failed to meet its targets at a time when national sentiment was high. Also, any milk chocolate derivative would draw much of its sales from their current offering.

After considering these arguments the marketing director decided to abandon this initiative.

Tasks

1. Examine the thinking which led to this project.
2. Review its development.
3. Explore the final argument.
4. Evaluate the final decision.

3

The Marketing System

Understanding the environment and marketing system in which the firm and its competitors, suppliers and customers do business is central to effective marketing. Managers must fully appreciate:

The business environment: the conditions, primarily economic, political, cultural and technological, under which the marketing system(s) exists or is developed.

Adapted from the Oxford English Dictionary

The marketing system: the set of significant institutions and flows that connect an organization to its markets.

P. Kotler, *Marketing Management[1]*

The traditional trading farmer is perhaps the simplest illustration of the system (Figure 3.1). Although perhaps the oldest marketing system, it persists throughout the world, although adaptations have taken place even here, perhaps to capitalise on new opportunities or imposed by law. Although the system is still basically the same, from the farmer direct to the customer, the roads have opened up a massive new travelling market, and cultural changes have encouraged motorists to buy direct from the farm.

Throughout the world, environmental factors have interacted with the marketing system to produce change and adaptation in both. (The systems view of the market views it as a series of interrelated processes made up of a number of parts (sub-systems) operating in a more or less complex environment. The parts of the system demonstrate an ordered pattern of behaviour designed to achieve certain goals, either their own or the system's.) The results are markedly varied in different parts of the world. The political, cultural,

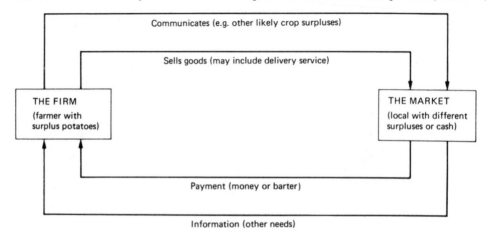

Fig. 3.1 A simple marketing system.

economic and technological history and conditions of Britain have created many areas in which the systems differ dramatically from those in North America and the white Commonwealth (perhaps those nearest culturally) and in Europe (nearest physically). There are, however, some areas of similarity. For example, advertising/sales ratios in the UK have tended to be nearer US levels than European ones, and the Co-operative (retail and wholesale) movement is powerful throughout Europe, including Britain, but in this semi-political form is virtually unknown in the USA.

The environment is continually changing, partly from interactions with other systems (much of our thinking about marketing is derived from ideas and research originating in the USA) and partly from internal factors (with the improving quality of British and European marketing has come a recognition of the real differences which exist and the confidence to recast some ideas and explore new areas). Two of the most dramatic areas of change in Britain over the last hundred years have been the decline in primary production (agriculture and mining) and the growth in the service industries (Table 3.1).

Table 3.1 *Percentage distribution among industries of working population (UK)*

	1861 (%)	1902 (%)	1921 (%)	1951 (%)	1971 (%)	1979* (%)
Primary						
Agriculture and mining	23.2	14.8	14.4	8.9	4.4	4.1
Secondary						
Manufacture	38.6	37.9	36.2	39.0	34.9	31.3
Intermediate						
Transport, communication, utilities, construction	11.3	16.3	12.2	14.0	15.4	19.6
Tertiary						
Services, white collar	21.2	25.1	35.1	37.7	45.3	46.0
Other	5.6	5.9	2.2	0.4	—	—

Reproduced with permission. Gershung, J., *After Industrial Society*. London and Basingstoke: Macmillan, 1978.
*C.S.O.

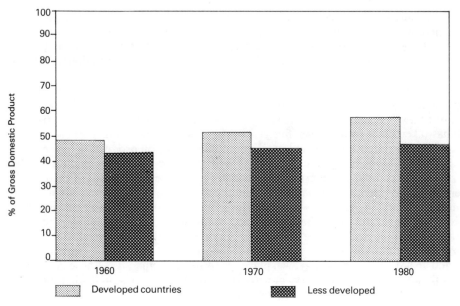

Fig. 3.2 The growing importance of the white collar services. (*Source*: UNIDO, 1982.)

Over half the working population of the UK is already employed in service-related industries. It is a pattern which can be seen across the developed world. In the USA, estimates now place the 'white collar' group as by far the largest sector of the population, with every indication that their relative significance is increasing rapidly with the introduction of new technologies.

Until recently attention has been concentrated on the impact of marketing on commercial and consumer services such as banking, tourism and catering. The pressure for 'deregulation' of accountancy, law and architecture has forced many professional groups to face up to the challenges of competition. The more sophisticated have become conscious of the potential impact of marketing on professional practice development. Shostack[2] has explored the impact of marketing as well as the differences in role that will emerge. In Britain many professional groups are seeking ways of building it into their client development strategies:

> 'It is not a question of whether professionals should adopt the marketing concept to assist in practice expansion, but whether they adopt it to survive and how well they undertake the tasks involved.'
>
> A. Wilson, *Practice Development for Professional Firms.*[3]

New technologies are currently associated with major changes in patterns of employment and consumption to transform markets and commercial relationships.

Table 3.2   *Exports of high technology products by selected countries*

Country	1972	1976	1978	1980	1982	1983
FRG	26	22	22	20	17	15
FRANCE	11	11	10	10	8	8
UK	14	12	12	13	11	10
SWITZ	4	4	4	4	3	3
JAPAN	13	18	19	18	20	25
USA	32	34	34	35	40	37

Source: Deutsche Bundesbank, 1984

This gives only a partial picture of the situation. It demonstrates the changing pattern of trade. There has been a major shift in the balance of trade during the period covered in Table 3.2. As recently as 1975, western Europe had a trade surplus of $1.7 billion (in high technology). In 1983 this was a deficit of $5 billion, which is expected to double by 1986 unless effective action is taken.

The transformation is not restricted to economic change. Policy initiatives by the Government have had a profound impact on commercial systems over a relatively short period of time. In Britain this can be seen in the extensive programme of 'privatisation' which has taken place over the last five years. This has led to actual or proposed drastic reductions in the state's involvement in telecommunications, oil production, gas production, air travel, shipbuilding and banking, as well as motor vehicle production. Kotler[1] suggests that the company system and environment can be viewed in terms of three levels: the general environment, different publics, and the marketing system. These are in a state of constant interaction, not only within each level but across different levels (see Fig. 3.3).

This figure illustrates how the general environmental forces—economic, political, cultural and technological—shape the marketing system and the commercial relationships within it. A free market economy, with competing political parties but sharing certain values and an advanced technology, will place very different demands on those involved in business than a closed, single party, underdeveloped economy. The individual firm will have far more freedom of action but can expect far less protection from commercial difficulties. Management will be far more mobile but so will competitors. The company

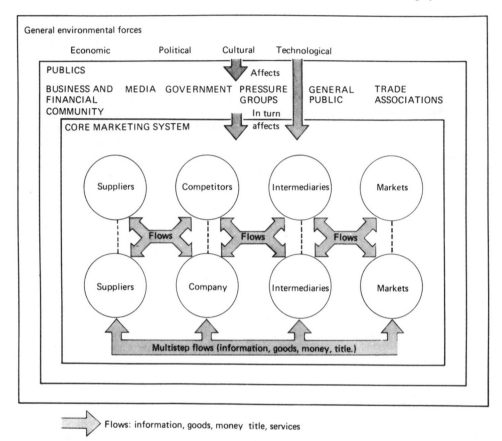

Fig. 3.3 The interaction between the different environments and the marketing system.

will have access to high technology but will need to meet high research and development costs while being vulnerable to novel offerings.

The precise form and shape of the commercial relationships within these broad patterns will be determined by the publics which surround the 'core marketing system'. The financial community can affect many areas of action, ranging from investment programmes to international trade. In Britain it has been suggested that the banks do not provide as much support for R&D and innovation as do banks in the US, Japan and West Germany. At the same time foreign competitors look with envy on the skills in international trade and finance which the UK Banks have acquired over the years. The approach of the media to industry has a direct effect on confidence and relationships. Many criticisms have been lodged against the UK media over the last few years; for example,

> The media are determined to send up industry as making profits out of innocent, ill-informed members of the public.
>
> Michael Shersby, M.P.

The earlier comments on 'privatisation' illustrate the way in which direct intervention by government can shape commercial relationships. Perhaps even more important is the way in which government can use its legislative, administrative, purchasing and other powers to shape markets. In turn, government is affected by pressure groups. These can influence markets directly, as the activities of groups such as the 'Consumer Association',

'Friends of the Earth', 'The British Clay Pipe Manufacturers Association' show. A clear illustration of this has been the pervasive influence over many years of the 'Lord's Day Observance Society'. Even when the Society was moribund, its policy was taken up by trade unions opposing (on very different grounds) proposals for repeal of the restrictions on Sunday trading in England.

In isolation or in concert, these forces shape the pattern of the market. Looking at them in terms of one country can be deceptive. These systems interact internationally. This was seen in the early 1980s, when US legislation on restricting access to new technologies by the Soviet Union came into direct conflict with the policies of other countries.

In some markets other 'environmental' forces play a major part. Agricultural and food markets can be affected immediately and dramatically by climate or ecology.[4]

GENERAL ENVIRONMENT

Britain is a mixed economy in which both the state and private enterprise are directly involved in the marketing process. A series of political decisions, stretching back into the last century, have led to the state becoming directly involved in both the management of the systems and the operations of specific industries, through direct intervention, regulation, inducement and direction, legislation and economic policies. The specific strategies of governments can vary considerably even over relatively short periods of time. The differences between, say, the Labour Government of 1974 and the Conservatives in 1983 illustrate this. The former was committed to direct intervention through such agencies as the National Enterprise Board. The latter adopted a policy of 'privatisation' designed to reduce public sector direct involvement. Despite these differences in policy, both recognised the profound impact their programmes could have on markets and business relationships.

Pressure for 'de-regulation' can be seen in many industries and a number of countries. Airlines, trucking, banks and professional services have been transformed. The reluctance of British firms to espouse marketing has been linked by King (1985) with two aspects of recent industrial development: the emergence of 'producer bureaucracies' and the 'profit spiral'. Both reflect the declining competitiveness of UK industry. This has been linked with two contradictory explanations:

The growth of competition and progressive removal of protectionism.[5]

The increasing bureaucratisation of trading relationships and the expansion of regulatory interference.

The balance of evidence in those industries where de-regulation has occurred suggests that the latter explanation is closer to the truth. This may reflect the failure of British companies to respond to the increasing 'globalisation' of trade:

Many observers have contrasted the long tradition of protected markets for British firms which has led historically to both buyers and sellers being resistant to change and competition.

P. Doyle.[6]

The evidence of the reluctance of sellers to adopt a marketing approach in certain key sectors has been demonstrated in a number of studies, notably machine tools,[7] textiles,[8] and vehicles.[9] It is possible that a high import penetration of many UK markets indicates a less conservative approach among buyers.

The overall British strategy for economic development employs many of the approaches open to any similar government. In North America, different attitudes, decisions and traditions will produce variations in government policy within a broadly similar framework. In Europe a more directly interventionist approach has been adopted, especially in France and Sweden. In Japan the tradition of strong informal links between government and industry finds its expression in the dialogues held under the auspices of MITI (The Ministry of International Trade and Industry). Elsewhere, detailed national plans are produced to assist and/or direct industry along certain lines. In Britain, the review of the available alternatives and consideration of their strengths and weaknesses in this context have led to a particular pattern emerging.

Direct intervention

The last five years have seen more substantial change in this area than at almost any time since the late 1940s. It is an area in which the greatest overall contrast exists between Britain and Europe on the one hand and the USA and Japan on the other. Despite recent changes, well over half the commercial transactions taking place in Britain today involve the state. The list of industries which the state owns or has a stake in, or which are directly dependent on government or local authority purchasing or help, is vast.

Among them, the top nationalised industries (the Electricity Council and Boards, the Post Office, British Steel, the National Coal Board, British Gas, British Railways, the National Bus Company, the South of Scotland Electricity Board, the National Freight Corporation, and British Shipbuilders) had a turnover in 1983 in excess of £35 billion, and employed over one million workers.

Table 3.3 *Britain's nationalised industries for sale.*

Organisation	Revenues (millions)	Net income (millions)	Assets (millions)
Electricity Council	$15,353	$554	$53,834
British Telecom	$10,657	$610	$16,251
British Gas	$9,957	$315	$20,137
British Steel	$5,399	($1,452)	$5,170
British Leyland	$5,374	($512)	$3,730
British Railways	$4,927	($304)	$3,142
British Airways	$4,172	$129	$2,232
Rolls-Royce	$2,612	($234)	$2,008
British Shipbuilders	$1,826	($214)	$949
National Bus	$1,184	$29	$590
Royal Ordnance Factories	$750	$147	$487
British Airports Authority	$474	$35	$1,489

Source: Fortune.

Areas in which the government has a direct interest through ownership or a major shareholding include basic utilities (gas and oil), strategic materials (BP, Britoil), communications (British Telecom), consumer goods (British Leyland) and a number of other spheres of interest, including chemicals, shipbuilding, and machine tools.

The process of intervention is so far advanced that even a government committed to reducing it faces severe limitations on its freedom of action, at least in the short to medium term. Some continuing involvement has been acknowledged by the Conservative Government, at least until the free market institutions are in a position to take over a more active supporting role. This process of intervention has direct effects on the marketing system both at home and overseas. It is important to recognise that the UK is not atypical among European countries, most of which have adopted direct intervention under specific circumstances (Table 3.4 and Figure 3.4). The massive industrial enterprises in Table 3.4 are part of a world-wide pattern of government ownership of key industries, services and utilities.

Marketing in the nationalised industries represents, in many ways, a very different competitive situation from that of the traditional free market. In some instances the firm

Table 3.4   *The fourteen largest state-owned manufacturers in Europe in 1977*

Company	Country	Industry
Aérospatiale	France	Aircraft, missiles
Alfa Romeo	Italy	Automobiles
British Leyland	Britain	Automobiles
British Steel	Britain	Iron, steel
Charbonnages de France	France	Coal mining, chemicals
DSM	Netherlands	Chemicals, fertilisers, plastics
Italsider	Italy	Steel
Renault	France	Automobiles, tractors, machine tools
Rolls-Royce	Britain	Aircraft engines
Saarbergwerke	Germany	Coal mining, rubber products
Salzgitte	Germany	Steel, shipbuilding, machinery
Stätsforetag Group	Sweden	Mining, paper products, steel
VIAG	Germany	Aluminium, chemicals
VÖEST-Alpine	Austria	Steel

Adapted from the *Harvard Business Review*, March-April 1979.

has a monopoly of supply or service, e.g. gas, electricity, post, telecommunications and rail. This imposes special responsibilities, and may impose very real constraints on activities throughout the system. For example, even though a firm controls 80 to 90 per cent of customer sales, it may be restricted in the following ways:

1. Supply policies. It may be unable to apply maximum leverage to suppliers, e.g. Parkinson-Cowan.
2. Competitive strategy. It may be unable to act with complete freedom against retail competition.
3. Intermediary behaviour. It may be unable to develop price and distribution policies to maximise profits, e.g. refuse to supply.
4. End-customer service. It may be unable to act with complete freedom on product usage or promotional strategy.

Pressure can come from Parliament to 'buy British' or from special interest groups, e.g. the Association of British Domestic Appliance Manufacturers. Even when the utility resists it can be overruled; e.g. the Department of Energy, consumer councils and other groups can by-pass management, by exerting political and media pressure.

The use of nationalised industries to add weight to government policies can also directly affect their marketing, and wage restraint can cut recruitment in key areas, e.g. service. It even appears that the 'public' character of public ownership means that consumers are far more critical and demanding of the nationalised industries.

Despite these features, some nationalised industries have demonstrated the scope for creative marketing. In 1977 the *Financial Times* described the Gas Corporation as one of the best marketing organisations in Britain. Unfortunately, there has been very little substantial research into marketing and the nationalised industries.

Regulation, inducement and direction

In most industrial economies in the western world some degree of regulation, inducement and direction of marketing activity is accepted. In Britain this ranges from the definition of technical standards (under the auspices of the British Standards Institute) to the direction of investment in certain parts of the country through Regional Aid.

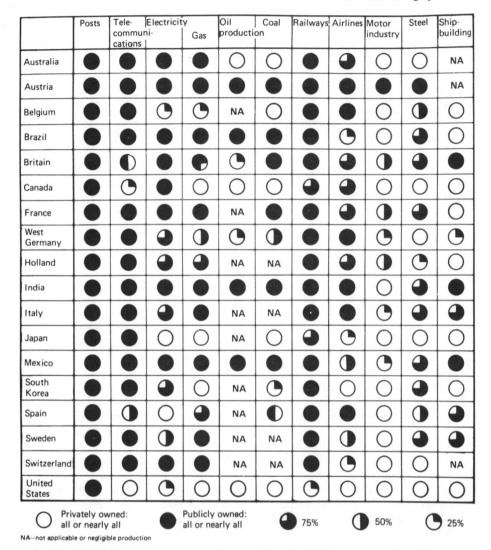

○ Privately owned: all or nearly all   ● Publicly owned: all or nearly all   ◕ 75%   ◑ 50%   ◔ 25%

NA—not applicable or negligible production

Fig. 3.4 The scope of state ownership. Reproduced with the permission of *The Economist*.

Regulatory systems

These include technical standards, building regulations and requirements for health and safety at work.

Regulatory systems can create new opportunities as well as impose rules, and there is now a service industry advising firms about the regulations.

Inducement

Inducements are often offered to persuade firms to implement government policies. Export policies are backed by an array of inducements from the British Overseas Trade Board, and innovation and investment are often grant aided.

> The Market Entry Guarantee Scheme (MEGS) is designed to help smaller and medium-sized firms in manufacturing industry to deal with the financial risk and problems associated with a venture to develop a new export market.
>
> British Overseas Trade Board Brochure, 1978.

Direction

The Government sometimes attempts to direct firms into specific areas of activity, e.g. investment in North Sea oil and related activities, or even towards specific business stances.

Great attention needs to be given (by industry) to 'non-price' factors. It is important that we all bring our products up to date, deliver them on time and provide full back-up service.

National Economic Development Office, 1978.

Legislation

The last forty years have seen an ever-increasing pace of legislation affecting the ways in which the firm operates in the market-place. Much of this legislation has been directed towards encouraging competition.

In the immediate post-war period the first major legislative move was the passing of the Monopolies and Restrictive Practices (Inquiry and Control) Act 1948. The overall aim of this Act was to establish a commission to enquire into business practices in industries in which one-third or more of an industry was held by one firm, cartel or less formal group, in order to establish whether this was in the public interest.

Partly because of a report of the Commission on restrictive practices in industry, the Restrictive Practices Act was passed in 1956. This set up a Registrar of Restrictive Trading Agreements and a Restrictive Practices Court. In the Court, judgement was made according to fixed provisions as to whether any restrictions were not against the public interest. In a series of important judgements the detailed framework of case law has been established. For example in 1962 the Court ruled that net book agreements designed to enforce retail price maintenance were acceptable, as their removal would affect the viability of many bookshops and reduce the ability of publishers to publish small-volume texts. In 1959 the Court ruled that price fixing and agreements on discounts by carpet manufacturers were not acceptable, as they were arbitrary and contrary to the public interest. The 1956 Act was amended in 1968 and also by the Fair Trading Act of 1973. This led to the appointment of a Director General of Fair Trading.

In 1965 the relatively short-lived National Board for Prices and Incomes was set up with a brief to examine pricing policies referred to it by the Government. The Board was abolished by the 1970 Conservative Government. Within three years the Price Commission was established to scrutinise prices in private industry, and during the period of the 1975 Labour Government the Price Commission played an increasing part in counter-inflation policies.

One of the first acts of the 1979 Conservative Government was to introduce the Competition Act 1979. This abolished the Price Commission, transferring a number of its powers to the Office of Fair Trading and the Monopolies and Mergers Commission. These bodies were provided with additional 'competition reference' powers. As a result, Britain's competition laws are based on the Competition Act 1979, the Fair Trading Act 1973, the Restrictive Practices Act 1976, the Restrictive Practices Court Act 1976 and the Resale Prices Act 1977. These Acts generally operate under the auspices of the Ministry of Trade and Consumer Affairs.

Since its re-election in 1983, the Government has maintained the same broad approach. This has been based on selective action in areas such as environmental protection while pursuing a strategy of minimum intervention elsewhere.

Although specific approaches by government have changed significantly over the last twenty years, all would probably subscribe to a general commitment to act by legislation if necessary

to attack anti-competitive practices and to ensure the proper operation of the market.

Mrs Sally Oppenheim, former Minister for Consumer Affairs

Also, although there are very real differences in policies, there has been a broadly consistent direction of thinking about overall competition practice.

A major plank of the present government's programme has been the reduction of statutory and voluntary restraints on trade. This process of 'de-regulation' can be seen in areas as diverse as banking services, optical supplies and transport.

The Acts noted above reflect some of the major areas of policy and legislation, but government action has also been directed at a number of specific areas of marketing activity and particular industries. Pricing is directly affected by both the Resale Prices Act 1977 and the work of the Office of Fair Trading. Advertising for certain commodities (cigarettes, gambling, food, drugs etc.) and in some areas (e.g. affecting health and safety) is controlled by a number of statutory instruments, e.g. the Consumer Protection Act 1961 (as amended by the Consumer Protection Act 1971). Product and warranty are governed by such legislation as the Sale of Goods Act 1893 and the more recent Supply of Goods (Implied Terms) Act 1972, and the broad area of the Law of Contract. Other important legislation is the Trade Marks Act 1938, the Copyright Act 1956, the Trades Descriptions Act 1968–72 and the Patents Act 1977.

As a member of the European Economic Community, Britain falls under the auspices of its competition laws, which have always played an important part in the community. They are encompassed by Articles 85 and 86 of the Treaty of Rome. Article 85 deals with agreements and practices which hinder the free play of competition, and Article 86 focuses on the abuse of a dominant market position. They apply only where trade between member states is affected. Responsibility for implementing these Articles lies with Directorate-General IV. All rulings by the Commission in this area fall into the scope of the European Court of Justice, to which firms can appeal if they are dissatisfied with the Commission's findings. Although there are areas of overlap between US and European practice, a fundamental difference exists in the approach to restraint on trade. Unlike the USA, the EEC is prepared to accept restraints which are economically useful and do not substantially reduce competition.

These two areas of legislation, EEC and UK, directly affect British firms both at home and in Europe. Firms operating overseas must learn to cope with the specific legislation of the markets in which they operate. Most industrially developed western economies have legislation and statutory bodies to protect customers and facilitate competition; a few are listed below:

Belgium: Consumer Council, General Economics Inspectorate, Commercial Economics Service.
France: Directorate General for Internal Consumers and Prices, Service de la Répression des Fraudes et du Contrôle de la Qualité, National Consumer Institute.
West Germany: Although no specific ministry has responsibility, policies are co-ordinated by the Inter-Ministerial Committee on Consumer Matters.
Japan: Conference on Consumer Protection, Economic Welfare Bureau of the Economic Planning Agency.
Sweden: National Council for Consumer Goods Research and Consumer Information, Market Court, Consumer Ombudsman.
United States: Federal Trade Commission, Anti-Trust Division of the Attorney General's Office.

Even in the countries listed many other government departments, ministries of finance or economics, are involved in what has become an almost worldwide movement by governments to legislate to achieve specific goals in competition policy and consumer protection. There is generally a close link between these and attempts to manage the overall economic progress of their countries.

Economic policies

Although the supply and demand issues which are the basis of any free market were discussed in Chapter 1, many other aspects of the economic environment help create the conditions under which firms operate.

Britain is one of the most economically developed countries in the world, accounting for about 5 per cent of the output of the 24 member states of the Organization for Economic Co-operation and Development. Although there has been a marked decline in the country's position relative to her major trading rivals, the British consumer has experienced significant real growth in living standards over the last decade, and much of British industry remains highly competitive and capable of winning business in highly sophisticated and technologically advanced markets, as Table 3.5 shows.

Table 3.5   *Winners of the Queen's Awards for Exports*

Firm	Technology	Markets
Avalon Chemicals	Synthetic resins and adhesives	Scandinavia, North America
Biozyme Laboratories	Biochemicals	Western Europe, Japan, USA
British Aerospace	Aerospace	Worldwide
Crosfield Electronics	Electronics	Worldwide
Davy International	Contracting	Japan, USSR
JCB	Materials handling	USA, Europe

Adapted from *Trade and Industry*, 11 May, 1979

Marketing policies are directly affected by worldwide, regional and domestic economic forces. The scale of Britain's dependence on exports (over 20 per cent of the Gross National Product) means that movements in the world economy influence both foreign and domestic operations. The apparent slowing down of the world economy,[3] caused by a mixture of energy shortages, inflation, protectionism and other factors, is forcing many firms to recognise the need to face up to new, slow or nil growth markets. Marketing in recession may become part of the business reality of the 1980s. These conditions highlight the importance of effective marketing:

1. Targeting will be critical; overall growth may be low but specific sectors will be far more resilient. During the slump in the UK furniture market in the mid-1970s the high-price, high-quality sector continued to grow while the low-price sector suffered.
2. Effective use of the marketing mix will be critical. According to a study of the economic recession of the early 1920s, 'the firms which increased their advertising also increased their sales'.[4]
3. Continual monitoring of the changing character of customer attitudes and behaviour will be essential. There appears to be an increasing professionalism among consumers, who are seeking solutions to their new economic circumstances.
4. The balance of a firm's business will probably require a broader market base, increased added value and a rigorous approach to pricing, notably in industrial markets. 'In the post 1973 recession, the Third World was the most buoyant market.'[5]

Membership of the EEC has subjected British firms to new economic pressures. The ten years between 1972 and 1982 saw a major shift in Britain's balance of trade as industry learnt to cope with new, sophisticated industrial markets (Figure 3.5).

Figure 3.5 illustrates how Britain's overseas trade has been influenced by membership of the European Community and other developments over the last twenty years. As recently as the mid-1960s the 'English speaking' world of North America, the old and new Commonwealth plus the less developed countries accounted for over half of UK exports. They were twice as important as the EEC. This situation has virtually reversed. The EEC is Britain's major partner, and its impact goes far beyond the members. The signing of the

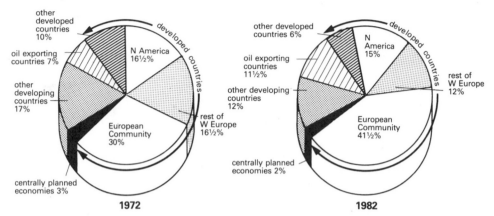

Fig. 3.5 Distribution of UK exports by areas. Reproduced with permission, Annual Report of the British Overseas Trade Board, 1983.

Lomé treaty between the EEC and 46 developing nations demonstrates how the economic and trading implications go far beyond the confines of the Community itself. As the EEC expands, this widening impact will continue.

There is increasing recognition of the extent to which the domestic marketing systems of most firms are influenced by external economic circumstances. However, it is the state of the domestic economy which generally has the most profound impact on the system.

Incomes (real and monetary), prices, interest rates, credit, output and savings all have a direct influence on the fortunes of companies. The high levels of inflation of recent years have given way more recently to fairly low rates. These reductions in the rate of inflation are coinciding with significant improvements in the Gross Domestic Product after a decade of stagnation.

This figure illustrates how the 1970s and early 1980s saw a significant slowing down in the rates of economic growth experienced since the end of the Second World War. The period 1983–84 has seen a reversal of this position, with the average growth for the 24 members of the OECD running at 3.5 per cent for this period.

The notion of the strong domestic economy as the basis for international competitiveness has influenced much government thinking. To encourage growth some form of economic management, through either fiscal (tax) or monetary policies, has been tried by most British governments. Marketing men now pay close attention to actions in these areas, but their freedom to react is directly affected by their lead times. Fluctuations in the domestic economy often lead to high imports, as intermediaries respond to demand by buying from countries with larger industrial bases in order to satisfy consumer demand before local firms can respond. Stability or consistency are vital for long-term planning particularly investment in technology.

Technology

Britain has been familiar with the impact of technology on the marketplace for longer than any other country. The Industrial Revolution which started here during the late eighteenth century affected all parts of the system from raw materials to the manufacturers, inter-mediaries and ultimate consumers. There has been continuing change and development for the last 200 years, and the process shows relatively little sign of slackening: in 1978, 50 000 patents were applied for in Britain alone.

Keeping pace with technological change is a challenge to which all firms have to

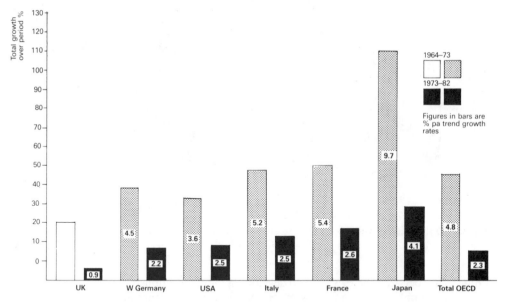

Fig. 3.6   Growth in real GDP over the periods 1964–73 and 1973–82. (*Source*: OECD.)

respond. Large firms invest vast sums in basic and applied research and smaller firms, although they may lack the absolute resources, have flexibility and commitment, which go a long way to compensate for resource limitations.

The large-scale investment of major firms, perhaps allied to government, university, college or other institutional research, plays a major role in advancing technology. The joint success in winning the Queen's Award for Technology of BDH Chemicals Ltd, Royal Signals and Radar Establishment and The Department of Chemistry, University of Hull, for the development and large-scale commercial production of biphenyl liquid crystals, illustrates the potential in this area. The emergence of a significant group of new technology based firms, which are generally small, highly specialised, and with significant added value, in Britain and other advanced industrial countries, brings out the continuing

Table 3.6   *Assistance with technology and innovation*

Country	Aid	Organisation
UK	Licensing, patents and new product development, encouragement of collaborative efforts, technical information services	National Research and Development Corporation, PatsCentre International, Design Council
France	Development credits, regional technology transfer and information centres, stimulation of collaboration between various institutions and firms	Fonds de la Recherche Scientifique et Technique, Délégation Générale à la Recherche Scientifique et Technique
West Germany	Venture Capital Bank, transfer of patents, investment grants, 'reshaping old firms into a more progressive and innovative mould'	Technological Advisory Service, Institutes Fraunhofer-Gesellschaft (research institutes), Deutsche Wagnisfinanzierungs GmbH (Venture Bank)
Japan	Finance, co-operative associations, tax concessions, joint research facilities	Small Business Promotion Corporation, Small Business Credit Insurances Corporation, Research Development Corporation of Japan

Adapted from R. Rothwell and W. Zedreld, *Small and Medium Sized Manufacturing Firms: Their Role and Problems in Innovation, Government Policy in Europe, the USA, Canada, Japan and Israel 1977.*

role of smaller firms in this sphere of activity. The contribution is now seen as so important that many nations have devised special support schemes (Table 3.6).

New technologies have an impact throughout the marketing system in shaping availability, cost and ultimate consumption of goods (Figure 3.6).

Marketing management's role in this area is to provide the spur to the company's innovation while supplying marketing insights into the broad patterns of technological change. Some new technologies marketeers directly, notably videotext for information transmission, mini and micro computers for handling problems and analysis, besides videofilm and cable television.

Culture

The ways in which any society responds to the various pressures described above depend to a considerable extent on its history and culture. Britain, as the first industrial power, has made adaptations which are very different from those of other countries, both those which are industrially developed and those which are undeveloped. Language, religion, attitudes, social organisation, education, the law, the arts and the very attitudes towards industry and materialism interact to create the special milieu in which the firm operates.

The existence of a single, shared language distinguishes the UK from many countries where tribal and 'national' sub-groups sustain wide variations in dialect and language. This means that mass communication through large-circulation newspapers, magazines, TV and radio is possible. The cohesiveness of British society has itself helped to create a broader-based national system of media, unlike countries such as the United States and Germany.

Changing attitudes and values continually create new opportunities. The emerging importance of a young, design-conscious, middle-income group in the 1960s provided the foundation of the success of Habitat stores. Growing geographic mobility, allied to the increasing desire of families to eat out but remain confident of consistent levels of quality, service and cleanliness, paved the way for the success of MacDonald's hamburgers in the USA.

The cultural and ethnic subdivisions in society create their own marketing opportunities. In the USA the negro market emerged as a powerful and important market sector, its impact ranging from product development to the models used in advertisements:

> If you want to reach the heart of a $20 billion-a-year market, you'll have to recognize that the negro is nobody's fair-haired boy.
>
> *Ebony Magazine*

In Britain ethnic heterogeneity is slowly being recognised as a factor in creating marketing opportunities and problems. For example: individual products may need to meet special religious needs, e.g. kosher foods; tastes may differ, e.g. Cadbury Typhoo's Poundo Yam, the Nigerian equivalent of instant mashed potato; intermediaries may be different, e.g. the importance of small, local, Asian-run shops; languages can be a barrier, e.g. 77 per cent of Pakistani women and 43 per cent of Pakistani men could not speak English, according to one survey. The impact of these sub-groups frequently extends beyond their confines into the broader population.

THE DIFFERENT PUBLICS

Although the system operates within the general environment created by the forces described above, many are interpreted and gain immediacy from the impact of more specialised and cohesive publics.

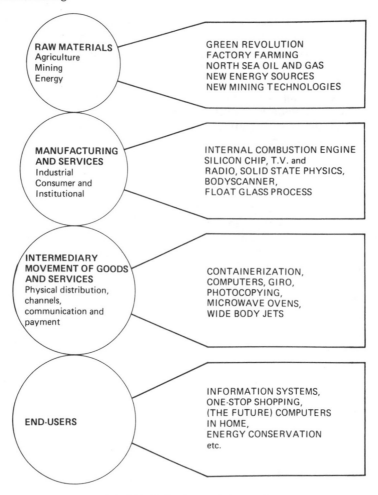

Fig. 3.7 Technology and the system.

The business and financial community

The community helps to create the trading and financial environment in which the firm operates. The confidence of manufacturers in very different sectors of the economy affects their willingness to recruit workers, give wage increases, invest and provide the overall stimulus to the market. The financial community provides the capital and credit to sustain this process. Its resources can be directed to both industrial and consumer credit. The confidence of a manufacturer in the sustained demand for his products may lead him to seek funds for new machinery, which creates demand not only for the machinery supplier but also for all his component suppliers. Equally, the prevailing rates of interest and availability of credit will determine the firm's real returns from investment in capital and plant.

The media

The media can have a direct impact on business confidence besides influencing specific firms and markets. The mass national media can have a substantial effect on markets. For example, the link between the TV series 'Life on Earth' and the book of the same name helped keep the book in the best-seller lists for over twenty weeks.

In fashion markets, the impact of magazines such as *Vogue* and *Harpers and Queen*, allied to the relatively new phenomenon of newspaper supplements, is considerable. It extends far beyond the £3 billion clothing and footwear market into general tastes and attitudes from domestic furniture to shop, office and even factory canteen layout.

The trade and technical press play a critical part in disseminating news and information. The authoritative position they can adopt in specific circumstances, e.g. in reviewing new developments or in featuring a firm and its activities, can enhance both the firm and its offering.

An important manifestation of the emerging interest in consumerism has been the publication of special-interest magazines. In some instances they are purely commercial, such as *What Car*, *What Buy*, or the short-lived *Value Today*. Many of these periodicals are linked to national consumer associations (Table 3.7).

Table 3.7 *Some European consumer magazines and associations*

Magazine	Association	Country
Which	Consumer Association	Great Britain
Consumentengids	Consumentenbond	Holland
Test	Verbraucher Rundschau	West Germany

Pressure groups

These have long been recognised as a vital part of the economic and social system. The emergence of the consumer movement and the organisation of formalised pressure groups play a major part in the context in which the firm operates. These bodies examine specific industries, and over 100 industries were studied by *Which* during the period 1975–1977. Their influence includes Parliamentary lobbying (The British Consumer Association actively supported the passing of the Unfair Contract Terms Act 1977 and Consumer Safety Act 1978) and international co-operation through bodies such as the International Organization of Consumers' Unions and the Bureau Européen des Unions de Consommateurs.

The influence of groups with direct interests in particular consumer and industrial goods can be considerable. In some areas, such as photography, motoring, sport and travel, their role can be very important, for example the International Air Travellers' Association in the DC10 groundings of 1979.

In industrial markets groupings of manufacturers and retailers can exercise great power over supplier industries, especially when acting to encourage improved standards. The work of trade associations illustrates very clearly the role that pressure groups of industrialists can play. For example, the British Plastics Federation has recently argued for changes in the British Standards Institution, the technical specifications of the nationalised industries and clay pipe regulations.

Trade associations

Throughout the world trade associations play a major part in advancing the interests of their members, besides providing them with a range of support services. In some countries, notably West Germany, trade associations play a consistently powerful role in policy formulation and implementation.

THE MARKETING SYSTEM

In examining the ways in which the firm operates within the marketing system, it is useful to think in terms of a conversion process. The company obtains an array of inputs which it converts into a selection of offerings for the market with a view to achieving some overall or specific goals (Figure 3.8).

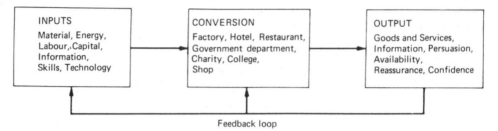

Fig. 3.8 The conversion process.

All members of the system are involved in some type of conversion as they seek to satisfy an array of needs and goals. The Rand Corporation propose that system analysis is:

Inquiry to aid a decision maker choose a course of action by systematically investigating his proper objectives, comparing quantitatively where possible the costs, effectiveness and risks associated with the alternative policies or strategies for achieving them, and formulating additional alternatives if those examined are found wanting.[10]

Even the smallest organisation may find that its inputs are extensive, complex, numerous and subject to change, while the conversion process and array of output demand effective management and control

The primary producer

The primary producer, whether in extractive industries or agriculture, faces the problems of bringing together equipment, labour and capital to ensure the effective exploitation of the minerals or land at his disposal (Figure 3.9).

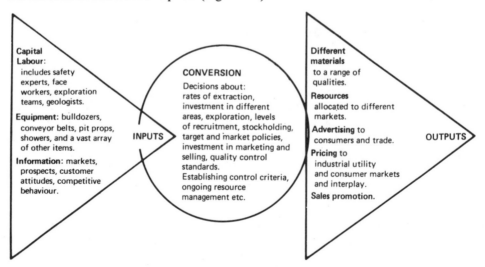

Fig. 3.9 The mine: a conversion process illustrated.

The manufacturer

The manufacturer of finished goods or components faces basically the same problems. These are complicated by the frequent need to introduce new products, which may mean extensive information-gathering, investment in large stocks of new materials and a large-scale logistics problem to ensure that all the elements come together at the optimum moment for introduction. The large number of product offerings by most firms adds a further dimension to the management of the system. A company's activities may extend into many distinct areas (Figure 3.10).

The systems approach

The systems approach tends to underplay this competitive element within a framework which emphasises the process of integration and adaptation. An alternative 'action' approach, while accepting many of the systems assumptions, emphasises the role of men, either individually or acting together, in shaping the market and environment to their own ends.

The power of the creative element in marketing, the achievements of managers, both entrepreneurs and working organisational managers, and the continuing dynamic of competition support this approach. In the overwhelming majority of successes in the marketplace, individuals interpreting the interacting forces around them, willing to take risks and adopting a creative marketing approach have played a vital part.

Mapping

The data from the analysis of the marketing system can be used in the production of maps of the market. These help the firm to:

1. Clearly identify its competitive position.
2. Identify the relative strengths and weaknesses of rivals.
3. Highlight the major features of current offerings in the eyes of customers.
4. Spot gaps in the market.

Mapping provides a way of performing these useful analytic tasks in a graphic and easily understood way.

The first step in building a market map lies in identifying the major product/market features or dimensions. Illustrations of this could be:

Market	Feature 1	Feature 2
Margarine	Price	Health
Bank	Convenience	Range of services
Breakfast Cereal	Nourishment	Novelty
Shampoo	Medication	Cosmetic
Dentifrice	Tooth care	Taste
Beer	Strength	Flavour
Yogurts	Range	Diet/Health

These features can be used to construct scales along which specific offerings can be located.

The map in Figure 3.11 indicates how the brands in a market can be distributed. Specific gaps can be identified, e.g. the one that existed in the 'mild' end of the market prior to the launch of 'Once' and 'Timotei' in 1983.

The same type of analysis can be used to explore the positioning of competitive companies, even retailers and advertising media.[11]

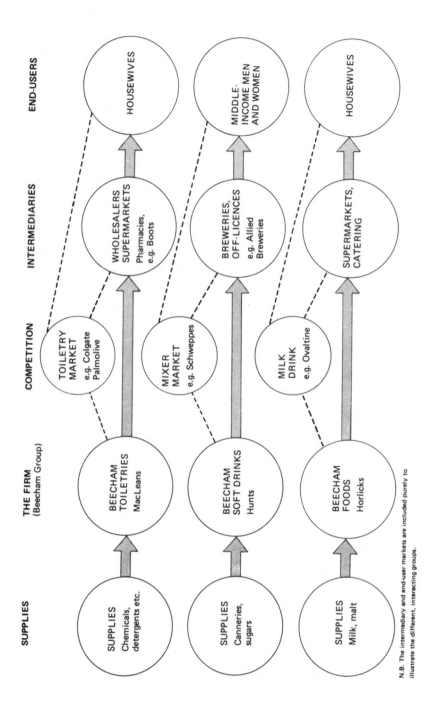

Fig. 3.10   The multiple-market conversion process.

N.B. The intermediary and end-user markets are included purely to illustrate the different, interacting groups.

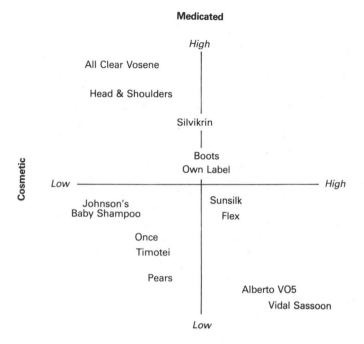

Fig. 3.11 Mapping the shampoo market.

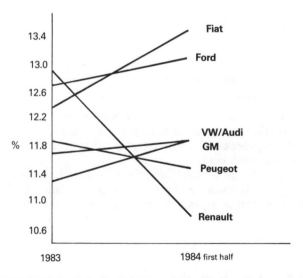

Fig. 3.12 Manufacturers' share of the European car market. (*Source*: *Fortune*, 12 November 1984.)

PARTICIPANTS AND PARTNERS

Analysis of the marketing system and effective use of techniques such as 'market mapping' calls upon firms to understand the character and role of all the other members of the markets in which they operate. Typically they will be only one of the participants in a complex and changing set of relationships (as in Fig. 3.12). The marketing orientated firm needs to know almost as much about its suppliers, competitors, immediate customers, competitors and end users as it does about itself. Managers ought to be able to conduct a SWOT analysis (Strengths, Weaknesses, Opportunities and Threats) about each, individually, and in terms of his own company.

It is as important to comprehend the limitations and potential of suppliers as it is to understand customers. It is not unknown for a very efficient producer to be faced with decline because its immediate customer failed to compete effectively in its market. This situation has faced the British components industry over the last twenty years, as domestic vehicle and white goods producers have lost their market share to European and Japanese producers. Those firms which built up their trade in Europe before the crisis of the late 1970s–early 1980s found that their sales to the growth firms went some way to compensate for the decline of others.

WINDOWS OF OPPORTUNITY

Although the type of technique identified above can indicate opportunities, it is just as important to realise that most gaps in the marketplace are temporary. Other firms can move to fill them. Changed conditions can eliminate the need for the particular offering. Customers can find an acceptable substitute. The 'windows of opportunity' that exist can close with surprising speed.[12]

This does not mean that firms should move without thoroughly researching the market and analysing the situation. It requires managers to continually seek for ways of matching care with decision.

KEY POINTS

A number of points which are central to understanding modern marketing relationships have emerged in this chapter. They have focused around four central points:

1. Marketing relationships involve sets of interrelationships, many of which go far beyond the specific transaction or immediate customer.
2. These relationships are continually changing as they are influenced by, and in turn influence, their environment.
3. Techniques and approaches have been developed over the years to help managers understand and draw lessons from this network of relationships.
4. Effective management involves linking this appreciation to decisive action.

Notes

1. Kotler, P. *Marketing Management; Analysis Planning and Control*. Englewood Cliffs: Prentice-Hall, 1984.
2. Shostack, L.G., 'Designing Services That Deliver', Harvard Business Review, January–February 1984.
3. Wilson, A., *Practice Development For Professional Firms*. London: McGraw–Hill, 1984.
4. Cannon, T., 'Marketing Problems in the Food Chain', *Food Marketing*, **1**, No.1, 1985.

5. King, S., 'Has Marketing Failed or Was It Never Tried?', *Journal of Marketing Management*, Summer 1985.
6. Doyle, P., 'Marketing and The Competitive Performance of British Industry', *Journal of Marketing Management*, Summer 1985.
7. Parkinson, S., 'Successful New Product Development', *British Graduate*, Spring 1982.
8. Amine, L., *Marketing and the Performance of the British Textile Industry*. PhD Dissertation, University of Bradford, 1976.
9. NEDO, *Industrial Performance: Trade Performance and Marketing*. London: HMSO.
10. McDaniel, G. 'The Meaning of the Systems Movement to The Acceleration and Direction of the American Economy', in *Analysis for Military Decisions*, ed. E.S. Quaile, California: Rand Corporation, 1975.
11. Wind, Y. & Robinson, P.J., 'Product Positioning: An Application of Multidimensional Scaling', in *Attitude Research in Transition*. Chicago: The American Marketing Association, 1972.
12. Abell, D.F., 'Strategic Windows', *Journal of Marketing*, July 1978.

Further reading

Ballance, R.H. and Sinclair, S.W., *Collapse and Survival; Industrial Strategies in a Changing World*. London: George Allen and Unwin, 1983.
Gershung, J. *After Industrial Society*. London: Macmillan, 1978.
Hammarkvist, K.O. 'Markets as Networks'. Cranfield, Marketing Educators Group Annual Conference, 1983.
Pickering, J.F. and Cockerill, T.A.J. (eds.), *The Economic Management of The Firm*. London: Philip Allan, 1984.
Udell, J.G. and Laczniak, G.R., *Marketing in an Age of Change*. New York: Wiley, 1981.

Glossary

Consumers' Association. Non-profit making organisation which provides a range of services associated with attempting to ensure effective representation of consumers to producers and government.

Demographics. The measurable, structural characteristics of a population, such as age, sex, income, family size, class, occupational distribution. Used a great deal to provide firms with profiles of the groups who may make up their market.

De-regulation. The process of reducing or eliminating the legislative interference in markets.

Environment. The context and set of forces which exist around the market and which shape it and determine its character.

Gross Domestic Product. The total value of all goods and services produced in an economy.

Inflation. Those increases in price which cumulatively produce a reduction in purchasing power or the real value of money.

M1. The measure of the money supply, defined as currency plus demand deposits.

M2. *M1* plus savings and time deposits at the commercial banks.

Market. The arrangement individuals or groups have for trading with each other.

Services. Those offerings which involve no tangible or manufactured product but attempt to satisfy needs. The service industries include: banking, tourism, leisure, entertainment and communication, as well as numerous government activities.

System. The set of interconnected and interdependent relationships which as a whole is greater than the sum of its parts.

Key organisations

Consumers' Association
14 Buckingham St.
London WC2N 6DS.

Department of Trade and Industry
1 Victoria St.
London SW1H 0ET.

4
Offerings and Organisations

The organisations or individuals existing within the system, described in Chapter 3, introduce into it their own history, technology, skills and other resources. These internal factors play a large part in determining the precise ways in which they respond, both as buyers and sellers, to environmental and system pressures.

Recognition of an opportunity or threat emanating from outside the firm is likely to be followed up by a series of organisational and operational adjustments before market-orientated action can be taken. Examples illustrating this are:

1. The would-be restaurateur might take months to find a site, obtain planning permission, meet fire and hygiene regulations and decorate and promote his premises before he can start serving customers.
2. It has been estimated that it will be at least twenty years before sufficient oil can be extracted from coal, tar sands and oil shale to make a significant impact on US oil imports, despite its importance and a forecast involvement of $88 000 million.

These time lags can affect the buyer as much as the seller, as the following examples show:

1. Lead times for certain types of plant or equipment can stretch into years if order, installation and running-in are included. This may effectively preclude some types of fast response to opportunities in the environment.
2. The British plastics industry has been precluded from capitalising on some market opportunities over the last decade because of shortages of skilled tool-makers.

The nature of the supplying industry and the purchasing groups directly affects the character of the buyer–seller relationship and the ways in which the firm operates. For simplicity, this chapter will concentrate on the single-industry, single-customer-type situation. In reality, however, many firms work within a number of situations or face special organisational or communication problems. For example, BICC Ltd produces raw materials (BICC Metals Ltd), processed goods (Telcon Plastics Ltd), components (Dorman Smith Ltd), finished goods (BICC Telecommunications Cables Ltd), services (SD Graphics NV), and plant (Balfour Beatty Construction Ltd). This is a pattern which is repeated in other firms from other parts of the world. For example, Mitsui Group encompasses raw materials (Mitsui Mining Co. Ltd), processed goods (Toray Industries Inc.), components (Mitsui Miike Machinery Co. Ltd), finished goods (Mitsui Norin Co. Ltd), services (Mitsui Mutual Life Insurance Co.), and plant (Mitsui Construction).

In some of these highly complex organisations, identifying the key personnel to approach when attempting to sell can be very difficult. A small rubber company in South London eventually tracked down the key decision-maker, for their area, of the giant German company Kraftwerk Union, at an exhibition in Brazil.

Occasionally the purchasing or consumption function is difficult to separate from the selling or supply role. End users may specify the use of certain components in the final item. For example, the Saudi Arabian Government may give the contract for fully equipping a new hospital to a German firm such as Labsco GmbH, but specify that all clean-air equipment is supplied by a UK firm such as Envair Ltd. In many government markets, policies of supporting local industry through directives such as 'Buy British' or 'America First' may be adopted. Sales and marketing may insist that certain types or grades of material or components are used; for example, a Yorkshire footwear manufacturer gradually replaced synthetic materials with leather as sales staff noted the growing popularity of natural materials. Vertical integration may predispose the firm to use materials or products from a sister firm. For example, when PVC-coated aluminium power cable was introduced into the UK market in the 1960s, the dominant cable manufacturer had little to gain in the short to medium term from introducing aluminium as it had an extensive interest in copper refining and no involvement in aluminium.

Despite the importance of these behavioural dimensions of the market, most managers find that much of their flexibility and the customers' responses are directly affected by established patterns of behaviour. These are determined, at least in part, by their industrial situation as producers of raw materials, processed products, components, finished goods, services, capital or plant.

Table 4.1 illustrates the broad structure of how expenditure in Britain is allocated between different areas. It brings out the significance and scale of Government expenditure: this alone accounts for almost a quarter of direct expenditure. It covers a vast assortment of items, from military equipment through equipment for the National Health Services to supplies and services for all government agencies. Dealing with the Government calls for many skills and disciplines. Some are common to all marketing areas, but others are highly specialised; for example, competitive tendering is more important in public sector activity than in most areas of the commercial activity.

In international trade the same broad patterns exist. In some countries the state plays an even more central role. Considerable variations exist in the ways in which commercial dealings are handled between countries. The researchers of the Industrial Marketing Group[1] indicate the degree to which organisational purchasing behaviour in different countries is influenced by:

1. The domestic environment.
2. The networks of relationships between suppliers and customers.
3. The nature of the offering.

The detailed discussion of this work will take place in Chapter 10, 'Industrial Markets'; here the emphasis is on the interaction between the offering and the organisation.

The conventional division between international and domestic markets has been challenged by those who have studied the 'global' marketing strategies of Japanese firms. Beal[2] indicates that in recent years:

> Although domestic demand has been sluggish, Japanese manufacturing industry has continued to grow and prosper.
>
> T. Beal, 'Domestic Consumer Demand and
> Japanese Global Marketing Strategy',
> *Proceeding of the 2nd World
> Marketing Congress*, 1985.

RAW MATERIALS

Raw materials, sometimes described as 'primary products', are so called because of their 'raw' or untreated state. The only processing they undergo will generally be for reasons of safety, economy, handling or avoiding deterioration. They are normally from extractive industries (mining, oil, gas and timber), agriculture and fisheries. In Britain these account

Table 4.1 Gross national product by category of expenditure 1977-81

	£000 million At current prices					£000 million At constant 1979 prices				
	1977	1978	1979	1980	1981	1977	1978	1979	1980	1981
Consumers' expenditure	85	98	117	135	151	64	68	71	71	72
General government expenditure	29	33	38	48	55	23	24	24	24	24
Gross domestic fixed capital formation	26	29	34	40	39	20	21	21	21	19
Value of physical increases in stocks and work in progress	1.6	1.1	2.5	-3.6	-4	1.1	0.8	1.5	-2.0	-2
Exports of goods and services	43	47	55	63	68	31	32	33	33	32
Total final expenditure on goods and services at market prices	185	209	247	284	309	140	145	151	148	145
Less										
Imports of goods and services	43	46	55	58	61	31	32	35	34	34
Taxes on expenditure	20	23	30	37	43	14	15	16	16	17
Add										
Subsidies	3.3	3.6	4.4	5.2	6	2.4	2.3	2.4	2.6	3
Gross domestic product at factor cost	125	143	166	193	212	99	102	103	101	97

Source: Central Statistical Office

for about 6 per cent of the GNP, employing about 5 per cent of the workforce. Figure 4.1 gives a breakdown of the 'industrial profile' of the UK and four other major industrial nations.

Although the dominant feature of this figure is the considerable similarity between these countries, some differences are worth noting. The sharp reduction in the proportion of the Japanese labour force employed in the 'primary sector' between 1962 and 1980—from 12.9 per cent to 3.9 per cent—reflects the successful growth of that country's industrialisation programme. The relative stability of this sector in Britain is partly a function of the earlier industrialisation of Britain, the efficiency of the agricultural sector and new extractive industries, e.g. North Sea oil.

Britain's extractive industries and her richness of resources, from coal to North Sea oil, have long played a major part in the economic prosperity of the country, and the marketing of these extracted materials is conditioned by a number of specific features. One of these aspects, the finite nature of these materials, is central to current thinking about marketing in this area, notably in fossil energy (although it has been argued that this 'finite' nature is exaggerated, particularly since large areas of the world's surface are as yet unexplored). This is clearly illustrated in the marketing problems of North Sea oil and gas. Although new discoveries are likely, the time span for depletion can be estimated at any given point in time. Achieving an effective balance between conservation and the effective exploitation of marketing opportunities is critical.

The scale of operations which is often necessary to open up a pit head or to explore for oil on the Continental Shelf has created a great deal of concentration in many of these extractive industries. The National Coal Board, the British Gas Corporation and the 'Seven Sisters' in oil illustrate this. (The Seven Sisters is the name given to the seven major oil companies: Exxon, Royal Dutch Shell, Texaco, Gulf, Mobil, Standard Oil of California and British Petroleum.) In some cases their control extends to the delivery of the product, sales and service.

In consumer markets this means that the primary area of competition is between the different energy sources: oil, gas, coal and electricity. There is generally a close link between sales of the basic material and appliance sales. For example, an estimated 80 per cent of all domestic gas appliances are sold through the Gas Corporation's own showrooms. Once an appliance has been purchased, conversion to an alternative energy source is expensive, and this is true for both industrial and consumer markets.

In the marketing of extractive industries the real price is a combination of material and installation costs. Distribution costs are often extremely high, leading to a tendency for industry to concentrate near the sources of raw materials. The cost and bulk factors have led some businessmen to doubt the scope for marketing in such product areas. In fact, however, the scope, particularly when recognised by creative marketing men, is considerable. For example, a quarry in Northern England sends sand to Kuwait because top management recognised that its sand had technical characteristics lacking in Kuwaiti sand.

Raw material marketing, trading and usage are increasingly affected by political decisions. The types of fuel used in power stations, the rates of exploitation of forestry reserves and even the willingness to sell certain raw materials are influenced by government action. In much of the world, industry is being directed to move its materials further 'downstream', to add value or use in manufacturing in the home market rather than export. Third World countries have responded to fluctuating primary product prices by attempting to introduce local manufacture. For example, many European tanneries are suffering from shortages of untreated hides as Eastern European and Third World countries stop exporting and open their own tanneries, and acute shortages of certain types of timber have occurred as countries like Malaysia and Indonesia build up their furniture, giftware and other timber-consuming industries. Over time these considerations are likely to affect the operations of the London Metal Exchange and the other primary product exchanges. Although the conditions of rapid price escalation which occurred on

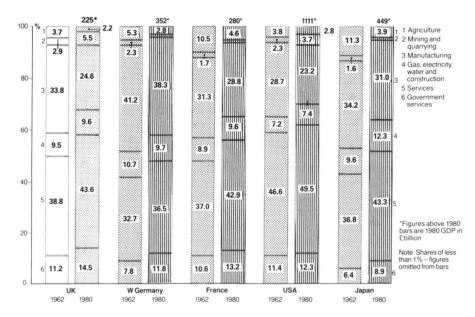

Fig. 4.1   Industrial profile: GDP activity shares. (*Sources*: OECD, CSO.)

the Rotterdam 'Spot' market for oil in 1979 are unlikely to be paralleled in other primary markets, some hints of the challenges inherent in finite, even restricted supplies and substantial excess demand are given by this situation.

The dramatic movements in prices in the extractive industries are matched by similar fluctuations in world agricultural and, to a lesser extent, fishery prices. In Europe, North America and many other parts of the world, determined efforts have been made, through policies like the Common Agricultural Policy (EEC) and the Agriculture and Trade Redevelopment and Assistance Act 1954 (USA), to introduce mechanisms to improve the basic stability of domestic (here including EEC) farm prices.

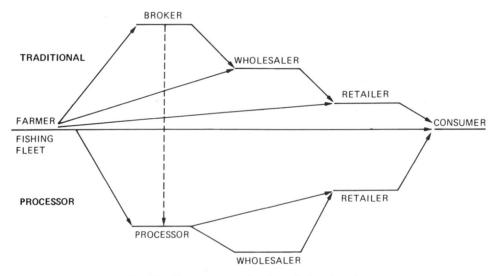

Fig. 4.2   The route to market for agricultural products.

The marketing of agricultural and fishery products follows two broad routes: traditional, untreated path to end use, and food processor to market (Figure 4.2). Although for many years the traditional path was dominant, the emergence of the giant processors during this century has revolutionised food marketing. Through canning and freezing they have offered assured long-term supplies, besides reassurances of quality. The farmers and fishing fleet operators have won long-term contracts to supply, resulting in freedom to plan and fully realise their potential.

AGRICULTURAL MARKETS

The last few years have seen a rapid growth in interest in agricultural markets and marketing. A number of factors have helped to stimulate this:

1. The clear success of initiatives such as those taken by Danish bacon, Jaffa oranges and French apples.
2. The demonstrated desire by consumers for quality reassurance and consistency.
3. The power of major retailers and their insistence on consistent quality.
4. Pressure and support from the UK government through programmes such as the 'Food for Britain' campaign.
5. The wish by farmers to improve their returns.
6. Actions by the EEC.
7. Research which has indicated the potential value and benefits from action in this area.[3, 4, 5]

It is useful to think of agricultural marketing in terms of the challenges posed to the farmer within the type of marketing system discussed earlier. All systems are to some degree unique, but also show certain important similarities. The farmer wishing to develop his markets needs first to understand the structure of his market (conduct an audit).

The institutions in the marketplace*

There are a very large number of private and public concerns and agencies active in agricultural markets, some long established, others relatively new. The three basic intermediary groups have existed in some form for many centuries, i.e. as long as farmers have wanted to move their output from the country to the city.

The merchants. These are the various retailers and wholesalers who buy from the farmer and supply to the consumer. They take many forms: the fruit and vegetable wholesaler based at one of the major markets in London or any big city (e.g. Vauxhall), the market trader operating in city centres such as Birmingham's 'Bull Ring', the major retailer such as Tesco, Sainsbury's or Marks and Spencer.

The agents. These act on behalf of their client suppliers to seek out opportunities and trade in them. They are particularly important in two areas: horticultural products and international trade.

The speculators. Agricultural markets are characterised by serious problems of control of output. Periods of glut can be followed by severe shortage. The speculator attempts to profit from this variability of output level by attempting to predict patterns before the rest of the market. The extent to which his/her forecast is accurate determines the degree of success.

The precise form and pattern of relationships varies considerably between countries and over time.

More recently, two other organisations have grown in scale and importance.

Processors, packers and manufacturers. These take the raw product, convert it into a

---

*Much of the following discussion is based on J. Barker, *Agricultural Marketing*.[4]

different form for onward sale. In scale, typically, they are much larger than farmers. They can exercise significant controls over the market. However, their capital investment often makes them vulnerable to supplier pressure. This has been very evident in the fishing industry over the last decade as fishing fleets have won major concessions from the processors in return for assurance of supply.

Government agencies and facilitators. These exist on a national and international scale. The UK government has had a long tradition of involvement in the working of the agricultural marketing system. It acts directly through legislation on standards and regulations, such as 'The Food Hygiene (General) Regulations, 1970', and indirectly through the various 'community commissions'. The EEC has had a major impact through the workings of the Common Agricultural Policy. Besides these bodies, many farming groups have organised themselves into co-operatives in attempts to achieve their marketing goals.

It is within the structures described above that farmers must design and develop their marketing strategies. The task is made more demanding by three unusual features of agricultural markets:

1. The importance of climate and related forces in determining the amount, range and quality of output.
2. The relatively small size of the producers (farmers) compared to their customers (the processors and middlemen).
3. The 'distance' between the supplier and the ultimate customer.

A number of approaches have been adopted by farmers to overcome these problems. Among the most significant are the Marketing Co-operatives. These have been set up on both a national and local level. Some concentrate on particular commodities while others are more broadly based. There has been a rapid growth in interest in recent years in the role new technologies, especially computers and telecommunications, can play in developing the market potential of farmers. Especially important has been the use of these technologies in providing accurate market intelligence, especially on prices and in increasing the scope for effective management control.[6]

The food chain

This has been described as stretching from the farm to the shopping basket. However, in this section attention is focused on the steps from the food processor/broker/dealer to the retailer in Figure 4.2. Marketing has grown in importance in this sector until it is now estimated that marketing and distribution costs now exceed production costs in this area.[4] This has occurred at a time when there has been a marked increase in concentration among middlemen, notably wholesalers and retailers.

Table 4.2 *The number of auction markets in Great Britain*

	1968	1974	1976	1978	1984
England and Wales	453	369	354	332	254
Scotland	74	65	65	65	65

The reduction in the number of outlets imposes greater power and responsibility on existing middlemen while restricting the choices open to producers.

A similar pattern can be seen among grocery retailers, with equally rapid and substantial increases in the market shares for the multiples (e.g. Tesco, Sainsbury's, Dee, Asda). This pattern poses major problems, especially for smaller producers. Major retailers require significant minimum order quantities as well as high standards in quality and consistency. It was reported recently that for fish products, a major retailer required a

Table 4.3 *The growth of the grocery multiples*

Year	1971	1976	1979	1982
Multiples	44	48	53	65
Co-operatives	13	16	15	13
Independents	43	36	32	22

Based on 'Institute of Grocery Distributions' and Nielsen data.

minimum annual throughput per line of 500 000 to stock any of the products.[7]

The scale of competition goes some way to explain the very high rate of new product introduction, price rivalry and advertising levels in this area.

At the same time, new technologies are having a major impact on food retailing. Electronic point-of-sale, laser scanning and bar coding are widespread at retail level. Companies such as Tesco and Sainsbury's are investing heavily in this area. These are likely to increase the pressures on smaller distributors while challenging the ability of major manufacturers to keep pace with developments.[5]

PROCESSED PRODUCTS

The dividing line between processed goods and raw materials is sometimes very fine indeed. Generally, sufficient treatment has taken place to make them qualitatively different from their natural state. Processed goods include pig-iron, steel, concrete, cement, chemicals and solvents, resins, and processed rubber and plastics. Their form is frequently changed by the buyer before being assembled or inserted in the final end product.

A typical processed product is plastic moulding: extruded, injected, vacuum formed, sprayed or hand-layered. It ranges in scale from the small, injection-moulded, plastic pegs used in games like 'Mastermind' to the glass-reinforced plastic hulls of boats such as the new Royal Navy Minesweeper. The vast majority of the output of the processing industries goes into industrial markets for inclusion (as in the case of the game), modification (for example when used in cars or domestic appliances) or assembly with other goods (as with the Minesweeper). The scale of process industries is seldom fully appreciated: plastics processing alone employs over 154 000 workers in approximately 2600 firms in the UK.

Marketing of processed products poses special problems, because in fact there is no product as such. The supplier generally works to the specifications of the customer, who will generally be incorporating the item into his own end product or component. The supplier will be providing machine capacity allied to his technical, engineering and design skills, perhaps allied to tool making. The key purchasing decisions occur very infrequently, i.e. when laying down the tooling, designing the item or placing initial orders. Once a project is initiated repeat orders may be frequent, but are often a routine purchasing operation. This pattern of behaviour leads to an emphasis on two key areas: winning initial orders and sustaining quality standards and prompt delivery. A skilled technical representative, capable of interpreting buyer needs and adapting them to the material or technology, is invaluable. These requirements, as well as the limited scope for 'off-the-shelf' buying, reduce the middleman's contribution in many sectors.

Strong, direct, customer–producer relationships may lead to powerful supplier loyalties. The customer depends a great deal on his suppliers, since moving tools[2] can cause a great deal of disruption in supplies. At the same time, however, no customer can afford to have his entire production line disrupted because of poor delivery or low quality from a supplier whose item may be a very small part of a major line. For example, a mattress manufacturer cannot afford to have his bulky and expensive product held up because the polythene-bag supplier's deliveries are late; and the production lines of a cooker manufacturer can be quickly reduced to chaos if the silicon rubber seals on the doors are substandard or late.

In some industries intermediaries do play a major role. In steel, stockholders play a major part in distribution, generally to smaller customers or where analysis of the 'cost of possession' has indicated the scope for economies by larger buyers. (The 'cost of possession' differentiates between the monetary costs of buying direct, probably in bulk from producers, and the real costs of larger stock holding and labour for handling and warehousing. See Chapter 15 for a fuller discussion.)

COMPONENTS

In this area, as well as the ability to make to specification where necessary, there is the need to develop lines of the producer's products for direct insertion in the buyer's product. Girling Brakes, Lucas Electrics, NSF Cooker Timers and Perkins Engines all offer lines of proprietary products to industrial customers but generally provide scope for adaptation or modification to special customer needs. In certain circumstances items are made to specification but probably only if the volume justifies it.

The cost per unit of components tends to be higher than that of processed goods, emphasising the importance of price. However, in many fields reputation and appropriate technology play an equal role. In a rapidly advancing field such as electronics, decisions about technology are critical. Today, many component manufacturers face the electronic/electromechanical dilemma. Although the technology may exist for the immediate step to electronics, the customers, i.e. the appliance manufacturers, are unclear about the medium-term end-user response to it. This places the component firms in a dilemma about the pace of their own shift to these systems: too soon and there is no market, too late and it has gone. The relatively small size of many component manufacturers limits their scope for stimulating any end-user pull for their chosen step. Firms like Perkins Engines have demonstrated the role that effective marketing can play in ensuring long-term profitable business.

Normally demand for an item is inelastic, but it may be met from a number of sources. This has created an environment in which distributors can play a major role for both suppliers and customers. There have been some elements of vertical integration in this area, with distributors becoming involved in limited assembly work. The complexity of the resulting distribution systems can be quite considerable, as illustrated in the case of hydraulic hose and couplings in Figure 4.3.

FINISHED GOODS

These are sold to all the different customer groups. Although they may require energy to drive them, operators to work them or machines to employ them, no other additions are normally required for their use or consumption. The majority of consumer marketing behaviour is directed towards finished goods, from fish fingers to motor-cars.

In industrial markets finished goods are made up primarily of equipment and supplies. Equipment ranges from large capital items destined to be part of fixed plant and fundamental to the manufacturing process, to everyday items such as small tools. The purchasing decision in equipment will normally be occasioned by one of four situations: replacement of old equipment; expansion of capacity; change of production process; or production of a new product.[8] Suppliers in some areas may be able, through their own innovation policies, to create a fifth situation in which capital investment will take place: the opportunity for differential advantage from adopting new technologies. In most

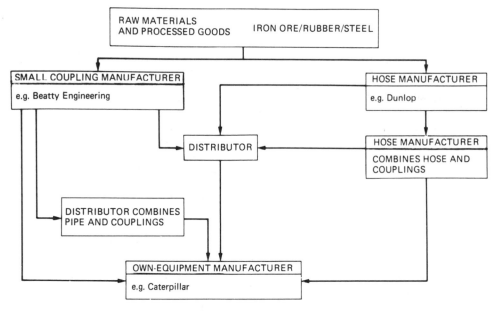

Fig. 4.3 A distribution system for industrial products.

situations customer investment is non-routine and involves substantial investment and, from the buyer's perspective, a certain element of risk. In today's inflation- and energy-conscious markets, the life-span of equipment and primary energy sources are increasingly important.

Supplies can generally be divided into two broad groupings: accessory equipment and operating supplies. Accessories include office equipment, tills, sales-force cars, promotional materials, photocopiers and computers (although the increasing extent to which computers are aligned with production may make this classification more and more inappropriate). Operating supplies have been described as the convenience goods of the industrial field. They include such diverse items as pens, stationery, cleaning equipment and books.

In many of these areas the relatively small unit investment and the repeat-order character of much of the buying have led to the emergence of powerful middleman groups such as Universal Stationers and Rymans.

In certain parts of the commercial environment supplies constitute, after labour, the largest single area of direct expenditure. Handling other types of finished goods provides intermediaries with their primary source of revenue.

The massive government markets concentrate much of their expenditure on finished goods. Their requirements include machinery and machine tools for colleges and government training centres and defence, and medical and educational equipment.

SERVICES

Throughout the developed world the service sector of the economy is growing, and in many countries it is the most rapidly growing sector. Service workers can be broadly divided into two groups: those employed in other key areas, e.g. doctors employed by the NCB and marketing staff of large manufacturers; and those directly involved in the service industries.

The main service industries are transport, post and telecommunications, communication, entertainment, holidays, hotels and tourism, government, intermediaries, maintenance and repair, domestic help and laundry, design, research and consultancy, medical, educational, legal and other professions, and finance.

Some important features of the marketing of services are as follows:

1. There is a broad division between profit and non-profit operations, with government, education and health dominating the latter.
2. Most offerings are of an intangible nature.
3. There is a tendency for the lack of a physical product to reduce the need for distributors and most forms of middlemen.
4. There have emerged agency systems in some markets, mainly those with very diffuse franchises, e.g. holiday, travel, tourism, some types of transport, some aspects of entertainment, communication, insurance and credit.
5. In the commercial sphere low barriers to entry often occur, leading to considerable emphasis on skill differentiation, reputation, availability and a high degree of responsiveness to the market.
6. In many areas of government services the conventional pattern of demand stimulation is replaced by demand control, even rediction.

Services are used by all the customer groups. The consumer uses travel agents and the postal service, watches TV, goes to the cinema and theatre, has his car repaired, raises funds and comes into contact with the law, education and medicine. The organisations which provide these services attempt in various ways to manage the exchange with the prospective user, the travel agent promoting holidays and the university recruiting students.

Industry provides much of the demand for the service sector, often requiring special talents or skills. For example the travel agent may develop a special business travel service, and the telecommunications needs of businessmen have led to the emergence of telex. Some services are highly specialised, e.g. management or marketing consultant, consultant engineer, fashion designer, market research bureau and advertising agent.

Commercial markets are closely linked to the service sector. The retail groups demand specialised logistics and location analysts, and the management service companies such as computer bureaux may need freelance systems analysts.

The state's need for services is perhaps the most extensive. The Central Office of Information is by far the largest advertiser, at one time employing over 27 advertising agencies. State requirements include architects, engineering research and consultancy, specialist advisers on areas of policy, and decision makers. As well as these specialists, they make use of almost all the other service organisations.

The scale of Britain's invisible trade illustrates the importance of this area overseas. Foreign governments make extensive use of UK services, such as the Engineering Industry Training Board's International Unit (helping countries to establish engineering training), PA Management Consultants' extensive foreign links, or the Crown Agent's buying skills.

CAPITAL

Capital is the life-blood of the market-place. It is the mechanism for exchange, and as such it provides a vital service to consumers, industrialists, commerce and government. The marketing of capital or money is dealt with in the general section on services. However, in Britain it is only over the last decade or so that finance has been recognised as a commodity like any other.

During the early 1970s financial advertising was by far the most rapidly growing sector of UK advertising. Although the rate of growth has slackened, the general awareness of the need for a more positive approach to marketing this most intangible of commodities has grown. To a considerable extent the newer forms of credit and finance, e.g. credit cards and charge cards, have led the way, followed by personal financial services through the major banks.

Perhaps the slowest area to change has been the area of corporate finance. The growth of competition in this area, partly from overseas (Citi Corp, Chemical Bank, Banco d'Italia, Bayerische Landesbank, Unico Banking Group) and partly from new institutions such as the Industrial and Commercial Finance Corporation, is already having a noticeable effect on policies and practices.

PLANT

Plant, sometimes called capital projects, constitutes some of the largest individual market opportunities. They range from the construction of houses and industrial and commercial properties to the giant projects to construct power stations, harbour installations and sometimes, in the Third World, whole townships. Their very scale can be daunting to even the largest international construction groups.

Although individuals may commission private projects, most of the activity is industrial, commercial and governmental. The scale of some projects is so great that tendering is increasingly conducted through consortia (Consortium: 'a partnership of corporations, firms or partnerships, generally for a specific project or time period'). The scale of some of the projects is illustrated in Table 4.4.

Table 4.4 *Giant projects in the Middle East (1975)*

Location	Type of project	Amount	Contractor and nationality
Saudi Arabia	Design engineering and construction supervision of a water desalination and power generating complex at Al Jubayl	$200 million	Sanderson & Porter Inc. (subsidiary of International Systems & Controls Corp., US)
Dubai	Construction and design of a trade centre	$128.3 million	Bernard & Sons (British)
Egypt	Sponge iron plant	$212 million	Arab Asian Development Partners, joint venture formed by Development Consultants International Ltd (Indian) Bancom International (Philippino) Arab Export Trade Co. (Egyptian)
Iran	Hospital	$235 million	United Kingdom Hospitals Group (coordinated by Orion Bank & Allied Medical Group Ltd) (British)
Algeria	Integrated steelworks plant	$690 million	W.S. Atkins (British)
Jordan	Third-stage expansion of the national petroleum refinery	$187 million	Industrialexport (Rumanian)

Adapted from the *Harvard Business Review*, Jan.–Feb., 1976.

The traditional pattern of winning business in these areas is through successful tendering: the Government or a firm announces a project, provides specifications and calls for tenders. Inevitably this system places considerable emphasis on the price element in the project. Despite this, other aspects of marketing can play a major part in building up a pattern of successful tendering. Preparing the ground is vital. Many firms find that close links with governments and other bodies prior to formulation of the project through advice and technical guidance may help sway judgement towards factors more favourable to them. The notion of systems selling is particularly important in the Third World. Firms which provide a more complete service (design, development, management and assembly of associated parts) meet the needs of countries with very limited resources in skilled management.

The scale of some projects and the central importance of finance have led many governments to sponsor or establish support schemes such as the UK Export Credit Guarantee Department's Specific Guarantee. The merchant banks are very active in contracts of over £1 million. They help to build up the loans necessary for the project, establishing competitive interest rates and agreeing the premium. In some instances groups of banks, perhaps in association with international agencies such as the World Bank, provide special 'lines of credit' for a country, a development plan or a specific project, as Table 4.5 shows.

Table 4.5   *Typical lines of credit for development projects*

Country	Donor	Amount and Purpose
Bolivia	IDB	A loan of US$5 million to finance pre-investment studies under the 1979–80 National Development Plan.
Brazil	LBI	Lloyds Bank International has granted a loan of US$10 million for the development of telecommunications in the north-east of the country.
	International	A loan of US$200 million from an international group of banks, managed by Lloyds Bank International, for the 'steel railway' between Belo Horizonte and Itutinga, and Sao Paulo and Volta Redonda.
Cameroon	IFC	An equity investment of US$889 000 for a US$5.6 million project for the improvement and expansion of production on a rubber estate, and to diversify output into palm oil and kernels.
Costa Rica	IDB	A loan of about 650 million colones (approximately US$75 million) towards a programme of rural road construction.
Dominican Republic	IDB	A loan of US$3.9 million towards the US$5.65 million expansion of a university involving the construction of buildings, the purchase of laboratory and workshop equipment, furniture and bibliographic materials, and the contracting of teachers and consultants.

Source: Lloyds Bank Limited, Overseas Department, International Trade Promotion Section, 1976. Reproduced with the permission of Lloyds Bank Limited.

For the firms entering this type of activity, notably turnkey projects ('the construction, under contract, of a project up to the point of operation, at which time it is turned over to the owner'[9]) the potential returns are enormous. The costs and risks are commensurate, notably in areas of political and economic turmoil, demanding the highest levels of marketing and financial and strategic management commitment. In many cases the monetary price will be less important than the form of payment, the availability of funding and follow-up service and support.

CONCLUSION

In these very different product, process or service areas, the intrinsic character of the industry and the firm plays a major role in determining the possible and appropriate marketing responses. The effective marketing man will need to build upon these internal capabilities to design offerings to meet the real needs of the customers, whether they are less developed countries seeking coastal shipping but lacking the foreign exchange and needing new lines of credit, or students looking for low-price travel during the summer holidays.

KEY POINTS

In this chapter it was noted:

1. How the fundamental nature of the industry in which the firm operates—raw

material, agriculture, etc.—does much to shape the possible and appropriate form of marketing.

2. That changes in many of these areas are posing increasing challenges to traditional ways of developing business.
3. That there are various ways in which marketing techniques can be used to modify, design or change offerings to increase their appeal to existing and new customers.
4. How effectiveness in many of these areas calls for skills in integrating marketing actions with technical and financial skills and resources.

Many of the areas presented here as separate and discrete for the sake of discussion also need to be reviewed in terms of their interrelationships, if a proper appreciation of their character is to be achieved.

Notes

1. Cunningham, M., 'International Marketing and Purchasing of Industrial Goods', Edinburgh, Marketing Education Group Annual Conference, 1980.
2. Beal, T., 'Domestic Consumer Demand and Japanese Global Marketing Strategy', Second World Marketing Congress, Stirling, 1985.
3. Nerlove, M. & Waugh, F.V., 'Advertising without Supply Control', *Journal of Farm Economics*, November 1961.
4. Barker, J.W., *Agricultural Marketing*. Oxford University Press, 1981.
5. Cannon, T., 'Marketing Problems in the Food Chain', *Food Marketing*, 1, No.1, 1985.
6. Graff, C., *The Marketing of Prestel to Farmers*. Strathclyde, Unpublished PhD Thesis, 1984.
7. Goulding, I., *New Product Development in the UK Trout Industry*. Aston, Unpublished PhD Thesis, 1983.
8. Hill, R.W. and Hillier, T.J., *Organisational Buying Behavior*. London: Macmillan, 1977.
9. Robinson, R.D., *International Business Management*. Illinois: Dryden Press, 1978.

Key organisation

Department of Energy
Thames House South
Millbank,
London SW1P 4QJ

CASE STUDY 3: WESTWARD PLASTICS

In 1978 Charles Price, the managing director, could look back on three years of sustained growth by Westward Plastics. The firm was a general plastics processor, with injection moulding dominant but some foam-extrusion capability, and was part of the giant Marchmont Group.

The firm had been acquired in the late 1960s with two basic objectives in view: entering into a new area of business; and meeting some of the group's own plastics processing needs. Despite the latter goal, the group is committed to the notion that all units are independent profit centres. This means that Westward have no special advantages in inter-group trading. In 1976, 1977 and 1978 sales within the group never accounted for more than 15 per cent of the turnover.

Business profit

When the company was acquired by Marchmont it was located in High Wycombe, near London. Much of the firm's business was drawn from the local furniture industry. The proximity of London had given access to a much wider industrial base. Their customer list encompassed both the manufacturing industry (a number of lorry manufacturers, with ERF particularly important) and telecommunications (both the Post Office and key suppliers such as Plessey). Just before the takeover important new accounts had been opened with South East and North Thames Gas (components for equipment used by service engineers in North Sea Gas conversion).

In 1971 it was decided by the group to shift the firm's factory from High Wycombe to a new plant in the North West of England, to capitalise on various regional development grants. Just before the move the composition of the company's output was: furniture, 35 per cent; goods vehicles, 20 per cent; telecommunications, 15 per cent; gas regions, 10 per cent; and others, 10 per cent. On 1 January 1971 forecast income for the year was £750 000.

The new location

The immediate fears that the move would seriously weaken the company's business base, especially in furniture and gas, rapidly proved to be unfounded. In fact the furniture industry was in the process of becoming more evenly distributed across the UK.

Growth during the 1970s

In the early 1970s business boomed: the furniture industry prospered; the gas conversion programme accelerated; and the telecommunications industry expanded. In September 1973 record monthly sales of £100 000 were recorded. This had been achieved almost entirely from the same industry profile as the firm had held before moving north.

The technical expertise and wide contacts of Ian Graham, the sales director, had played a major part in holding on to these accounts. Despite the distances involved, he kept close and regular contact with these accounts. Ian was viewed as an important part of their 'problem-solving capacity'.

Economic recession in the mid-1970s

A number of their key customers were hit very hard by the economic recession of the mid-1970s. Furniture companies were particularly seriously affected. Their largest single customer, Johnson's Furniture, cut back orders from £12 000 per month in September 1973 to under £3000 per month a year later. The gradual ending of the gas conversion programme by the British Gas Corporation posed further problems. At its lowest point the firm's turnover was less than £60 000 per month.

The workforce was pruned severely as part of a general economy programme. At the same time a number of avenues for new business were sought. Three major paths were followed: new own products; new industries; and new processes.

The first new product introduced was a Do-It-Yourself brick mould. The product was designed to enable the DIY enthusiast to manufacture his own garden-wall bricks. They launched the product at Interbuild (the building industry's main exhibition), and considerable initial interest was shown. A major Midland DIY group stocked the product during the first year. Unfortunately, consumer 'pull' was very limited. The launch of a more expensive competitive brand backed by a heavyweight advertising campaign led Westward to abandon active promotion of the mould in the trade.

This coincided with the skateboard boom at the end of 1977. Westward introduced a medium-priced skateboard in September 1977, and sales rapidly built up through the major supermarket and department store groups. In November 1977 £30 000 worth of boards were dispatched. Attempts were made to open up accounts with Alpine Sports (the leading specialist retailer) and other 'better quality' outlets, since it was felt that the supermarkets and others would stock only while the boom was on. Therefore they wanted to obtain outlets with a greater commitment to the sport. The demands of these outlets for ex-car selling supported by advertising created real problems. The firm was willing to invest in promotion but the company's very small, highly qualified sales force were very reluctant to carry large stocks of the product to sell to small skateboard outlets. By mid-1978 the firm's skateboard sales had almost disappeared.

The pressure of these developments was reduced by the company's achievements in new industries and new processes. The major new industry is toys. From very small sales to toy manufacturers even before the move north, this has become a major new source of sales.

Discussions with ICI have also led to the company's developing the capacity to process non-rigid, skinned, polyurethane foam. A number of existing customers are already showing interest in its possible applications. ICI have provided a great deal of help in seeking out possible buyers and new applications. This has proved so successful that all existing capacity for foam is taken up.

The current situation

In late 1979 the profile of business is: furniture, 25 per cent; toys, 20 per cent; goods vehicles, 13 per cent; telecommunications, 10 per cent; gas regions, 7 per cent; electrical, 7 per cent; group, 5 per cent; and foam, 10 per cent. The projected turnover for the year is £1.75 million.

Charles Price is determined to sustain this success. The overall target for the forthcoming year is to achieve sales in the region of £2.25 million. He feels that it is important to adopt a positive attitude to this, believing that they cannot afford to rest on their success.

A number of areas of development appear to present themselves: explore new products again; seek new markets, e.g. export; and build up local strength, since very little business comes from the North West.

Task

To fully realise these and to identify new avenues in which to capitalise on their strengths, Charles Price feels that a stronger marketing orientation is needed. Explore what this will mean for Westward Plastics.

5

Marketing Research

The growing importance of marketing has been paralleled by the emergence of marketing research as a major area of business activity. In 1977, it was estimated by Simmons[1] that £55 million was spent on commissioned research. More recently (1979), Crisp placed the estimate at £80–£85 million, or 7–8p for every 100p spent by customers. The latest indications are that the turnover of the industry in 1984 was approximately 120 million pounds. The Market Research Society is the professional institute of market research practitioners in Britain: it has over 3,000 members. Three useful definitions of market research are:

> Market Research is the means used by those who provide goods and services to keep themselves in touch with the needs and wants of those who buy and use those goods and services.

> The systematic collection and objective recording, classification, analysis and presentation of data concerning the behaviour, needs, attitudes, opinions, motivations etc. of individuals and organizations (commercial enterprises, public bodies etc.) within the context of their economic, social, political and everyday activities.
>
> International Chamber of
Commerce, European Society
for Opinion and Marketing
Research

> The systematic and objective search for and analysis of information relevant to the identification of any problem in the field of marketing.
>
> Paul E. Green
and Donald S. Tull[2]

These definitions go beyond the confines of market research, with its emphasis on the measurement and analysis of markets, 'to solve a particular company's marketing problem'[3] in an attempt to understand the broad field of marketing.

Four factors have been instrumental in encouraging the development of both market and marketing research:

1. The size of firms has increased, with the resulting increased distance between marketing decision-makers and consumers, buyers and users.
2. The scale of the market has increased notably as costs and risks increase with the shift from local to national, even international, markets.
3. The commitment of marketing men to look outside the firm, particularly at buyer needs, for clues to the company's future.
4. Increased awareness of the forces affecting both need creation and the choice process has highlighted the extent to which many and complex non-price factors influence behaviour.

These four factors have interacted to place a massive premium on information for effective marketing decision-making.

To manage a business well is to manage its future: and to manage the future is to manage information.

M. Harper Jnr[4]

Traditionally, information management was a personal and subjective process. Top management had close, day-to-day links with their customers, and a continual process of review and up-dating was possible. The personal links were often strong, response was swift, and the number of customers small enough to be managed. In many of these situations an overall pattern of stability existed, posing no challenges to assumptions about market behaviour.

The four factors listed above, however, have gradually undermined these traditional patterns of behaviour. The growing scale of operation and the increasing size of risks required the development of new approaches to information gathering and use. At the same time the accelerating rate of change in markets and research in other areas created a need for a deeper understanding of the more fundamental features of the marketplace. In seeking insights into these issues marketing followed the example of the other social sciences and looked to the model of empiricism, objective and systematic study, set by the natural sciences.

THE 'SCIENCE' OF RESEARCH

In raising the issue of the scope for considering marketing research as a scientific pursuit one is posing a question which has long been central to the study of human behaviour. The founders of the three major disciplines from which much marketing thought has evolved, sociology, psychology and economics, saw the 'scientific' status of the enquiry as a matter of considerable importance:

> Our principle . . . demands that the sociologist puts himself in the same state of mind as the physicist, chemist or physiologist when he probes into a still unexplored region of the scientific domain.
>
> Emile Durkheim[5]

> The goal of psychological study is the ascertaining of such data and laws that, given the stimulus, psychology can predict what the response will be; or on the other hand, given the response, it can specify the nature of the effective stimulus.
>
> John B. Watson[6]

> The . . . period, from 1820–1830, was notable in England for the lively scientific activity which took place in the field of political economy.
>
> Karl Marx[7]

These writers saw the achievements of the natural scientists as evidence of the enormous power of the approach to investigation employed by workers in these fields. Adoption of a scientific approach was therefore seen as the best route to matching their achievements. However, this is an attitude which has been strongly challenged by others. Some question the relevance of this approach to the complex and changing world of human behaviour, while others doubt the scope for working within the basic disciplines of scientific methodology. The two major elements of these disciplines are a firm commitment to empiricism, i.e. the importance of observation and experimentation, and the search for objectivity by researchers. Beyond these there is no general consensus on the specific nature of a science.[8] The key questions are: the relative status of scientific knowledge versus other forms, e.g. common sense; the roles of theories, laws, hypotheses and models; and the relationship of the hypothesis, the law, the model and the theory.

In modern marketing research we can see examples of the two broad approaches to the accumulation of knowledge and the explanation of behaviour which exist in the social sciences:[9]

1. Inductivism: the observation of the world with a view to identifying regularities which are then, once having been verified by repeated empirical studies, raised to the status of universal laws.
2. Deductivism (encompassed by the hypothetico-deductive theory of explanation): 'explanations require the adducing of general laws, with the status of empirical hypotheses about the natural order, from which, in conjunction with statements of initial conditions, we can deductively infer statements about empirical consequences,'[10] which are then subject to attempts at falsification.

In the overall approach to statistical inference in some modern research there are clear links with the inductivist approach:

Ehrenberg[11] indicates that several hundred cases examined support the relationship (but) provides no clues as to how the relationship fits existing knowledge.[12]

The approach of Zaltman et al[13] is much closer to the deductivist approach, with its nine steps:

1. Assessment of relevant existing knowledge.
2. Concept formulation and specification of hypotheses.
3. Acquisition of meaningful data.
4. Organising and analysing data in relevant ways.
5. Evaluating and learning from results.
6. Dissemination of research information.
7. Providing explanations.
8. Making predictions.
9. Engaging in necessary control activities.

But also with a vital tenth step: *integration into existing stock of knowledge.*

Both routes are part of powerful strands of scientific knowledge, the former encompassing Bacon, Copernicus and J.S. Mill, the latter Newton, Laplace and, more recently, Popper.

As Hesketh[14] states, 'marketing research is as close to science as we get in this field', when properly conducted with rigour, objectivity and a clear empirical base. Although the emphasis is on the 'scientific' method, there are different ideas of precisely what that means, and also, it is important that the notion that creativity and insight have no role is avoided. The history of the natural sciences abounds with individuals whose methodological discipline was a launching pad for their genius, not a strait-jacket.

RESEARCH IN THE FIRM

Despite the importance of information to effective marketing, there has been a tendency in many firms to narrowly define the role of the market or marketing research department as simply to gather data, and this is a role which has been welcomed by some researchers whose dedication to their methodologies has outweighed their desire to make a real contribution to corporate effectiveness.

Many involved in both marketing and research recognise that this approach diminishes the contribution that research can make to improving the quality of planning and decision-making, as well as the more conventional information-gathering to answer more or less urgent questions. In playing this larger part in the firm's activities the fundamental disciplines retain their importance but become part of a larger system.

For many firms the first step towards this has already been taken by giving a manager specific responsibility for marketing research or establishing a marketing research department.

Market research deals with data for specific studies or to a particular brief, and usually involves specific aspects of customer or buyer behaviour. Most of this work involves a combination of secondary (employing existing sources) and primary (original studies usually involving direct market contact) data. Sales research is generally associated with the analysis of patterns of customer behaviour as manifested in purchase patterns or through syndicated research. It attempts to forecast sales or quantitative response to specific company actions. Invariably there is considerable overlap between these two areas of the firm's research activity.

As research departments have grown or been started by firms, management of their relationships with outside agencies has become a large part of their work. Very few manufacturers, financial institutions or service companies can fully employ a substantial, national field force of researchers. The Market Research Agency (including the large research departments of advertising agencies who work to outside clients' briefs) can do this, as well as providing the variety to keep staff motivated, giving clients access to different levels of expertise and skill, as well as objectivity, that vital element in research.

Although some agencies with field forces will simply recruit respondents from a firm's own staff to interview, most clients avail themselves of a wider array of agency services. Most marketing research departments are actively involved in reviewing prospective agencies, assisting marketing management in the formulation of briefs, briefing agencies, helping with the analysis of information, participation in the dissemination of acquired knowledge, and setting quality standards and managing costs. To perform these tasks effectively, while contributing to the general activity of the department, requires staff of very high calibre. The research manager in particular must be able to deal with the techniques involved, at the same time contributing his and his department's special skills to corporate policy and decision-making. To fully realise the inherent potential of the area, direct access to decision-makers is necessary.

BRIEFING FOR RESEARCH

In order for these tasks to be undertaken efficiently the relevance and quality of the information collected must be carefully scrutinised. Nowhere is the saying 'rubbish in, rubbish out' more true than in the process of briefing for a research study.

Deciding on the topic to be examined is central to all scientific investigation. Unfortunately, it is often glossed over in some broad description of an area of interest with few clear clues to specific issues or likely courses of action.

In a succinct and practical paper on the subject, Ehrenberg[15] proposes seven basic rules for effective briefing for a marketing problem. The research brief should:

1. Mean the same thing to all concerned. This may call for detailed discussion of the problem and the goals of the marketing staff. It is better to invest time before the study than lament failure afterwards. Often the research firm's proposal for the study following their briefing highlights these misunderstandings.
2. Not ask for irrelevant information. All research involves some pay-offs between cost and time. Irrelevancies cost time and money and can easily detract from the time spent on the substantial issues, as well as clouding the findings.
3. Define the population(s) to be sampled. This focuses attention on the specific contribution that the particular sample is seen as making to the project's findings.
4. State the variables to be measured. Most activity likely to be researched is multi-dimensional, involving many variables. A rigorous approach here will force the manager to review his existing knowledge carefully as well as making him think through the problem fully.
5. Give some indication of the required accuracy of the results. Almost all research is

geared to planned or likely action by the firm, so a clear view of the likely courses of action and the criteria for judging results will be of importance in designing a good brief.

6. Give an order of priority for the required accuracy of the various specified breakdown analyses.
7. Ensure that the research brief does not prejudge the selection of research techniques and procedures.

THE SCOPE OF RESEARCH

The scope of research which can be encompassed by this type of brief is enormous. A number of typologies have been put forward, of which the most generally accepted is that of Crisp, which is as follows.[16]

1. Research on markets:
   (a) analysing market potentials for existing products and estimating demand for new products;
   (b) sales forecasting;
   (c) characteristics of product markets;
   (d) analysing sales potentials;
   (e) studying trends in markets.
2. Research on products:
   (a) customer acceptance of proposed new products;
   (b) comparative studies of competitive products;
   (c) determining new uses of present products;
   (d) market-testing proposed products;
   (e) studying customer dissatisfaction with products;
   (f) product-line research;
   (g) packaging and design studies.
3. Research on promotion:
   (a) evaluating advertising effectiveness;
   (b) analysing advertising and selling practices;
   (c) selecting advertising media;
   (d) motivational studies;
   (e) establishing sales territories;
   (f) evaluating present and proposed sales methods;
   (g) studying competitive pricing;
   (h) analysing salesmen's effectiveness;
   (i) establishing sales quotas.
4. Research on distribution:
   (a) location and design of distribution centres;
   (b) handling and packing merchandise;
   (c) cost analysis of transportation methods;
   (d) dealer supply and storage requirements.
5. Research on pricing:
   (a) demand elasticities;
   (b) perceived prices;
   (c) cost analysis;
   (d) margin analysis.

Even this list, however, fails to encompass such important areas as international and export studies, economic and business forecasting, lifestyle research and corporate responsibility research.

Research, like most other areas of marketing, responds quickly to developments and new ideas. Until fairly recently motivational research was seen as being very important, but now interest has shifted to lifestyle and psychographics or qualitative research. Overall there is a constant process of accretion, with the basic skills and techniques constantly supplemented by new ideas. The pattern of research conducted in the UK in 1968 and 1976 is shown in Table 5.1.

Table 5.1   *Research agencies by type in UK, 1968 and 1976*

	1968		1976	
Total research agencies	88		170	
	No.	%	No.	%
General research agencies	34	39	47	28
Industrial research;				
management consultancy	20	23	19	11
Qualitative research	6	7	13	8
Advertising media research	6	7	1	1
Retail audits	3	3	3	2
Product development;				
packaging research	3	3	13	8
International research	3	3	13	8
Fieldwork specialists	3	3	19	11
Data processing	3	3	9	5
Pharmaceutical; medical	—	—	5	3
Consultancy; market intelligence	—	—	5	3
Other research specialist	7	8	23	13

Reproduced with permission. Martin Simmons, *The British Market Research Industry*

SECONDARY SOURCES

The search through secondary sources ('data neither collected directly by the user nor specifically for the user, often under conditions that are not well known to the user'[17]) should be the first step in any marketing research project. It is sometimes called desk research, although this may encompass a slightly broader operation, involving the collection of information from internal staff, salesmen and even outside individuals.

The firm itself is a vast store of marketing intelligence, ranging from the insights of top management to the detailed, day-to-day information of which delivery or sales staff have knowledge. The major sources of quantitative material are:

1. Production: output, inventory, costs, utilisation etc.
2. Distribution: goods in transit, stock levels and locations, stock turn rates and absolute throughput.
3. Purchasing: costs, rate of change of costs, materials, sources.
4. Sales: distribution and location of accounts, value and volume of trade, major developments.
5. Marketing services: expenditure, forecasts of turnover or likely developments.
6. Finance: costs, depreciation, overheads etc.
7. Personnel: staff and wage costs, trends, shortages and efficiency levels.

Much of this information can be matched with industry statistics collected and distributed by trade associations, industry research associations and, in specific contexts, chambers of commerce and development agencies. For example, Table 5.2 shows information provided by the Furniture Industry Research Association.

The 'information revolution' of the middle of the twentieth century emerged as large numbers of organisations became involved in the gathering of data. This has created a rich field of potential insight for the marketing man. Although the development of data

Table 5.2   *Product groups by percentage of annual sales*

	1970	1971	1972	1973	1974	1975
Upholstery	35	34	34	33	32	34
Bedroom	20	20	19	20	20	20
Kitchen	19	21	23	24	23	22
Dining/living	23	21	21	20	16	16
Occasional					7	6
Other	3	4	3	3	2	2
Total	100	100	100	100	100	100

Reproduced with the permission of the Furniture Industry Research Association

processing systems has greatly facilitated the handling of this material, coping with the sheer scale of the information does pose many problems.[18]

The information revolution of the 1980s has added a new dimension to this with electronic transmission of information through Prestel and other systems.

Government and international agencies

In Britain researchers are fortunate in having access to invaluable directories of both UK and international marketing information: *Sources of UK Marketing Information* compiled by E. Tupper and G. Wills, Ernest Benn, 1975; and *International Directory of Published Market Research*, sponsored by the British Overseas Trade Board. The task of keeping this material up to date is generally beyond the scope of any individual or commercial concern, although magazines such as the Department of Industry's *Trade and Industry* play a vital role here. Fortunately the Central Statistical Office (CSO) of the UK has adopted a very positive marketing orientated approach. Every student should be familiar with the CSO's *Annual Abstract of Statistics*, *Daily List of Government Publications*, and *Government Statistics: A Brief Guide to Sources*.

Many other countries have a similar interest in providing a statistical picture of their country and its economy. International and export marketing researchers should be familiar with the data provided in their target market, for example *Statistical Abstract of the US*, US Department of Commerce and *Das Arbeitsgebiet der Bundesstatistik*, Statistisches Bundesamt.

International bodies such as the United Nations, EEC and OECD are making a growing contribution. It is impossible to list more than a few organisations and publications here, but important sources are:

1. United Nations:
   (a)   Directory of International Statistics
   (b)   Demographic Yearbook
   (c)   Yearbook of Industrial Statistics (formerly Growth of the World Industry)
   (d)   Statistical Yearbook
   (e)   Yearbook of National Accounts Statistics
   (f)   Monthly Bulletin of Statistics
2. International Monetary Fund:
   (a)   Balance of Payments Yearbook
   (b)   Direction of Trade (annual).
3. Statistical Office of the European Communities:
   (a)   General Statistical Bulletin
   (b)   Agricultural Trade in Europe (various reports)
   (c)   Bulletin of the European Communities
   (d)   Economic Survey of Europe.

4. Organisation of Economic Co-operation and Development:
   (a) Economic Surveys of Member Countries
   (b) Economic Outlook (biannual)
   (c) Consumer Price Indices (monthly)
   (d) Financial Statistics
   (e) Food Consumption Statistics
   (f) International Tourism and Tourist Policies in OECD Member Countries
   (g) Main Economic Indicators.

Commercial and semi-official sources

General data

The main sources of general data are: The Statistical Information Service at Warwick University Library; Extel Statistical Services; the British Middle Market Directory (Dun and Bradstreet); the Guide to Key British Enterprises (Dun and Bradstreet); and Companies House. Most banks also offer their clients some form of economic or commercial information service.

Specific data

Data specific to particular areas of business activity or industry can be obtained from: trade associations, identifiable through the Directory of British Associations (CBD Research) (although it should be noted that most offer a very limited service to non-members); industry research associations, generally restricted to members; the Advertising Association; the Incorporated Society of British Advertisers; the Institute of Practitioners in Advertising; the Confederation of British Industry; the Market Research Society; the Industrial Market Research Society; the Institute of Marketing, an important recent development of which is the publication of *Marketfact*, the Institute's weekly digest of marketing news and information; and various magazines and newspapers (the Mirror Group publish the excellent *Advent*, which deals with the creative side of newspaper advertising). Some advertising and research agencies also issue special bulletins or reports on particular issues and general topics. Notable among these are AGB Research's *Audit*, A. C. Nielsen's *Researcher* and Ogilvy Benson and Mather's *Planning and Research Bulletin*.

A number of organisations publish excellent subscription-based industry or marketing studies: *Retail Business* (Economist Intelligence Unit); *Mintel* (Maclaren); *IPC Consumer Marketing Manual*; and *IPC Industrial Marketing Manual*.

Occasionally, studies of specific markets are published by research companies, e.g. *British Toys and Games Industry 1976*, Jordan Dataquest Limited, London.

Research for overseas markets

This is carried out by broadly the same set of organisations. In most countries this is complemented by the work of the national export promotion bureau. The British Overseas Trade Board supports UK firms with such facilities as the Export Intelligence Service. A number of commercial UK and international research agencies are active in this field of published information: Economist Intelligence Unit, *Marketing in Europe, Multinational Business* and *International Tourism Quarterly*; Frost and Sullivan Ltd, special industry studies, e.g. *Food Service: USA*; Predicasts Inc., *Plastic Trends*, etc.

Libraries

Every student and researcher should become familiar with the rich store of information available throughout the UK in libraries: local, central, college and polytechnic, university, industry and trade association. Even relatively small local libraries are likely to have various relevant publications, and the central libraries of the major cities such as Birmingham, Manchester, Bristol, Liverpool, Newcastle, Glasgow and Cardiff have specialist staff and a large stock of material. (Birmingham public library and a number of others publish short guides to their business information collection.)

Colleges and polytechnics frequently have major data sources and subscribe to such periodicals as *Retail Business*. Many universities have enormous stocks of economic information, although some have much to learn from the colleges about making it available to industry.

Industry research associations, trade associations, chambers of commerce and specialised bodies such as the Advertising Association, the British Institute of Management and the Institute of Marketing frequently hold material relevant to their members or specialisation.

Particularly important libraries are: the City Business Library (renowned for its helpful and informed staff); the Statistics and Market Intelligence Library (notably the Exporter's Reference Library); the University of Warwick Library (financial statistics); Birmingham Central Library; and the British Library of Political and Economic Science (restricted access).

In his paper on the topic, however, Nigel Newson-Smith[19] makes the point that desk research cannot 'fulfil the field research role of putting the supplier in direct touch with the consumer'.

Videotex

Electronic transmission of information is already transforming both the range of available information sources and the ways of handling information.

Two basic forms exist. *Teletext* is transmitted through the broadcast media of the BBC (Ceefax) and the IBA (Oracle). Although Teletext is useful, more commercial material is organised through *Viewdata*, which provides access to a vast store of data through the telephone network. In Britain, British Telecom have made major strides through *Prestel*, though systems in Europe and North America are beginning to catch up, e.g. Canada's Telidon system.

In the medium term, the real breakthrough is likely to come through *interactive* (two-way) systems. Rex Winsburg's *Viewdata in Action* is an invaluable source book.

PRIMARY STUDIES (FIELD RESEARCH)

Field research provides access to primary information, normally through direct contact with consuming, buying, intermediary or influencing groups. As indicated above, the specific design of field research should be based on a thorough review of secondary sources of information and a carefully designed and agreed brief. Research is generally divisible into qualitative and quantitative studies for one of a number of client groups, e.g. consumer, industrial, intermediary, commercial or governmental.

Although quantitative studies commissioned by consumer-goods producers and the Government have tended to dominate research activity, there has recently been a growth in qualitative research and research commissioned by industrial and commercial firms, notably banking and tourism.

Sampling

Once a project has been initiated the first set of decisions normally involve the sample of respondents to be studied. 'A sample is a subgroup selected from the market, chosen usually to provide insights into a larger population with a view to drawing general conclusions about the population.'[20]

In research, samples are generally used instead of censuses (surveys of the total group), primarily on the grounds of cost and speed. In some limited industrial studies, however, the prospective purchasing population is small enough to justify a census.

The skill in sampling determines to a considerable extent the degree to which accurate statements about the total population can confidently be made. Two important factors are the sample size and selection of the sample.

The size is usually computed on the basis of acceptable levels of accuracy. The extensive literature[1] in the field highlights the importance of this decision, which is occasionally influenced by cost factors. All too often decisions or findings are based on samples with little statistical credibility, especially when sub-samples of the main group are discussed; e.g. rejection by 10 per cent of the population in socio-economic groups A and B living in the Merseyside area and aged over 35 might mean rejection by one person.

P.G. Moore[21] identifies four basic approaches to selecting samples:

1. Random sampling: every member of the population has an equal and constant chance of being selected.
2. Systematic sampling: a set numerical routine is used to select the sample, e.g. every twentieth passer-by or house.
3. Stratified sampling: this attempts to bring out the differences which may exist in particular strata or groups in the population. Quotas are often used by the researcher to achieve this; i.e. the interviewer is given a quota of respondents in a group.
4. Cluster sampling: the respondents are selected on the basis of their grouping or clustering around a particular area or location. They may then be randomly selected within this area.

Although these approaches have been developed primarily for use in quantitative studies, they may also be used to provide a framework for selecting respondents in a qualitative study. However, it must be recognised that a qualitative study is not a substitute for quantitative investigation.

Piloting

Far too often in modern marketing research the pilot study is omitted. However, it plays a vital part in both interview approach development and questionnaire design. It should be carefully planned and the objectives clearly understood. The goal of the pilot is to assist in the development of full-scale investigations, and this should be borne in mind when briefing the interviewers and designing the format of the questionnaire. The pilot study should not be confused with 'dip-stick' research (designed to obtain a quick and limited insight into the market) carried out by managers who start looking for conclusions about the substance of the investigation rather than the research design.

Researchers in the UK have available to them the Market Research Society's *Handbook for Interviewers*. This provides a practical guide to the problems and issues associated with the personal interview. Interviewing, however, is only one of a number of methods of establishing a direct link between the firm and the respondent in order to gather data, as Table 5.3 shows.

Table 5.3   *Research methods other than personal interview and experimentation*

Method	Some uses	Some advantages	Some disadvantages
Telephone	When simultaneous interviews are needed; when individual calls are very far apart	Cost, speed	Lack of rapport, interviews must be fairly short, cannot use showcards or pictures, low incidence of telephone ownership
Mail	When respondents are difficult to contact	Cost, no interviewer 'interference'	Unrepresentative sample, lack of control of questionnaire completion
Self-completion	When interview should be carried out but interviewer cannot be present	Cost, accuracy of reporting close to action reported	As with mail survey (e.g. misunderstanding bias; only short questionnaire possible)
Psycho-galvanometer	When respondent unlikely to be aware of own responses	Prestige and similar answers need not be considered	Unreal surroundings, little data about 'why', cost of large samples
Tachistoscope etc.	To test detailed physical behaviour, particularly of eye reaction	Ability to measure action in a detail not available by other methods	Unreal surroundings, little data about 'why', cost of large samples
Count	When requirement implies total numbers of people involved in certain actions	Cost, speed, large samples	Little data about 'why', no analysis possible by profile of individual
Observation	When the concern is more with *how* people act than *why*	Direct observation of what people do rather than what they *say* they do	Cost, sample structure
Participant observation	When only information at a very detailed level is of value	Depth of response	Very high cost and very long time taken, problems of representative sample

Reproduced with permission. England, L., 'Telephone, Mail and Other Techniques'. In *Consumer Market Research Handbook* (Ed.) Worcester, R.M. & Downham, J. London: Van Nostrand Reinhold, 1978.

It is in situations involving direct personal contact with the respondent that the role of the interviewer is of real importance. Personal interviewing calls for a range of professional skills normally requiring careful selection, training and close monitoring of the staff involved. In most consumer research the interviewing is conducted by part-time staff. This places a special responsibility on the firm to ensure that the field force of researchers involved is well managed, the briefing for the project is carefully conducted, the piloting involves the field force, continual effort is invested in minimising 'interviewer bias', and close control and monitoring of the work of the field force is carried out. (Interviewer bias is the introduction of bias into the research situation through behaviour, comment, appearance or other features of the interviewer.)

In industrial markets there is a far higher likelihood of the interview being conducted by the research company's own full-time staff. They can bring a high level of training, skill and knowledge into situations which may require the ability to probe and analyse in the course of the interview. Despite this, the basic control and management disciplines retain their role. In industrial situations careful management is necessary to maintain a level of consistency and comparability between interviews.

The questionnaire

The questionnaire is central to proper management of the interaction between researcher and interviewees. The basic rules of good questionnaire design are easy to state—keep it short, keep it simple and make sure that it is understood—but very difficult to put into practice. This is because the purpose is usually to elicit meaningful answers, from what is often a large and disparate group of respondents, to questions which may have little immediate relevance to those interviewed.

Planning the questionnaire is very important. The briefing, the initial discussion and the pilot all provide clues to the key issues under investigation, the forms of response required and likely reactions to particular formats, and these should be built into the overall structure of the questionnaire. The effect of the sequence of questions has been widely discussed and the following pattern found useful:

1. Open with a few factual, easy-response questions.
2. Lead into a small number of factual multiple-choice questions.
    Follow with questions designed to gauge whether the interviewee has thought about or knows about the topic(s) under review.
4. Move into a series of structured and semi-structured questions designed to cover very specific issues.
5. Introduce a selection of open-ended or wide-open questions so that the respondent can fully express himself.
6. Close with 'filter' questions, i.e. questions designed to locate the respondent according to the sampling frame.

In the questionnaire there should always be some double-check questions to check for consistency of response and control questions to compare answers with information from other sources.

Although this framework has worked in a number of situations it is not a universal model. The brief, the topic, the sample and the pilot should determine the appropriate structure for each situation.

Questionnaires are part of a broader research study, so it is their overall contribution that is important. Computer-based data-handling techniques are normally used to handle aggregate data, so coding frames and the pattern of information should be borne in mind when designing the questionnaire.

The rules mentioned earlier – simple, short and easily understood – are doubly relevant to specific questions within the overall goal of gathering the required information. Work by Belson[22] has demonstrated the frequency with which respondents fail to fully understand the interviewer's questions. Some common causes[23] of these failures are ambiguity, the use of unfamiliar words, difficult and abstract concepts, overloading the respondent with too many instructions, vague concepts, and trying to ask two questions in one. In a very good report on the subject the Market Research Society of Great Britain highlights the potential contribution of standardised questions.[24] The report also provides a practical summary of the principles and substance of good question design and the many forms questions can take.

Questionnaire and question design in industrial market research poses special problems for the researcher.[25] The project may be probing into highly specialised areas where:

1. Technical terminology in the questions is unavoidable, posing real problems for the interviewer.
2. There may be only a small number of possible respondents in a particular sphere.
3. Major problems and reservations about confidentiality can occur.

Careful control of the response rates is essential to all forms of questionnaire-based research. Although it is virtually impossible to avoid some level of non-response, particularly in mail or telephone studies, sustained follow-up to minimise it and a close watch on its possible effects are necessary.

Completion of the fieldwork is not the end of a research effort. The project was set up to make a contribution to policy formulation and decision-making and to assist in resolving certain issues. The presentation of the findings and their dissemination are therefore two critical final steps.

Presentation usually involves a written and a verbal report. The Market Research Society's minimum acceptable content of a written report involves overall purpose and specific objectives, details of the principals and researchers, a description of the population covered, sample and sampling frame, methodology, details of research staff, timings, the questionnaire, findings, the data base and locations of interviews.

The report must face up to the problems posed by the client. The researcher has the responsibility to ensure that technical terminology which may be necessary for effective communication between specialist researchers does not become a barrier to understanding for the non-expert general marketing staff.

So far discussion has concentrated on questionnaire-based studies. However other approaches to market intelligence-gathering, experimentation and observation, also have an important role to play.

Experimentation

This is the corner-stone of investigation in the natural sciences, and as such it has always been of special interest to the behavioural scientist. However, its use in the social sciences has been restricted by the difficulties of setting up experimental situations and the dangers of the experimental situation itself affecting the research behaviour. Despite these difficulties the need to study, under certain circumstances, in a closely-monitored situation, specific behaviour and responses has led many researchers to sustain their commitment to experimental marketing.

'A subject that covers the entire range of situations involved when a company first decides to introduce changes into a small part of its market so as to gain information before becoming committed to innovation on a wider scale.' In using this definition we go beyond the traditional area in which experimentation is used—test marketing of new products—into a much broader sphere of testing changes in controlled market situations.

As an area of investigation it has the scope for providing management with the opportunity to explore the impact of their ideas and developments in the real world. Attention is focused not on respondents' intentions or stated attitudes, but on their actual behaviour. The potential power of the approach is matched by the need for considerable skill in setting up the experiments and rigour in its application. Without doubt it is the most demanding area of marketing research.

To overcome some of the problems associated with real-world experiments, some researchers have explored the scope for simulation.[26]

The process of modelling things, problems or concepts.

Definitions Committee of the AMA

Techniques for manipulating a model of some real-world process for the purpose of finding numerical solutions that are useful in the real process that is being modelled.

T. Kempner[27]

Although there is considerable interest in this approach, particularly in the USA, its contribution in the UK has been largely confined to new product development, physical distribution and brand choice. A number of recent studies[28] have highlighted both the capacity for its use in other areas and the scope for its simplification in order to overcome the recurrent problem of complexity in simulation research techniques.

Observation

This approach has been extensively used in the social sciences and has played a major role in a number of important studies of behaviour, notably in the workplace and the small community.[29] The basic idea is that by watching the behaviour of specific respondents in controlled situations, insights into their reactions can be achieved.

Its most popular uses are:

1. Direct observation: examining how people behave in specific situations. Although until recently direct observation was largely confined to retail studies, a number of industrial researchers are now exploring its use, notably for views of how machinery is used and opportunity spotting.
2. Recording devices: in this controversial area a number of electromechanical devices have been developed for monitoring respondents' reactions. Two commonly used devices are the eye camera, for recording eye movements (generally in advertising testing) and the psychogalvanometer, for measuring perspiration as a gauge of involuntary physical response, usually to advertisements.

The real value of observational studies lies in their ability to describe routines and patterns of behaviour. The nature of the approach calls for the researcher to infer causality if that is sought by the study.

Qualitative research[30]

As well as the data provided by quantitative studies of the market size and composition, there exists a mass of material required for a deeper understanding of the customer. Perception, motivations and attitudes cannot readily be discovered at an acceptable cost in large-scale quantitative studies. Qualitative research focuses on the less easily measured facets of perceptions, thoughts, motivations and attitudes in new, unfamiliar or changing markets. It deals in concepts rather than numbers.

Three methods of inquiry have been developed:

1. Non-directive group discussion: this brings together members of the target group to explore and discuss specified themes. It can lead to a heightened willingness to contribute besides highlighting the special features of group-influenced behaviour.
2. Non-directive individual interview: this provides the opportunity to probe in depth the respondent's behaviour, attitudes, opinions and needs. It is particularly relevant in industrial market research where in-depth analysis of confidential material is sought.
3. Projective techniques: these involve different forms of stimuli—story-boards, sentence completion, Rorschach ink blot tests—to prompt the respondent to talk in an unstructured manner about specific topics. By letting the respondent range freely over a subject it is hoped that some unconscious or hitherto unmentioned views will emerge.

Qualitative studies play a significant role in current research, but place tremendous demands on the skills of the researcher and those involved in briefing and reporting.

Syndicated research

Syndicated research is performed for a combination of firms involved in a sphere of activity which provides the research firm with scope to conduct large-scale and regular studies of a selection of consistent topics. In Britain it takes four basic forms: trade audits, consumer panels, omnibus surveys and TV ratings.

The general pattern of development involves the identification of a broad sphere of activity, e.g. consumer purchasing of fast-moving non-durables. The research firm conducts regular studies of a sample, providing a number of clients with the information gathered.

Trade audits

These are conducted among panels of wholesalers and retailers. The research firm sends 'auditors' into the selected outlets on a regular basis to count stock and record deliveries, thus providing a measure of throughput. From their raw data a number of basic tabulations can be arrived at, notably consumer sales, stocks, price and brand distribution. A firm may find that, although its sent-out sales (from the factory) are high, retail stocks are growing rapidly. This may require immediate corrective action. Another company might note a weakness in a specific type of outlet, e.g. retail off-licences, and specific tactics can be considered to overcome this problem.

A number of highly specialised services have emerged, notably specialised area studies, e.g. Nielsen Drug Index, Nielsen Food Index etc., special analysis of particular topics, and test market studies. The leading retail audit company in Britain is A.C. Nielsen and Co.

Consumer panels

These provide a continuous survey of a consistent and large sample of consumers. A complete picture of their purchasing pattern can be built up over time, and this can provide an incomparable base for statistical and econometric analysis of patterns of behaviour.

Two types of panel exist: home audit (an auditor visits the home to check purchases, stocks and used cartons, wrappers etc.) and diary panel (the respondent completes, on a daily, weekly or other regular basis, a diary of his or her purchasing). Panels can be either long term or set up on a short-term basis to study specific patterns or situations. A relatively recent development has been the establishment of specialist panels in certain markets (Table 5.4).

The availability of continuous time-series data has provided the framework for the use of sophisticated forecasting and diagnostic techniques in research. One of the earliest uses of consumer-panel data was in Brown's classic studies of loyalty and repeat purchasing.[31] It is an approach which has been employed by a number of more recent workers.[32]

Omnibus surveys

As implied by their name, these represent an attempt by firms to minimise the costs of surveys by participating in a single large study made up of a large number of small questionnaires.

Normally responsibility for designing the firm's questions will lie with the client company. They will invariably be required to meet certain conditions imposed by the research company concerning number, location and support materials. As the majority of omnibus surveys are operated on a continuous basis (e.g. British Market Research Bureau (weekly), Gallup Poll (weekly), the firm will be able to build up a picture of performance over time, as well as making savings.

Table 5.4 *Different panels operating in the UK in 1978*

Panel service	Date of formation	Reporting sample size	Data collection method	Type of data collected	Standard reporting periods
Attwood Consumer Panel	1948	4800 households	Postal diary	Purchases of household consumer goods	4-weekly and/or quarterly
AGB Television Consumer Audit	1964	5800 households	Home audit	Purchases of household consumer goods	4-weekly
JCPI (Individuals Panel)	1973	8000 adults 1500 children	Postal diary	Purchases of personal consumer goods	One or two monthly
Attwood AMSAC Personal Panel	1970	12 000 individuals	Postal diary	Purchases of personal consumer goods	
RSGB Baby Panel	1967	1150 mothers with babies	Diary and interviews	Purchases of consumer goods for use by babies	4-weekly and/or quarterly
RBL Motorists Panel	1964	4000 individual motorists	Postal diary	Purchases of petrol, oil and car accessories	4-weekly
Agridata Farming Panels	1971	Two panels of 1500 and 2500 farmers	Personal interview	Purchases of sprays, fertilisers, feeds, etc.	Quarterly
AGB Index	1978	11 500	Personal	Spending habits, savings, insurance	Monthly

Reproduced with permission. Parfitt, J., 'Panel Research'. In *Consumer Market Research Handbook* (Ed.) Worcester, R.M.

TV ratings

These are probably the most famous forms of syndicated research. They are sponsored by the TV companies to build up a picture of patterns of viewing behaviour. A number of different approaches are used, notably:

1. Meter recording of sets: a meter is attached to the set to monitor the precise times of watching and the channels (and hence the programmes) viewed. (As the meter is automatic there is no guarantee that the viewer is actually in front of the set.)
2. Interviewing: this is conducted soon after the evening's viewing. A mixture of aided (prompted) and unaided (non-prompted) recall approaches are used.

SPECIAL AREAS OF STUDY

So far the particular problems associated with areas such as industrial market research have been noted as the discussion progressed. A few comments are necessary about the major non-consumer goods fields: industrial market research; services, notably finance, research; and non-profit organisations. All require special skills and disciplines for effective marketing research.

Industrial marketing research

This usually calls for grounding in the specific industries being studied. When managers are being interviewed they will frequently respond negatively to the failure to have thoroughly conducted preliminary investigations. At the same time it is often difficult to identify the responsible decision-makers in the areas being studied, since formal job titles may have only limited relevance to the work done. In many instances no one individual is responsible; a purchasing coalition (formal or informal) may exist. Respondents are likely to be more conscious of the real cost of their time, so this calls for a disciplined approach to questionnaire length.

Services

The major banks, unit trusts and insurance companies conduct research regularly. They are often working in areas that are seen as personal and often highly confidential, e.g. salaries, tax levels, investments. Respondent reservations have been made greater by the use of false questionnaires by some firms. Research here therefore requires considerable tact to overcome these problems.

Non-profit organisations

Probably the largest sponsors of research in Britain are the Government and the local authorities. Studies of social problems, leisure and the elderly are becoming an increasingly important part of the research environment. Much of this research is focused on the poor, the aged and the disabled, groups which have in the past posed considerable recruitment and communication problems for researchers.

There is an increasing interest in research among non-government, non-profit-making bodies, from pressure groups to colleges. This has been marked by an almost anti-professional stance by those conducting the research, and has usually been associated with unsystematic and subjective accumulations of dubious information. Although it is possible to self-conduct limited types of research,[33] the disciplined approach still retains its importance.

MARKETING INFORMATION SYSTEMS

The collection, communication and dissemination of data in all areas is seen by more and more marketing men and researchers as part of the continuing process of building up a corporate marketing information system.

The notion of constructing marketing information systems is fundamental to the entire approach of this chapter. Marketing intelligence is the life-blood of the firm. It is not sufficient that it exists; managers must be in a position to use it to formulate policies, make decisions and resolve problems. As such the marketing information system is best described as:

> A structured, interacting complex of persons, machines and procedures designed to generate an orderly flow of pertinent information, collected from both intra- and extra-firm sources, for use as bases for decision-making in specified responsibility areas of marketing management.   Smith, Brien and Stafford[34]

All the salient features of good MIS design are encapsulated in this definition:

1. 'A structured, interacting complex of persons, machines and procedures': it is carefully planned and constructed to achieve the maximum pay-offs for the organisation, within specified goals.
2. 'An orderly flow of pertinent information': this emphasises the need for the patterns of communication to be thought through to ensure that those needing the information get it at the right time and in the required form, but at the same time

ensuring that other managers are not swamped by irrelevant material.
3. 'From both intra- and extra-firm sources': the total network of contacts with the environment and sources of relevant data are effectively tapped and built into the system.
4. 'Bases for decision-making': these flows of material are directed to the areas of need,where new information can help managers to more effectively resolve problems or minimise the risks involved in their decisions.

Constructing a marketing information system calls for a careful study of both the information needs of the company and its managers and the methods of acquiring the material required.

In 1972 Briscoe[35] identified the problems faced by the British Steel Corporation in matching the various sources of marketing intelligence with the information needs of management. More recently, Jobber and Rainbow[36] found that almost 50 per cent of the large firms responding to a questionnaire on the topic had established, or were in the process of establishing, a marketing information system. The advent of the microprocessor is creating many new opportunities and demands for system design and use.

DECISION ANALYSIS

One of the primary roles in market and marketing research is to gather information to assist managers to resolve uncertainties, generally with a view to more effective or lower-risk decision-making. Information cannot make these decisions or eliminate the risks. As information cannot eliminate the risk, but merely reduces it, some might ask why money should be spent on collecting it. It is the issue which is faced by modern theories of decision, notably the Bayesian approach to decision-making under conditions of uncertainty.

Although there is not the scope for a full review of this complex and controversial topic here, the major aspects are:

1. It is possible to identify for any decision a series of likely outcomes.
2. These outcomes can be identified and the returns for the firm in each situation detailed.
3. A subjective probability can be assigned to each outcome.
4. By multiplying each outcome by the appropriate probability and summing, the products and expected return can be established.
5. Where a manager has imperfect information upon which to base his probabilities, he can elect to gather more information if the value of the additional information is greater than the cost of obtaining it.

Bayesian statistics provide a framework for handling this computational problem.

CONCLUSION

Marketing research is one of the most dynamic and rapidly developing areas of study and effort in modern marketing. In Britain large numbers of skilled managers and researchers are actively involved in improving and developing research techniques and working on approaches to the effective managerial use of market information. It is a context in which both the power of discipline and the potential of creativity must come together to produce more effective company marketing. The breakthrough made possible by electronic systems will produce dramatic changes over the next few years.

Notes

1. Simmons, M., *The British Market Research Industry*, Annual Conference of the Market Research Society, 1977.
2. Green, P.E. & Tull, D.S., *Research for Marketing Decisions*. Prentice-Hall International, 1978.
3. Hund, S.D., *Marketing Theory*, Columbus Grid Inc., 1976.
4. Harper, M. Jr, 'A New Profession to Aid Management', *Journal of Marketing*, January, 1961.
5. Durkheim, E., *Rules of Sociological Method*, 1895.
6. Watson, J.B., *Psychology from the Point of View of the Behaviouralist*, 1919.
7. Marx, K., *Capital*, **I**, 2nd Edition, 1873.
8. Kaplan, A., *The Conduct of Inquiry*. New York: Chandler Publishing, 1964.
9. For a full review of this topic the interested reader is referred to Alan Ryan's excellent textbook *The Philosophy of the Social Sciences*. New York: Macmillan, 1971, or Sir Karl Popper's classic *The Logic of Scientific Discovery*. London: Hutchinson, 1972.
10. Ryan, A., *The Philosophy of the Social Sciences*, Macmillan, 1971.
11. Ehrenberg, A.S.C., 'Laws in Marketing: A Tail-piece'. In *Consumer Behaviour* (Ed.) Ehrenberg, A.S.C. & Pyatt, F.G. Harmondsworth: Penguin Books, 1971. (Title in these readings, 'Regularities of behaviour'.)
12. Hund, S.D., *Marketing Theory*, Columbus Grid Inc., 1976.
13. Zaltman, G., Christian, R.A., Angleman, P. & Angleman, R., *Metatheory and Consumer Research*. Holt, Rinehart and Winston, 1973.
14. Hesketh, J.L., *Marketing*. New York: Macmillan, 1976.
15. Ehrenberg, A.S.C., 'The Research Brief'. In *Marketing Research* (Ed.) Seibert, J. & Wills, G. Harmondsworth: Penguin Books, 1970.
16. Crisp, R.D., *Marketing Research Organization and Operation*, Research Study No. 35, pp.39–47. New York: American Management Association, 1958. Reproduced with the permission of the American Marketing Association.
17. Definition Committee of the American Marketing Association.
18. Ehrenberg's *Data Reduction* is a good guide to a practical approach to coping with large amounts of raw data.
19. Newson-Smith, N., 'Desk Research'. In *Consumer Market Research Handbook* (Ed.) Worcester, R.M. & Downham, J. London: Van Nostrand Reinhold, 1978.
20. See Moser, K. & Kalton, G.G.W., *Survey Methods in Social Investigation*. London: Heinemann, 1971.
21. Moore, P.G., *Statistics and the Manager*. Macdonald, 1966.
22. Belson, W.A., *Studies in Readership*. Business Publications, 1962.
23. Much of this discussion is based on Jean Morton-Williams' article 'Questionnaire Design' in *Consumer Market Research Handbook* (Ed.) Worcester, R.M. Van Nostrand Reinhold, 1978.
24. Market Research Society of Great Britain, *Standardized Questions*, MRS, 1976.
25. Perhaps the most important work in this area is Wilson, A., *The Assessment of Industrial Markets*. London: Hutchinson, 1968.
26. For a useful overview see James, G., *Simulation for Business Decisions*. Harmondsworth: Penguin, 1973.
27. Kempner, T., *A–Z of Management*. Harmondsworth: Penguin, 1973.
28. Beazley, D. & Westwood, D., *Modelling Choice Behaviour*, Market Research Society Annual Conference, March, 1976.
29. Gouldner, A.W., *Patterns of Industrial Bureaucracy*. New York: Free Press, 1975. Whyte, W.F., *Street Corner Society*. Chicago: University of Chicago Press, 1954. Both these studies employed the specialised form of observational study known as participant observation. Very little use has been made of this approach in marketing, except for some limited use in industrial studies.
30. This discussion is based on the Report of the Market Research Society's Research and Development Sub-Committee on Qualitative Research, published in the *Journal of the Market Research Society*, April, 1979.
31. Brown, G.H., 'Brand Loyalty'. In *Consumer Behaviour* (Ed.) Ehrenberg, A.S.C. & Pyatt, F.G. Harmondsworth: Penguin, 1971.
32. Ehrenberg, A.S.C., 'The Pattern of Consumer Purchases', *Applied Statistics*, Volume 8, 1959. Parfitt, J.H. & Collins, B.J.K., 'The Use of Consumer Panels for Brand Share Prediction', *Journal of Marketing Research*, May, 1968.
33. For a review of some basic rules see Bassford, G. & Schlacter, J.L., 'Practical Market Research for Executive Decisions'. In *Marketing: Contemporary Dimensions* (Ed.) Robicheaux, R.A., Pride, W.M. & Ferrell, O.E. Houghton Mifflin Co., 1977.
34. Smith, S.V., Brien, R.H. & Stafford, J.E., 'Marketing Information Systems: An Introductory Overview'. In *Readings in Marketing Information Systems* (Ed.) Smith, S.V., Brien, R.H. & Stafford, J.E. Boston: Houghton Mifflin Co., 1968.
35. Briscoe, G., *The Sources and Uses of Marketing Information in the British Steel Corporation*. London: British Steel Corporation Fellowship Scheme, 1972.

36.   Jobber, D. & Rainbow, C., 'A Study of the Development and the Implementation of Marketing Information Systems in British Industry', *Journal of the Market Research Society*, **19**, No.3, July, 1977.

Further reading

Green, P.E. & Tull, D.S., *Research for Marketing Decisions*. Prentice-Hall International, 1978. This fourth edition, with its confirmed quantitative and decision-making approach, sustains the commitment to quality of the earlier works.
Wilson, A., *The Assessment of Industrial Markets*. London: Hutchinson, 1968. A thorough review by Britain's leading authority in the area.
Winsbury, R., *Viewdata in Action*. London: McGraw Hill, 1981. Essential reading for those seeking to keep in touch with this dynamic and changing field.
Consumer Market Research Handbook (Ed.) Worcester, R.M. & Downham, J. London: Van Nostrand Reinhold, 1978. An excellent compilation of articles from some of Britain's leading researchers, its range and the quality and practical relevance of the papers included go far in demonstrating the vigour of UK market research.

Key organisations

Market Research Society,
15 Belgrave Square,
London SW1X 8PF

Central Statistical Office,
Great George Street,
London SW1P 3AQ

Industrial Market Research Society,
Bird Street
Lichfield, Staffs

CASE STUDY 4: PRICE AWARENESS IN THE TOILET SOAP MARKET

Background

The toilet soap market is a large, fairly stable market. Toilet soap is a household staple with a high purchase frequency. There are many brands but only three major manufacturers: Procter and Gamble, Unilever, and Colgate Palmolive. Demand is concentrated among the top five brands. There is a high brand advertising, industry advertising/sales (A/S) ratio, and earlier work indicates a relatively high degree of brand loyalty. However, price cutting is endemic and appears to be growing.

Objectives of the research

Putting ourselves in the position of a leading manufacturer we hope to discover:

1.   Consumer price awareness: how knowledgeable consumers are about the price of a block of soap, particularly the brand they bought last and the brand they buy regularly (if different). As there is some variation in sizes, e.g. standard and bath, interest is focused on the size they purchased and the size they regularly purchase.
2.   The relationship between awareness and the outlet from which the product is purchased. Thus we need to know:
     (a)   where the product was bought;
     (b)   whether that outlet stocks an own-label brand;

    (c)   whether the consumer considers purchasing the own-label brand;

    (d)   where he does (or does not) buy it;

    (e)   what the effect of the outlet is on the consumer's price perception.

3. The assumptions made about the consumer's knowledge of the price of other brands; thus we need to know:

    (a)   how aware customers are of the price of brands other than those recently or regularly purchased;

    (b)   whether they actively compare prices in stores;

    (c)   whether they compare the recommended prices, the size of the price cut or the final price;

    (d)   whether there is any concept of a fair price for soap;

    (e)   whether the research can support Gabor's contention that definable price brackets exist in a market.

Target population

Women aged between 25 and 55, with particular emphasis on married women with two or more children under 15.

Annual size/value of the market

The figures for production of toilet soap seem to offer very little indication of the probable trends in the retail market: variations between 107.2 and 70.9 thousand tonnes in 1962 and 1972 respectively seem to suggest a seriously declining volume in total in a period when, with rising standards of living, greater attention to hygiene and a growing population, one would expect that volume would be rising slowly.

    The value of the retail market was estimated at £30-35 million (1973).

Table 5.5   *Production of toilet soap ('000 tonnes)*

1962	1968	1969	1970	1971	1972	1973
107.2	91.3	99.6	96.7	93.4	82.8	98.2

Table 5.6   *Business monitor series (sales by UK manufacturers)*

	1972	1973
Home market/wholesale, retail, '000 tonnes	65	72
Home market/other	n.a.	5
Export	29	38
		(£43.5 million in total)

Principal advertisers and brands

(those spending £100000 or more in 1973 or 1974)

Table 5.7   *Press and TV advertising (£'000)*

		1973		1974			
Advertiser	Brand	TV	Press	Total	(%)	TV	Press
Procter and Gamble	Camay	294	3	300	(10)	298	3
Cussons	Imperial Leather	188	—	279	(9)	248	31
Procter and Gamble	Fairy	410	—	394	(13)	386	8

Table 5.7 *contd.*

| Advertiser | Brand | 1973 | | | | 1974 | |
		TV	Press	Total	(%)	TV	Press
Lever Bros	Lifebuoy	280	2	202	(7)	200	2
	Lux	414	11	326	(11)	325	2
Colgate	Palmolive	322	—	406	(14)	404	2
	Fresh Lemon	230	6	155	(5)	155	—
	Fresh Mint	5	—	155	(5)	155	—
Gibbs	Pears	134	27	193	(7)	178	14
Total for group	'Soaps Toilet'	2425	315	2965	(100)	2660	305

Channels of distribution

The main channels of distribution are grocers (predominantly), variety stores, chemists and departmental stores. Supermarkets and self-service grocers may account for half of the purchases.

Indications of brand shares

The pattern presented suggests that the overall (or sub-group) leadership could be continually changing within the top brands.

Mintel suggests that Camay, Lifebuoy and Fairy are rather further behind Lux and Palmolive and that Fresh Lemon had reached a 5 per cent share.

Private label brands were estimated by Mintel to account for 16 per cent (including Boots).

Table 5.8 *TGI (1974) brand choice*

Lux	16%
Palmolive	16%
Camay	14%
Lifebuoy	14%
Cusson's Imperial Leather	15%
Fairy	15%
Boots	11%
Knights Castile	6%
Wrights' Coal Tar	5%
Fresh	4%

Other points of interest

Virtually all housewives buy toilet soap. 10 per cent were classified as 'heavy users' by TGI in 1974. On the other hand IPC recorded an 86 per cent usage level among women, for 'use on the face'. Non-users were biased towards younger women and towards London and the South East.

Below-the-line activity (price-offs etc) is used very extensively in this market. The launch of Fairy was very heavily supported 'below the line': price-offs, coupons, sampling etc. Colgate launched Fresh Lemon in 1972.

Only Lifebuoy seems to have been able to establish and maintain itself as a deodorant soap. The other leaders are all essentially 'cosmetic' soaps.

Heavy users occur disproportionately in the 35-44 age group, in the C_2D class and among families with children aged 10-15 (TGI 1974). In this latter group 22 per cent of housewives were classified as 'heavy users'.

Sources: IPA 'Total Market Sizes'; EIU 'Retail Business' No. 93 and No. 138;
BMRB Target Group Index, 1974; MEAL 1973 and 1974 Digests; IPC
'Cosmetics' Survey, 1972/74; Mintel, December 1973.

Decisions required

As the major manufacturers are engaged in considerable price competition, particularly
through the major supermarket groups, we need to know the following:

1. Is this an efficient means of competing and can we consider discontinuing it?
2. Should we give greater prominence to price in our advertising?
3. Are brand loyal customers impervious to price cutting, i.e. do they even bother
    checking?
4. How important are the brand loyal customers and should we concentrate on giving
    them rewards, e.g. improved imagery?
5. Is our policy of giving bonuses and discounts to the supermarket groups paying off
    or are we merely lining ourselves up for price comparisons in store?
6. Does the concept of a fair price exist and, if so, what promotional or product
    development opportunities does it stimulate?
7. Can we identify any new brand or new product opportunities through pricing?

Buyers, Consumers and Influences

In Chapter 2 some of the factors that make up demand for a firm's product were introduced. It was noted that the market's requirements were usually the results of the needs of a number of different customers (although in industrial, commercial and government markets this is not necessarily the case; Marks and Spencer's take all the output of some suppliers, and firms in the medicare and defence fields may sell all their output to the government). Each customer purchases the product for his own reasons, some shared with others, some individual. At the heart of the marketing concept is the proposition that the firm's ability to understand and meet the needs of sufficient numbers of buyers is the essential precondition for long-term success.

In this chapter the implications in consumer markets of this notion will be explored in depth. Consumer markets are those concerned with the private end-users of a product, service or other form of offering. Our knowledge of the forces shaping consumer and buyer behaviour is built on the foundations laid in the more general behavioural sciences. Although this was once a highly dependent relationship, advances in this area in marketing, notably the increasing amount of empirical study, have altered the balance over the last decade.

Despite the considerable amount of investigation carried out, no current theory or approach fully satisfies the needs of the marketer or researcher. The forces affecting behaviour are complex and wide ranging. They have been viewed from a number of different perspectives: economic, psychological, physiological and sociological. In an attempt to understand the buying process more fully, models of the buyer's or consumer's approach to purchasing have been constructed. A model is an attempt to represent visually or verbally the most important element in a real world situation as a basis for achieving greater understanding or conducting experiments to test the part or the whole.

The extent of the factors which influence the buyer are illustrated in Figure 6.1. These affect the consumer not only directly but also through their interaction. For example, Mr Khan's desire for a sports car may be affected by his economic circumstances and his wife's fears for his safety.

Kotler[1] suggests that a useful way of considering this process is to think of purchasing in terms of four broad characteristics:

1. Objects: the classifications of goods and services.
2. Objectives: the factors affecting the customer's search for satisfaction and choice.
3. Organisations: the groups involved in achieving this satisfaction.
4. Operations: the actions needed to carry out this process.

These four 'O's can be matched against four 'P's of the marketing mix (see Figure 1.5).

Buying can be seen in terms of a simple 'black box' system (Figure 6.2). The idea of the 'black box' is used to show the fact that what goes on inside is not fully understood.

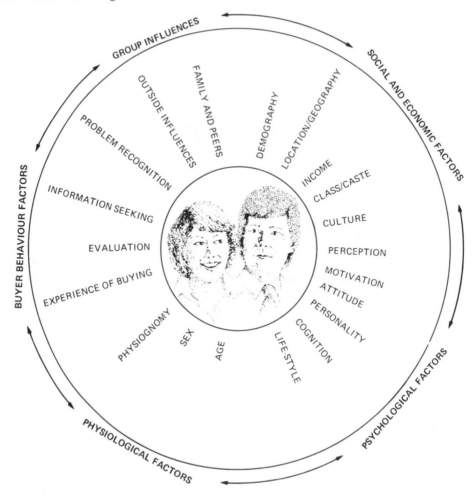

Fig. 6.1   Influences on the buyer.

In order to understand the factors that influence the consumer we must return to some of the concepts introduced in Chapter 2.

SOCIAL AND ECONOMIC VARIABLES

The socio-economic forces of demography, location, income and class establish many of the preconditions for particular types of needs, drives and actions. These pressures are not constant. They change over time for both the total society and the specific individual or family. Some major socio-economic changes occurring now in Britain are: the increasing economic power of women, from 30 per cent of the labour force in 1951 to over 40 per cent now; a progressively older population profile; the increasing terminal education age of population; the shift from manufacturing industry to services; and the growth in leisure time.

These create problems for some firms and types of organisations while opening new opportunities for others. For example, the traditional male-only pubs and clubs are being forced more and more to admit women, and organisations such as the tour operators 'Saga' are catering for the increasingly important subgroups.

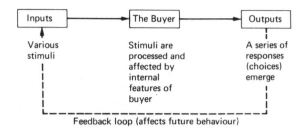

Fig. 6.2 The 'black box' system.

In exploring these patterns and trends the danger of thinking in terms of single, mass, homogeneous markets has been recognised.

MARKET SEGMENTATION

Market segmentation, as an approach, emerged from the recognition of this danger. It is based on the proposition that, if a holiday package is being designed for a market consisting of three age groups (14 to 25, 26 to 45 and over 46) and three different types of participant (single, married with children, and married with grown-up children), and each group is willing to spend different amounts (up to £400, £800 and £1000), then two different methods are available. A single general holiday—a low-price, two weeks' full board holiday in an English holiday resort—could be offered. All the potential holiday-makers would be able to afford this, but younger holiday-makers may want more freedom, family units may need 'evening supervision' for the children, and older groups may require a greater educational or cultural interest. Therefore the approach of 'any holiday so long as it's full board in Blackpool' will succeed only until competitors satisfying the basic 'affordability' requirement also start meeting other needs.

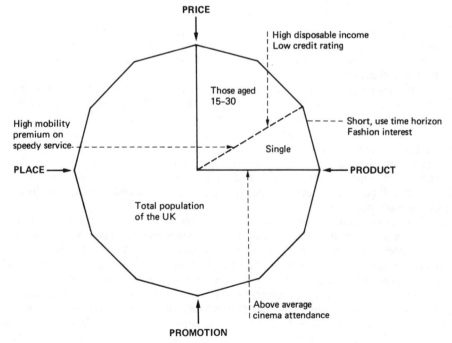

Fig. 6.3 Subdividing the market.

Market segmentation is 'the subdividing of a market into distinct and increasingly homogeneous subgroups of customers, where any group can conceivably be selected as a target market to be met with a distinct marketing mix'.[2] There are two important features of this definition: the segments are more homogeneous than the market from which they are chosen; and they can be reached through a marketing mix which is probably specific to them. The basic aims are to meet the needs of subgroups, protect the firm's offering from competition on price, and improve customer loyalty and company returns (Figure 6.3).

The routes which can be taken to reach different segments are as varied as the different perspectives towards understanding consumer behaviour and the forces prompting purchase action.

Segmentation by location

This is probably the oldest and most established method. Here firms target their offerings on specific local communities or groups. The retail trade has traditionally adopted this approach, since the shop serves its own community, and the range of goods offered reflects their needs rather than national or regional patterns of brand share or market power. There may be 'stottie cakes' in the bakers' shops on Tyneside, 'black puddings' in the butchers' shops in Lancashire, enormous arrays of exotic fish in the Birmingham Bull Ring fish market, and kosher food in East London. The local shop probably often meets convenience needs, and this fact is reflected in their pricing policies. Until very recently the growth in personal mobility had created a very high failure rate in small local shops, but now the energy shortages and high petrol prices may reverse this trend. Location is very important in certain industrial markets.

Socio-economic factors

Socio-economic factors are used as a basis for segmentation. Shared economic position and broadly similar incomes, levels of literacy and viewing habits, as well as some shared values, are seen by many firms as clues to the appropriate product offering, pricing, promotional and distribution mixes.

This is an approach to the market which is particularly important to the media, especially newspapers. Segmentation by class helps them to design their own special mix to appeal to specific groups. Equally important, the newspapers and magazines can use the make-up of their readership as part of the offering to prospective advertisers.

Increasing research into segmentation has highlighted weaknesses in these approaches, emphasising as they do external, non-product-related criteria. It is implied that 'differences in reasons for buying, in brand choice influences, in frequency of use or in susceptibility will be reflected in differences in age, sex, income and geographical location. But this is usually not true.'[3]

Out of this emerged a number of specific new approaches to segmentation and a new perspective on the entire process. *Benefit segmentation* attempts to get to the roots of the causes of action in particular markets. The customers' opinions and attitudes to specific brands and products are explored in depth and from this a number of segments with shared product requirements are identified. Recent developments in the toothpaste market illustrate this approach clearly. Consumption is dominated by families with children, but they share with other groups a specific requirement or benefit: protection from tooth decay. This theme is developed in product promotion: in 'fluoride reduces decay' promotion, fairly classless groups are used to communicate the message and pricing and distribution are geared to maximise availability.

Life style

A development of this approach, but drawing on research going on in other fields, is segmentation by life style. 'Life styles are the patterns in which people live and spend their money.'[4] These patterns are determined by three behavioural components: activities, interests and opinions (AIO). Activities are observable behaviour, interest is the attention given and its importance, and opinions are the responses to various stimuli, especially questions.

Life-style analysis, by examining the patterns which emerge when these issues are explored in a population, seeks to identify groups which behave in a broadly consistent manner, have shared interests, share certain values and opinions, and are probably consistent demographically. A manual worker in a factory who actively plays soccer, is home centred, adopts conservative, traditional standards for judging products, and has two sons and a daughter is likely to respond to product, promotional and other mix stimuli in a manner broadly similar to others with this life style.

Life-style analysis is seen as particularly useful in helping the firm to reconsider its markets. Traditional structures such as 'our target audience is ABC males in NE England' can be re-examined, and even retitled 'traditionalist executives'. This may provide clues to new customers who share all the needs satisfied by the product but who are located elsewhere or are not approached for other reasons. Equally important, this perspective can provide creative clues for advertising and new product development. For example, a soccer-playing worker may respond very positively to promotion of clothes for himself and his children using soccer stars, while a traditionalist executive may provide a market for an array of new products designed to meet the needs which underlie his values.

Although these groupings can be identified it should never be assumed that the members of the groups will respond in exactly the same way to the stimuli they receive. Many internal, psychological forces intervene.

MOTIVATIONS

When an individual or group embarks upon the act of purchase, even the so-called impulse buy, he is driven by motives. These may be personal and idiosyncratic, but still exist for the person. These in turn are probably only part of a complex of forces determining and motivating actions. Some aspects of the notions described earlier—the economic or social roots of behaviour—are relevant here. Much of the study of motives has developed from the work of psychoanalysts and psychologists.

Psychoanalytic views

These views of motivation are founded on the ideas put forward by Freud that man's needs operate at various levels of consciousness. The most important of these needs are unconscious and not readily observable. Although many psychoanalysts have rejected Freud's ideas on the specific drives, most concur with the emphasis he places on the subconscious.

The study of unconscious motivation has been rich in theories of the best way to stimulate required responses among buyers. In the USA the success of a number of products has been ascribed to the extent to which they effectively capitalise on these unconscious drives. In Britain over 80 per cent of market research agencies have used or still use research techniques to probe into the unconscious.[5]

There have been a number of fruitful outcomes of this area of investigation. Unfortunately, a recurrent problem in the study of unconscious motivation has been the lack of any objective or replicable evidence. In fact, the researcher appears to affect the results appreciably.

The behavioural approach

This approach to motivation contrasts diametrically with the interpretative study of the unconscious favoured by Freud. Emphasis is placed on the observable and measurable aspects of behaviour. The individual is seen as responding to various stimuli, so a drive originating from some inner need (e.g. thirst) leads to specific responses to particular cues or stimuli.

The pattern of responses is conditioned by the effects which follow a specific response. Thus a severe headache, when associated with taking an aspirin and the response of pain relief, reinforces the belief that aspirins relieve pain. A pattern of aversion will emerge if the response is discomfort, e.g. a particular food gives stomach-ache. In this framework we see the foundations of one of the most important aspects of consumer behaviour—the notion of learning. This approach has been closely associated with the work of J.A. Howard[6] and will be discussed later in this chapter.

In the study of motivation in marketing the work of A.H. Maslow[7] occupies a particularly important place. Maslow suggests that we are motivated by individual motivating factors which interact in terms of recognisable hierarchy (Figure 6.4).

Although this approach provides some useful clues about generating ideas and organising the manager's thinking about his offerings, its predictive and diagnostic value in specific situations is very limited. At the same time Chisnall[8] has placed emphasis on the need to recognise that wants do not exist in isolation.

ATTITUDES

Any individual considering a purchase or entering a buying situation takes into it certain attitudes:

> An attitude is a mental and neural state of readiness to respond, which is organised through experience and exerts a directive and/or dynamic influence on behaviour.[9]

We all have attitudes of one kind or other. When we watch TV in the evening, our attitudes to the advertisements, and hence to the products they promote, are influenced.

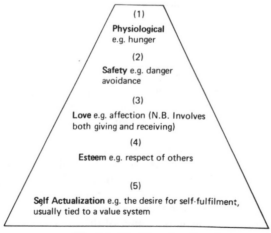

Fig. 6.4   The hierarchy of needs.

Unfortunately, beyond the knowledge that attitudes exist, very little else is actually known about them. This is particularly true of the critical relationship between attitude and behaviour. The traditional assumption in advertising has been that change in attitudes would be followed by change in behaviour:

> to result in a sale an advertisement must bring about a positive change in the attitude of the reader or viewer.
>
> Grey Advertising Inc., 1968

It is a viewpoint which contains a certain logical appeal. 'I like the image of Guinness portrayed by advertisements.' Result: favourable attitudes to Guinness, 'I value the ideas inherent in Ford's advertising.' Result: favourable attitudes to Ford. 'I recognise the merits displayed in Sony's advertising.' Result: favourable attitudes to Sony. Therefore I should drink Guinness, drive a Ford and install a Sony hi-fi. The crux of the attitude dilemma is that *I* don't. This does not mean that my favourable attitudes turn me against the brands: it merely means that the relationship is far more complex than traditionally has been assumed.

Bird and Ehrenberg,[10] in a series of important empirical studies, examined this problem and the closely related view that people's attitudes are influenced by their use of particular goods and services. They found that spontaneous awareness, intention-to-buy and favourable attitudes were all closely related to past or current usage patterns. At the very

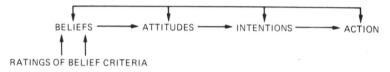

Fig. 6.5   The relationship between attitude and behaviour.

least this suggests that attitude–action relationships are two-way rather than unidirectional, as was supposed in the past.

This lack of empirical corroboration for the relationship between attitude and behaviour provided the starting-point for Martin Fishbein's study of attitudes.[11] He rejected the more complex definitions of attitudes, preferring instead 'a relatively simple unidimensional concept connected with the amount of affect or feeling for a particular object'.[12]

These attitudes are in turn determined by certain beliefs. From the attitudes are derived not specific actions but merely intentions. The link between intention to buy and actually buying therefore becomes the key point for further research (Figure 6.5).

Even in this newer formulation it appears that the predictive power is fairly limited. Engel, Blackwell and Kollat[13] suggest that this is because 'we still have not taken into account the full range of situational influences'.

IMAGES OF REALITY

In this examination of the consumer it has become clear that the marketing man faces a continuing conflict between two goals. On the one hand he needs a greater understanding of the buyer in order to design suitable offerings, and on the other hand this understanding must be matched with profitable action. It is always a problem in research that the search for averages and consistencies to guide behaviour is tempered by the fact that these may merely cloud judgement (Figure 6.6).

Segmentation studies illustrate one solution to the problem. They recognise that 'The world is made up of minority markets' (Winston Fletcher, *Adweek*, 22 March, 1974).

The firm can explore its own information to arrive at target segments. Outside sources

Fig. 6.6   The dangers of averages blurring real differences.

such as BMRB's *Target Group Index* (an annual study of 25 000 self-completed questionnaires) can also be employed. Ultimately, however, segmentation gives only limited insight into the behavioural processes. More recently, there has been a growing interest in the modelling of behaviour to obtain some further insight into the processes of consumer behaviour.

MODELS OF BUYER BEHAVIOUR

J.A. Howard[14] has long believed in the potential contribution that models of behaviour can make to our understanding of the processes involved. In his book he introduces the notion that behaviour could be thought of in terms of a learning process. He suggests that when people are purchasing an item they rely heavily on experience. If the item has been bought before and was satisfactory, the chances that it will be bought again (repeat buying) are increased (higher probability), as Figure 6.7 demonstrates.

The curve can be divided into three distinct phases. Initially a buyer's experience is very limited, so cannot draw on it to help him choose brands or products. Therefore he goes to various sources of information for help. At this stage he is involved in extensive problem-solving (Figure 6.8). This involves the most conscious and rigorous active evaluation of alternatives. Theoretically, it is closest to the idea of economic man. In a market such as the hi-fi market, the individual may be buying his first stereo system. He

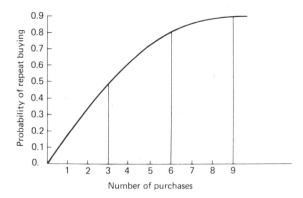

Fig. 6.7 The learning curve. Adapted from J. A. Howard, *Marketing Management*. Illinois: R. D. Irwin, 1963.

therefore asks friends for information and reads *Popular Hi-Fi*. He visits shops such as Dixons to listen to different makes. He may already have some biases or preconceptions such as 'big speakers give the best response'. He may even defer his decision because events led him to spend money elsewhere. All these factors affect the marketing of both the retailers and the manufacturers.

A major change occurs as the buyer's experience builds up. He relies increasingly on his own knowledge and experience of purchasing. Information may be sought, but usually only when some outside event, for example a new product or a bad purchase experience, triggers it. What he is now doing is termed limited problem-solving (Figure 6.9), when only a few alternatives are considered. Under certain circumstances, especially when buying low-cost, frequently bought items, buying becomes totally routine. This is known as automatic response behaviour (Figure 6.10).

Like all valuable contributions to marketing knowledge, this approach provided the starting point to investigation, not a conclusive statement.

It has prompted research into the following areas to provide guidance for the marketing man:

1. The influence of the outside variables which directly or indirectly influence purchasing: the housewife's decisions are affected by family pressures; the individual may be buying for himself but is conscious of the effect of his purchase on friends or colleagues.
2. The ways in which people process the information they receive from a battery of sources: a statement on a consumer affairs programme might conflict with information from advertisements.
3. The process of motivation itself.
4. Under certain circumstances the search will be active and rigorous: what prompts this, how can the firm capitalise on it, and what type of information is sought?

Ultimately, firms seek methods of measuring these forces and weighting actions by them (usually at a cost) against returns.

Almost inevitably, as information and knowledge have increased, the complete model has become more complex and the relationship more tortuous.[15] Partly to overcome this problem, as well as to provide a model to give a clearer insight into such areas as information processing, Kotler and Engel, Blackwell and Kollat introduced models based on stages in the buying process (Figure 6.11). Although these stages provide a useful vehicle for analysing buyers and their behaviour, particularly exploring the objectives of marketing mix strategies, the full specification of the relationship requires more research.

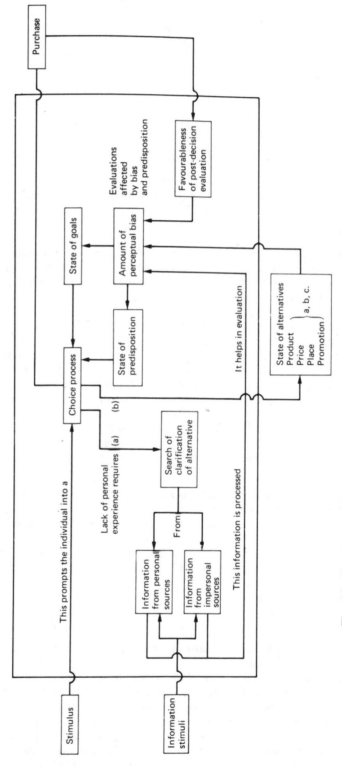

Fig. 6.8 Extensive problem-solving. Adapted from J. A. Howard, *Marketing Management*. Illinois: R. D. Irwin, 1963.

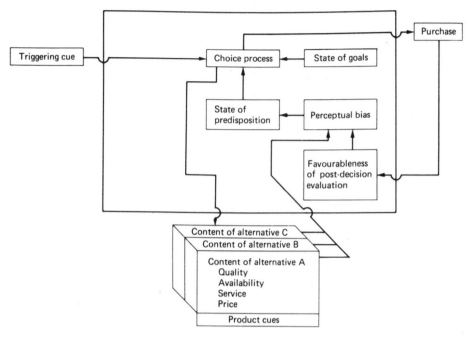

Fig. 6.9 Limited problem-solving. Reproduced with permission. Howard, J. A., *Marketing Management*. Illinois: R. D. Irwin, 1963.

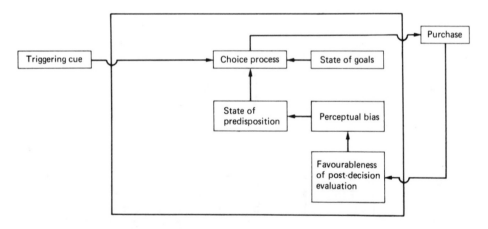

Fig. 6.10 Automatic response behaviour. Reproduced with permission. Howard, J. A., *Marketing Management*. Illinois: R. D. Irwin, 1963.

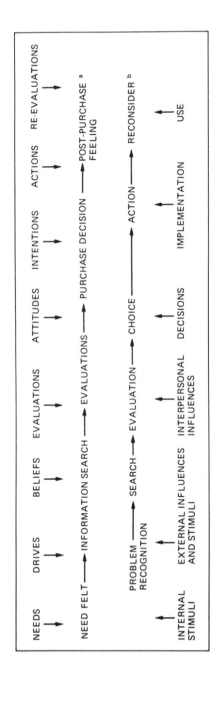

Fig. 6.11 Different visions of the stages in the buying process.
[a] Kotler, P., *Marketing Management.* Englewood Cliffs: Prentice-Hall, 1976.
[b] Engel, J.F., Blackwell, R.D. and Kollat, D.T., *Consumer Behaviour*, 3rd edition. Hinsdale, Illinois: Dryden Press, 1978.

DIFFUSION AND ADOPTION OF A NEW PRODUCT

One area in which an understanding of the processes described above is critical is in the study of innovation and new product development. In his research into this area Rogers[16] suggested that a pattern similar to that described above occurred in the adoption of new products: need exists (conscious or unconscious) ⟶ awareness (as potential means of satisfying this need emerges) ⟶ interest (thus created leads to information search) ⟶ evaluation (of information, tempered by beliefs) ⟶ trials (probably preceded by 'intention to buy') ⟶ adoption (or rejection) occurs.

Although this is what occurs on an individual basis, the producer's main interest is in aggregate behaviour. The entire target population is unlikely to respond immediately, even if awareness were instant (Figure 6.12).

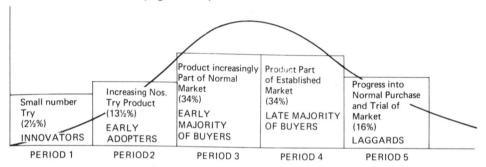

Fig. 6.12 Relative time of adoption of innovation. Adapted from E.M. Rogers, *The Diffusion of Innovations*. New York: Macmillan, 1962.

Rogers' model seems to make sense, but although he introduces a breakdown of the population he studied in terms of unconsciousness, early adoption etc., there is little support for this as a universal formulation. Equally important, there is no evidence to suggest that the groups are consistent across product fields. For example, the well-educated, self-confident farmer may innovate in terms of new machinery or hybrid crops, but be a laggard in terms of music. His innovativeness may be related far more to his peer group than to the product category; e.g. in fashion goods an innovative farmer may be a member of the late majority of the total population.

LOYALTY TO STORE AND BRAND

The study of customer loyalty demonstrates the importance of research into behaviour. Brand loyalty is the tendency of some consumers to purchase a brand consistently. In a fast-moving consumer market it was seen as manifesting itself in such patterns as those shown in Table 6.1

Table 6.1 *Buying profile of detergent*

Weeks	1	2	3	4	5	6	7	8	9	10
Mrs Osborne	A	A	A	O	A	A	O	B	A	A
Mrs Turner	B	A	B	B	B	A	A	O	O	B
Mrs Griffiths	A	B	D	D	D	D	O	O	B	A
Mr Marrion	–	–	A	–	–	–	A	–	–	A

(A = Ariel, B = Bold, D = Daz, O = Others.)

Some customers, it was believed, show undivided loyalty; others have either unstable or no loyalty. The phenomenon was seen as so important that Cunningham[17] commented:

Brand loyalty is a substantial asset . . . in promotional planning. They (firms) should consider brand loyalty carefully.

However, some authors, notably Ehrenberg, question the value of aspects of the basic concept, preferring instead the notion of patterns of repeat purchasing. It appears that the levels of loyalty are virtually a constant for all brands, suggesting that loyalty-building advertising policies have not changed the levels of loyalty. In Table 6.1 Mr Marrion, the most 'loyal' customer, was a light user, a pattern consisent with research in the field.[18]

CONCLUSION

Over the last twenty years the study of consumer behaviour has emerged as one of the central themes of modern marketing, but in a short chapter such as this only a few of the central themes could be explored. Important contributions such as those of Nicosia,[19] Sheth[20] and Kuehn[21] have been excluded largely on the grounds of space.

A potentially fruitful start has been made in the study of consumer behaviour, and concepts such as segmentation, learning and motivation are already playing an important part in policy making. In the future the marketing manager will need to be as familiar with these as he is with the notions of media selection, sales force territorial allocation etc.

One issue that should be borne in mind is that the construction of models and theories is of extremely limited value if a large-scale and firmly empirical stance is not adopted to their evaluation and modification.

Notes

1. Kotler, P., *Marketing Management*. Englewood Cliffs: Prentice-Hall, 1979.
2. Adapted from Kotler, P., *Marketing Management: Analysis, Planning and Control*. Illinois: Prentice-Hall, 1976.
3. Yankelovich, D., 'Market Segmentation'. In *Consumer Behaviour* (Ed.) Ehrenberg, A.S.C. & Pyatt, F. G., Penguin, 1971.
4. Engel, J.F., Blackwell, R.D. & Kollat, D.T., *Consumer Behaviour*, 3rd edition. Hinsdale, Illinois: Dryden Press, 1978.
5. Collins, L. & Montgomery, C., 'Whatever Happened to Motivational Research: End of the Messianic Hope', *Journal of the Market Research Society*, Volume 2, 1969.
6. Howard, J.A., *Marketing Management*. Illinois: R.D. Irwin, 1963.
7. Maslow, A.H., *Motivation and Personality*. New York: Harper and Row, 1954.
8. Chisnall, P.M., *Marketing: A Behavioural Analysis*. London: McGraw-Hill, 1975.
9. Allport, G.W., *Handbook for Social Psychology*. Massachusetts: Clark University Press, 1975.
10. Bird, M., Channon, C. & Ehrenberg, A.S.C., 'Brand Image and Brand Usage', *Journal of the Market Research Society*, Volume 7, 1970.
11. Fishbein, M., 'The Relationship between Beliefs, Attitudes and Behaviour'. In *Cognitive Consistency* (Ed.) Feldman, S. New York: Academic Press, 1966.
12. Chisnall, P.M., *Marketing: A Behavioural Analysis*. London: McGraw-Hill, 1975.
13. Engel, J.F., Blackwell, R.D. & Kollat, D.T., *Consumer Behaviour*, 3rd edition. Hinsdale, Illinois: Dryden Press, 1978.
14. This section draws heavily on Howard, J.A., *Marketing Management*. Illinois: R.D. Irwin, 1963.
15. Kotler, P., *Marketing Management*. Illinois: Prentice-Hall, 1976.
16. Rogers, E.M., *The Diffusion of Innovations*. New York: Macmillan, 1962.
17. Cunningham, R.M., 'Brand Loyalty: What, Where, How Much?', *Harvard Business Review*, Jan.–Feb., 1956.
18. Cannon, T., Ehrenberg, A.S.C. & Goodhardt, G.J., 'Regularities in Sole Buying', *British Journal of Marketing*, 1970.
19. Nicosia, F.M., *Consumer Decision Process*. Englewood Cliffs: Prentice-Hall, 1966.
20. Sheth, J.N., 'A Review of Buyer Behaviour', *Management Science*, August, 1967.
21. Kuehn, A.A., 'Consumer Brand Choice as a Learning Process', *Journal of Advertising Research*, December, 1962.

Further reading

Chisnall, P.M., *Marketing: A Behavioural Analysis*. London: McGraw-Hill, 1975. A lucid drawing-together of the various strands which make up our current knowledge, providing an insight into a consumer-behaviour perspective on marketing. Note particularly Chapters 1 and 8.

Ehrenberg, A.S.C., *Repeat Buying: Theory and Applications*. Amsterdam: North Holland, 1970. Brings together the results of perhaps the most sustained empirical examination of this complex phenomenon. Note particularly Chapters 1 and 2.

Engel, J.F., Blackwell, R.D. & Kollat, D.T., *Consumer Behaviour*, 3rd edition. Hinsdale, Illinois: Dryden Press, 1978. This balanced and comprehensive work provides an excellent overview of the current state of knowledge. Note particularly Chapters 2 and 19.

CASE STUDY 5: THE BUYING PROCESS IN THE TOILET SOAP MARKET

Using the information obtained from the research project in Chapter 5, highlight salient aspects of the buying process for key subgroups in the toilet soap market.

7
Marketing Analysis

In December 1984 a series of announcements by Philips of Eindhoven suggested that one of the longest-running battles 'against the market' of recent years was coming to an end. The struggle by Philips to introduce 'Laser Vision' as an alternative to video recorders for consumer markets in Britain and North America appeared to be coming to an end. It would be difficult to estimate the costs of this project, but they are likely to be many millions of guilders, pounds and dollars. This was not a unique event. The same month saw Dysan Corporation (the US floppy disc manufacturer) give up its attempts to introduce a new standard 3¼-inch disc, British American Tobacco sell off their loss-making 'International Stores' Group, and Hewlett-Packard announce further re-organisations of their consumer products division in an attempt to achieve their targets for personal computer sales. What makes sophisticated companies with technically excellent products misjudge the temper of the market and lose vast sums of money? This is a question which observers have posed ever since the launching of Ford's Edsel, Du Pont's Corfam, and Imperial Tobacco's NSM (New Smoking Material). The evidence suggests that the clearest explanation for these and the myriad earlier, and future, similar products lies in the inadequate attention firms give to the analysis of their markets.[1]

The weakness is not confined to the management of new products and services. Wills saw the sales of 'Woodbines' collapse when novel packaging was introduced, to modernise the image of the brand. Unfortunately for the firm, existing customers preferred the old image and new customers did not want to smoke 'Woodbines' in any guise. The decision by British Leyland to cut back on their dealer network gave foreign manufacturers their opportunity to build their distribution system. Tesco almost left it too late to replace their large numbers of small (relatively inefficient) stores with smaller numbers of larger outlets. This almost led them to follow the Co-Operatives into decline and losses. There is repeated evidence the firms fail to invest the time and effort into systematic analysis of the market that its importance demands.

The growing interest in planning and strategy has highlighted the critical role of marketing analysis as the foundation stone on which future policies must be built.[2]

ANALYSING THE MARKET

Effectiveness in this area is built on the implementation of a series of relatively simple steps in a rigorous and systematic way. The approaches that can be used vary in complexity, but virtually all are founded on:

1. Asking basic questions, especially the *who, what, where, when, how* and *why* of the markets the firm is in or seeks to enter.

2. Challenging assumptions, especially those which fit neatly into the way the firm wishes the market to be operated.
3. Never taking *anything* for granted.

On these fundamentals, most techniques for marketing analysis can be built. The procedure can be seen in terms of two parallel processes.

Steps in the process	*Exploring the issues*
1. Define the market.	Measure its scale, character and key features.
2. Diagnose the purchasing process.	Describe the needs, goals and benefits sought by customers in their terms.
3. Define the target groups and segments.	Explore the levels of satisfaction, potential, saturation and structure of the market.
4. Describe the groups and segments.	Detail the salient features objectively with maximum accuracy.
5. Analyse competitive positions.	Conduct brand and market share analysis and distribution studies, as well as likely competitor action.

This process of market analysis should go alongside the regular internal audits of *P*otential *A*nd *N*eeds, *I*nvestments and *C*apabilities (PANIC).

Defining the market

This is based on building an up-to-date picture of the parameters of the market; its size, composition, consumption patterns and internal structure. This needs to be done regularly, as changes can occur rapidly with little apparent warning. The basic data can be built from consumption and usage statistics. The current and previous buyers can be measured using either company statistics or data gathered by public or private agencies. Wider issues can be brought into this analysis, such as the impact of unemployment on demand. It is normally necessary to extend this analysis to look at trends in development as well as the current position.

The success of Krona margarine was based on wedding this type of analysis to a distinctive offering. Van den Bergs, the producers, highlighted a number of key features in the market:*

1. It is huge, worth £600 million at RSP in 1979.
2. It is generally static.
3. It has experienced major shifts in demand over previous years, a large post-war move to butter, followed by a trend to margarine as quality improved and customers became interested in diet and health-related products.
4. There is increasing price sensitivity.
5. There has been a history among consumers of seeking 'a butter substitute'.

The product was targeted on a key sector of this market—a group who were both

---

*This section is based on 'How Advertising Helped Make Krona Brand Leader', in S. Broadbent, *Twenty Advertising Case Histories*.[2]

significant in buying potential and likely to be responsive to the particular characteristics of this product:

> Housewives currently spreading salted butter, who are being forced to trade down because of the increasing price of butter, but who do not wish to sacrifice the taste and texture of butter.[2]

A media campaign and budget were established to achieve awareness, trial and repeat purchase among this group. Following its launch in October 1978 it achieved 'brand leadership' with a market share of 18 per cent of the margarine market by August 1979, with 43 per cent trial and 80 per cent prompted awareness.

The ability to define the market as tightly and accurately as possible is the measure of a marketing staff which is on top of the job. Many companies have the practice of maintaining a 'marketing fact book' for each product and brand area in which they have an interest. In industrial markets, problems can be caused by the difficulties faced when attempting to define markets in categories such as components or processed products. This places greater pressure on the marketing executive to produce specific measures for his area of activity.

Diagnosing the purchasing process

In chapter 6, considerable attention was paid to issues of buyer and consumer behaviour. Understanding the purchasing process is vital to any manager seeking to develop an effective marketing strategy. The examination of buyer characteristics such as demographics, location, lifestyle (in consumer markets) and professionalism, training, discretion and reporting systems (in industrial, commercial and government markets) is only part of the picture. It is important to be able to build up models of the buying process to explore the benefits sought, the stages in decision-making through which the buyer passes in order to understand the information sought, and the best means of influencing actions.

Parkinson's research[3] on the adoption of new manufacturing systems indicated the different roles adopted by customers in two situations. Industrial buyers in West Germany expected to play a more 'proactive' role in the development of products for their own use than their British counterparts. They were willing to invest considerable time and effort in supporting the development process and expected to be sold total 'systems' rather than individual items.

In consumer and commercial markets, the same pattern of diversity in purchase behaviour can be seen. This highlights the importance of understanding the buyer's approach to the decision, ability and willingness to buy, as well as the influences which bear upon decisions in this area.

Defining the target groups and segments

The greater the firm's awareness of a market, the more management will become conscious of the different groups which make it up. This process of breaking up large, heterogeneous groups into more homogeneous target audiences is central to the marketing process.

The notion of differentiation has grown in importance along with marketing. It is based on the proposition that the firm's competitive position is strengthened and its appeal to customers is greatest if based on a combination of meeting generic needs *and* supplying special benefits to customers or groups of buyers. This usually calls for greater specificity in offering (avoiding the attempt to be all things to all men). Often it can lead to reduced marketing costs and increased productivity in expenditure. Effectiveness in this area turns on:

1. The ability to define the market.
2. The skill to provide offerings which the customer group sees as providing sufficient added benefit to buy.

Analysis of these segments should be linked with some appreciation of the market potential provided by these groupings. The potential will vary considerably over time and between sectors, and can be influenced to some degree by the action of firms and their customers.

The growth of the 'pot snacks' market in the UK illustrated this in the late 1970s. The sector grew from nothing to over £20 million (RSP 1980) within three years. A number of successful new products were launched during the early part of the period. However, the market soon began to show clear signs of saturation as rates of trial of new brands declined, advertising expenditures rose and retail discounting increased.

The purchase patterns on which this type of analysis is based can change considerably over time as economic and other circumstances change. The early stages of recession frequently see the phenomenon of 'deferred purchases', as certain customer groups put off their buying of certain items until they feel more economically secure. The furniture market has been especially prone to this, as householders re-schedule purchasing of major items. The pattern is not uniform across all categories. The mid- and late 1970s saw a much more dramatic drop in purchases at the lower price end of the market than among premium price lines.

Describing the target groups

The discussion in Chapter 1 of the nature of marketing placed considerable emphasis on its *action*, its *operational* role. This is critical to successful targeting and segmentation. Once the different groups within a market have been defined, the optimal means of reaching them should be detailed. A sector that cannot be accessed cannot be a meaningful target market. In this context the notion of 'access' refers to the firm's ability to reach a sector in a way which delivers the benefits sought by the customer.

Paliwoda's analysis[4] of the French packaging industry indicated the scope for segmentation. Out of it, specific strategies for reaching these groups can be described.

> The French carton market is highly fragmented, served by some 550 small and medium-sized companies. Whilst it must be acknowledged that the economic crises of the 1970s led to many companies going out of business there is still substantial over-capacity in the carton industry and competition is intense. With margins being low over the last decade many companies have been unwilling to invest and there is thus great inequality in the technological sophistication levels of the companies. It is to be noted that whilst printing methods may remain fairly stable, there is much innovation in machinery, and as machines modernise there are greater demands on the mechanical properties of the cartons, to obtain higher performance and greater productivity.

> The French carton may be divided into three broad sectors; 50 per cent of carton producing companies serve the food industries, 40 per cent serve the pharmaceutical industry and only 10 per cent serve diverse industries of which the perfumes and cosmetics industry is one.

Within these sectors, three sub-groups can be identified: 'commodity producers' (large volume/low margins); 'systems producers' (offering integrated ranges of multi-packs), and 'high quality packaging suppliers'. A technique such as gridding can be used to define specific segments for which suppliers of machinery, supplies and services can develop unique and distinctive marketing mixes.

Gridding the French Packaging Market

Type of output

		Commodity	System	High added value
	Food			
Market	Pharmaceuticals			
	Other			

A paper company might decide to target their product on system producers supplying the pharmaceutical industry. They would be in a position to specify very clearly the range and qualities of product acceptable (product). They could tailor their advertising and exhibition policy to reach this group with messages that would appeal to them (promotion). At the same time, the pricing policies could reflect their detailed knowledge of acceptable levels and price structures (price). The ability to identify them and analyse their demand patterns would make distribution and servicing more effective (place).

Analysing competitive positions

The identification of a market and the presentation of distinctive offerings to the target group are only the first stages of effectively developing a market. Having taken the ball and run with it, the firm must hold on to it. This involves competitor analysis. Frequently firms develop approaches to their markets which assume that they and their customers exist in a vacuum. This gives the competition the chance to develop approaches which learn from their mistakes and exploit weaknesses. The most obvious form of this is in the area of new product development where certain firms deliberately adopt the policy of 'poisoned apple marketing'. This involves never being the first into a market. The competition is allowed to take the first bite and take the biggest risk. There are clear risks to this approach, especially where lead times are long or the innovator has recognised the risks and done all in its power to avoid them.

A regular feature of the marketing analysis should be the review of the competition. This should range very widely to include external threats to the firm as well as immediate rivals.

NEW INFORMATION TECHNOLOGIES

New developments in information technology are having a wide-ranging influence on marketing. They are making data available more quickly, in larger volumes and in relatively easily manipulated forms. McFarland[5] suggests that this will change the nature of business 'fundamentally'. Piercy[6] argues that the impact will be so great that the most basic marketing concept will need to be revised:

'Information processing should be regarded as the fifth 'p' in the marketing mix.'

The availability of the new technologies should not be confused with their use. Many managers are reluctant to employ the technology that is available today. They often lack the skill to use it effectively. Others believe that experience and intuition can be substitutes for new technology-based data. Lyons[7] has highlighted the challenges that the combination of these traditional attitudes and the potential of the new technologies will

"Ford have done well with the Fiesta's roadholding and handling too. It almost matches the grip of the Polo..."

"We expected the Fiesta to leave the Polo standing when it came to performance. Not so..."

"The Fiesta's engine emerges as a satisfactory one, rather than an outstanding one like the Polo's..."

"...the Fiesta does not body roll much at all. It just isn't as beautifully crisp as the Polo, and it won't go around corners quite so stunningly quickly..."

"...on the open road when the Polo accelerates hard, the Fiesta has to summon every last ounce of horsepower to make a serious impression..."

"...the Fiesta's engine is fairly quiet, though nowhere near as smooth as the Polo's..."

"Ford's careful body engineering shows through when the weights are compared; the 1510lb Polo is brilliant in this respect, and at 1543lb for the basic model, the Fiesta comes respectably close."

MEL NICHOLS, *car* MAGAZINE, AUGUST 1976.

Making a car that looks like a Volkswagen is not the same as making a Volkswagen.

Polo. Ⓥ

Shown here: Polo N £1999, Fiesta L £2079. Prices include car tax and VAT. Delivery and number plates extra. Seat belts extra on Polo.

Please send me a 20 page colour brochure on the Polo plus a facts analysis on the Polo, Fiesta and other competitors.

Name_____

Address_____

Volkswagen (GB) Ltd , Pembroke House, Campsbourne Road, London N8 7PT.

Fig. 7.1 Knocking copy.

pose to marketing education. The widespread use of electronic spreadsheets will give managers the scope to ask the type of 'what if' questions that were impossible to handle manually.

EXPERIENCE, SHARES AND COMPETITION

Examination of competition and competitiveness in business is intimately associated with issues of returns to relative effort, productivity and profits. These topics provided the focus for a programme of research conducted in the USA to examine the 'Profit Impact of Marketing Strategies'. This work is more usually referred to in terms of its initials, PIMS.[7] More specifically, the study sought to establish the marketing factors which had the greatest impact on return on investment (profits). The initial study was based on 50 companies with 600 business units. This has been expanded to over 240 firms with 1800 business units. A number of specific conclusions were drawn from the research, especially the close relationship between market share and profitability.

Table 7.1   *The relationship between market share and profit*

Market share	Profitability (return on investment)
Under 7%	9.6%
7–14%	12.0%
14–22%	13.5%
22–36%	17.9%
Over 36%	30.2%

Source: Buzzell et al.[8]

These results appeared to demonstrate a strong and clear link between increased market shares and increased profits. The concept was taken further with the notion that this increased performance was a function of an experience or learning curve, i.e. the more the firm learnt about its market the better it would perform in both sales and profits. This has been spelt out more fully as:[9]

1. A high market share requires high output.
2. Production costs go down as output increases.
3. Reducing production costs plus stable prices equals higher unit margins.
4. Higher unit margins equal greater return on investment (ROI).

Assuming this relationship holds true, the optimal strategy for most firms would be to seek out policies to increase market shares.

However, the research indicated a number of significant additional factors and limitations on these findings, notably:

1. The strong relationship between product quality and ROI.
2. The poor return on heavy marketing expenditure where product quality is low.

More recent research has highlighted weaknesses in the PIMS work, especially in terms of the weakness of the claims for causal links between the variables.[10] Kotler[11] has raised questions concerning the strength of the relationships for very high share business.

Hammermesh[12] tackled the converse of this problem which concerned the strategies open to firms either operating in 'low market share' businesses, i.e. where the market was highly fragmented, or low share brands. He highlighted the importance of:

1. Segmentation and targeting of specialist sectors.
2. Seeking improved returns through the more efficient use of R & D.
3. Exploiting relative smallness through short lines of communication, decisiveness and creativity.

In sum, he appears to be reverting to the traditional marketing strategy: 'If you have problems competing with your rival in his market, on his terms, redefine the market and fight on ground of your choosing'.

Key issues

This chapter highlighted:

1. The role of marketing analyses as the foundation stone on which marketing policy is built.
2. The need to bring together objectivity, systematic study and appropriate techniques in marketing analysis.
3. The links between profitability and market share.

However, this process is dependent on the existence of an effective marketing information system and reliable marketing research.

Notes

1. Hopkins, D.S., 'New Product Winners and Losers', Report Number 773. New York, The Conference Board, 1980.
2. Broadbent, S. (ed.), *Twenty Advertising Case Histories*. London: Holt, Rinehart and Winston, 1984.
3. Parkinson, S., 'The Role of the Buyer in Successful New Product Development', *R & D Management*, 12, No. 3, July 1982.
4. Paliwolda, S. & Thompson, P., 'Industrial Product Classification and Market Behaviour', Manchester, *Proceedings Research Developments in International Marketing*, 1984.
5. McFarland, 'Information Technology Changes the Way You Compete', HBR. May–June 1984.
6. Piercy, N., 'Information Processing: The Newest Mix Element', Marketing Education Group Annual Conference, Cranfield, 1985.
7. Lyons, H. & Thakur, S., 'New Information Technologies; The Educational Implications for Marketing Management', 2nd World Marketing Congress, Stirling, 1985.
8. Buzzell, R.D., Gale, B.T. & Sultan, R.G.M., 'Market Share—The Key to Profitability', *Harvard Business Review*, January–February, 1975.
9. Runyon, K.E., *The Practice of Marketing*. Columbus, Ohio: C.E. Merrill, 1982.
10. Anderson, C.R. & Paine, F.T., 'PIMS:A Re-examination', *Planning Review*, January 1978.
11. Kotler, P. & Bloom, P.N., 'Strategies For High Market Share Companies', *Harvard Business Review*, November–December 1975.
12. Hammermesh, R.G., Anderson, M.J. & Harris, J.E., 'Strategies for Low Market Share Businesses', *Harvard Business Review*, May–June 1978.

Further reading

Ackoff, R.L., *Creating the Corporate Future*. New York: Wiley, 1981.
Drucker, P.F., *Managing in Turbulent Times*. London: Heinemann, 1980.
Strategic Planning Institute, *The PIMS Programme: The Strategic Planning Institute Brochure*. Cambridge, Massachusetts, 1980.

Glossary

Benefit. The perceived advantage or satisfaction sought by a customer or potential buyer.

Differentiation. The process of establishing a distinction between one offering and another.

Lifestyle. Usually employed in terms of 'lifestyle analysis', the programme of research designed to explore the differences in behaviour which emerge from the different ways of living and different attitudes of groups who behave in similar ways.

Market share. The percentage of a market or sector held by a specific brand or company.

Return on investment (ROI). The amount earned in proportion to the capital invested.

Segmentation. The subdivision of a larger, more diverse market into smaller more homogeneous parts.

CASE STUDY 6: DETTOL*

Introduction

In this case history we have set out to demonstrate in two distinct ways that Dettol's advertising works and is effective.

Firstly we show that, by virtue of a change in creative strategy that was implemented at the beginning of 1978, consumer attitudes to Dettol have been modified in the directions intended. The research also shows that the use and purchase of Dettol have increased in this period.

Secondly, an econometric analysis of factors affecting Dettol's sales during the period 1974-78 is used to demonstrate that the sales response to the advertising expenditures put behind Dettol generated profitable increases in sales.

Other factors influencing Dettol's sales are also identified and it is clear that two 'non-marketing' variables—seasonal factors and consumer's purchasing power (disposable income)—have a major effect.

We conclude however that it is the long term effects of Dettol advertising that lead consumers to purchase Dettol when these factors are favourable.

In consequence the dramatic decline in Dettol sales that occurred in 1975–77 was converted into an equally dramatic improvement in 1978 and maintained in 1979 (Table 7.2).

Table 7.2   *Dettol ex-factory sales index*

1973	100
1974	100
1975	85
1976	87
1977	83
1978	100
1979	100

Many brands enjoyed increased sales as a result of rising consumer prosperity in 1978, but not to the extent of these figures, which underline the importance of maintaining a brand franchise by sustained and effective advertising support.

Background

Dettol has been marketed in the United Kingdom since 1933.

It is promoted as both an antiseptic and a disinfectant and is used in a wide variety of ways ranging from personal antisepsis of cuts and grazes, through to disinfection of surfaces in the kitchen and bathroom and, in some instances, as a more general disinfectant down lavatory bowls, waste pipes and drains. It is sold in three sizes, 100, 250 and 500 ml.

Dettol is not only a mature brand but an extremely well established one. There is universal awareness of it by housewives; 70 per cent of housewives claim to use it nowadays—a figure which has not changed over the past eight years—and it has virtually 100 per cent distribution in chemists and grocers.

Although there are many alternative antiseptics and disinfectants on the market, including many low priced retailer own brands, there is only one other product that is promoted as a direct alternative to Dettol in its range of uses, Savlon Liquid. For many

*This case study has been reproduced from *Advertising Works*, papers from the Institute of Practitioners in Advertising's 'Advertising Effectiveness Awards, 1980', edited by Simon Broadbent and published by Holt, Rinehart and Winston, 1981.

years Savlon had been available only through chemist shops, but since the beginning of 1979 has been heavily advertised and its distribution widened into grocery outlets also.

Advertising support for Dettol has been provided consistently over the last 20 years and is considered to have been a major factor in the brand's development to the position it now occupies (as described above). The case history described in the following pages, however, relates to the period 1974–1979 and describes, in particular, the changes to the advertising campaign that were implemented in 1978.

The 1977 scenario

Sales of Dettol had reached a peak in 1973–74. However, a combination of factors—rapid inflation and declining consumer purchasing power, reduced advertising investment, some production problems—had led to a sharp decline in sales in 1975, 1976 and 1977 (see Table 7.2).

Additionally, a situation had been developing which was of concern to the future promotion of Dettol. A significant personal use of Dettol was in bathing which involved claims which could not be proved or disproved. Therefore, the ITCA would not permit the claims for this area of usage to be advertised.

So the problem that Reckitt & Colman and the agency faced in 1977 can be concisely expressed as: 'How can we restore sales volumes to the 1973–74 levels when a major usage area of Dettol is no longer open to direct advertising, and inflationary pressures are affecting sales volumes?'

Development of the 1978 strategy

Where is increased volume going to be obtained?

Research had shown that amongst Dettol users its use as an antiseptic was virtually universal; fewer housewives used it in its disinfectant role. Further research using diary panel techniques showed that there were certain household cleaning functions where Dettol was more widely used than others, e.g. in wiping lavatory seats, cleaning up after pets, but even in these instances Dettol's share of products used was relatively low.

We nevertheless argued that, to increase Dettol volume sales to any marked extent:

1. We could not expect to obtain additional users—household penetration was extremely high (70 per cent).
2. And that increased volume was more likely to occur from the advertising of *disinfectant* uses of the product.

But this conclusion presented its own problems.

1. The earlier success of Dettol had been built on the personal/antiseptic uses of the product: heavy promotion of disinfectant uses could well destroy the extremely favourable attitudes housewives had with regard to its personal benefits.
2. Dettol's price was considered to be a problem in the market place (dictated by the high cost of ingredients). If Dettol is looked upon primarily as a disinfectant then the price differential with its main alternatives becomes particularly large—in some instances two or three times the price of own label disinfectants.

How should we approach the problem of price?

An econometric analysis (described in full later) had shown that consumers appeared to be relatively insensitive to changes in Dettol's *price*, but sales were found to be affected by the decline in *disposable income*. This apparent anomaly can be explained by the fact that the housewife's need for Dettol has a lower priority than essential items such as food. In other words, for Dettol to be included in a housewife's grocery purchases, she must have sufficient money left after buying the essential items; and relatively small variations in the price of Dettol do not therefore affect her decision to buy. As a result the decision was taken to allow the price to rise generally in line with inflation and to confine any price cutting to short term, tactical retail promotions.

A new creative strategy based on disinfectant usage

In developing a creative strategy for Dettol based on disinfectant usage it was essential to be aware of consumer perceptions of Dettol and to provide advertising consonant with them. Research had shown that advertising centred on the *scientific* basis for Dettol's performance in killing bacteria was ineffective in changing consumer attitudes and behaviour. The high regard which consumers have for Dettol is based on confidence and trust derived from its history, its name, its smell and clouding in water. As one interviewee commented: 'You can't see germs being killed. I have to use Dettol to be sure.'

New advertising for Dettol had to reflect such attitudes.

1978 advertising

At the beginning of 1978 we introduced new TV and press advertising for Dettol which took account of the thinking outlined in the previous section.

TV: Two TV commercials, entitled 'Beginning' and 'Discovery'. These two commercials addressed themselves to the need for environmental protection in the home in the context of a newborn baby and a toddler, Dettol providing protection and confidence. In parallel a TV commercial for Dettol Cream—an antiseptic cream—was also transmitted, assisting in the reinforcement of Dettol's traditional first aid usage.

Press: Full colour page advertisements were produced in both 1978 and 1979 pinpointing specific disinfectant usage areas for Dettol. The subjects chosen were ones in which Dettol already had relatively high usage, although still low in absolute terms, viz: the lavatory seat, kitchen waste bins, cleaning where pets have been, e.g. the kitchen floor.

Media: In each of 1978 and 1979, TV advertising amounted to approximately 20 weeks at an average of 50 to 60 TVR per week in all ITV regions. The press advertisements appeared in women's weekly and monthly magazines providing 70 per cent cover and 7.0 OTS.

To summarise the advertising changes:

Content. A switch from advertising which had been primarily concerned with the antiseptic uses of Dettol to its environmental/disinfectant role.

Weight. Although the budget was maintained in cash terms in 1978, due to media cost inflation the effective weight of advertising was reduced by about 20 per cent compared to 1977.

Results and evaluation

1.   Volume sales of Dettol increased substantially in 1978, and this achievement was maintained in 1979.

2. Consumer research clearly indicates the improvements in consumer attitudes to Dettol that occurred during the period of the 1978–79 advertising campaign as well as changes in consumer usage of Dettol.
3. An econometric analysis of the factors affecting Dettol sales volume conducted over the period 1974–78 shows the profitability of the advertising investment throughout that period and suggests also that the long term investment in advertising is a major factor in determining consumer purchasing of Dettol.

It should be noted that the periods covered by the econometric analysis and the consumer research are not exactly coincident. The reason for this is simply that the two pieces of research were not planned as a co-ordinated programme.

Consumer research

Two disinfectant and antiseptic usage and attitude studies have been carried out amongst consumers: the first in January 1978, the second in January 1980. These two surveys reflect the extent to which the advertising for Dettol has been successful, both in increasing its usage and changing perceptions of the brand.

The broad objectives of these studies were to monitor trends in the usage and image of disinfectants and antiseptics in terms of the following:

1. Brand awareness.
2. Brand penetration.
3. User profiles.
4. Usage patterns for the major brands.
5. The image of the major brands.
6. Detailed purchasing habits.
7. Usage and purchase patterns of antiseptic creams.
8. Advertising recall.

The research method. For each of the studies, 1200 housewives were interviewed at 120 sampling points throughout Great Britain by Public Attitude Surveys Ltd. They were located by means of Random Location Sampling. In each case the sample was restricted to housewives aged 15 to 64.

A non-interlocking, two-way quota was set on working status (working full time/others) and whether they had children.

Weighting factors were applied to ensure that the sample was representative of the population.

The findings. In the two year period since the beginning of the new Dettol strategy, research indicates that Dettol has:

1. Retained its leading position in terms of the penetration measurements.
2. Achieved increases in terms of the frequency with which it is bought and used.
3. Achieved increases in the applications for which it is used, reflecting the success of the advertising strategy of the past two years.
4. Achieved positive shifts in its image as a disinfectant.
5. Retained its positive image as an antiseptic.

There has been a substantial and significant increase in the frequency with which Dettol is used (Table 7.3). Just over one quarter (an increase of 7 percentage points) of users now use Dettol every day: 53 per cent of housewives use it on average every two to four days.

Table 7.3   *The frequency of using Dettol*

Base: all current users	January 1978 835 %	January 1980 849 %	Change 1980 vs. 1978
Every day	19	26	+ 7[a]
Every 2–3 days	28	27	− 1
Every 4–6 days	12	11	− 1
Once a week	19	18	− 1
Once every 2-3 weeks	6	6	−
Once a month	7	5	− 2
Less often	8	7	− 1

[a]Statistically significant at 99.9 per cent confidence level.

There has been a substantial and significant increase, of 10 percentage points, in the number of housewives buying Dettol once a month or more often (Table 7.4). These findings are consistent with the increase in ex-factory dispatches during 1978 and 1979 and the improvement in consumer sales audited by Nielsen, which is described overleaf.

Table 7.4   *The frequency of buying Dettol*

Base: all current users	January 1978 835 %	January 1980 849 %	Change 1980 vs. 1978
Once a month or more often	39	49	+ 10[a]
Once every 6 weeks	22	18	− 4
2-3 times a year	29	26	− 3
Once a year	7	5	− 2
Less often	3	2	− 1

[a]Statistically significant at 99.9 per cent confidence level.

In terms of usage, Table 7.5 shows increases in the areas of Dettol usage which clearly reflect the positive effects of the advertising strategy over the past two years. This table also shows that increased household usage has not resulted in a decline in personal usage—in fact, upward movements have been noted in some areas of personal use.

Table 7.5   *The usage occasions for Dettol*

Base: all current users	January 1978 835 %	January 1980 849 %	Change 1980 vs. 1978
Selected household uses			
Cleaning lavatory seat	51	56	+ 5[a]
Lavatory bowl	43	46	+ 3
Bath and handbasin	32	36	+ 4
Kitchen rubbish bins	29	34	+ 5[a]
Kitchen sink and waste pipe	28	32	+ 4
Kitchen floor	23	32	+ 9[c]
After pets	23	25	+ 2
Kitchen surfaces	16	23	+ 7[c]
Outside dustbin	13	14	+ 1
Selected personal uses			
Cuts and grazes	64	71	+ 7[b]
Bath	55	55	—
Bites and stings	38	45	+ 7[b]

Statistically significant at:
[a]95 per cent confidence level.
[b]99 per cent confidence level.
[c]99.9 per cent confidence level.

The image of Dettol: method. The image questions were structured so that respondents could make a free association with attitude couplets by brand. Thus, the respondents were introduced, by a preamble, to mention whatever brands on the list were appropriate to the Stimulus (attitude couplets). The respondents were free to mention as many or as few brands as they wished. In each study half the sample were given a list of antiseptic brands to associate with the attitude couplets while the other half of the sample were given a list of disinfectant brands.

Table 7.6 shows the number of positive mentions achieved by Dettol over several selected dimensions. Aside from illustrating the positive overall image of Dettol, it also shows upward shifts in perceptions of the brand's image in those areas for which it has been advertised.

Table 7.6 *The image of Dettol as a disinfectant*

Base: all rating the disinfectant products	January 1978 583 %	January 1980 592 %	Change 1980 vs. 1978
A product you can really trust	91	94	+ 3[a]
Particularly effective against infection	90	90	—
Strong enough for my needs	83	82	− 1
Goes a long way	73	73	—
Particularly suitable for cleaning the lavatory	52	56	+ 4
Particularly suitable for sinks and drains	47	50	+ 3
Particularly suitable for kitchen surfaces	37	41	+ 4

[a]Statistically significant at 95 per cent confidence level.

Table 7.7 shows the number of positive mentions achieved by Dettol when the product is rated amongst a list of other antiseptics, and illustrates the overall stability of the brand in this area.

Table 7.7 *The image of Dettol as an antiseptic*

Base: all respondents rating the antiseptic products	January 1978 614 %	January 1980 602 %	Change 1980 vs. 1978
A product you can really trust	92	92	—
Particularly effective against infection	88	86	− 2
Strong enough for my needs	82	82	—
Particularly suitable for adding to bath water	78	77	− 1
Goes a long way	66	66	—

Economic analysis of the factors affecting Dettol sales

Outline of method of analysis. Common sense dictates that variations in the weight or content of the advertising are not the only factors which will influence a brand's sales. Even with the benefit of a carefully controlled area test specifically designed to measure the effects of advertising, it is usually necessary to check and allow for the influence of other marketing factors which may have caused a differential sales effect between areas. In the case of Dettol, no controlled experiment was carried out and thus the evaluation of the sales effects of Dettol's advertising requires that any other influences on sales are isolated.

In essence, the method involves setting up a simple hypothetical model of the market which describes the likely relationship between the brand's sales and the marketing factors which are believed to influence sales. For example, a very simple model might be of the form:

$$\text{Brand Sales} = K_1 \text{ Advertising} - K_2 \text{ Price} + \text{Constant}$$

This means that for each unit increase in advertising weight the brand's sales increase by K_1 units; and for each unit price increase sales will decrease by K_2 units. The technique of multilinear regression analysis is then used to find the values of the constants in the model (the K's) which provide the best fit to the historical sales data.

There are, of course, many different formulations of the model which are hypothetically possible, which then raises the question as to which is the right one. To answer this, the chosen model must satisfy three basic criteria:

1. The model must agree with common sense. In other words, the variables influencing sales must satisfy our intuitive understanding of the market.
2. The model must be capable of accounting for a large proportion of the historic sales variation. Unless this is so, one cannot tell whether the marketing variables in the model really do significantly affect sales.
3. The model must be able to predict sales once the new values of the various marketing variables are known. This last condition is an acid test of whether the model really does explain the behaviour of the market.

The mechanics of the analysis involve the use of real-time computer facilities. With this aid it is possible to evaluate many different models rapidly and at low cost, and thereby find a model which meets the three conditions described above. The following sections describe the evaluation of Dettol's sales performance. Details of the statistical analysis are shown in the appendix at the end of this chapter.

The construction of the model. Dettol occupies a unique position in that it is used both as a disinfectant and an antiseptic; consequently the definition of its competitors, and hence its market share, is somewhat arbitrary. In the event, we found that the most satisfactory explanation of the brand's sales performance was achieved by modelling Dettol's actual volume sales rather than its share of a defined market.

The model was constructed from Nielsen bimonthly consumer sales audit data covering the period 1974–77, and the 1978 data was then used to test the model's predictive capability. (In the initial stages national data were used, which provided 30 observations, and the analysis was subsequently expanded by including the data for five individual regions, giving a total of 150 observations.)

Four factors were found to have a statistically significant influence on Dettol sales; they were:

1. Real personal disposable income.
2. Dettol's price (adjusted by the retail price index).
3. An underlying seasonal variation (this is common to all disinfectants and antiseptics, sales being higher in the warmer summer months).
4. Accumulated advertising weight (described in detail in the next section).

Figure 7.2 shows how each of these factors has varied over time. When combined they account for 90 per cent of all the variations in Dettol's national sales. This is demonstrated in Figure 7.3, which shows the bimonthly sales of Dettol as recorded by Nielsen from 1974 to 1977, together with the fit to these data provided by the model which has the four factors above as its components. In statistical terms the correlation between sales and the component factors is highly satisfactory; the chance that the result is merely a random coincidence is substantially less than one in a thousand.

The significance of the relationship between sales and each individual factor is demonstrated by the cross-plots shown in Figures 7.4 to 7.7. For example, Figure 7.4 shows the correlation between the variation in accumulated advertising weight (expressed as an effective advertising weight in TVRs) and Dettol sales after removing the effect of the other three factors (price, disposable income and seasonal variation).

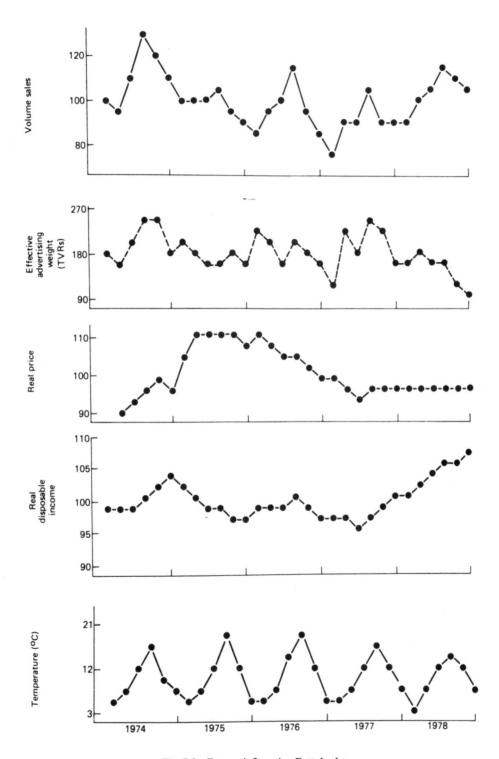

Fig. 7.2 Factors influencing Dettol sales.

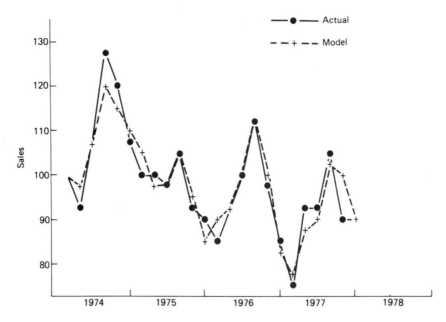

Fig. 7.3 Fit of model to actual sales. National sales, 1974–77.

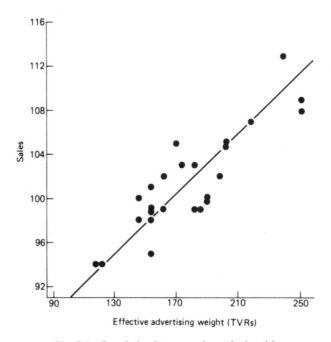

Fig. 7.4 Correlation between sales and advertising.

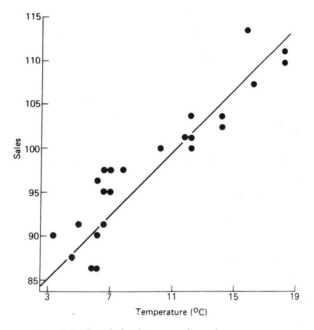

Fig. 7.5 Correlation between sales and temperature.

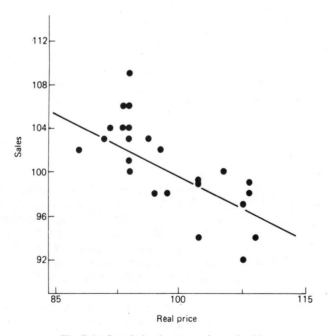

Fig. 7.6 Correlation between sales and price.

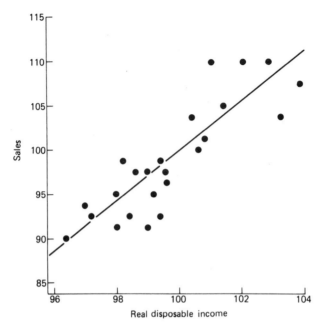

Fig. 7.7 Correlation between sales and disposable income.

An important feature of the analysis is the substantial effect that the 'non-marketing' variables have on sales. Together, the underlying seasonal variations and the influence of disposable income account for more than half the total variation in Dettol's sales. This underlines the need to take account of such effects before examining the influence of factors which are within the control of the advertiser, i.e. price and advertising.

The predictive capability of the model was tested by comparing the model's sales forecasts (based on the known values of the four variables during 1978) with the actual sales achieved in that period. This is shown in Figure 7.8. The model estimates closely follow the actual sales achieved, which is a very satisfactory result, particularly in view of the fact that the reversal of the previously declining sales trend has been correctly predicted.

The effects of advertising. The weight of advertising was expressed in terms of television rating points. Press expenditure, which formed only a small proportion of the total, was included in the television figures assuming it to be equally cost efficient. Using the larger sample of 150 observations available from the regional Nielsen data, it was possible to investigate the duration of the advertising effect, i.e. previous advertising influencing sales in the current period. The analysis (which is described in the appendix) provided strong evidence that the advertising effect decayed over time at a rate of about 10 to 15 per cent per month, i.e. half the full sales effect is achieved within about four months. This is an important result since it means that it is the accumulated weight of advertising which influences sales and not simply the advertising in the current period.

The economic implications. One of the most important features of this type of statistical analysis is that it is possible to quantify the effects on sales of changing the price and the weight of advertising. Because Nielsen reports at bimonthly intervals, and hence the number of observations is limited, only the average effect over a number of years can be calculated with any degree of reliability. The results in Table 7.8 are presented in the

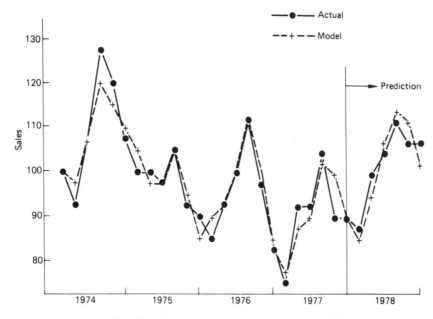

Fig. 7.8 Model predictions vs. actual sales in 1978.

form of elasticities, i.e. the percentage change in sales that results from a 1 per cent change in each of the four variables.

Table 7.8 *Elasticities calculated from economic model, 1974–78*

	Best estimate	95% confidence range
Advertising elasticity	.19	.11–.26
Price elasticity	– .44	– .64– – .23
Disposable income elasticity	2.26	1.66–2.86
Temperature (pr⁰C)	1.85	1.49–2.21

The price and advertising effects are clearly of most interest to the advertiser, since they have a direct bearing on decisions regarding the marketing strategy. The most useful way of interpreting these results is to compare the estimated elasticities with the 'breakeven' values (Table 7.9).

Table 7.9 *Estimated elasticities compared with breakeven values*

	Best estimate	Breakeven
Advertising elasticity	.19	0.16
Price elasticity	– 0.4	– .20

For example, the breakeven price elasticity of -2.0 means that a 1 per cent increase in price would generate an increased profit for the brand provided that sales volume did not fall by more than 2 per cent. The estimate of the actual price elasticity is substantially less than this breakeven figure; had price been increased by 1 per cent the best estimate is that sales volume would have declined by 0.44 per cent. Thus, there is strong evidence that the brand has been underpriced.

By contrast, the estimate of Dettol's advertising elasticity, 0.19, is higher than the breakeven figure of 0.16 (this is the percentage increase in sales required to recover the costs of a 1 per cent increase in advertising expenditure).

The implications of this are:

1. *The advertising expenditure over the period 1974–78 has generated profitable increases in sales for the brand.* Even allowing that a degree of uncertainty is associated with every statistical estimate, there is only a 1 in 5 chance that the advertising was not profitable (i.e. the advertising elasticity was actually less than breakeven).

2. Given that our best estimate of the advertising elasticity is correct, the level of expenditure should have been higher to maximise the profit returned. By definition, at the optimum expenditure level the breakeven and actual elasticities will be equal. However, it is not possible to say what the optimum level should have been; to do so requires that the precise shape of the advertising/sales relationship is known.

The consumer research described above showed that the 1978 advertising campaign had generated significant improvements in consumers' attitudes, accompanied by increases in claimed usage. This certainly suggests an increased advertising effectiveness in 1978. Unfortunately, it is not possible to confirm this finding via the econometric analysis, for two reasons:

1. Firstly, as previously stated, there are only a limited number of sales observations for any one year, which means that an estimate of the advertising elasticity based on one year's data will be very unreliable. In fact, a statistically significant result would only have been obtained had the advertising doubled in effectiveness.

2. Secondly, 1978 was a period when consumers' disposable income rose rapidly. In this situation it becomes very difficult to separate the contributions that advertising and disposable income made to the improvement in sales. (A very small change in the weight of importance given to disposable income would allow a substantial improvement in the effectiveness of the 1978 advertising.)

However, the assessment of the average advertising effectiveness over the period 1974–78 almost certainly understates the contribution that advertising made to the substantial improvement in sales during 1978. The rapid increase in consumers' spending power was a necessary precursor, but it is not axiomatic that this increased prosperity should have been directed to purchases of Dettol. Consumers must have a reason for purchasing the brand which involves a belief in its value, and this in large part must depend on the image built up by many years of advertising. Such benefits cannot be readily quantified, but they nevertheless provide additional justification to the value of Dettol's advertising.

Conclusion

The change in advertising strategy that occurred in 1978 provided us with the opportunity of demonstrating that Dettol's advertising does influence attitudes and behaviour. There were shifts in consumer usage and attitudes along each of the desired dimensions.

The econometric analysis conducted between 1974 and 1978 has shown that the advertising expenditure on Dettol in this period has been profitable.

Further, in 1978, the combination of past and current advertising allowed Dettol to capitalise on the growth in consumer spending power.

APPENDIX: TECHNICAL APPENDIX TO ECONOMETRIC ANALYSIS

1. Model based on national sales data

The results shown below were achieved using stepwise multilinear regression on 24 observations, covering the period 1974–77.
The regression equation is:

$$\text{Sales Volume} = 1.7 \times \text{Temperature} + 2.2 \times \text{Disposable Income} \\ + .183 \times \text{Accumulated Advertising} - .241 \times \text{Real Price} \\ - 131$$

With the exception of temperature (which is expressed in degrees centigrade) all other vehicles were computed as indices about their mean values and hence the coefficients represent the elasticities for each variable. The key statistics for the regression equation are as follows:

$R^2 = .909$ This shows that 91 per cent of the variation in sales volume has been explained and thus it is unlikely that another factor of major importance has been ignored.

F ratio = 35.85   This means that the chance of such an explanation being due to random chance is less than one in a thousand.

Standard error as % of mean volume = 4.13
    This is a measure of the likely forecasting error.

Durbin-Watson statistic on residuals = 1.8
    It is important that the error term (residual variation) is randomly distributed. If this is not the case, then the variables are not independent of each other, and errors in estimation are likely. There is no evidence here of colinearity (a value of 2.0 is ideal, with 1.5 to 2.5 being acceptable limits). Table 7.10 below shows key statistics for each of the variables in the regression equation.

Table 7.10

	95% confidence limits			T	Partial
	Mean[a]	upper	lower	statistics[b]	F[c]
Temperature	1.7	2.15	1.24	7.89	62.2
Disposable income	2.2	1.11	4.25	4.25	18.1
Advertising	0.18	0.07	3.47	3.47	12.1
Real price	− 0.24	− 0.52	− 1.82	− 1.82	3.3

[a]The mean is the most likely estimate of the coefficient for each variable, and the 95 per cent confidence limits indicate that there is a 5 per cent chance of the coefficients lying outside the range shown.
[b]The T statistic is a measure of the extent to which the coefficient is significantly different from zero (i.e. the variable has no effect on the regression equation). A value greater than 2.0 is significant at the 95 per cent confidence level.
[c]This is a test of whether the variable in question explains a significant amount of the sales variation. A value of 4.0 would be significant at the 95 per cent confidence level.

2. Model based on regional data

The regional model was based on 150 observations using Nielsen data from the five largest areas (London, Midlands, Lancashire, Yorkshire, Wales and West). Each variable was expressed as its index about the regional mean.

The existence of long-term advertising effects was established by first testing for an immediate advertising effect and then by introducing lagged advertising variables, examining whether the fit of the model (R^2) improved significantly (an R^2 lower than that for the national model is to be expected, since the regional Nielsen shop sample is smaller). With only immediate advertising considered, the R^2 was .50 and the F ratio for immediate advertising 19.1; by including advertising variables successively lagged up to six periods ago, the R^2 improved to .58.

A plot of the lagged advertising coefficients is shown in Figure 7.9. Compared with the coefficient for immediate advertising, those for the lagged variables diminish the longer the lag. The rate of advertising decay implied by this is of the order of 25 per cent per bimonthly period.

This information was used to construct a transformed advertising variable, representing the accumulated advertising effect, assuming a decay rate of 25 per cent per bimonth, viz:

Accumulated Advertising Weight $= a_0 + .75a_1 + (.75)^2a_2 + \ldots\ldots$
where $a_0 =$ current advertising
where $a_i =$ advertising lagged by i periods

Using this variable the R^2 achieved was .65, with the F ratio for advertising increasing to 57.5
The full results were as follows:

Sales Volume $= 1.85 \times$ Temperature $+ 2.26 \times$ Disposable Income
$+ .188 \times$ Accumulated Advertising $- .44 \times$ Real Price
$R^2 = .653$ F Ratio $= 44.7$
Standard error as % of mean volume $= 8.3$
Durbin-Watson statistic on residual $= 2.1$

Table 7.11

	95% confidence limits		T	Partial
	upper	lower	statistic	F
Temperature	2.21	1.49	10.04	100.82
Disposable income	2.86	1.66	7.4	54.9
Advertising	0.264	0.111	4.86	23.6
Real price	− 0.23	− 0.64	− 4.15	17.25

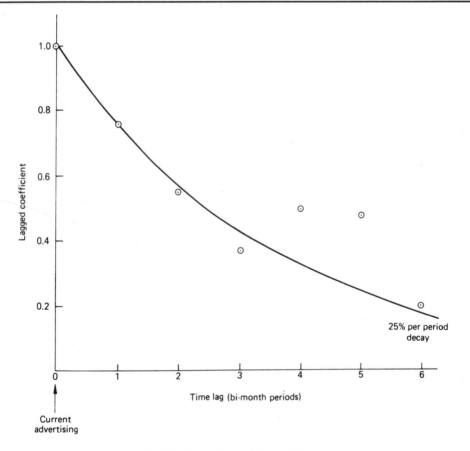

Fig. 7.9 Lagged advertising coefficients.

8

Marketing Information Systems and Technologies

Although the gathering and analysis of the data has continued to be a central pre-occupation of marketing personnel, attention over the last few years has swung increasingly towards the issue of organisation and application of information. Three factors have contributed to this trend:

1. The scale of the 'information revolution'.
2. Technological progress in handling data.
3. Recognition that effective strategic and operational management requires good quality, usable and manageable data.

These issues provide the central focus for this chapter.

It is difficult to arrive at a totally satisfactory definition of 'information technology', as it is largely:

> A new label for a collection of old ingredients, technologies which up to now have enjoyed disparate natures and histories.
>
> J. Eaton and J. Smithers,
> *This Is IT* [1]

Any definition will need to encompass both the diversity of the area and the debate on the range of activities which can be incorporated into the field. This may be best achieved through an approach which recognises its eclectic and dynamic nature.

> Information technology is the generic term used to describe those technologies concerned with the collection, storage, transmission and reception of information. It incorporates both the 'hardware' needed to handle these activities and the 'software' required to organise and process the data.

There can be little doubt today of the interest of both government and industry in this area. Despite the economic problems of the last decade, progress here has done much to 'cast a steady glow of light over the industrial nations' economic horizon' (*Time Magazine*, Nov. 26, 1984). It has provided the driving force for the growth of key firms, industry sectors and countries. Companies such as IBM, Apple, Control Data, Hewlett-Packard and Wang have continued to grow and prosper at a time when the more common pattern has been retrenchment and decline. It has been the firms which have effectively applied the new information technologies, investing to stay ahead rather than saving to survive, which have prospered.

Internationally, a similar pattern has been seen. The lead established by the US in information technology appears to have been a major factor in its recent economic growth. The gap that has emerged between North America and Japan on the one hand, and Europe on the other, goes some way towards explaining the latter's relatively poor recent economic performance. Acknowledging this has prompted the British Government

Fig. 8.1   The Information Technology Year symbol.

to embark on a range of initiatives to support the development and application of new information technologies. They range from the ALVEY programme, designed to support research, through assistance with applications projects such as CAD/CAM, to the designation of 1983 as 'Information Technology Year'.

International initiatives have been introduced in parallel with these, notably the ESPRIT programme in the EEC to promote the development and use of new information technologies.

Marketing is at the centre of these developments, both in the introduction of the technology through existing and novel products and services, and in the use of information technology to assist its own operations. The pace and scale of change has absorbed the attention of increasing numbers of researchers, who see this as an area of vital significance to the marketing operations of industry and commerce.[2]

IT AND ITS IMPACT

Hitherto research has tended to focus on developments in hardware or the even more diverse software developments. Relatively little attention has been paid to the impact of these innovations on established organisations and their operations. It is an effect that could transform many industrial, commercial and public agencies from engineering design to library services. Current evidence suggests that the challenges posed will go far beyond the technical and procedural difficulties imposed in the recent past when innovations or new products became available. The change could be as profound as the previous 'industrial revolution'. This saw changes on two levels:

1. The nature of the goods and services sought by customers.
2. The ways in which companies organised themselves to produce, supply and distribute these goods.

In this chapter both these areas will be examined.

The new technologies provide a range of technological and commercial opportunities for firms, based on the accelerated transmission and recovery of data and the scope for rapid organisation and close specification of material. This is occurring at a time when the real cost of the new technologies is declining almost as rapidly as the technological performance is increasing. In a recent speech, Dr. D. Dekker for Philips pointed out that the amount of information that could be stored on a 'chip' had doubled virtually every year for the last decade. At the same time the price had approximately halved! More graphically it has been pointed out that:

> If the internal combustion engine had developed at the same pace, it would cost about 25p, generate enough energy to drive the QE2 and fit inside a match box.

The existence of this potential will not guarantee a relevant response by current providers of equivalent services. In other areas, the opposite has generally held true.

> The railways were providers of transport services but did not respond to the transport revolutions of the 20th Century.

> The department stores provided mass retailing but failed to move into supermarket trading.

> The manufacturers of mechanical calculators completely missed out in the move to electronic calculators.

> Producers of TV sets in North America and Europe almost wholly failed to establish themselves in the video cassette recorder market.

There is now sufficient evidence available to suggest that established providers find it very difficult to respond to 'discontinuous' changes, prompted by technologies which call for major modifications of behaviour. This is the case in information technology.

Four features of the new technology will create new options for provision and call for new patterns of behaviour:

1. *High Availability*. Access points can be large in number and highly diverse. Britain has the highest per capita computer ownership in the world. It is estimated that a town such as Northampton now has more computing capacity than existed in the world fifteen years ago.
2. *High Customer-Specificness*. Services and products can be designed to very close tolerances, jointly by customers and suppliers. This degree of tailoring has only been possible in relatively high-price products in the past. The 'Cabbage Patch' dolls of 1983 and 1984 are forerunners of this technology.
3. *Recurrent Adaptation*. The rate of change is now so fast that the notion of a fixed product or service may disappear.
4. *Interaction*. The facility now exists for users and suppliers to set up a communications network capable of virtually instantaneous interaction and response.

Few areas illustrate the potential impact of the new information technologies more clearly than Computer Aided Design/Computer Aided Manufacturing (CAD/CAM). This allows those working on projects to design, draft and analyse their offerings using computer graphics on a screen. It eliminates enormous areas of routine and 'chore', while giving the designer opportunities to analyse, review alternatives and experiment which would have been impossible in the recent past. The newer systems enable the firms to take the newly-designed offerings and use the computer to conduct a range of simulated tests on the product.

The application of CAD/CAM is making traditional procedures more efficient and providing avenues for innovation and new development. The use of the system by car manufacturers illustrates both sides of this process. A traditional task, such as designing the boot of a car to ensure maximum capacity, used to require models and mock-ups. This was expensive. Building a full-size wooden model of the boot could take days and cost thousands of pounds. Now it can be done in moments with optimisation techniques displaying the alternatives open to the producer. The even more expensive and time-consuming tasks of producing and testing new body designs has seen the same process of change. The more demanding, expensive and complex the area, the greater the potential for change.

The evolution of 'expert systems' is likely to take this process of applying the technology even further. These systems are based on attempts to build models of how the mind works. Typically, they are built from two parts. The first, i.e. 'the knowledge base', provides the loosely structured collection of rules which summarise the state of 'expertise' in a field. The second provides the 'logic' for the system which allows the 'knowledge base' to manipulate and combine data. It is an attempt to mimic the way an expert in a field handles a question or issue. The strengths of expert systems are likely to lie in the type of structured selection tasks often handled today by libraries.

It is clear that change at this rate, with the diverse array of alternative avenues, cannot be tackled with traditional tools. It requires a re-examination of roles as well as tasks. Traditionally these have been based on the services offered or the facilities provided. Priority has been given to either widening services or reaching more potential users: these are akin to the production and distribution tasks of manufacturers or service companies. Faced with the current environment, a new perspective is required. This emphasises the needs to be met rather than the means used to satisfy them. Emphasis will be placed on *needs*, such as leisure or information, rather than specific and potentially outdated means of meeting them.

In marketing, four variables are seen as critical to this process of tailoring services to target groups: the product or service; its availability; awareness or attitudes; and cost. Specific customer groups will seek particular combinations of these variables. The new information technologies enhance the scope for novel combinations while increasing the competitive pressures on providers. The four features of the new technologies mentioned earlier each illustrate this, while having differential scope to influence the above variables.

The high availability of home and personal computers allied to the increasing penetration of TV-based information services will dramatically reduce the cost of information search while raising questions about the viability of established cataloguing and referencing procedures. Already, almost half-a-million homes in Britain have access to on-line data through Oracle, Ceefax or Prestel.

In France, government policies designed to stimulate domestic information technology-based industries allied to incentive pricing are stimulating demand for Teletel.

The introduction of interactive videotext will transform the current cumbersome access procedures while expanding the capacity for downloading material for reference and analysis.

Table 8.1   *Computerised interactive videotext.*

Country	Name of system
Austria	Bildschirmtext
Canada	Telidon
Denmark	Teledata
Finland	Telset
France	Teletel
Germany	Bildschirmtext
Italy	Videotel
Japan	Captain
Netherlands	Viditel
Norway	Teledata
Spain	Videotex
Sweden	Data Vision
Switzerland	Videotex
United Kingdom	Prestel
United States	Various systems

A number of important initiatives have already been taken. The links between ASLIB in Britain and services such as DIALOG, ESA–IRS, Pergamon–Infoline, SDC–Orbic and Polis give some indication of the networking potential. Parallel developments across Europe and in North America incorporating novel and existing technologies to provide access to national and international data bases are illustrating the potential of both computer-based and telecommunication systems. There is revitalised interest in computerised interactive videotext. Preliminary research results suggest that the process of adoption of these new technologies is broadly following the Rogers model of the line-process of adoption as indicated in Figure 8.2.

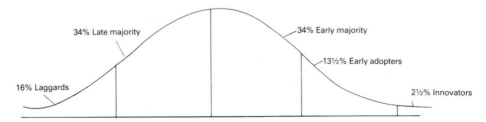

Fig. 8.2   From E. M. Rogers, *Diffusion of Information*. New York: Free Press.

In the UK the success of MicroNet 800's software downloading system vividly illustrates the potential for developments associated with specific market segments or opportunities in this field. More recently the expansion of Gateway Technologies, through Prestel, will increase access to specialist 'information providers' in business markets.

In the United States, innovative systems are being developed which seek to capitalise on distinct market opportunities. In West Germany the progress with Bildschirmtext has been greatly stimulated through links with the banking sector. The Canadian Telidon system has developed through public and private sector co-operation to meet sectoral needs. In the near future it is likely that increased scope for interaction will expand demand for these systems.

In the different sectors of the market—consumer, industrial commercial, and services (public and private)—this type of pattern can be seen. However, it is clear that a high degree of variation exists. This is affected by a number of factors. Techno-commercial factors, especially the need for real-line access, have assisted the rapid diffusion of this type of technology in sectors such as travel agencies. Techno-cultural factors are causing resistance to adoption among certain groups, e.g., older, less well-educated males.

Despite these factors, the pace of change is remarkable. The diffusion curves for a number of media can be compared:

Newspapers   Expansion of the market to virtually all households took almost 80 years (from 1850s to 1930s).

Films   The same pattern of access took place over less than 40 years (from early 1900s to late 1930s).

Radio   The expansion of the network took just 25 years (from mid-1920s to early 1950s).

Television   The penetration of TV took place in about 12 years (from late 1940s to early 1960s).

Electronic Calculators   The widespread adoption of these took less than 10 years (from early 1970s to late 1970s).

Home and Personal Computers   It has taken less than 3 years for over 5 per cent of all households to have a personal computer.

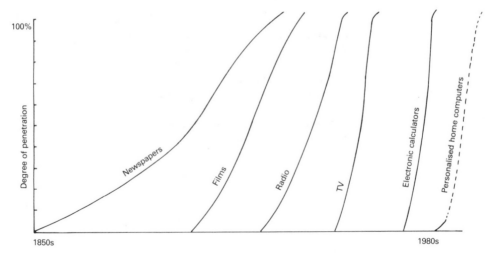

Fig. 8.3   Diffusion curves for a number of media.

The rate and scale of changes will challenge many of our pre-conceived ideas.

It would be a mistake to assume that there are no potentially negative consequences other than those indicated above. Perhaps the most fundamental change may occur in organisational relationships and structures. Traditionally these have been hierarchical and localised; that is, the overall structure of the commercial firm or public body has been based on a relatively simple internally-structured hierarchy, often with localised centres of knowledge and power.

This pattern may be challenged in both the short and long term. In the short term, the pace of change is likely to pose serious operational problems of adaption and absorption to hierarchically- or bureaucratically-structured entities. Innovation is generally achieved more easily and effectively through open organic structures. These permit information flows, rather than structure, to be directed. A parallel pattern can be seen with task- versus purpose-orientated structures. The latter finds the management of change easier than the former. Absorbing, responding to the innovations indicated above, will require profound short-term organisational adaption.

The direction taken within this general phenomenon will be influenced by the nature of the technologies themselves. Researchers are only now becoming fully aware of the broader implications of the relationship between the nature of the technology and the appropriate organisational structures within a wider society. The introduction of the factory system, widespread mechanisation and industrialisation were major factors in the emergence of the type of bureaucratic, hierarchical structure dominant throughout modern industrial society. This pattern of organisation extended far beyond the factory or commercial firm to a point where it is sometimes perceived as a 'natural' way of organisation.

However, modern information technologies are built around a different model. Here networks, rather than flows or hierarchy, predominate. Multiple access points, vertical as well as horizontal communication, unit separation, gate-keeping are replacing the single access, hierarchical structure implicit in older systems. Organisational forms will inevitably change as 'loops' replace 'lines', and 'open' rather than 'closed' systems become the norm.

The organisational changes and the diffusion process mentioned earlier will have a social cost, at least in the short term. D. Boddy and D. Buchanan suggest that although the direct effects on manufacturing employment have been less dramatic than earlier anticipated, a number of issues need to be born in mind.

1. Firms introducing new information technologies so far (the innovators) have tended to be the more prosperous, more successful enterprises. Their growth has compensated for potential job losses.
2. The increase in turnover associated with new information technologies has been accompanied by increased added value per job, not new jobs.
3. The greatest impact has been on older, less well-educated males, i.e. a sector which is particularly difficult to reach through retraining and other schemes.

The work of L. Sawyers in the retail sector has arrived at broadly similar findings, but has noted that among female workers there is evidence of:

1. Resistance to developing the skills to use the new technologies at a level far greater than their male counterparts.
2. De-skilling, as first and second levels of supervisory management are cut back in numbers as central control becomes easier.

These broader organisational and social consequences will need to be overcome if the potentials inherent in the technologies are to be realised.

COMPUTING AND TELECOMMUNICATIONS

The emergence of Viewdata systems is one of the symbols of the most obvious outputs of information technology: computer-based systems providing a wide range of data to a diverse array of users. The computer itself remains the most potent symbol of the information revolution of the second half of this century. It has been the basis on which major corporations have been built, attitudes challenged and new skills developed and demanded.

Table 8.2 *The major computer companies*

Name	Country of origin	Employees (000s)	Sales (1983) $billion
IBM	US	350	40
Philips	Holland	343	16
NEC	Japan	73	6
Honeywell	US	76	6
Sperry	US	77	5
Hewlett-Packard	US	72	5
Control Data	US	56	5
Burroughs	US	63	4
Digital	US	73	4
Wang	US	22	1.5
ICL	UK	22	1.3

The initial stages of the development of this area have seen *the introduction of mainframe computers into industry, commerce and government.* These were generally expensive and required highly specialised staff to operate them efficiently. The primary role of the computer in these early years was the performance of traditional computation or calculation—'number crunching'. Markets for these items were highly specialised, generally based on the notion of 'expert to expert' sales and service. The customer expected a high degree of customising of product, software and services. Many organisations structured their internal operations around their 'data processing' department. Typically these were responsible for all policy and development.

The 1960s saw *the launch of the 'mini computer'.* Generally these sought to meet the same broad array of needs, but they were smaller, cheaper and generally more tolerant of their operating environment. The rapid growth of the producers of 'minis' was based on the combination of low price and robustness. This meant that they could be used for applications and in areas closed to the traditional mainframe and the data processing specialists. They rapidly penetrated in a range of novel areas, as users with specialist needs explored potential uses. Marketing and sales relationships were generally based on the applications-orientated non-computing expert in dialogue with the supplier firm. Buyers still expected a great deal of client service, but tempered this with a recognition of their responsibility for 'applications packages'.

Despite these developments, the computer remained a highly specialised 'expert'-orientated tool until *the introduction of the micros*. The dramatic reduction in entry costs mentioned earlier meant that access to the technology was opened to a vast array of non-specialist users. The limitations were primarily in user-awareness and software. This era has seen the computer change from a highly specialised tool to a universal aid in every area from work to entertainment.

It is very difficult to predict the direction that computer technology will take over the next decade. It is clear that the range of applications will continue to increase as customer confidence and the range of technology increases. At the same time, it seems likely that research into 'expert systems' will bear some fruit. Perhaps the most important likely development for marketing personnel will emerge from the developing links between computers and communications systems (more precisely, telecommunications). The last year has seen a number of important initiatives, including the attempt by IBM and British Telecom to develop a partnership arrangement in the area. Although this was blocked by the Government, the challenges posed by the expanding task of transporting data between computers is likely to force developments in this field. The slow progress in Britain of Prestel is likely to force British Telecom to explore ways of making their role as 'information provider' more relevant to newly computer-literate users.

INFORMATION TECHNOLOGY AND DISTRIBUTION

Retailers, wholesalers and distributors have been using computers and their associated technologies to perform the types of functions described above for many years. However, their new lower price, easier-to-use systems provide a potential for the introduction of a range of innovations especially suitable to the trading practices and traditions of the retail and distributive sector. In particular, they provide:

1. Opportunities for decentralisation.
2. Scope for storage, assembly and analysis of the vast number of transactions whose volume defeated earlier attempts to gather and use it effectively.
3. Increased opportunities for effective management control in key areas such as stock control, inventory management and order/payment processing.
4. The potential to link transactions into 'electronic funds transfer'.

Besides these general opportunities, there is increasing interest in the integration of retailing with the new technologies in a more active way. Tesco recently announced an initiative designed to explore the scope for 'armchair shopping', i.e. where the items for sale are listed on the TV screen. They can be bought by using a special keyboard to indicate choices. Similar experiments, based on the Birmingham 'Club 403' and the home banking initiative of the Bank of Scotland, indicate some avenues which are likely to open over the next few years.

However, it is at the 'point of sale' that most immediate changes have taken place. The introduction of *electronic point of sale systems* (EPOs) and associated bar coding systems gives firms the opportunity to:

1. Check and monitor prices.
2. Store and retrieve accurate up-to-the-minute information.
3. Print detailed till receipts.
4. Measure performance.
5. Improve cash control (even eliminate cash if electronic funds transfer is introduced).
6. Price goods more accurately and easily.

These improvements in the management functions will have direct impact on the marketing policies of the retailers and distributors and their relationships with manufacturers. Traditional problems such as 'out of stock' difficulties should be drastically reduced, while the ability of the trader to monitor the performance of products will pose major challenges to producers.

Traders and suppliers will be able to use the new technology in merchandising and promotion to improve layouts, quickly introduce special promotions (especially those based on price), and provide accurate information and promotional material for customers, perhaps using Prestel and videos.

ISBN 0-03-910603-9

9 780039 106034

Fig. 8.4   Illustration of a bar code.

A bar code, such as that in Figure 8.4, contains coded information which can be read by a laser scanner or light pen linked with a computer.

THE MARKETING INFORMATION SYSTEM

The increased access to data provided by the new information technologies imposes extra responsibilities on management to use it effectively. This requires the construction of carefully planned and well-organised *marketing information systems* (MIS).

> The MIS is the organised arrangement of people, machines and procedures set up to ensure that all relevant and usable information required by marketing management reaches them at a time and in a form to help them with effective decision making.

This definition highlights the important features of a Marketing Information System.

Management control

Central to Marketing Information Systems is that they are deliberately set up and organised to ensure the most effective use of marketing intelligence. This normally calls for a programme of planning, research, experimentation and introduction to ensure that the objectives of the MIS are achieved. Establishing these 'goals' for the system is the first step. These should be as clearly defined and as fully understood as possible. Specific responsibility for managing and monitoring the system has to be allocated, to ensure continuing system efficiency as needs change and the range and variety of data develops. The system will only work if it is operated effectively.

This calls for the integration of people, machines and procedures. People are frequently the primary sources of information, as well as being responsible for its efficient allocation and distribution. Machines are the tools of the system. It is a common fallacy that equipment can solve the problems in this area. It is generally more accurate to say that machines can only make good solutions work better (or worse). Procedures for review, access and allocation are vital to system maintenance.

User friendliness

Despite these organisational and control considerations, it must be recognised that Marketing Information Systems exist for only one reason: to assist with effective decision making. It is critical that those responsible for decisions, the users of the data, provide the basis on which the system is designed. This means involving line management at an early stage in specifying their requirements. Frequently this does not mean additional information:

> Some Management Information Systems (MIS), as well as much of the literature on MIS, are based on a significant misconception. The assumption is made that the computer system will benefit the management of the enterprise by providing more historical or projected data, of greater accuracy, in a more timely fashion, directly to the line manager for use in managing ... (but) very few line managers want more data than they now get whether historical or projected; most managers are inundated with data.
>
> V.A. Vyssotsky[3]

The design of effective Marketing Information Systems calls for the integration of the sources with needs.

Figure 8.5 illustrates the twin processes which come together in an effective information system.

Watkins[4] identifies the three essential features of a Marketing Information System as

1. Sources of information.
2. Mechanisms for handling and manipulating data.
3. Decisions requiring information.

Although these features are found in numerous commercial situations, information systems are used in a relatively restricted number of situations. Piercy[2] examines these while exploring the limitations on the effective application of these procedures. In Britain, Fletcher[5] identified eight common uses for information systems: these are listed in order of frequency.

The uses of information systems

1. Customer Analysis.
2. Profit Analysis.
3. Sales Force Control.
4. Competitor Analysis.
5. Cost Savings.
6. Improved Data Retrieval.
7. Sales Forecasting.
8. Planning and Decision Making.

Information gathering   Information processing   Information utilization

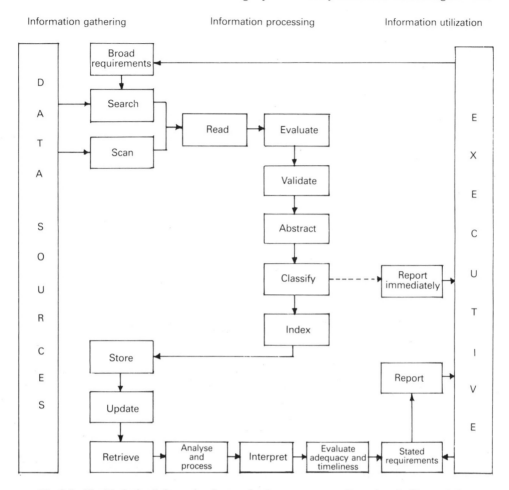

Fig. 8.5   The Marketing Information System development process. Reproduced with permission.

Modern microprocessor-based information technologies are leading to many changes in the way information is organised and used in firms. Among the most important of these are:

1.   The increased access to technology.
2.   The erosion of information boundaries.

The rapid reduction in the price of information storage has made it relatively cheap and easy to distribute micro-computers widely in firms. There has been a dramatic increase over the last twenty years in the amount of computing power that can be purchased for each pound. The data in Figure 8.6 suggest that the cost of information processing capacity measured in MIPS (Millions of Instructions Per Second) has dropped dramatically over this period. Parallel improvements in software, especially in 'user friendliness', have increased the willingness of managers to use this data. Piercy[2] has highlighted the degree to which conventional institutional barriers are eroded by modern information technologies. The integration of data from 'scanning', 'cable TV', 'Viewdata' sources, besides more conventional means of gathering data, provides many opportunities for manufacturers and retailers to co-operate to improve customer services.

At the same time, new avenues for competition will emerge as firms realise that whoever controls the information system controls the market. Piercy's Product-Market Macro-Marketing Information System illustrates how the data sources of suppliers and intermediaries can dovetail through the 'Central Market Data Base'.

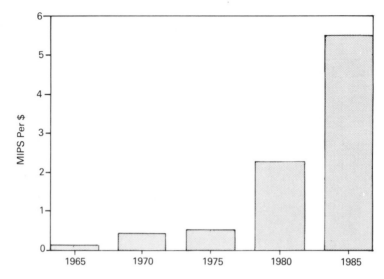

Fig. 8.6   The reducing cost of information.

Key issues

In an area as complex and dynamic as this it is difficult to be confident that the aspects identified as central today will remain so. However, the following points should be borne in mind:

1. Information technology is transforming a wide range of commercial relationships.
2. It is influencing both the nature of the goods on the market and the ways firms organise themselves.
3. Historically, those firms already established in markets have faced very real difficulties in coping with the type of discontinuous change taking place today.
4. The retail and wholesale distribution sector is at the centre of many of the innovations in the application of IT in customer transactions.
5. The access to data places special demands on those involved in information systems design and implementation.

Notes

1.   Eaton, J. & Smithers, J., *This Is IT*. London: Philip Allan, 1982.
2.   Piercy, N. & Evans, M., *Managing Marketing Information*. London: Croom Helm, 1983.
3.   Vyssotsky, V.A., 'Computer Systems; More Evolution Than Revolution', *Journal of Systems Management*, **13**, No.2, 1980.
4.   Watkins, T., 'Marketing Information Systems in Insurance', 2nd World Marketing Congress, Stirling, 1985.
5.   Fletcher, 'IT and Consumer Decision Making', Marketing Education Group, Annual Conference, Cranfield, 1983.

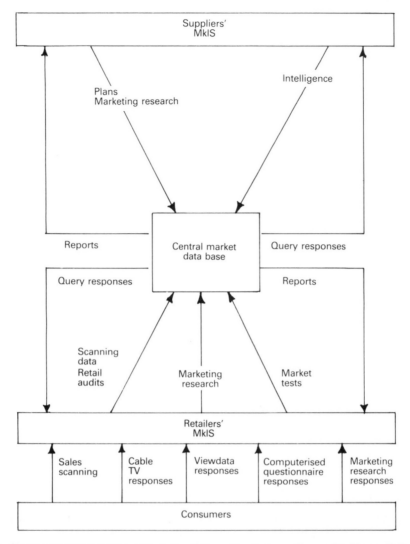

Fig. 8.7 The Product-Market Macro-Marketing Information System. (*Source*: N. Piercy, 'Information Processing—the Newest Mix Element', Marketing Education Group Conference, 1983.

Glossary on information technology*

Alpha numeric key pad. A small calculator-type keyboard containing both numbers and letters, used to give instructions to the computer in a Viewdata system.

Auto-teller machines: ATMs. A machine provided by the bank which enables cash to be withdrawn electronically, and can be installed in any location outside a bank. A plastic card is inserted into a card-reading device and a personal identification number (PIN) is entered in order to make a demand. The service can also be used to make account enquiries.

---

*This glossary is reproduced with permission from *Technology. The Issues for the Distributive Trades*. Distributive Trades Economic Development Committee. London: NEDO.

Bar codes. A series of black lines of varying widths, each width representing a number from 0 to 9. Used in combination they form a digital code which can be identified by a laser scanner or light pen linked to a computer.

Computer language. A form of written instruction which enables a user to make a computer carry out the function required. See also 'user friendly' language.

Computer terminal. A device that provides input/output facilities to a computer, often from a remote location.

Data base. A larger computer file of information, often made up of smaller files linked together.

Data processing. The receipt, transmission and storage of information by computer, and its organisation in the required manner.

Dedicated lines (also known as private circuits, private wires, or lease lines). Private lines leased from British Telecom for use in company telephone networks.

Digital exchanges. A method of telecommunications which carries data or speech in a digital rather than analogue form.

Electronic cash register: ECR. A device which serves as a cash register but because of its electronic components can be enhanced to perform calculation and price look-up functions.

Electronic funds transfer system: EFTS. A system which communicates information about payments electronically instead of on paper and, as with cheque payment, minimises the physical handling of cash.

Electronic point of sale systems: EPOS. A general name for systems which record sales data at the point of payment on to cassette tape or computer file.

Electronic pricing. Price information that is held in computer files and is communicated automatically to the cash register upon the manual or automatic entry of a product code.

Encodation. The process of incorporating a code, usually into the magnetic strip on a credit or charge card.

Fibre optics (or optical fibres). An optical system that uses one or more glass perspex fibres as a light guide. The fibre optics systems now used for telecommunication purposes use electronic signals from a transmitter to modulate a laser beam, which is then transmitted through the fibres. Many more signals can be carried through a bunch of fibres than through a conventional copper cable of the same diameter.

Hardware. A general term used to describe all the electronic and mechanical components of the computer, together with those devices, such as printers, used with it. See Software.

Information provider: IP. A supplier of information to British Telecom for use on Prestel.

Laser scanner. A fixed, flat-bed device which uses a laser beam to measure the width of the black lines of a bar code when products incorporating such a code are passed over it. Since each different width has a unique numerical identity the scanner is able, when linked to a computer, to convert the series of lines into a digital code for product identification purposes.

Light pen or wand. A similar concept to the laser scanner except that the beam emanates from a hand-held device resembling a pen or wand which is moved across the bar code by hand.

Machine readable code. Any form of coding which can be identified by an electronic device, e.g. bar code.

Microcomputer. A term used to describe computers which are smaller than minicomputers in both size and capacity.

Minicomputers. A term used to identify those computers, generally physically small, with a limited amount of storage capacity. Typically such computers would be dedicated to a single task.

Modem. A device which fits between computing equipment and British Telecom equipment to convert data into a form which allows it to be transmitted over telephone lines.

Off-line. A term which identifies those items of equipment that are part of a computer system, but are not controlled by a central computer. Information that is to be communicated to the computer is stored on magnetic tape, cassette, or disc, which is then despatched by post or messenger service.

On-line. A part of a computer system is on-line if it is directly under the control of a central processor.

Optical character recognition: OCR. A form of coding in which standard typewriter characters and numbers can be read by an optical device connected to a computer, as well as the human eye.

Packet switching. A technique in which data is transmitted across a data network in discrete, addressed blocks (called packets). Terminals on a packet network may send and receive packets to and from a number of other terminals simultaneously.

Personal identification number: PIN. A confidential and unique number allocated by banks to customers for the operation of an ATM with a plastic authorisation card. The PIN is known colloquially as the 'electronic signature' as it verifies the customer's identity.

Portable data capture unit: PDCU. A device like a calculator which acts as a small, portable computer. Typically it can be used by a salesman, or stock checker, to record information for subsequent entry into a computer.

Price look-up: PLU. A facility for obtaining price information that is held on the computer and using it to record a sale through the cash register, usually by means of entering a product code.

Program. A set of instructions written in the language of the computer and used to make it perform a specific task or series of tasks.

Protocols. A formal procedure for the exchange of data between computers or computer terminals.

Software. A set of computer instructions contained in programs that are needed to make the computer hardware function and carry out the tasks required. See Hardware.

'User friendly' language. A form of computer program in which the computer is instructed to guide the user through the tasks he needs to perform in order for the computer to carry out the function he requires.

Visual display unit: VDU. A computer terminal comprising a video display and keyboard which allows data to be entered, displayed, despatched or received from a computer.

Wanding. The process of moving a light or magnetic 'pen' or 'wand' across a machine readable code in order to record the coded information into a computer.

9

Intermediary Markets and Marketing

In 1969 David Morrel, then Assistant Managing Director of Tesco Stores, gave a talk at a conference in London. Two interrelated themes dominated his lecture:

1. The lack of proper consultation of the retailer by the manufacturer. 'All manufacturers in this country are concerned about is "what can we get in the store?", not "what does the supermarket operator want?".'
2. From the trader's perspective, retail marketing and selling (in this case supermarkets) are very different from manufacturer marketing. 'The principles of supermarket selling are quite simple: pile it high and sell it cheap; the best selling line in the best selling position; if you have any money to spend at all, spend it on discounts, spend it on incentive.'

Less than a year later, the Annual Conference of the Advertising Association returned to these issues when the main topic at the Conference was: 'Is the growing power of the retail chains against the public interest?'. The recurrent theme was that the power of the retail groups was so great that competition, innovativeness and profitability among manufacturers were being seriously eroded. Geoff Darby of Beecham's summarised these views later with the comment:

> So much buying power is today concentrated into the hands of so few retailers that these retailers are able to exert considerable influence upon the marketing activities of the manufacturer.

In the decade which followed, the discussion of retail or trade power has been a recurrent feature in marketing. Although the views have mellowed, the discussion has spilled into other areas of intermediary behaviour:

1. The BETRO Report on Britain's exports suggested that UK exporters were overdependent on agents.
2. British Leyland criticised many of their dealers for failing to increase their throughput.
3. Appliance manufacturers have demanded better service and repair facilities.

These discussions clearly demonstrate the importance of effective intermediary relationships and the central part they play in the marketing system. Despite that, there has been a tendency to view intermediary marketing as largely a service to manufacturers.

The success of many intermediaries has been based on the recognition that building up their business and its prosperity is dependent on understanding the needs of their customer. This goes far beyond the customer's need to have specific products stocked, and encompasses location, price, stock levels, range of goods, hours of opening and many other elements that make up the customer's relationship with his store.

CHANGES, DEVELOPMENTS AND COMPETITION

An intermediary or middleman is any firm or individual who provides a service between manufacturers and end-users in a channel of distribution (Figure 9.1). Continual pressures to improve channel services and reduce costs, along with relatively low costs of entry, result in intermediary patterns being in an almost constant state of change and development. For example, Electronic Brokers Ltd, a wholesale electronics merchandiser, started in 1967 with £4500 capital, and by 1979 had a turnover of £1 000 000; and Cartiers Superfoods (food supplies for home freezers) had initial capital of £79 in 1969 and when it went public in July 1979 it was worth over £4 000 000. Although the cost of entry can be low and the potential enormous, substantial risks face the intermediary. In fact, the largest single group of bankruptcy cases each year are normally drawn from the retail trade.

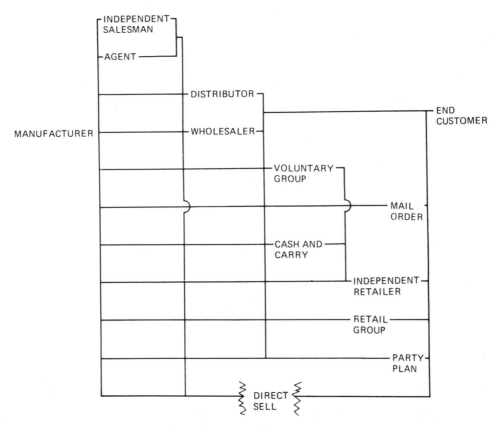

Fig. 9.1 Trading patterns.

This pattern of change and development is so significant that the concept of the 'wheel of retailing' has been coined to describe how new retailers can enter markets, generally as low-status, low-profit-margin, low-price operators. As they move up market, through improved customer service, better design and display etc., opportunities are created for new types of retailer. This useful rule of thumb can partly explain some of the major changes (Figure 9.2). However, it fails to explain either the persistence of certain types of outlet (e.g. fruit and vegetable markets continue to prosper) or some relatively high-price entries (e.g. vending machines and craft shops).

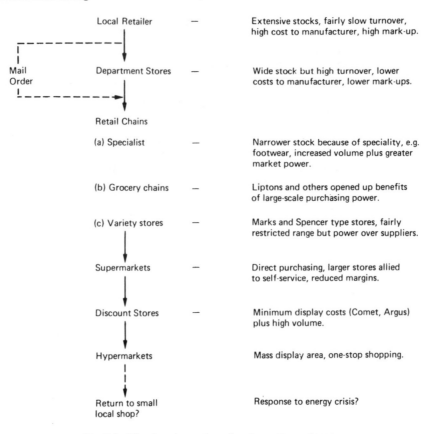

Fig. 9.2   The changing and overlapping pattern of trade.

AGENTS, DISTRIBUTORS AND WHOLESALERS

These can be described as the middlemen's middlemen. Their primary role for the customer is to provide access to a broad range of supplies so that the customer does not have to deal with each individual manufacturer.

Independent salesmen

These are sometimes called factory representatives, although they are not employed by any one firm. They act partly as salesmen and partly as intermediary managers. In the western industrial economies their role has generally been taken over by the selling agent, but in the Third World countries they provide local retailers with access to goods or opportunities to become dealers or distributors.

Agents

The major role of agents is the management of relations between customers and manufacturers. They do not become principals in the purchasing transaction but usually operate for a fee or commission. The agent's skill lies in selecting his client list carefully and then effectively selling their goods to appropriate wholesalers, distributors, and even end-users.

Although the pure selling function is important, the more sophisticated recognise that they are at the centre of a two-way communication process. Their customers will often have a number of different needs, and the agent's task will be to transfer information about these needs to his current clients as well as to seek new suppliers.

Distributors and wholesalers

Distributors and wholesalers share a willingness to hold stock, thus providing access to the physical product (rather than order processing by agents). Traditionally the distributor has been linked to a single supplier for each line he carries, while the wholesaler will often carry a number of competing lines.

The direct link between distributor and supplier usually means that far more extensive support facilities are provided, often in return for regional or industry exclusiveness. The provision of back-up services, as well as more extensive stock-holding, is critical to effective distributor marketing.

In the past, wholesalers played a dominant role in the distribution of many goods, and their scale of operation permitted them to exercise considerable power over their retail customers. In the first half of this century, however, this position of leadership was eroded by the giant manufacturers who stimulated customer 'pull', in part through media advertising and promotion. Since the 1950s their position has been further eroded by the growth of the major retailers, whose market power enabled them to bypass the wholesaler to deal direct with the manufacturers.

Fig. 9.3 The trade-marks and names of leading cash and carries.

More recently, wholesalers have exploited a number of inherent strengths to stage a limited come-back. A number have made use of their tradition of strong retailer links (primarily with the small independent stores) to build up voluntary groups such as VG, Mace and Spar. The sales forces of wholesalers (especially those in voluntary groups) have become skilled in providing advice and guidance to customers which goes far beyond the traditional sales task. The voluntary groups also conduct joint advertising.

Credit, delivery and high service levels are critical to their success. The restricted financial resources and limited staffing characteristic of most smaller retailers make the 'service' cost well worth paying. This pattern of support has been helped by the move by many manufacturers to restrict their selling and distribution services to smaller accounts.

For example, in the cigarette market these patterns created a gap in the mid 1970s that Philip Morris successfully exploited. Their launch into the UK was targeted on the wholesaler. They capitalised on the cutting back of direct supplies by some of the UK majors to small outlets with their inevitable move to wholesalers. At the time the UK majors were slow to react to this increased wholesaler significance.

The most important growth area in wholesaling has been in cash and carry operations (Figure 9.3). The idea behind these is simple: retailers, hoteliers and caterers are given the opportunity to 'supermarket shop'. Acting almost as giant supermarkets, with suitable trade discounts, they keep their overheads down while providing traders with access to goods. Normally located in out-of-town areas, their low overheads keep costs and prices down. A recurrent problem for cash and carry outlets is the 'rogue' buyer, i.e. the individual who uses the outlet for personal shopping. Retailers are hostile to any cash and carry which permits this to develop to proportions threatening their own livelihood.

The skill with which the major full-service wholesalers, such as Palmer and Harvey, the cash and carry firms and the voluntary chains have employed the marketing approach, often in the face of adverse trading conditions, demonstrates its relevance, in its fullest sense, in this sector.

RETAIL MARKETING

The direct nature of the relationship between the retailer and his customer has always given a sense of immediacy to the satisfaction of buyer needs in this area. The great retail entrepreneurs—Thomas Lipton, Lord Sainsbury, Marcus Sieff, Isaac Wolfson, Terence Conran and many others—have succeeded by adapting their complex offerings to customer needs. Over the past twenty years this traditionally intuitive approach has been matched by a determination to fully exploit the marketing concept.

Fig. 9.4 Advertising and retailing.

Retail advertising (Figure 9.4) leapt from £56 million in 1970 to £307 million in 1978. This was an increase of 548 per cent against an overall national increase of 33 per cent. Although main media advertising plays an important part in the promotion of the retail trade, the stores themselves still dominate their image. The character of the store, F. W. Woolworth, Marks and Spencer, Boots, Tesco, Sainsbury's, Habitat, John Lewis and almost every retail outlet, is created to a considerable extent by the design, layout, appearance and staffing of the store itself. The pattern of increasing retail concentration mentioned earlier has created a situation in which the store groups are increasingly investing in these areas to ensure their continued growth and prosperity.

Major types of retail outlet

The following are the main retail outlets:

1. Independent retailer: corner grocer, independent chemist, small group of retailers (probably not more than fifteen outlets).
2. Retail chains: typified by the large supermarket chain but including some speciality stores, e.g. W. H. Smith or Boots.
3. Department stores: large general-goods stores offering an enormous array of goods.
4. Co-operative societies: usually 'owned' in some way by consumers. Traditionally, profits are returned to them by dividends or stamps.
5. Voluntary trading groups: alliances of independent traders who act together to realise economies.
6. Door-to-door delivery: specialist carriers, usually delivering a limited selection of goods to customers.
7. Cash and carry discount shops: retailers offering a minimum of service and presentation at low prices, e.g. Comet.

The post-war period has seen an increasing concentration in this sector, with the independent retailers, co-operative stores and department stores steadily losing ground to the retail groups and chains.

Successful marketing among retailers is based on the effective management of product array, location, pricing and promotional policies.

Product

The product mix offered to the customer provides the customer with his clues to the type and fashions change. An illustration of this is the problems which faced the Burton Group product offering.

Adaptability in this area is a major problem, as strengths can become liabilities as tastes and fashions change. An illustrtion of this is the problems which faced the Burton Group in 1977. The established strength of the group in providing reasonably priced, made-to-measure suits, with substantial vertical integration (from sheep to shop), caused major problems when tastes moved to ready-to-wear, high-fashion clothing.

Stock is not there merely to attract customers. Stock turn-around is a major factor in determining retail profitability, and therefore requires a thorough appraisal of all lines in terms of their contribution to income and the part they play in moving other items and lines. The idea of the loss leader in supermarket shopping illustrates this interdependence of lines. Specific products are sold at very low prices, perhaps even at a loss, with the aim of drawing in customers who will purchase enough other items to pay off the firm's investment. As a concept, it has become linked in supermarkets and hypermarkets to the notion of one-stop shopping, where the customer is encouraged to do all his shopping in one outlet. This saves him time but also gives significant boosts to the average shopper's expenditure.

'Own label', sometimes called 'private-label', brands play an important part in retailing:

Own-label products are defined as consumer products produced by, or on behalf of, distributors and sold under the distributor's own name or trade-mark through the distributor's own outlet.

Economist Intelligence Unit,
'Own Brand Marketing',
Retail Business, October, 1968

For a time during the late 1960s and early 1970s the growth of own-label brands in supermarkets was seen as a threat to the viability of many manufacturer's brands:

> The manufacturer finds that his brand is under fire from the private label products which usurp what he has come to regard as his own shelf space in the store and consequently part of his sales.

G. Darby[1]

For a time the strength of own-labels such as St Michael and Sainsbury's, allied to the appearance of own-label products in most major retail groups and the voluntary associations, seemed to confirm this. However, over the past few years the share of own-label brands has stabilised, although individual own-label brands have grown. The policies of particular stores vary (see Table 9.1).

Table 9.1   *Private-label share of grocery sales*

Twelve weeks ending	Aug. 1975	Aug. 1976	Aug. 1977	Aug. 1978	Aug. 1983
Tesco %	24	24	23	23	24
Sainsbury %	67	65	62	57	63

Source: AGB/TCA.

Private-label is now recognised as a tactic which can play a part in building a product mix and reinforcing imagery, but only one aspect of this. The key factors in introducing own-label are: improved gross or net margin; low prices; own-label brands which are good value becoming associated with the store and assisting in building loyalty; supply problems with established brands.

Location

Perhaps the most important decision facing a retailer or distributor is the location of his outlet. In many senses his primary offering to the consumer is location, or availability. In the past such decisions have been simplified by the desire to establish outlets in or near shopping centres or on the high street. More recently, however, some major stores have established an ability to attract custom. A Marks and Spencer shop nearby might ensure sufficient interest in the location to justify the high rents involved in siting near Marks and Spencer.

One of the earliest attempts to provide a more systematic approach to retail location analysis was the work of Reilly[2] on the gravitational pull of specific positions on trade from adjoining areas. This model has been developed further to incorporate such issues as the relation between distance and size, the topography of the area, ease of access (public transport, road networks and parking) and communication (catchment areas of local radio, TV and newspapers) (Figure 9.5).

Checklists are commonly used to gauge the potential of specific locations in terms of such criteria. An example of a location checklist is: rent; rates; frontage (to main street); area of shop; local expenditure on items held; competition in area; distance from firm's other outlets; local population (catchment area defined); composition of population; physical characteristics of outlet; availability of labour; character of area; adjoining outlets.

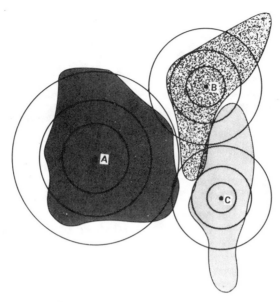

Fig. 9.5   The drawing power of different outlets A, B and C, weighted by ease of travel. From T. Cannon, *Distribution Research*. London: Intertext, 1973.

Prices

A glance at the type of advertising used by retailers or in store promotion shows the importance given to price in retail promotion (Figure 9.6). Most retail pricing is a mixture of mark-up prices, specific promotions and targeting on specific markets. The overall level of prices and the prominence given to price in promotion (both in and out of store) are generally conditioned by the store's target market and desired image. For example, price may be an aspect of the appeal of Sainsbury's but it generally receives relatively little prominence.

The major exception to this in retailing is the sale. Sales are used by retailers for a variety of reasons: clearing stock, ironing out seasonalities, renewing interest in the store, and publicity. They have the special characteristic that even a store which targets itself on upper-income groups, such as Harrods, can run a sale with no risk to its overall image.

Until now the discussion of retailing has focused on semi- and non-durable goods. The trader in durables (cars, household appliances etc.) faces many of the same stocking, pricing and location problems, but his marketing also needs to take into account the high value (per unit) of his items and the service and warranty requirements of his customers. Stock turnover is critical when the item could be worth anything between £1000 and £20 000. This places particular importance on the role of the salesman in the transaction. Generally the durables salesman will be expected to do far more than simply collect an order. He may need to arrange credit, handle technical questions, negotiate trade-ins and handle immediate post-sale problems. The scale of this involvement and the need for manufacturers to be confident that these transactions were being conducted effectively contributed to the growth of producer franchising.

FRANCHISING

Until very recently franchising in Britain was associated with manufacturer-led operations. Two forms dominated:

Fig. 9.6 Consumer advertising by retail group highlights the importance of price. Reproduced with the permission of Key Markets.

1.   Agencies: in areas such as cosmetics, it is frequently the policy of manufacturers to give individual pharmacists or other outlets sole rights to retail a product in return for some agreements about display and support service, e.g. a trained beautician on the staff.
2.   Dealerships: in the case of many consumer durables, such as cars, the dealer is given exclusive rights to an area. Normally he is not allowed to handle competitive lines. He may also be required to meet a number of predetermined conditions and be subject to inspection.

The operations of dealer-owned petrol stations and tied houses in brewing meet the broad definition of a franchise: 'a contractual agreement allowing a customer to use a supplier's name and receive assistance in location, merchandising, or other matters in return for the purchase for resale of the supplier's product or a separately specified franchise fee'.

Recently, there has been a surge of interest in franchising[3] as new firms, building on the American experience, use franchise arrangements as a spur to growth. In the USA it is estimated that franchise operations account for just over 30 per cent of all retail sales and 10 per cent of the gross national product.

The appeal of franchising is threefold:

1. To the customer it offers a reassurance of quality and service based on previous awareness or experience of the franchise.
2. To the prospective franchisor it offers fast growth with minimum strain on his capital.
3. To the prospective franchisee it offers the chance to become an entrepreneur while having the reassurance of a tried and tested product or service, backed by promotion and support services.

Although there has been criticism, there is little doubt that many existing franchises are operating very effectively and that scope for growth, in both the concept and the range of industries encompassed, exists.

THE FUTURE

If franchising provides one insight into the future, a number of other aspects are likely to play at least as significant a role. Marketing under conditions of recession and the energy crisis present the intermediary with specific problems.

The major retailers have responded to the prospect of difficult trading conditions by:

1. Reducing the service offered: the pay policy has hit hard an industry which is both low-wage and labour-intensive. Consequently, retailers have been looking for ways to reduce their labour bill, such as staff reductions, less overtime and greater use of part-time staff.
2. Reducing stock levels: retail stocks are down in volume terms compared with 1974. Most retailers claim to carry fewer brands and fewer variations within product lines so as to reduce the capital tied up and improve cash flow.
3. Closing smaller outlets.
4. Pushing own labels: there has been a swing back to own labels in some retail chains.
5. Offering more price-off deals: recession has meant that price offers are the only guaranteed way of moving stocks.
6. Operating differential price policies: as price has become more and more important to the consumer store loyalty has weakened.

Almost universally, major retailers have de-stocked during the recession: only one of those interviewed in recent research was going against this trend.

The fact that there has been a general de-stocking in the retail trade does not mean that there is any less interest in new products. If anything, the reverse is true. There is one phrase that seems to be universally used to describe new products: they are 'the life-blood of the business'; they are welcome any time.

The larger retailers, particularly in the food field, no longer think so much of the terms that they can get from manufacturers, but rather of the total 'deal' or 'package' that they can negotiate.

There is no doubt about the importance that retailers attach to 'price' as the key factor in determining consumer purchasing patterns: all put it at the top of the list and say that its importance is increasing.

The main development over the next decade is expected to be large-scale, out-of-town retail units.

The energy crisis may have a dramatic effect on the move towards out-of-town shopping, since increasing petrol prices and the prospect of shortages may lead to a revival of the local store. This, however, is unlikely to be a mere copy of the traditional outlet. The history of innovation and dynamism that has characterised intermediary marketing suggests that a radical new development, perhaps based on new data-processing techniques or the entrepreneurial flair of an individual, will emerge.

Notes

1. Darby, G., 'A Manufacturer's Views on Below the Line Activity', *Admap*, 4th World Advertising Workshop, 1971.
    Reilly, W. J., 'Methods of Studying Retail Relationships'. In *Research Monograph 4, Bulletin 2994*. Austen: University of Texas Bureau of Business Research, 1929.
3. The reader is referred to the excellent review of the current situation in franchising, Stanworth, J. & Curran, J., 'Franchising at the Crossroads', *Marketing*, April, 1978.

Further reading

Cannon, T., *Distribution Research*. London: Intertext, 1973.
McNair, M. P. & May, E. G., 'The Next Revolution of the Retailing Wheel', *Harvard Business Review*, September–October, 1978. A stimulating review of the problems and opportunities in retailing today.
Snadden, P., *Starting a Retail Business*, Small Firms' Information Service, 1976. A useful brief introduction to the issues facing the small retailer (free).
Note. There is an urgent need for sustained research and writing in the UK in this field. At the moment journals such as *Marketing, Journal of Retailing* (US) and *Forbes Magazine* (US), and the biographies of leading figures in the industry, provide the best insights.

Key organisations

Retail Consortium,
Commonwealth House,
New Oxford St,
London WC1

National Union of Small Shopkeepers of Great Britain
   and Northern Ireland,
Westminster Buildings,
Theatre Square,
Nottingham

Economist Intelligence Unit (Publishers of *Retail Business*),
Spenser House,
27 St James's Place,
London SW1 1NT

CASE STUDY 7: PANDORA (ARTS AND CRAFTS) CONSIDERS A NEW OUTLET

History

Pandora is a group of three retail craft shops based in South-West England. It was started in 1972 by John Jackson and Graham Lonsdale, two graduates of Bristol Polytechnic's BSc. in Management Studies.

Their first shop was in Bristol. Eighteen months later a store was opened in Bath and two years after this an outlet in Cardiff was added. Since then, the shops' turnover and range of items carried have grown steadily. John and Graham have been reluctant to consider further shops while consolidating their existing business. This has not prevented their moving premises twice in the last three years as superior sites in Bristol and Bath became available.

The range carried

Their original concept in starting Pandora was to provide an outlet for the increasing numbers of individual craftsmen, both those already working and those just starting up, in the South-West and South Wales. Although individual local craftsmen, potters, jewellers, brass-workers etc. continue to provide a large part of their range the business has expanded in a number of other directions.

Links have been built up with a number of cottage industries, primarily knitwear. Graham in particular has played a substantial role in encouraging a few of their better 'designer/craftsmen' to expand in this direction, recruiting knitting or dressmaking outworkers.

A recurrent problem of obtaining good-quality stock has encouraged this development. This problem led to a more widespread search for stock, and they now have goods coming from all parts of the UK. This has led to links being established with craft guilds in the Midlands, the Lake District, Northumbria and Scotland, as well as with local groups.

A few years ago the stock problem was so serious that quite large quantities of goods were being imported from Europe and North Africa. This led to some adverse comment from some craftsmen and arguments between John and Graham, as Graham was very worried about losing their high-quality craft position in the market. However, the problems have eased as their supplies of UK crafts have increased. Imported items are now less than 15 per cent of turnover (by volume) and are concentrated in the low-price end of their range.

The current situation

The financial period 1978/79 was the best year Pandora have ever had. Profits were good while the range and quality of the items carried were probably better than ever before. They held a number of exhibitions for well-known artist-craftsmen, which gained excellent publicity both locally, with major features in the *Bristol Evening News* and BBC South-West, and nationally, in a number of craft magazines.

In the light of these developments, John is keen to open a new outlet. Although an equal partner, he has a full-time job as a lecturer in computer science at Portsmouth Polytechnic, and would like the shop to be in this area. Graham, however, who works full-time in the business, is uncertain about this. Both agree to a more wide-ranging review of their options, and this results in the following choices:

1. Continual consolidation with a progressive improvement in range: Graham greatly prefers this as it would probably free him to develop his own craft interest as a carpenter/toymaker.
2. Open a new outlet but in the same general South-West region, in Cheltenham, Exeter or Plymouth.
3. Use their links with the craft community to develop a wholesale side to their business, perhaps even involving them in exports.

4.   Open the outlet in Portsmouth suggested by John, but bearing in mind that he will still work only part-time in the business.

This is perhaps the most critical problem facing them at the start of the 1980s.

Task

Advise on a policy.

10

Industrial Markets

In 1965 Aubrey Wilson introduced a collection of readings on the subject of marketing industrial goods with the comment:

> Industrial marketing is so broad a subject, so vital for individual firms and for the economy, that it is truly remarkable why so few books specifically on this subject have appeared in the UK.

This book itself is now out of print and, apart from a relatively small number of exceptional contributions, the area is still badly neglected, relative to consumer-goods marketing. This does not reflect any relative insignificance of the sector: there are more firms and more areas of activity encompassed by industrial marketing than by consumer marketing. Britain's exports are dominated by industrial goods: an estimated 60 per cent of manufactured exports.

One of the fundamental objectives of this text is to seek to give a better balance in coverage. As a deliberate policy, discussion of the implications for industrial marketers of many of the points made are included in the specific sections. In this chapter some of these points will be brought together and the special character of industrial markets reviewed.

ARE INDUSTRIAL MARKETS DIFFERENT?

Two definitions help show the areas in which industrial markets may have their own special character:

> Industrial marketing: All those activities concerned with purchases, sales and service in industrial markets and between organisational buyer and seller.
>
> A. Wilson[1]

> Industrial buyers are those buying goods and services for some tangibly productive and commercially significant purpose.[2]

The character of industrial marketing lies partly in the goods and services offered, partly in the goals of buying and partly in the buyers themselves.

The goods themselves are not necessarily unique. A manufacturing firm buys paper, tea, tools, food, banking services, telephone and postal services, cars, travel, adhesives, pens, pencils and many other items that end-users buy. In these days of Do-It-Yourself, the handy-man might even be buying bricks, sanding equipment or gravel, items which are traditionally associated with builders, manufacturers and other industrial markets. However, in the purchasing of many items, such as heavy lifting gear, many components, manufacturing and processing equipment and advertising and promotional services, no ambiguity exists. These 'industrial' goods and services are identifiable, but the borderline, if we use products to differentiate, is hazy.

The purpose for which items are purchased provides a clearer area of difference. The industrial firm buys goods and services for a 'tangibly productive and commercially significant purpose'. The company wants to earn some form of tangible return from its purchase. Paper for correspondence is part of the communication process, and assists internal efficiencies or external relations. At least in theory, a balance between pay-offs and expenditures can be specified. Tea might be bought for the works canteen, itself an element in the effective management and operation of the organisation.

This should not be taken to mean that behavioural factors do not affect choice or even the decision to purchase specific items. In a now famous experiment, Levitt[3] demonstrated how a minor design change enhancing the appearance of a piece of industrial equipment significantly improved its sales. More recently, a northern plastics moulder used Penthouse Pets to promote his chair mouldings at an exhibition, with startling improvements in orders taken. This does not mean that this type of tactic *will* improve performance, merely that it *can*, even in a relatively undifferentiated area such as chair mouldings.

Although in consumer markets there are cases in which goods or services are purchased with a view to returns (e.g. housing repairs and specific items such as installing central heating may be viewed as improving the selling price, or individuals may get their car serviced and buy touch-up paint in order to improve the car's price), in the normal course of events the purchaser probably owns the items concerned for reasons other than their resale value.

The part played by the industrial buyer or purchasing officer is an important area of differentiation. They enter the purchasing process for commercial reasons, and it is their job to ensure that efficiencies exist and that optimum policies are adopted by the firm in all areas of organisation purchasing. Organisational purchasing is the process by which organisations define their needs for goods and services, identify and compare the suppliers and supplies available to them, negotiate with sources of supply or in some other way arrive at agreed terms of trading, make contracts and place orders and finally receive the goods and services and pay for them. The buyer may be a senior executive of a large corporation, versed in value analysis, material management and other developments, or the chief executive of a small firm.

Although the housewife, car buyer, photo-freak or house buyer may be able to invest considerable expertise in specific areas, the continuing need to weight consequences and alternatives is far more real for the industrial buyer. His position may be enhanced by greater market power, closer relationships and technical expertise.

Although industrial markets and consumer markets often merge, there are substantial qualitative differences, with which the industrial marketer must learn to cope.

DERIVED DEMAND

Holding together the points of difference mentioned above is a central, common element: the demand state of the industrial customer derives from the demand by others for his offerings.

For the consumer-goods producer in Figure 10.1, his demand for the various items he buys is a function of the state of his markets. He might open up a new export market generating a further 10 per cent demand. This will increase his raw material needs and perhaps his equipment and labour requirements, but probably not his plant. Loss of a market such as (b) will probably reverse these trends. Over time, equipment ordering and labour needs will be affected, particularly if other losses occur. It will be only when the business has ceased to be viable that the plant needs change.

This derived demand goes some way towards explaining the lags that occur in demand for industrial goods. Increased demand will show itself first to the consumer-goods producers, then in the demand for raw materials, and later in the equipment, labour and

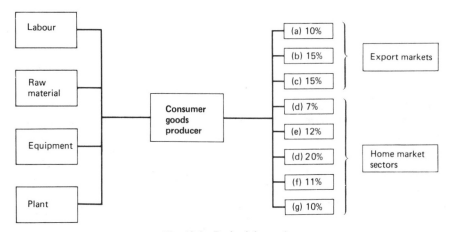

Fig. 10.1 Derived demand.

plant markets. Similarly, these markets tend to be slower to respond to downturns. External factors can directly affect these patterns: the much heralded economic downturn of the late 1970s has been accompanied by firms' deferring plant, equipment and labour recruitment decisions in anticipation of a future decline in demand, even if their own order books are not yet affected.

The derived nature of demand places an onus on industrial-goods suppliers to think their systems through. Customer 'pull' can be a more important determinant of demand than any sales effort.

> To effectively break these (resistances to new products) down, the manufacturer must accept the prime responsibility for approaching all levels of the system.
>
> Briscoe, Cannon and Lewis[4]

> The rapid growth in the market for silicon rubber heat seals in cookers derived in part from fears among consumers of asbestos seals.
>
> Managing director of silicon rubber producing firm

An awareness of the customer markets and an understanding of the forces affecting them can play a major part in ensuring the firm's long-term prosperity.

SELLERS AND BUYERS

It would be a mistake to see the industrial buyer as a passive participant in this push–pull process. It is as much his job to buy as it is the salesman's to sell, and to that extent they are in partnership. Clearly this does not mean that the buyer is under an obligation to buy from a specific salesman. It does mean that understanding marketing is becoming an increasing feature of the purchasing officer's job.

In many industrial buying situations the industrial, technological and negotiating skills, as well as the overall professionalism of the buyer, are important factors in the selling/purchasing context. Often the buyer is operating in a fairly narrow and technical area, e.g. he might be responsible for all packaging requirements of a large consumer-goods manufacturer. His knowledge places a considerable 'product knowledge' requirement on the salesman.

This professionalism means that industrial buyers are capable of seeing criteria other than price on which to judge a firm's offerings. At the same time, the behavioural forces mentioned earlier influence decision. In studies of how industry buys[5] it was found that: a significant proportion of buyers would not switch suppliers for price cuts of up to 10 per cent; and assured delivery was normally more important than quick delivery. However, perhaps the results of empirical testing of the relationship between these attitudes and buyer actions should be known before it is totally accepted. Nevertheless, it suggests that the professional buyer recognises the relevance of product development, service levels, and communications as much as price in his purchase choice.

The emerging recognition of this broader purchasing role has led to significant advances in 'the art and science of source management' over the last decade. Procurement, supplies and source management are becoming key areas of management decision. In a wide range of industrial goods purchasing staff are adopting a more active role in:

1. Resource planning: evaluation of likely resource situations is becoming a part of corporate planning. This in turn places extra responsibilities on purchasing staff to recognise the impact of political, economic and other environmental forces.
2. Purchasing research: some companies are attempting to make routine the search process itself. Technical staff may be given responsibility for seeking ways of improving purchase performance, even to explore current manufacturing procedures.
3. Value analysis: the firms adopting this perspective call upon their buyers to review the whole purchase act, not just the price but also specification, stocks and delivery times, in order to bring out the real savings that are possible.
4. Materials analysis: this focuses on two aspects of supplies: the total costs of key items and the real returns from being involved in these expenditures. Materials-analysis teams involve staff who have a range of functions, enabling them to get to the root of total product make-up and hence procurement policies.

Purchasing staff are being directed more and more toward a constant scanning of the horizon. There is some evidence that besides placing pressures on the salesman's product knowledge, demands on the supplier's communication, and calls on suppliers to consider carefully their service and delivery levels, these developments are posing questions for supplier technology. The product life-cycle is likely to shorten if the purchaser actively searches for newer, superior or simply cheaper ways of more effectively meeting his procurement goals.

Hitherto in this discussion a critical aspect of the buyer's situation has been played down: this aspect is risk. All his purchasing involves some degree of risk. For example, a new supplier may not deliver, thus disrupting product schedules; a new material may not run properly, costing large sums in machine time and waste; or an established supplier's service may deteriorate. The risks involved directly affect all the buyer's evaluation processes, and his response to salesmen is affected by this.

Risk avoidance, allied to certain minimum 'satisficing'[6] policies, may lead to a considerable degree of conservatism in purchase policies. Swedish researchers[7] found that procurement staff were reluctant to buy from smaller overseas firms: when trial orders were placed, they kept in very close, almost daily contact, for reassurance. Breakdowns or problems in communication, e.g. home staff not passing on messages or being unable to speak any foreign languages, created severe tensions even when not accompanied by a failure to perform well. This Swedish research has much in common with Levitt's findings[8] on the interplay between communication and industrial setting, discussed later. Important recent European research with contributions by Cunningham and Ford[9] have highlighted the interactive and continuous nature of the purchasing process.

FACTORS AFFECTING THE DEGREE OF RISK FROM BUYER'S VIEW

The following are the factors which have the greatest effect on the degree of risk:[9] size of expenditure; degree of novelty; extent to which product is essential; source of purchase decision; self-confidence of buyer (general); self-confidence of buyer (in this specific situation); experience; purchasing history; professionalism; size and financial position of firm; company purchasing structure.

All these factors do not come into play every time a purchase is made. There are a number of different buying situations faced by the buyer, which in turn pose problems for the prospective or actual supplier. These can be broadly compared with the problem-solving situations noted in consumer behaviour.

The most complex purchase situation is probably the first-time purchase, involving new products, new material, new services, new suppliers or even a new buyer. In this situation there is likely to be an extensive search. This provides the supplier with a major opportunity, as the customer is looking for solutions to a recognised problem. An important difference between consumer and industrial 'extensive search' is that the technical knowledge and buying power of the industrial customer provides the scope for far more substantial dialogue. In many instances the customer will specify, in considerable detail through drawings or a specification sheet, his requirements. The most extreme case of this is when individual projects are put out to tender, allowing a number of firms to bid for particular work.

A recurrent problem of firms supplying industrial customers is deciding which of the many requests to quote that they receive they should follow through completely. A typical medium-sized engineering firm may receive as many as thirty invitations in a single week, both from home and from overseas, so quoting fully for each would take up a considerable amount of time and resources. There is no simple answer to this problem. It involves having a clear strategy indicating the types of business desired and continuing research into the market-place to more effectively estimate which business can be won.

A great deal of industrial business involves modified rebuys. Here changes may have been introduced internally, perhaps in the product sold by the firm, in required technical specifications, or in purchasing policies or personnel. The degree of source loyalty will generally determine the extent of and commitment to the search (comparable with 'limited problem-solving').

Under normal circumstances the modified rebuy involves approaching a restricted number of prospective suppliers. It will be more extensive when a technical or material change is being introduced, i.e. when existing suppliers cannot adapt, as in the case of asbestos cooker seals mentioned earlier.

For the supplier the most intractable situation is the straight rebuy. The customer is likely to have established suppliers and no immediate, internal reasons to look for alternative sources. These situations can encompass items like stationery, raw materials and mouldings. In the case of moulds or components the situation may be more complex because ownership of tools is often shared. An injection moulder may have part ownership of the tool, and to move to another supplier could mean £12 000 to £15 000 for a new tool, or a proportion of this to buy the old tool from the current supplier. The problems are compounded by the likelihood of reduced services while the account is being changed.

These situations apply to service requirements as well as to physical goods. Advertising agency services are an industrial supply. An agency looking for business must consider: accounts where they have been asked to 'pitch' because the business is being moved; situations where the current agency will be making a presentation of its own, to try to hold on to the account; those occasions on which it is believed that the client is dissatisfied with the performance of the existing agency; trying for some desired accounts where there is no current movement. Another aspect of industrial buying is introduced by this situation. The purchasing officer is very unlikely to be involved in recruiting, selecting, or managing advertising agencies. In most firms this is firmly rooted in top management or marketing.

In many industrial selling situations, identifying exactly who controls, specifies and even places the order can be a major part of the selling task.

THE BUYING COALITION

In many industrial buying situations other members of the firm's management and staff will be directly involved in deciding whether to buy, specifying the product, and considering alternative offerings and supplier choice. The location of those members of the firm and their influence can vary enormously (Table 10.1).

Table 10.1   *Those involved in buying*

Group	Areas
Top management (board level)	Plant, capital equipment, key services, e.g. banking .
Product management	Raw materials, printing and packaging, main energy sources
Engineering	Equipment, tools
Marketing	Raw materials and components, advertising, promotional services

In some firms and in certain areas purchasing may not be directly involved at all: a secretary ordering an airline ticket for a director is buying, but this may not involve purchasing. In the majority of firms and in most situations the purchasing staff will be involved, but as part of a buying coalition, which is a group, organised formally or otherwise, of staff or management involved in industrial procurement policy through: specification, advice, information, transference or discretionary authority.

It has been suggested by Hill and Hillier that it is useful to compare the firm's buying operation with the structure of an atom (Figure 10.2). Next to the core (1) lie those directly involved in the decision (2). The company may be introducing a new product, so

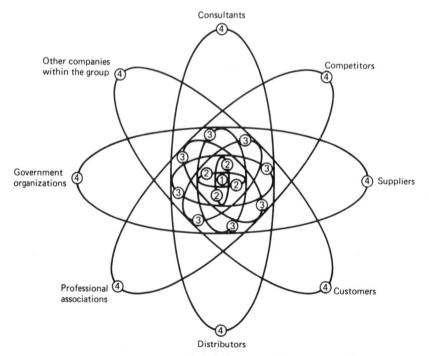

Fig. 10.2   The buying operation. Reproduced with permission. Hill, R. W. & Hillier, T. J., *Organizational Buying Behaviour*. London and Basingstoke: Macmillan, 1977.

purchasing staff, production, research and development and marketing will be directly involved. Other members of the firm (3) may be requested to provide specific or general information, e.g. distribution management on problems of packing or transport, market research on market testing. Outside the firm are various other individuals or organisations (4) who may exert influence, e.g. the advertising agency might point out that delivering the advertising promise calls for product improvements, or the Motor Industry Research Unit might point out that the specifications fall short of UK or overseas standards.

Most industrial marketing is directed at the buying centre (those directly involved), so identifying them is the first stage in the selling effort. Their relative positions and relationships are critical. For example: marketing may have the final say in display materials but consider it totally inappropriate for companies selling display materials to approach them, other than through the purchasing department; media salesmen may approach brand management with 'special deals', but the firm may take a very firm line that all bookings are made directly with the retained agency; in some firms minor modifications in product make-up, and even supplies, may be vetoed by sales and marketing, if it is felt that they will significantly affect sales.

A number of studies of how industry buys have been conducted which clearly show the importance of understanding these interrelationships.

TACKLING INDUSTRIAL MARKETS

The differences in the structure of the buying process and the types of buyer pose a challenge to the firm operating in industrial markets. In the past the supermarket philosophy 'pile it high and sell it cheap' has been echoed all too often. In an environment in which the range of skills invested in the purchasing process is considerable, the best approach is one which recognises the many variables influencing choice.

Price is important. Comparing prices is part of the buyer's job, and where no difference in the offerings of the suppliers exists it is his duty to purchase the cheapest. Competing on price and seeking ways to keep prices down is part of the marketing effort in industrial markets. It also exists in consumer markets, but the consumer may lack the time or skill to judge offerings, so some simple rule of thumb may be developed. Cost and price cutting should not mean merely biting into profitability. Standards can be checked. Some customers who are particularly sensitive to price may accept product adaptations (cheaper materials, shorter life-span) to keep prices low. Others may accept shorter credit, longer lead times or reduced warranty.

Many firms embarking on this type of exercise soon find that the single homogeneous price-conscious customer group is actually a far more complex group accepting rather than preferring certain standards. Minor adaptations to meet their particular needs can become a hedge against cut-throat price competition. Warranty and service policies can be particularly effective here. Machinery breakdowns or production lines out of action can quickly offset small price savings. Warranties have the important side-effect of reducing buyer risk.

It is not enough to introduce improved standards in these areas: communicating them to existing and prospective customers is vital. Considerable evidence now exists to illustrate how important a well thought-out promotion strategy can be to the industrial-goods producer. Buyers are constantly seeking information that they can use or store, and media advertising can do much to enhance awareness and the image of firms. Small companies often suffer from buyer reluctance to trade simply because they are small and unknown.

Brochures are probably the main non-personal promotional medium for the majority of firms. One merely needs to go into the sales office of a small engineering firm to see stacks of expensive brochures stored in cupboards or piled on shelves to realise the importance of planning the use of material.

The media balance in industrial markets shows great differences. It is, however, in the contribution of the salesman, technical representative or sales engineer that the difference in the promotion mix is most clearly demonstrated. The salesman is the main intermediary between the firm and its customers. His knowledge, skill and authority must at least match those of his customer. In smaller and medium-sized firms, top management often recognises this by becoming directly involved in the selling exercise. This is unfortunately an area in which Britain lags behind its major industrial rivals—in the qualifications and rewards of industrial sales staff as well as in active support for them. Expenditure on the sales force is estimated to account for 60 to 70 per cent of total promotional expenditure.

Systems selling has emerged as vital to the marketing effort in capital-goods markets. It is based on the proposition that the real cost to the customer includes his management and organisation of the project he is developing. The supplier, by taking over the functions of project control, purchasing related items, planning, and even construction, can offer significant savings to the buyer. As the seller is likely to have more experience of this type of exercise than the buyer, he has scope for further economies. The expertise of the systems selling team can become a major asset to the producer. They can seldom replace the individual representatives, but can become a major feature in his selling armoury.

Selling agents play a major part in the marketing of industrial goods, particularly in overseas markets. The carefully recruited, selected and managed agent can play an important role in the firm's success. It is an unfortunate feature of the approach of some firms that, instead of seeing agents primarily in terms of the special contribution they can make, they view them in terms of the money saved through not employing salesmen. A well managed agent need not save money but should provide expertise, knowledge and access to markets.

These large capital-goods projects introduce into the marketing effort a need to appreciate the workings of the financial and credit systems. The probability that any industrial order involves issues related to cash flow means that finance and credit are integral parts of industrial marketing. Negotiating the length of credit and chasing up late payments may be part of the industrial marketing man's job. Judging the credit risk in dealing with specific customers is a recurrent problem, and credit policies are a major feature of the industrial marketing mix. Recent interest in rental and leasing policies reflects the priority given to this area.

SEGMENTS AND MARKETS

The concept of subdividing markets into more homogeneous segments has been one of the more successful transfers of a consumer marketing idea to industrial markets. The basic notion of geographical segmentation has guided industrial operations, at least unconsciously, for many years. A good illustration is the concentration of certain supply industries around the main fabricator industries. (The word 'fabricator' is used here merely to describe a company making some item from some other firm's goods. It is often used to describe producers of final customer lines.)

Shipbuilding in the North East and Scotland attracted large numbers of companies serving their needs, providing everything from welding equipment to steel. Motor-car production in the East Midlands and the South East has helped create and sustain major supplier industries, many of whom are not independent of the motor trade.

Standard Industrial Classifications provide guidelines for segmentation for some firms. The company targets its efforts on, for example, the foundry industry or small boatbuilders. Government statistics can then provide information about numbers of firms, their average turnover and other aspects of their operations. As in the case of consumer markets it has now been recognised that these externally measured (organisational) demographics are, at best, a very crude mechanism of targeting.

Approaches focusing more closely on behaviour and need are emerging from the study of industrial buying. Some of these are based on actual operations. For example: firms in industries such as plastics moulding, rubber processing etc. have a recurrent hopper-feeding need, and producers might concentrate on firms with this type of requirement; companies operating in overseas markets may require special types of financial services, so finance houses may introduce special types of credit factoring.

Other approaches focused on new buying are being conducted in specific firms. Sheth[10] raises the potential contribution of lifestyle as a determinant of buyer behaviour. As interest in this area grows the type of approach and the skill with which it is applied are likely to improve considerably.

INDUSTRY

So far in this chapter the complex nature of the industrial market-place has been played down to provide a fairly consistent basis for discussion. There is a considerable amount of variation in the types of industrial customer and industrial firm. Often there is some ambiguity in the approach to the topic of industrial marketing in this area: is the marketing *to* or *by* industrial firms? The answer is both. Many of the firms operating in the industrial market-place face special problems caused as much by the character of their offering as by the customers they deal with.

Process producers

Often process producers work entirely to customer specifications. To talk of their product is wrong, as their real offering is capacity, technology and service. The salesman's technical abilities are often the most important feature, but generally they need to be backed by flexible and fast-moving production units. As a result many process industries are characterised by large numbers of small firms built around sales-orientated, engineering entrepreneurs.

Capital goods

These are a total contrast to process industries. Since the scale of some projects is enormous, some of the world's largest firms have been daunted by the risks involved. Governments have become major participants in this area, by providing insurance and coverage against certain types of risk.

This area of business encompasses large construction projects, technological development, projects such as supplying a new engine for an aircraft project, shipping, aircraft and some specialised areas of engineering or exploration. In these projects even the smallest details can involve large sums of money, even determining the profitability of the entire venture. The sales and marketing men involved will need a breadth of vision capable of ranging over different types of payment systems, levels of liability and the form it takes, and perhaps relations with other members of a consortium. Stamina is necessary, since such contracts may take months, or even years, to finalise. Throughout that period an error of judgement can endanger the long period of time invested. With the costs involved, targeting on specific projects or areas of activity can be essential, and accumulated expertise can save considerable time and reduce costs dramatically.

Even in areas where there are traditions of operating all projects on a one-off basis, marketing principles can play a major part. The success of SD14 by Austin and Pickersgill exemplifies this. Shipbuilding has a long history of tailor-making every vessel to the owner's specification. Sunderland Shipbuilders reversed this by producing a standard vessel based on careful market appraisal. This resulted in one of the most noticeable success stories in British shipbuilding in recent years.

Engineering firms, highly technical companies and basic-material producers

These and many other types of firm face particular problems in trying to open up industrial markets. Marketing staff involved in these areas are recognising the scope for adapting the marketing concept to match their particular circumstances.

CONCLUSION

There remains a continuing need to invest time and effort in the study of industrial markets. Some of the researchers mentioned earlier, centres such as Aston, organisations like the Institute of Marketing and the CAM Foundation, specialised bodies, and journals such as *Marketing, Industrial Marketing* and *Industrial Advertising and Marketing* are making a real contribution to progress.

Notes

1. *The Marketing of Industrial Products* (Ed.) Wilson, A. London: Hutchinson, 1966.
2. Marrian, J., 'Marketing Characteristics of Industrial Goods and Buyers'. In *The Marketing of Industrial Products* (Ed.) Wilson, A. London: Hutchinson, 1966.
3. Levitt, T., *Industrial Purchasing Behaviour*, Harvard University Graduate School of Business Administration, 1965.
4. Briscoe, G., Cannon, T. & Lewis, A. L., 'The Market Development of New Industrial Products', *European Journal of Marketing*, **6**, No. 1.
5. Wilson, A. & Fowler, J., 'Marketing of Non-differentiated Industrial Products'. In *Marketing Concepts and Strategies in the Next Decade* (Ed.) Rodger, L. W. London: Associated Business Programmes, 1973.
6. The notion of 'satisficing' means setting certain minimum job performance criteria, enough to perform tasks with no risk to position. Cyert, R. M. & March, J. G., *A Behavioural Theory of the Firm*, Englewood-Cliffs; Prentice-Hall, 1963.
7. Wootz, B., *Communications Patterns in Industrial Purchasing*, Workshop on Industrial Marketing, Brussels, 1975.
8. Levitt, T., 'Communications and Industrial Setting', *Journal of Marketing*, April, 1967.
9. Hakansson, H. (Ed.), *International Marketing and Purchasing of Industrial Goods*. Chichester: Wiley, 1982.
10. Sheth, J. N., 'A Model of Industrial Buying Behaviour', *Journal of Marketing*. October, 1973.

Further reading

Alexander, R. S., Cross, J. S. & Hill, R. M., *Industrial Marketing*. Illinois: R. D. Irwin, 1961. Still unrivalled in the extent and depth of its coverage.
Hakansson, H. (Ed.), *International Marketing and Purchasing of Industrial Goods*. Chichester: Wiley, 1982. Describes some of the most valuable recent work in the field. A powerful, strongly empirical study of a critical issue.
Hill, R. W. & Hillier, T. J., *Organizational Buyer Behaviour*. London: Macmillan, 1977. Provides a valuable insight into a critical area of interest.
Wilson, A., *The Assessment of Industrial Markets*. London: Associated Business Programmes, 1974. Based on a wealth of experience.

CASE STUDY 8: HALFORDS DROP FORGINGS

Halfords Drop Forgings Limited is a small company, located in old-fashioned premises on the outskirts of Birmingham. They have been producing high-quality forgings for the last 60 years, and although they have been recently taken over by a larger general engineering group, they continue to operate fairly independently. The firm takes all the business it can and boasts in its literature that:

'We can supply any type of forging, and of any quality, from 10–10,000 units.'

They operate a wide range of hammers and all dyemaking is done on the premises, and a small technical and design service is available to all customers.

The Managing Director, Brian Day, has been with the firm 25 years, working his way up from the shop floor. His management team is organised as follows:

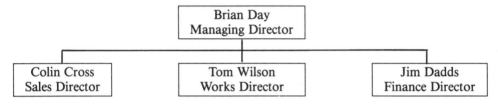

Halfords obtain business in three ways—they have a small proportional budget of £5000 for trade advertisements, and this generates some new enquiries. These leads are followed up by the Sales Manager. Existing customers tend to recommend Halfords to other customers, who in turn contact Halfords direct. They also manage seven field agents, who obtain sales leads on a commission basis. These agents report to Colin Cross, who complains:

I don't have enough time to manage or motivate them effectively.

Most of Halfords' business, some 60 per cent, comes from the automobile industry. Their major customers are British Leyland, Automotive Products, David Brown and Rolls-Royce, and Colin spends most of his time with these key accounts.

Halfords have dabbled in export markets and have supplied one order to Murphy Engineering in Dublin. Because of transport and clearance problems, there have been no follow-up orders. They have also received ad hoc orders via the Crown Agents and a London-based export house: these bodies arranged collection and delivery of the forgings. A recently appointed German agent has generated some enquiries, but these have not been converted into orders—price is the major barrier.

Brian Day is disturbed by the decline in the automobile industry and his firm's over-dependence on this sector. At the same time, by operating as a jobbing shop, he is unable to schedule in production effectively—the firm has recently reverted to a four-day week. The problems in the maket are compounded by the increasing level of Far East and Eastern European importers who are able to undercut UK manufacturers by up to 50 per cent on certain forgings. At the monthly sales meeting, the following discussions take place.

Brian Day: 'The holding group have expressed doubts about our recent sales performance and are recommending that, in line with other group companies, a Marketing Manager is appointed, to generate a more positive, marketing-orientated way forwards, both in the UK and overseas.'

Colin Cross: 'I could certainly use somebody to get those commission agents moving. But on a brighter note, the Maestro launch at BL has gone very well, which must mean more repeat business for us.'

Tom Wilson: 'That ball joint we developed for towing trailers—a new Marketing
                Manager could help promote that as a finished product and that
                could help my production scheduling problems.'
Brian Day: 'A new appointment could certainly help generate new business, but
                something needs to be done. There have been eight company closures
                in the forging business in the last six months and the price war is
                getting worse.'

Brian has to report back to the Group Managing Director before the next board meeting
on the best means to get the firm back into a growth position. At the end of the sales
meeting he feels that they cannot continue along their present lines.

11

The Marketing of Services

The growth of the service sector in industry is perhaps one of the most striking features of modern society. US writers are already beginning to dub the last twenty years of the twentieth century the 'post-industrial' or 'service' society.

> The United States is now pioneering a new stage of economic development. During the period following World War II, this country became the world's first 'service economy'.
>
> Fuchs[1]

The shift from agriculture to manufacturing is now being followed by a move from production (including agriculture, mining and fishing) to services. Britain and Western Europe are following the US pattern, with an increasing proportion of the working population involved in service (Table 11.1).

Table 11.1 *Percentage employed in services[a]*

	1960 (%)	1970 (%)	1975 (%)	1980 (%)
United Kingdom	47.6	52.0	56.4	59.3
Total for EEC (Eur. 9)	39.5	45.6	49.7	54.7

[a]There are differences between these figures and the figures quoted earlier, as they are derived from different sources. The EEC figures are for slightly broader categories.
Reproduced with the permission of the Office for Official Publications of the European Communities.

SERVICES: A DEFINITION

It is not easy to define exactly what is meant by the service sector. One of the main points of the market concept is that a firm's offering goes far beyond the physical product offering into a broader array of need satisfactions. This means that firms must recognise that everyone in business sells some element of service. This means that the standard definition of services:

> Those separately identifiable, essentially intangible activities which provide want-satisfaction, and which are not necessarily tied to the sale of a product or another service. To produce a service may or may not require the use of tangible goods. However, when such use is required there is no transfer of the title (permanent ownership) to these tangible goods.
>
> Stanton[2]

can usefully incorporate the notion that:

> The service is the object of marketing, i.e. the company is selling the service as the core of its market offering.
>
> Grönroos[3]

Even using this definition, organisations, individuals and offerings vary enormously in scale and type of offering (Figure 11.1).

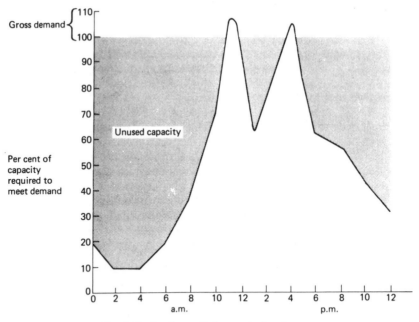

Fig. 11.1   Services, offerings and advertisements.

THE SOURCES OF GROWTH

A number of factors have contributed to the growth in the service sector. In consumer markets increased discretionary income and additional leisure time have stimulated the demand for education, grooming, travel and entertainment. In industrial and business markets, the growing complexity of the environment, along with specialisation and fierce competition, has created new service markets. Government has faced demands from articulate and powerful groups for action in specific areas. At the same time, broad economic and social movements have forced government action. For example, the importance of geographical mobility among the workforce and the growth of the nuclear family in modern industrial society have transferred many roles, e.g. caring for the elderly, away from the person onto the state. There is every evidence that these forces will continue in the future.

THE DIFFERENCE BETWEEN SERVICE AND PRODUCT INDUSTRIES

There are five basic differences between a service industry and a product industry. Services are usually *heterogeneous, intangible, inseparable, perishable* and *not owned by the buyer*. It is the combination of these five factors which creates the particular context in which the service company develops its marketing policies.

Heterogeneity

Services are usually designed around the specific requirements of the individual customer. For example, an insurance company will quote for each person a policy based on their specific industry, goods, prospects, even location, albeit using a fixed formula. There is an element of this in some product marketing, notably in industrial markets, but here there is usually a fair degree of standardisation, e.g. by machine capacity or specific industry types.

A move towards standardisation is now emerging in some service industries. An essential feature of franchising is the attempt to establish and comply with certain norms, which the customer can be confident of obtaining. For example, part of the 'Holiday Inn' offering is:

> Everything in our hotels must measure up to our 'no surprise' standards. From things you will notice, like every mattress in every room . . . specified 'manufacturer's top of the line' . . . to things . . . like cleaning your carpet every day.

Intangibility

You cannot touch, taste, smell or take apart to examine the working of a service. A lawyer's services cannot be evaluated in this way; nor can a hotel, club, consultant, or barber. The opinions or attitudes of others can of course be obtained, but the 'trial' element is lacking. Even when free or low-price trials are offered, e.g. by car hire firms, the trial will not be exactly the same as the actual offering; for example, the car may be different or the staff may change.

These are intangibles which may be involved in any purchase. The BMW may be dirty or earn a poor reputation for performance, but the physical offering is what is important. This introduces the 'no bench-mark' aspect of service markets. When purchasing a new TV or hi-fi, the service in the shop can be terrible and the staff unpleasant, but the product itself can compensate for this. The same does not apply with a service: the facilities of a restaurant, the attitudes of the staff and the quality of cooking determine to a far greater extent the customer's rating of the offering.

Inseparability

Production of the service and consumption occur at the same time. This concept is particularly important in the realm of personal services. It limits the scope to which dealers, distributors or agents can be effectively used, and places considerable emphasis on the skills and attitudes of those involved in selling. For example, in Britain, very few bank managers would see themselves as salesmen, but to a considerable extent that is their job. They are selling credit, financial services or advice to customers. Like all salesmen, they select their buyers (creditworthy?) when selling; the bank manager's service and consumption of the offering occur at the same time (although of course the credit may be over a much longer period). This is an area in which progress has been made by service companies trying to combine a degree of standardisation with opening up new markets. Insurance brokers, travel agents and some franchise operations achieve this very effectively.

Perishableness

Services cannot be stocked or held over: hotel rooms left vacant one night do not add to the following night's capacity. This creates massive problems when demand fluctuates, as in the case of some utilities, e.g. British Telecom. To cope with peak demand, massive capacity, much of it idle during the rest of the day or night, is needed (Figure 11.2). A variety of policies have to be developed to cope with this inability to store for more than a very short time, e.g. differential prices, promotion of evening use. It has even been

Fig. 11.2   Telephone demand patterns (hypothetical).

proposed that private telephones or home extensions are distributed free (although it has been suggested that unless some form of time lock (stopping peak hour use) could be installed, these would merely serve to amplify the trends).

Lack of ownership

In a service industry, access to or use of a facility does not mean that the customer obtains ownership of it. The hotel room, car, telephone or computer service is only hired for a period, and ultimately possession reverts to the firm offering the service. For example: 'This card remains the property of the issuing Bank.'—Access; 'This card is the property of American Express Company.'—American Express; 'This card remains the property of Barclays Bank Limited.'—Barclaycard. Payment is for the use of, access to, or hire of items. This does create some overlap with product markets, notably when an item is purchased but a warranty is attached.

THE RANGE OF SERVICE INDUSTRIES

Service industries are extremely wide-ranging. They encompass some of the largest commercial concerns, e.g. Barclays Bank, Lombard North Central (Finance), Marks and Spencer, Czarnikow Group (commodity brokers), Inchcape and Co. The largest organisation of all, government, is also a service concern. The following is a selection of just a few of the service industries: accountancy, advertising, airlines, architects, banks, barbers, brokers, cafés, car hire, circuses, cinemas, clubs, computer services, consultants, credit agencies, decorators, dentists, designers, doctors, dry cleaners, education, entertainment, factors, franchising, freight forwarding, hospitals, hotels, hairdressing, information collection, insurance, law, leisure, market research, office services, personnel counselling, post, recreation, recruitment, repairs, research laboratories, restaurants, sport, surveying, symphony orchestras, telecommunications, theatre, transport, travel, universities and colleges, valuations, and window cleaning. In reviewing these areas some broad generalisations are necessary. Some service industries are closer to the product model than others. Some authors[4] have suggested that the differentiation itself is of limited value. However, the combined effect of the areas of difference and, perhaps more important, the comments of practising managers, suggest that in a number of key areas of marketing the circumstances demand policy adaptations. Although there is some truth in the suggestion that this argument 'seems to result from a "production" as opposed to a "market" orientation', it is equally true that the problems appear so severe, the differences so significant, that the adaptation should be two-way, with marketing men themselves steering clear of a product perspective on their own offering.

Government services

The state is the largest provider of services in the UK and in most societies today. These services range from information, advice and counselling to health care, credit and education. Most are provided on a non-profit-making basis, but there are a few which act or have acted on a more commercial basis, such as parts of the Department of Trade and the Exports Credit Guarantee Department.

In many government services there is a growing recognition that they need to establish some form of effective control over their demand. This can encompass such actions as:

1. Overcoming objections to certain kinds of government actions, even persuading people to participate, e.g. in vaccination programmes: conversional marketing.
2. Creating demand among indifferent groups of the population for certain government priorities, e.g. persuading firms to employ more export salesmen: stimulational marketing.

When government activity was confined to the fundamentals of law, order and defence, the need to think seriously about the market was fairly limited, since legal enforcement and acceptance of specific social values dominated relationships. The extent of government involvement and the range of areas into which policy now intrudes have made the state very much an active participant in the market. The traditional roles of *regulator* and *customer* have been joined by *participant*. This is not, in fact, a totally new development, but is only now being recognised.

Choice is now a very real factor in many areas of government action. The industrialist can reject calls to export, invest or recruit. The mother can refuse to have her children vaccinated against certain diseases. The trade unionist can reject pay restraint. The family can refuse to insulate their home.

The traditional governmental approach is broadly similar to a sales orientation: heavyweight advertising backed by ministerial speeches. To a certain extent this is inevitable so long as ideological commitments by political parties broadly determine policies. There are, however, many areas in which these general perspectives do not intrude directly, and where a marketing perspective could play a very positive role, for example in export promotion, relocation of industry, health care and provision of educational services. In doing this some new and different approaches to marketing may have to be adopted. As the overwhelming majority of government departments are involved in services, the ideas built up in this area are perhaps the most relevant.

MANAGING THE SERVICE OFFER

People are at the centre of any business. They provide the direction and much of the motivation behind its development and success. In service industries the 'people dimension' gains added power from the lack of a tangible product offering:

> In product-orientated business, the physical reality of the product provides a simple but powerful base on which to build a business description.
>
> Dan R. E. Thomas[5]

> In goods marketing there is a tangible core around which the offering can be developed.
>
> Christian Grönroos[6]

In service industries people are this central core. The consumer defines the organisation in terms of the ways in which the personnel behave or respond to him. For example: the disinterested or hostile waiter defines the restaurant; the lax lawyer determines the client's view of the law firm; and the unhelpful official determines attitudes to the government department. The impact of this is made even greater by the ability of the service organisation's personnel to determine the character of the service and the form of the offering. For example, the consulting engineer is responsible for translating the customer's needs, using his own knowledge and expertise, into a clear project proposal. He may have more people to back him up, but he is the designer.

Even in a franchise operation the goals of standardisation and uniformity are interpreted and judged by the franchisee's and franchisor's personnel. Some mechanisation is taking place (automatic car washes, automatic bank services, launderettes), but to date its impact has been very limited and restricted to highly routine and low-skill areas.

The impact of the people element is taken even further by customer access and expectations. In industrial markets access to operatives is extremely limited: the industrial customer may meet the tool and jig maker but that will probably be all. No customer expects to meet the packers in a sweet factory, let alone expect them to have any responsibility for the total product offering. In service markets, however, access is far greater. The overwhelming majority of staff have some form of direct customer contact. The clerks in an insurance company, the operators in the telephone company and the porter at a business school all meet the customer and help form his impression of the institution. Equally important, the buyer has high expectations of these staff.

Staff management is a major part of the design of the service organisation's offering. The bank manager who refused to lend Caterham Cars £10 000 to buy the freehold of their premises can only watch while its turnover creeps up to £1 million per year.

In service markets the 'official' sales force tends to be more important than it is in industrial markets. Although the definition of a salesman is far broader, his role is significantly more substantial.

The extent of their knowledge and skill should reflect the importance of differentiation of skill, expertise and approach in most service industries. Among advertising agencies Rod Allen of Allen, Brady and Marsh, David Ogilvy of OBM and many other senior executives provide the basis of the skill/style differentiation which clients seek. Maintaining these standards throughout the organisation is particularly difficult in the larger organisations such as the Government, banks and insurance companies. A ministerial commitment to exports can be frustrated by a civil servant building barriers between himself, the services provided and firms.

The complex nature of this differentiation creates special problems in pricing policies. The price itself is often as intangible as the product. For example, it can be very difficult to work out exactly what is paid for bank services. Is the price the access to your deposits, the bank charges, special interest payments for loans, or some abstract combination of all three? Traditional cost-plus pricing poses problems when the primary costs are personnel. The low cost of entry in some service industries and problems of customer evaluation often keep prices very low. High levels of differentiation supported by individual negotiations occur, especially in situations where personal service is involved. In general, price information is difficult to obtain in these situations.

In some professions, regulatory agencies have been set up which exercise control over entry and sometimes fees. The bodies often adopt group policies towards advertising and promotion, prohibiting it in some cases, regulating it in others.

Advertising has long played a substantial and central part in the development of some services. Some of the finest creative advertising has been conducted for services, e.g. Toulouse Lautrec for the theatre. A number of specific opportunities for promotion do emerge in the service sector. Sports and entertainment are frequently featured on specialised television programmes and often have their own sections in newspapers. Conferences, seminars, symposia and journals may provide the opportunity to disseminate information about the individual or firm, as well as the formal topic.

Promotion has a particularly important role in those services where indirect representation through agents (travel) or distributors (franchising) is not possible, and where the client may need to initiate the search or approach, i.e. through briefing or invitations to tender for business.

Grönroos[7] suggests that the concept of accessibility provides a major clue to both the difference between service and product marketing and the direction service marketing should take:

> Resources influencing accessibility are, for example, human resources, machines, offices, buildings and other physical things as well as extra services.

His basic proposition is that service marketing should be centred round the notion of maximising access to the service industry for the target market(s). Barriers to access and factors interfering with access to the essential offering (or understanding this offering) should be overcome.

INNOVATION AND PRODUCTIVITY

The people-based nature of service industries has tended to mean that contrasting patterns of innovative activities have emerged. In highly skilled sectors innovation has frequently been individualistic. Sometimes this has been comfortably encompassed in existing organisations, e.g. the long and successful history of some research laboratories, but probably more often the low cost of entry and the close client contact have led to new enterprises being established. This problem of 'ownership' of new concepts may discourage some service organisations from formal innovation policies.

The larger people- or machine-based services have generally adopted a more formal policy toward innovation. The high labour content in services such as banking, travel, leisure and recreation has created considerable interest in productivity improvements through automation or standardisation. Low labour productivity is a recurrent problem in the service industries and is one reason why the percentage of the population involved has risen so dramatically. The productivity of manufacturing has improved while that of services has stabilised.

THE FUTURE

Productivity and people are the keys to the future of service industries. Microprocessors may provide a significant contribution to productivity in some industries, but past performance suggests that other, probably more labour-intensive services will emerge to satisfy new needs as the demand for skills and knowledge to cope with the new environment or leisure requirements increases.

Attitudes to service industries will play a part in their development in the UK. For a significant proportion of the male UK workforce there appears to be prejudice against service industries, reflected in reluctance to seek employment there, negative attitudes when working, and the low priorities given to the service sector. Many government support schemes in development areas specifically exclude service industries, despite their high employment potential. This situation is worsened by the poor marketing of many of Britain's major services. Service marketing needs to be considerably developed over the next decade.

Notes

1. Fuchs, V. R., *The Service Economy*. New York: National Bureau of Economic Research, 1968.
2. Stanton, W. J., *Fundamentals of Marketing*. New York: McGraw-Hill, 1978.
3. Grönroos, C., 'A Service-orientated Approach to Marketing of Services', *European Journal of Marketing*, **12**, No. 8, 1979.
4. Wyckham, R. G., Fitzroy, P. T. & Mandry, G. D., 'Marketing of Services', *European Journal of Marketing*, **9**, No. 1, 1975.
5. Levitt, T., 'Production Line Approach to Service', *Harvard Business Review*, September-October, 1972.
6. Thomas, D. R. E., 'Strategy is Different in Service Business', *Harvard Business Review*, July–August, 1978.
7. Grönroos, C., 'A Service-orientated Approach to Marketing of Services', *European Journal of Marketing*, **12**, No. 8, 1979.

Further reading

Ogilvy, D., *Confessions of an Advertising Man*. New York: Athenium, 1963. Amusing and well written insight into the ideas and actions which led to the development of one of the most successful advertising agencies in North America by a Briton.
Wyckham, R. G., Fitzroy, P. T. & Mandry, G. D., 'Marketing of Services', *European Journal of Marketing*, Volume 9, No. 1, 1975. The difference between service and product marketing in this article gives a comprehensive and penetrating review of the relevant research practice in the area.

CASE STUDY 9: MARKETING DEVELOPMENT AND EXPORT SERVICES

In 1979 Marketing Development and Export Services (MDES) completed a major development programme designed to draw up a framework for a specialist export course to meet the needs of small firms. A complete package of teaching aids, course notes and case studies had been drawn up following four years of extensive research. Pilot courses had been conducted with a number of key industries.

These pilot programmes had been very successful. The sponsoring bodies of these (primarily industrial training boards, but one or two trade associations had been involved) were very keen to greatly expand their involvement with these courses, and with MDES in general. Within a few months it became clear that conducting these courses for existing clients would take up all the firm's resources in this area for the foreseeable future.

Rapid expansion of facilities was not seen as possible by the firm's top management. The demands placed on tutors by the courses were so great that they could be involved in only a very small number each year. At the same time, severe problems had been experienced in recruiting staff with the thorough knowledge of export and small firms required to effectively conduct the courses.

Faced with the dilemma of meeting the needs of current clients or expanding, as planned, into new industries, it was decided to expand as intended. This meant that the desire of some current clients for courses in the near future was frustrated.

Top management felt that this extra exposure and the opportunity to establish extra networks of relationships were worth the risk of alienating existing clients. At the same time, it was decided to explore the scope for reducing the scale of tutorial involvement, perhaps through greater ITB training adviser involvement or working with other consultants or agencies.

Despite this decision there were still worries about the wisdom of this step and the choices that had led to this position. The company therefore set itself the task of examining the situation for clues to the ways in which a marketing perspective could assist them in the future. The first topic examined was the decision to follow the expansion route described above.

12

International and Export Marketing

The international market-place provides one of the most challenging environments for the marketing man. The scale is enormous: during 1977 world trade in manufactures exceeded £345 billion, world trade in invisibles, although much harder to calculate, was probably over £100 billion, and the population of the world was over three billion. This was a particularly important year for Britain, as there were signs during that year that the long-term decline in the country's share of world trade was levelling out. Over the past hundred years this share has dropped from about 27 per cent in 1877 to just over 9 per cent in 1984.

Although this decline has been very real, it is important to recognise that Britain is, and has been for a very long time, one of the world's great trading nations. In fact, the share of Britain's Gross National Product exported far exceeds many of our leading industrial rivals (Table 12.1). The picture of Britain's export performance is very mixed, with some very bright spots and some areas in urgent need of improvement. Exporting is perhaps, more than any other, the area in which a marketing perspective can earn the greatest returns.

Table 12.1 *Percentage share of Gross National Product exported (1984)*

Country	%
UK	31
West Germany	16
France	17
USA	6
Japan	7

A HISTORICAL PERSPECTIVE

Britain's long overseas trading history covers only a part of the time during which trade between independent communities has been important. It is possible that the earliest developed forms of commerce existed between autonomous groups, and it is this independence which characterises international trade. Although today the international market-place is dominated by the nation state, in the past groups from tribes, cities, regions and empires followed patterns of trade which in their broad principles would be familiar to today's international or export marketing man.

Four factors have determined the extent of trade: political stability, urbanisation, some medium of exchange (acceptable currencies) and, most recently, industrialisation. The rise of the nation state from the thirteenth century provided a high degree of domestic political stability. The growth of the cities over the last 700 years has been dramatic. Although specific currencies have declined during this period there has been greater convertibility of currencies. No single factor has been more important to the dramatic growth in world trade than the Industrial Revolution. Besides the surge in volume of trade, a continuing pattern of change and counter-change has typified this period.

Despite its importance and the complex problems it poses, international export marketing has been neglected in many books. Throughout Western Europe, and for Britain in particular, the application of a marketing perspective to all areas of export and international marketing is vital.

Although traditionally there has been a tendency to confuse the terms 'export marketing' and 'international marketing', there are very real differences between them. Export marketing is the marketing of goods, produced in one or more countries, in other countries. International marketing, on the other hand, gives weight to the development of business in a number of countries or regions, with a framework capable of incorporating the establishment of local manufacturing, distribution and marketing systems.

For most firms the majority of their overseas trading is directed towards exports although, notably among larger firms, there has recently been a move towards establishing overseas manufacturing capacity. Despite its importance even to some of Britain's largest firms (Table 12.2), there has been an unfortunate tendency to relegate the study of exports to problems of procedure. There is an urgent need to reverse this pattern of behaviour and firmly establish the marketing dimension of export, as well as international marketing.

Table 12.2 *Proportion of turnover exported*

	Turnover (£m)	Exports (£m)	%
Imperial Chemical Industries	3099	586	19
Unilever	2876	234	8
British Leyland	1868	589	32
General Electric	1407	315	22
Dunlop	1015	98	10

Note: All figures refer to accounting year ended 1975.

THE MARKETING PERSPECTIVE

At its most fundamental this involves viewing the world from a new perspective. The traditional, physical geography viewpoint has only a limited value. More important to the marketing man is the economic geography of the world. Population, national income, educational standards and levels of economic development provide better clues to opportunity for the marketing man than do land masses. Also important are variables such as culture, language, attitudes towards change, wealth or achievement and social systems, as well as the very different ways of conducting business around the world (Figure 12.1).

Success will go to the firm which, whether producing in Britain for dispatch overseas or considering production in the consuming market, opts to base its policies on an understanding of the market and its needs, drives and choice processes, rather than trying to impose home marketing overseas regardless of circumstances.

THEORY OF COMPARATIVE ADVANTAGE

Adam Smith (1776) pointed out that in the case of two countries like Britain and France, each has its own special characteristics and endowments enabling it to produce certain goods. If each could produce one product better than the other, absolute advantages would exist, and the profits from trade would be very clear. The warmer climate and special soil conditions of France may be more productive of grapes for wine, while the

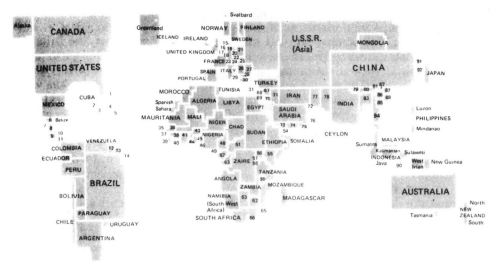

Fig. 12.1(a)   Diagram indicating national territories (1 mm² = 33 333 km²).

1 BAHAMAS	24 AUSTRIA	47 NIGER	70 JORDAN
2 JAMAICA	25 HUNGARY	48 CAMEROON	71 IRAQ
3 HAITI	26 YUGOSLAVIA	49 EQUATORIAL GUINEA	72 KUWAIT
4 DOMINICAN REP	27 ROMANIA	50 CHAD	73 YEMEN
5 Puerto Rico	28 BULGARIA	51 CENTRAL AFRICAN REP	74 SOUTHERN YEMEN
6 GUATEMALA	29 ALBANIA	52 GABON	75 OMAN
7 EL SALVADOR	30 GREECE	53 CONGO	76 QATAR
8 HONDURAS	31 CYPRUS	54 Afars and Issas	77 AFGHANISTAN
9 NICARAGUA	32 TUNISIA	55 KENYA	78 PAKISTAN
10 COSTA RICA	33 LIBYA	56 UGANDA	79 BANGLADESH
11 PANAMA	34 MAURITANIA	57 RWANDA	80 NEPAL
12 GUYANA	35 GAMBIA	58 BURUNDI	81 SIKKIM
13 Surinam	36 SENEGAL	59 MALAWI	82 BHUTAN
14 French Guiana	37 GUINEA BISSAU	60 ZAMBIA	83 BURMA
15 DENMARK	38 GUINEA	61 MOZAMBIQUE	84 THAILAND
16 NETHERLANDS	39 SIERRA LEONE	62 RHODESIA	85 CAMBODIA
17 BELGIUM	40 LIBERIA	63 BOTSWANA	86 LAOS
18 LUXEMBOURG	41 IVORY COAST	64 NAMIBIA	87 NORTH VIETNAM
19 WEST GERMANY	42 MALI	65 SWAZILAND/NGWANE	88 SOUTH VIETNAM
20 EAST GERMANY	43 UPPER VOLTA	66 LESOTHO	89 Kalimantan
21 POLAND	44 GHANA	67 SYRIA	90 Bali
22 CZECHOSLOVAKIA	45 TOGO	68 LEBANON	91 NORTH KOREA
23 SWITZERLAND	46 DAHOMEY	69 ISRAEL	92 SOUTH KOREA

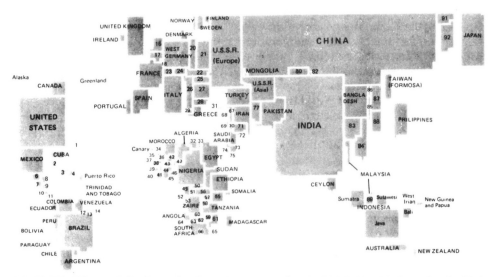

Fig. 12.1(b)   Diagram indicating national populations (1 mm² = 800 000 inhabitants). Reproduced with the permission of the Office of Official Publications of the European Economic Community.

cooler weather and different soils of Scotland are more suitable for grains for producing whisky. When each country specialises, the sum of production will be greater than if each attempts to produce both.

Problems emerge, however, when one country is more efficient than the other in producing every product. The question of whether there is still any point in trading then arises. The answer from the theory of comparative advantage is yes. So long as there are differences in the relative efficiencies of producing the goods in each country there is a value in trade. The more productive country would still benefit from specialisation in those goods it is best at producing while importing from the less productive country those goods it is comparatively worse at producing. Thus, in Japan it may take ten man-days to produce a car and one man-day to produce a TV set, while in Britain it may take 15 man-days to produce the same car and two man-days to produce the TV set, yet it still pays both of them to trade, as the total output will be greater than if they both try to produce both items.

Although economists such as Samuelson can state that 'The theory of comparative advantage is a closely reasoned doctrine which, when properly stated, is unassailable', many forces act against the implementation of policies based upon it. High tariffs, protectionism, local preference and the fear of competition are facts of life for the exporter, although attempts have been made, and continue to be made, to reduce these pressures.

DEVELOPMENTS IN TRADE

Since the end of the Second World War a number of major developments in international trading have taken place, generally with a view to facilitating trade and building up prosperity.

GATT (the General Agreement on Tariffs and Trade) is probably the most important attempt at international co-operation to reduce tariffs. The IMF (International Monetary Fund) was established to iron out the fluctuations in the international monetary system created by foreign trading. Credits are provided for countries with short-term trading deficits while longer-term assistance is given to countries with more intractable problems. The World Bank provides a more general banking role, supplying loans to people or countries unable to get private funding for apparently economically sound projects.

All these and other institutions operate to widen the scope for successful international trade and prosperity.

On a narrower base, but equally important, the last twenty years have seen a movement towards powerful regional or common-interest groupings. The formation of the European Economic Community (EEC) has revived interest in customs unions and other associations geared to stimulate world trade within a number of linked countries. The broad policy of the EEC has been to eliminate tariffs between member countries while setting up common tariffs against non-members. The Community is now only one, albeit probably the most powerful, of a number of similar groupings throughout the world. Even in Europe it is matched by the internally more cohesive but economically less developed association of socialist states, the Council for Mutual Economic Assistance (CMEA, more commonly known as COMECON). This pattern of establishing unions of states in particular regions is now being paralleled by the emergence of specific-interest groups such as OPEC (the Organization of Petroleum Exporting Countries).

The major economic groupings and customs unions are: European Economic Community (EEC), European Free Trade Area (EFTA), Council for Mutual Economic Assistance (CMEA), Caribbean Community and Common Market (CARICOM), Latin American Free Trade Area (LAFTA), Central American Free Trade Area (CACM), East African Community (EAC), West Indies Associated States (WIAS), Caribbean Free Trade

Area (CARIFTA), Central African Customs and Economic Union (UDEAC), West African States Customs Union (UDEAO) and Association of South East Asia Nations (ASEAN). Although all these organisations inevitably focus their attentions on their member states, most have established trade agreements or some associations with non-member countries or other associations. Countries which have trade agreements or are associated with the EEC are: Greece, Spain, Portugal, Turkey, Morocco, Tunisia, Algeria, Israel, Cyprus, Egypt, Malta, Lebanon, Yugoslavia, member states of EFTA, certain African Caribbean and Pacific states, Argentina, Uruguay, Brazil, Mexico, Bangladesh, India, Pakistan and Sri Lanka.

The majority of these developments are designed to reduce the barriers to trade either globally, as in the case of GATT, or in a specific region, as in the case of the EEC.

Although there has been progress in reducing the tariff barriers to markets, less success has been achieved in limiting the non-tariff barriers to entry. *Non-tariff barriers* to entry are all obstacles placed in front of prospective importers which are not incorporated in formal tariffs. They range from specific trade practices designed to limit competition to differential levels of skill and willingness to adapt. Japan in particular is often accused of conscious attempts to baffle would-be importers by 'Japanese methods of negotiating and the complexities of Japanese law and language', as well as by specific actions designed to limit imports in certain areas. The difficulties of penetrating the export market are nowhere more clearly seen than in attempts to understand the Japanese distribution system, in which products may go through the same trading company several times before they reach the market. The industrialised nations of the west are frequently accused of having similar policies designed to keep out of their markets goods produced in the Third World.

Even within groupings such as the EEC it is recognised that reductions in tariffs have only limited impact in the face of national preferences, trading advantages by local companies and specific regulations. The 'buy British' policies often adopted by government departments, local authorities and firms are real barriers to foreign firms, but they are matched by both formal rules and informal policies in most countries of the EEC. 'Italians always prefer their own goods', 'The French are fiercely patriotic', and 'The Germans never buy foreign goods when they can buy German' are all frequent comments of UK businessmen. It has been claimed that as fast as tariffs are removed non-tariff barriers are erected, thus holding back progress towards the 'single home market' goal of the member states. These are problems to which the export or international marketers must find solutions by superior marketing in all spheres.

THE INTERNATIONAL MARKETING SYSTEM

The need to understand the marketing system in order to effectively develop business is nowhere more important than in export and international marketing. The picture built up of a country or market is complicated by the differences and interrelationships which occur with foreign business, and by the recurrent problem, particularly in exporting, of viewing the market as an outsider. These can lead to grave errors and misunderstandings. It is important to recognise that, although a market may be foreign to the exporter, it is the user's home market. Too many firms believe that inferior service is acceptable because the market is so far away, because of logistics problems, or because of the costs involved, ignoring the fact that no buyer willingly accepts these propositions. Firms may find certain markets too difficult to manage effectively, but this poses questions about both their market selection and total product proposition.

Economic, political, cultural and technological factors determine both the international environment in which the firm operates and the specific circumstances of target markets.

Economic factors

The three major economic factors are the trading relations within and between countries, the economic structure and policies of specific nations, and the level of economic development.

In the first part of this chapter trade relations have been extensively reviewed. It is important to recognise that many countries have very different economic structures and policies from those of the UK. The overwhelming majority of countries in the world now operate within some form of economic or national plan. Even Britain had an industrial strategy identifying key areas of economic development until the election of the Conservative Government in 1979.

This is a pattern which is far more developed in the countries of Eastern Europe and the Third World:

> A total amount of 2.6 million tonnes of plastics materials was manufactured during the last five years. In the next five this figure will have to be brought to almost four million tonnes.
>
> Directives of the German
> Democratic Republic's Five-year
> Plan, 1976–1980

The level of economic development is extremely important for highlighting the kinds of opportunity overseas. Models such as that put forward by W. W. Rostow, suggesting five stages of economic growth (traditional agricultural society, transition from agriculture to industry, steady growth to a strong industrial base, drive to mature employment of modern technology, and high mass consumption), are helpful in organising our understanding of markets and grouping similar markets together to assist in identifying and meeting common needs.

Political factors

The nation state is the central feature of modern export and international marketing. Its domestic freedoms, national system and structure and links with other countries are critical to any picture of the available opportunities:

> Mexico (is) actively employing a policy of reducing its dependence on the US.
>
> Ann Cooper[1]

The federal nature of many countries, such as the USA, West Germany and Nigeria, can have a direct impact on factors as varied as local taxation and regulations on warehousing. The centralisation typical of the communist countries is in total contrast to this. Here all buying for an entire national industry is likely to be conducted through a single, state-controlled foreign trade enterprise. In international marketing in particular, a willingness to adapt to different political systems is critical to success.

Culture

This pervades all aspects of foreign trade, from the character of the needs and the forms of gratification which are acceptable to the response to particular forms of communication. No-one faces these problems more directly than the export salesman. He must be able to respond positively to the culture shocks which are always possible in new situations. Their impact can range from the simple and procedural:

> An American customer receiving a letter bearing a subscription 'dictated by Mr Exporter, and signed in his absence by A. Smith, Secretary' experiences a rising wave of personal insult,

occasioned by what is, to him, a plain condescension.

F. Posses, *Selling to the Americans*

to the profound rethinking of overall values and attitudes. For example, there is in many parts of the industrial world:

An increasing disenchantment with the artificial and man-made aspects of the modern world.

T. Mortmore and J. Siddall, *The Importance of Cultural Trends in Marketing Planning*

Technology

This provides the thrust behind the market economy. Under its pressure the past 200 years have seen a profound transformation which has reached almost all parts of the world. Technology, through direct sales, transfer of capabilities or adaptation, creates many opportunities in international trade. It has been proposed by Louis T. Wells Jnr that there exists an international product life-cycle, which is based on the proposition that innovations will generally occur close to the more sophisticated markets, those most capable of employing the new developments. From there, four distinct stages can be identified with potential policy responses. (In Figure 12.2 the USA is used to illustrate this proposition.) Although this suffers from the weakness of all life-cycle models, oversimplification of very complex phenomena, it does give some insight into key aspects of the spread of technology.

In exploring responses by the innovator or adaptor the importance of market-orientated research and development cannot be overstated, and it gains considerably in importance when the issue of export-led growth is raised.

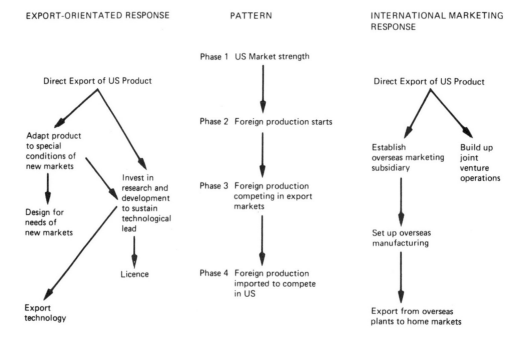

Fig. 12.2   The international product life-cycle.

EXPORT-LED GROWTH

Most national governments are committed to creating and maintaining domestic employment opportunities through manufacture at home and sales overseas. A healthy balance of payments created by this is generally seen as an indication of economic success. Besides this, it is generally argued that striving for domestic growth is far less risky when based on exports than home sales because there is less impact on inflation.

Many countries have built much of their prosperity on overseas sales. For example: British exports of wool and later of textiles were major contributors to growth in the last century; since the war both Germany and Japan have used earnings from exports to lead to home growth; and France has, over the last decade, successfully used export earnings to boost national growth. Although it is now becoming clear that domestic economic strength is as important as export earnings, these still have a major part to play in national prosperity.

Most countries offer an extensive array of incentives to exporters. In Britain the main government help is directed through the British Overseas Trade Board, operating through the Department of Industry and overseas through the Foreign Office (Table 12.3).

Table 12.3 *Resources for export promotion*

	1978/79	1977/78
Collection and dissemination of market intelligence	£16.9m	£15.7m
Trade promotions	£21.9m	£21.3m
Overseas trade fairs (including symposia)	£16.6m	£16.2m
British Export Marketing Centre, Tokyo	£1.1m	£0.9m
Outward Missions	£2.8m	£2.9m
Other	£1.4m	£1.3m
Help to individual UK exporters	£12.0m	£10.1m
Assistance to capital goods export projects	£3.3m	£3.1m
Export marketing research and advice	£0.9m	£0.7m
Market Entry Guarantee Scheme	£0.8m	nil
Assistance to UK businessmen visiting overseas and help to exporters in overseas representation	£4.5m	£4.0m
Other	£2.5m	£2.3m
Information and publicity, and support for Inward Missions	£12.8m	£13.4m
Overseas Information Service	£8.2m	£9.0m
Inward Missions and individual business visitors	£2.3m	£2.2m
Other	£2.3m	£2.2m
Miscellaneous, including administration and planning	£8.3m	£7.8m

Source: British Overseas Trade Board, Annual Report, 1978. Reproduced with the permission of the Controller of HMSO.

British exporters are fortunate in having access to assistance from many sources, including government departments (e.g. Ministry of Defence Sales), banks, trade associations, chambers of commerce, industry research associations, specialised bodies (e.g. British Standards Institution, which offers technical help for exporters), colleges and universities. It is a pattern of support paralleled in many other countries, but seldom equalled. One area of help, direct financial support for sales, is specifically forbidden by EEC rules.

Despite this help, the problems faced by the exporter and the international marketer are enormous. Unfortunately, many firms invest relatively little time and effort in overseas market analysis and selection:

> British companies appeared to sell to more markets, i.e. 40 per cent of the British companies interviewed sold to more than 100 markets compared to 32 per cent in France and only 20 per cent in Germany.[2]

Policies similar to the undifferentiated mass-market approach of the product- or sales-orientated firm seem to characterise many firms. Consequences such as greater vulnerability to fluctuating exchange rates because of simplified price competition tend to follow.

MARKET SELECTION AND DEVELOPMENT

Concentration on key markets or opportunities provides firms with the chance to build a fuller picture of market conditions, understand the details of customers' specific requirements, design and develop offerings adapted to meet buyer needs, establish and sustain a long-term marketing presence, and minimise costs while maximising the returns from individual markets. When key markets are examined it is essential to avoid the trap of equating a market with a country. A firm's target may just as easily be a segment within an overseas country or a segment crossing national boundaries as a specific country:

> Silentnight (Kenya) Ltd . . . has supplied the beds, furniture and furnishings for most of the tourist hotels developed in the area.[3]
>
> In its export range Van Heusen attempts to cater for the junior executive group . . . in all its export markets.
>
> British Overseas Trade Board, 15 Export Case Studies

In approaching and concentrating on target markets the progressive improvement in international statistical information is increasing the scope for constructive desk research and employing quantitative techniques to group or cluster markets. Organisations such as the EEC, UN, World Bank and the Organization for Economic Co-operation and Development (OECD) regularly publish data to complement national statistical information. Commercial organisations such as the Economist Intelligence Unit also gather data on a systematic basis both for publication and for specific clients.

There has been a progressive worldwide improvement in the facilities for good-quality market research, and many UK companies conduct research in foreign markets. ESOMAR (the European Society for Opinion and Market Research) has played a major part in the improvement of international standards. The ESOMAR Handbook and the American Marketing Association's *Green Book* list potential agencies and give an insight into the scope for obtaining good-quality research, at least in the industrially developed world.

Despite these developments there does appear to be some reluctance to conduct detailed studies. Many firms have got themselves into a vicious circle: large numbers of markets and lack of differentiation because of a reluctance to conduct detailed investigations caused, at least in part, by the costs of studying such large numbers of markets. Carefully planned investigations based on rigorously thought-out briefs, which take into consideration the differences in practice and approach which may occur overseas, can play a major part in identifying key market opportunities and the best means of developing them.

ADVERTISING AND SALES PROMOTION

The need for in-depth understanding of a market is nowhere more important than in designing advertising and sales policies. In some instances it has proved to be possible to transfer advertising campaigns overseas, either to specific markets or to many countries. The Esso tiger, the Marlboro cowboy and the Coca Cola bottle are recognised throughout the world. However, even here it has been found that such similar campaigns can mean very different things in different markets. The overwhelming majority of consumer-goods firms adapt or totally revise their message to fit into the culture, values and language of their target markets.

Language alone can make a dramatic difference to meaning. In some countries a direct translation of 'Come Alive with Pepsi' is 'Come out of the Grave with Pepsi'. In the UK, if a product went 'like a bomb' it would be a great success, but in the US it would be a total failure. Spanish and Portuguese as spoken in South America are very different from the languages of Spain and Portugal. An English manufacturer of KD kitchen furniture would have faced disaster if the buyer for a Canadian store had not noticed that the proofs of their instructions were in European, not Canadian, French.

Many industrial firms believe that they are immune to these problems, but translators of technical copy must be thoroughly conversant with the appropriate and current usage in the target market. The amount and form of technical information required vary enormously. In Eastern Europe, for example, far more detailed material is required than in Britain. The role of visuals in advertisements and brochures is also very important, since the relevance and impact can vary considerably. For example, pictures of female operatives may totally alienate buyers in some countries, specific colours may arouse very different sentiments, and in developing countries endorsements and acknowledgements by previous clients can be a very important form of reassurance. In the development of promotional and advertising material, local staff or agents can provide valuable insights.

Exhibitions and trade fairs probably play a more important role in export and international marketing than in domestic business. They bring buyer, intermediary and seller together, minimising for all the costs and time involved in the international search for supplies and custom. In scale they range from the giant international exhibitions and fairs such as Leipzig, Hanover, Paznan and Baghdad, to the highly specialised Telecom, London Boat Show and Semaine de Cuire, and national or local exhibitions, e.g. Scandinavian Furniture Fair, Royal Melbourne Show.

SELLING OVERSEAS

In the vanguard of much of this marketing effort is the salesman, whose continuing importance in modern marketing is discussed more fully in Chapter 20. In export markets new and different problems are often faced, and the salesman must learn to operate in alien, sometimes hostile, environments. The distance from head office makes communication difficult, and often the issues raised by prospective customers are new or unpredictable.

Some firms, particularly medium-sized or large ones, overcome some of these problems by employing only locals wherever they go. This effectively solves the language and culture problems, and also often gives access to contacts and leads. However, many firms find it hard to understand their foreign employees, and there can be problems about remuneration, especially in markets where wage rates are much higher than in Britain. Also, in relatively small markets there may be no scope for advancement, creating the risk of demotivation.

Maintaining the representatives' level of technical knowledge is vital in industrial markets, and partly for this reason industrial firms tend to use UK-based technical staff to a greater extent than do consumer-goods firms. Their technical knowledge enables them to reassure clients, and they can also fully appreciate the needs of both supplier and customer.

Recent research[4] has highlighted the importance of giving the overseas representative a great deal of discretion, since failure to do this can adversely influence customers. The same research highlighted the importance of a very high degree of technical competence in sales staff operating in conditions which may stretch their knowledge to its limit.

The export salesman is the main point of contact in many cases. Often he handles far greater volumes of business than his home-based colleague,[5] and therefore is likely to remain crucial to most firms' overseas success in the foreseeable future. However, because of the problems involved in operating an export or international sales force, many firms give intermediaries a far greater role than salesmen in foreign markets.

INTERMEDIARIES

It has been estimated that agents and distributors acting on behalf of overseas manufacturers or service companies handle about half the world's overseas trade, and these are only two of the many different types of intermediary available to the firm attempting to develop a foreign market. The term 'intermediary' is used to describe all those persons and organisations providing the service of representation between sellers and buyers.

Although intermediaries frequently represent the producer, a number of organisations act on behalf of the prospective purchaser, searching out suppliers using their specialist knowledge and expertise. The Crown Agents act for government and public bodies throughout the world. Principals of the Crown Agents are:

1. Governments, e.g. Abu Dhabi, Afghanistan, Alderney, Anguilla, Antigua, Ascension Island.
2. Local government, e.g. Capital Municipality Aden, Eldoret Municipal Council, Honiara Town Council.
3. Ports and harbours, e.g. Colombo Port Commission, East African Harbours Corporation.
4. Railways and transport, e.g. East African Railways Corporation, Ghana Railways and Ports Administration.
5. Banks and currency boards, e.g. Bank of Botswana, Bank of Ghana, Bank of Guyana, Bank of Jamaica.

There are also firms like Macy's (New York), 'the world's largest department store', who have offices in London to search out prospective suppliers. The great Japanese trading houses such as Mitsui have offices in London performing basically the same role in the Japanese market.

However, the problems of the majority of firms lie in finding the right type of intermediary, choosing the best individual or firm and establishing a system of management, motivation and control geared to win initial business, sustain customer loyalty and provide a basis for a profitable long-term presence in the market. There are many different ways open to the firm looking for overseas representation (Figure 12.3).

The initial decision faced by the firm is the best form of overseas representation: direct or through intermediaries. Policies adopted at this point are critical to the firm's future in a market. The position may be made more complex by the laws of the country in question. For example, in Sweden employee protection legislation is extremely rigorous, making the dismissal of Swedish sales staff extremely difficult, and in France, agency law classifies buyers as the customers of the agent, not of his client, the producer. In virtually no country is the termination of an agency agreement easy and without costs or risks.

An agent is a firm or individual acting on behalf of another, generally in the sales process but occasionally in a technical or advisory capacity. Agents and distributors are the main forms of representation of UK firms overseas, and agents are of three basic types: those acting with the exporter as principal; those acting with the buyer as principal; and those specialising in certain tasks, e.g. technical support. Remuneration systems vary considerably between industries and countries, but can be broadly divided into fee and commission based, with some involving a combination of both.

Distributors can generally be distinguished from agents by their willingness to invest in stock (they are the principals) and their ability to hold stock. They are often much larger

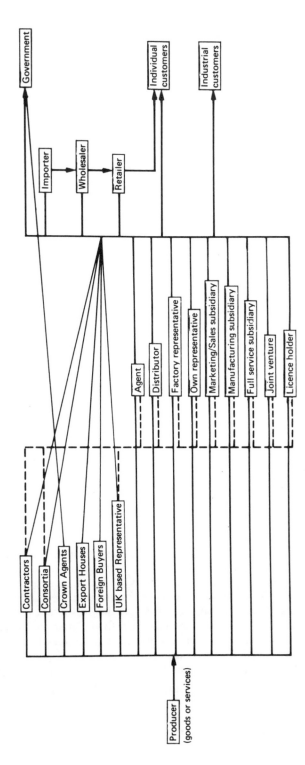

OVERSEAS MARKET BASED

HOME MARKET BASED

N.B. It is common practice to combine some of these e.g. UK representatives working with overseas agents, distributors etc (the dotted line indicates these links).

Fig. 12.3 Export representation, home and overseas based. Adapted from D. Tookey, *Export Marketing Decisions*. Harmondsworth: Penguin Books, 1975.

Table 12.4   *Projects and consortia*

Location	Type of Project	Amount	Contractor and nationality
Iran	Petrochemical complex at Bandar Shahpur	$2.3 billion	Iran–Japan Petrochemical Co., joint venture comprised of: Mitsui Group (Japanese) The Iranian government
Egypt	Sponge iron plant	$212 million	Arab Asian Development Partners, joint venture formed by: Development Consultants International Ltd (Indian) Bancom International (Philippino) Arab Export Trade Co. (Egyptian)
Jordan	Fertiliser complex	$180 million	Joint venture including: Agrico Chemical Co. (US) The Jordanian government International Finance Corp. (The World Bank) Jordan Phosphate Mines Co. (Jordanian)
Iran	Hospital	$235 million	United Kingdom Hospitals Group (co-ordinated by Orion Bank & Allied Medical Group Ltd, British)
Saudi Arabia	Desalination and thermal power generation facility	$167 million	Sasakura Engineering (Japanese) C. Itoh & Co. (Japanese) Brown, Boveri & Cie (West German subsidiary) Saline Water Conversion Corp. (Saudi Arabian)
Iran	Expansion of port of Bandar Abbas	$1 billion	Italian consortium of state-controlled companies, including: Condotte d'Acqua Co. Construzioni Motalliche Finsider Italedii Dragomar, Ing. Mangelli & Cia.
Saudi Arabia	Direct reduction steel plant	$200–$300 million	Marcona Mining (US) Gilmore Steel Corp. (US) Nippon Steel Corp. (Japanese) Nippon Kokan K.K. (Japanese)

Adapted from the *Harvard Business Review*, Jan.–Feb. 1976.

organisations with more extensive facilities and resources.

Both agents and distributors offer manufacturers a permanent presence on the market capable of making repeated customer contact, gathering information and clinching business. The fact that they are generally local firms (although there are some important international agencies providing world-wide cover) means that they understand and can adapt to local conditions. Equally important, they give the prospective customer a degree of reassurance. (The meaning of 'local' here must be fully understood. In some countries major social and political divisions may pose problems, e.g. a Greek Cypriot agent could gain very little access to Turkish Cypriot business.)

Despite these strengths some firms find that direct representation offers more advantage:

All our experiences (with agents), Britain excepted, were disappointing.

Their products need selling techniques that are much too sophisticated for the average agent.[6]

It provides a degree of control that is impossible to achieve through intermediaries. In technical areas many agents and distributors have neither the resources nor the desire to follow through opportunities in the way that the producer can. In some instances small firms have found it impossible to find good agents, but through careful market selection have built up business in markets close at hand:

> The 400 miles I drive to visit my customers in Benelux from Leeds is less than the distance to my customers in Glasgow, Aberdeen and Exeter.
>
> Managing director of a small giftware firm

Direct representation is wholly dependent on the personnel involved.

Some forms of access to foreign markets can be achieved through the home market. Sub-contracting for overseas contracts won by other firms is a major source of indirect exports, particularly for smaller firms. The very scale of some projects dwarfs the resources of even the largest firms. Consortia (groups of firms coming together to tackle projects beyond the resources of an individual firm) are becoming increasingly common, particularly for government projects in less developed countries (Table 12.4).

British firms trying to build up their overseas business at a low cost but capitalising on established market links are fortunate in having access to the expertise of Export Houses.

> An export house is any company or firm not being a manufacturer whose main activity is the handling or financing of British export trade and/or international trade not connected with the UK.
>
> British Export Houses Association, 1978.

In scale and expertise export houses vary enormously. Companies like Booker Merchant offer expertise equal to any of the larger British exporters, while other houses are highly specialised; for example, Jardines (Hong Kong) can trace its history back to the East India Company.

Choice of the type of intermediary is only the first step in a continuing process. The firm must match the exporter's needs and be able to work effectively to develop his business. Unfortunately, many firms lack method in their choice. Some choose to approach firms in a specific country, on the dangerous premise that 'we haven't got anyone there, so we've nothing to lose'. The marketing-orientated firm, however, draws up a clear brief describing the type of intermediary required, a detailed job description and a plan of their respective roles in building up a market.

Once an agent, distributor or other representative has been chosen, the task of sustaining their motivation and working together for long-term success begins. It will involve regular contact and repeat visits by the exporter to the market-place, but it provides the opportunity for fully realising the company's potential.

FROM EXPORT TO INTERNATIONAL MARKETING

As foreign business grows many firms are faced with pressure to establish a more substantial overseas presence. It is a problem that has faced many of today's giant corporations:

> In the first part of this century, when today's giants were embarking on international expansion, the term international marketing was practically synonymous with exports.... (Now) their quest for even larger markets has led them to invest in foreign production facilities.
>
> Business International Corporation[7]

This pressure can come from many sources: governments reluctant to see a continuing drain on their foreign exchange, local competition, a desire to spread the firm's risks, special opportunities or incentives, cost or marketing benefits.

Many of the problems discussed earlier—adaptation to overseas conditions, designing policies—are as important in international marketing as in exports. The advantages which can be gained from establishing a major presence overseas are matched by new problems.

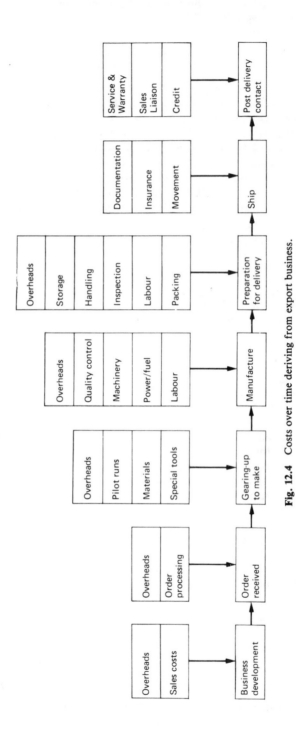

Fig. 12.4   Costs over time deriving from export business.

Many of the advantages centre on two recurrent and thorny issues of overseas trade: pricing and product development. This development from home to overseas is complex, full of challenges and potential setbacks—far from the simple process sometimes implied.

Pricing overseas

In launching a new product overseas a firm has open to it many pricing options. (These are discussed in Chapter 16.) Often firms use home-market prices plus cost for freight and insurance, but this fails to take into account the different market conditions the firm is likely to face in opening up new markets. Also, many hidden costs emerge which may directly affect the company's real returns (Figure 12.4).

In determining prices and agreeing terms, parties in international trade operate under the terms agreed in Incoterms 1953 (revised 1967 and 1974). These set out rules to avoid misunderstanding and dispute over the precise meaning of an agreed price.

The company setting up a manufacturing plant in the target market can avoid many of these trading problems, and may also benefit from lower production costs or distribution savings. It is generally in a position to price much more competitively. For the overwhelming majority of firms, overseas production involves establishing a limited number of plants (generally small in proportion to the number of markets), the location of which should be carefully considered by marketing staff to fully exploit their marketing potential as well as any production or financial benefits, e.g. development grants from governments.

Distribution

For many firms one of the main advantages in establishing manufacturing plants overseas is reduced physical distribution costs. Research by organisations such as the National Economic Development Office has highlighted the effect of service and other aspects of distribution on overseas trade. Poor delivery and service are seen as 'the British disease' by foreign buyers, and although a great deal of progress has been made in this area it remains a recurrent criticism by customers. It seems that if a UK firm delivers late the purchaser calls it typical, but if a German company delivers late the buyer sees it as an exception that will not recur. Regardless of the rights and wrongs of this, it is a situation British companies must work hard to resolve.

Manufacturing from a point much closer to the market can improve service levels and lower distribution costs. However, control of production and other operations can be a major problem, especially in plants at a considerable physical distance or operating in very different societies. Two fundamentally different approaches to this problem have been adopted in international marketing: centrist and devolved policies. *Centrist* operations are organised around and tightly directed by head office, while with a *devolved* policy the local operations have considerable authority. Most companies locate themselves somewhere between complete head office control and total operating freedom.

Products

One of the areas in which issues of central or local control come most clearly to the fore is in product development and management. The Wells' international product life-cycle discussed earlier suggested that offerings emerged from the home market out into new markets. The pattern emerging today is a continuous flow of ideas and products from many parts of the world. Although Britain and the USA are the only net exporters of licences, a study of new product directories will show inventions and innovations from all corners of the world:

> Gas alarm instrument using fixed electric current by a Japanese firm.
>
> Licence is offered by a US company for a patented process for disinfecting liquids by irradiation.
>
> A blocking mix against enzymatic action ... developed in Scandinavia.
>
> *Planned Innovation*, April, 1979

Overseas subsidiaries are increasingly geared to adapt existing products to their own special market conditions as well as producing their own innovations. These patterns of research and development require careful monitoring by the parent firm to maximise returns while minimising waste and duplication.

Recurrent issues when discussing with foreign buyers products originating in the UK are poor quality control, low service levels and inadequate stocks of parts in the customer markets. These are areas of immediate interest to export and international marketing management, since orders which have been won in the face of fierce competition can easily be lost by failure to sustain standards in these areas. Many products originating in Britain have received acclaim overseas when introduced only for this praise to be followed by a chorus of disappointment because of weaknesses in the areas mentioned above. In overseas trade the competition is so great and hard-won advantages so easily lost that communicating this message within the firm is an essential task of corporate management. The campaigns sponsored by the British Overseas Trade Board, 'Export Year' and 'Export United' appear to have made real progress in these areas.

Up to this point discussion has been focused broadly on British exports of manufactured goods. The rest of our trade falls broadly into the area of 'invisible exports', an area of recurrent balance of payments surplus.

TRADE IN 'INVISIBLES'

The trade in 'invisibles' is so called because it deals in intangibles, in contrast to the physical tangible nature of visible trade.

> The invisible account is concerned with the payments and receipts derived from the provision of services. It includes payments and receipts derived from shipping, air freight, tourism and insurance: income earned and paid on overseas investment and foreign-owned home investment; current government expenditure abroad on the maintenance of forces, the provision of grant aid to underdeveloped countries (and contributions to bodies such as the EEC).
>
> Kempner, T., *A Handbook of Management*, Penguin Books, 1976

Four broad areas are of interest to the marketing man: finance (including insurance); shipping, freight and related services; consultancy and advisory services; and tourism. These are becoming increasingly important areas of opportunity for marketing-orientated executives. Their long-term strength and sustained growth are leading some authorities to suggest that Britain's economic future is more closely linked with these service sectors than with manufacturing.

Although it will be many years, if at all, before the service sector can provide either the foreign exchange earnings or the job opportunities to make this type of forecast come to pass, its growing importance appears to be certain.

Finance

The City of London is still the banking and insurance capital of the world. Marketing financial services throughout the world is a major source of the UK's export earnings. Income is generated from returns on investment, loans, advisory and counselling services and the highly publicised but relatively small area of currency management.

> The government (Uruguay) in 1975 received capital from various sources including an allocation of SDR 46.6 million from the IMF's special oil deficit facility plus a loan for an initial amount of $110 million from a consortium of banks in London.
>
> Barclays Bank Report on Uruguay, 1976

The strength of the British banking system is matched by the power and authority of the insurance community. Lloyds coverage is sought throughout the world. Some brokerages earn the overwhelming majority of their income from export transactions in this complex and highly specialised field.

No discussion of international or export marketing is complete without a mention of the specialised trading companies, although these are not strictly speaking in the finance area. Merchants such as European Grain and Shipping (exports in 1974 were over £35 million), Frank Fehr and Co. (exports in 1974 were over £22 million) and Star Diamond Co. (exports in 1973 were over £17 million) play a vital part in international trade, especially in primary products and raw materials.

Shipping, freight and related services

Britain's long history as a trading nation has built up a wealth of knowledge and expertise in the international movement of goods and associated services which is unsurpassed anywhere in the world. The shipping lines and the air and road freight organisations have

Containerships

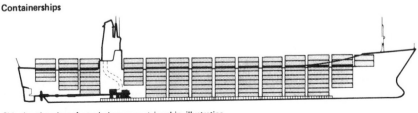

Side elevation view of a typical ocean containership, illustrating
container cells

Roll-on/roll-off vessels

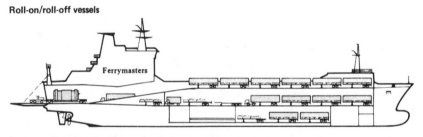

A cut-away illustration of a short sea stern-loading, freight-only
ro-ro vessel. Note access to the upper deck via a fixed vehicle
ramp, and to the lower trailer deck using a powered elevator

Fig. 12.5   Types of liner vessels. From Thomas Meadows and Co. *Understanding the Freight Business*, 1979.

accumulated expertise which is in demand throughout the world. Some companies, such as Overseas Containers Ltd, have established extensive networks of support services throughout the world to facilitate the movement of clients' goods. The operations of the transport firms are complemented by freight forwarders and other specialised organisations. It is an area in which radical change has occurred during the post-war era as the shipping firms have competed vigorously for a share of the movement of goods in world trade. A good illustration of the pace of development is the 'container revolution' which, from beginnings as recently as the mid-1950s, has changed the entire face of surface transport (Figure 12.5).

Consultancy and advisory services

Knowledge is rapidly becoming recognised as one of the most valuable international commodities. There has been a surge in demand for advice, technological skills and design, consultancy and other knowledge-based services over the last decade, particularly from the rapidly developing economies of the Middle East, Africa, the Far East and South America. The main demand in the initial period has been for technical assistance in areas such as construction and agriculture. Architects, designers and building, civil, mechanical, mining and electrical engineers have been at the forefront in opening up new markets. More recently, the scope for business development in this area has been recognised by consultants and advisers in many fields.

As the industrial base of these emerging countries grows there is a growing demand for management and marketing expertise. Business schools, polytechnics and colleges of further education, as well as the more commercial concerns, are finding opportunities based on the need in many overseas countries for expertise in these critical areas.

Tourism

Four statutory boards which gave official recognition to the growing importance of tourism and its related industries to the British economy were established in 1969 by Act of Parliament. These were the British Tourist Authority, charged with promoting Britain in overseas markets, and the English, Scottish and Welsh Tourist Boards, which had the authority to assist the promotion and development of tourism in Britain. This growth has continued, and today tourism is one of Britain's most important and vigorous industries. It provides employment to hundreds of thousands across the country, from museum keepers on Hadrian's Wall to waiters in London restaurants. It is, however, an area in which 'the marketing concept is yet to (fully) permeate'.[8] Although progress has been considerable since that comment was made, tourism remains an area of real opportunity for the creative marketer, from the large national concern catering to mass markets to the small local firm meeting the needs of special interest groups.

The requirements of customers go far beyond the 'tangible' aspects of the product. Also important are the attractions of the destination, the facilities (accommodation, catering, entertainments and recreation), the means of getting to and from the destination, the availability of goods and services, and the entire cluster of presentation, promotion, advice, finance, general atmosphere and, increasingly important, local attitudes to visitors.

A recurrent problem of tourism marketing is the impact of the 'total experience' on the holiday-maker or visitor and the number of uncontrollable factors which can influence their satisfaction. Weather, general impressions of the environment and interaction with residents can be as important as the stated purpose of the visit. Promotions geared to encourage overseas visitors can be nullified by hostility to them once they are here.

In tourism marketing there must be a recognition of the very different marketing opportunities which can arise from the varied holiday needs of customers from different parts of the world.

THE MULTINATIONALS

It is impossible to review international and export marketing without some discussion of the multinationals. Multinationals are firms which have direct investment in a number of countries, generally deriving 20–50 per cent or more of net group profits from markets other than their original or home country. Management makes policy decisions based on

Table 12.5 *Partial listing of major Third World multinationals*

Company	Country of incorporation	Industry	1977 sales in estimated millions of dollars
National Iranian Oil	Iran	Petroleum	22 315.3
Petróleos de Venezuela	Venezuela	Petroleum	9628.1
Petrobrás (Petróleo Brasileiro)	Brazil	Petroleum	8284.3
Pemex (Petróleos Mexicanos)	Mexico	Petroleum	3391.5
Haoi Omer Sabanci Holding	Turkey	Textiles	2902.7
Hyundai Group	South Korea	Shipbuilding, transportation	2590.7
Indian Oil	India	Petroleum	2315.6
Schlumberger	Neth. Antilles	Measuring and scientific equipment	2160.3
Chinese Petroleum	Taiwan	Petroleum	1920.1
Zambia Industrial & Mining	Zambia	Mining and metal refining—copper	1862.3
The Lucky Group	South Korea	Petroleum, electronics, appliances	1744.3
Steel Authority of India	India	Metal refining—steel	1447.6
Turkiye Petrolleri	Turkey	Petroleum	1376.7
Kuwait National Petroleum	Kuwait	Petroleum	1376.3
Korea Oil	South Korea	Petroleum	1341.1
Samsung Group	South Korea	Industrial equipment, electronics, textiles	1305.3
Thyssen-Bornemisza	Neth. Antilles	Shipbuilding, farm equipment	1258.7
CODELCO-CHILE	Chile	Mining and metal refining—copper	1231.2
Koc Holding	Turkey	Motor vehicles	1207.6
Philippine National Oil	Philippines	Petroleum	986.2
Daewoo Industrial South	South Korea	Textiles	851.8
Siderurgica Nacional	Brazil	Metal refining—steel	847.5
USIMINAS	Brazil	Metal refining—steel	826.4
General Motors do Brasil	Brazil	Motor vehicles	824.4
Vale do Rio Doce	Brazil	Mining—iron	824.0
Ford Brasil	Brazil	Motor vehicles	758.7
SANBRA	Brazil	Food products	707.3
Indústrias Reunidas F. Matarazzo	Brazil	Chemicals, food products, textiles	675.3
Grupo Industrial Alfa	Mexico	Metal refining—steel, chemicals	603.2
ICC	South Korea	Metal products, rubber, textiles	580.6
Sharat Heavy Electricals	India	Industrial equipment	525.4
Ssangyong Cement Industrial	South Korea	Chemicals	598.0
Sunkyong	South Korea	Textiles	467.6

the relative merits of alternatives anywhere in the world, and this feature places them in part, outside the scope of international or export marketing. They generally try to minimise, if not eliminate, the foreign or alien nature of their offerings. Wherever they operate, their aim is to become a local firm. Lever Bros (US) might be part of Unilever, but generally their actions are those of a US firm in the American market. The Ford Corporation is a giant US concern, but Ford UK is almost as British as British Leyland (Ford UK contributed exports of £452 million to UK trade in 1975).

Multinational corporations are now among the major forces in the world economy. Although it is impossible to obtain accurate figures, it is estimated that the 300 largest account for over 20 per cent of world trade, a proportion which is steadily growing. Their size, power and apparent independence from national governments have raised many fears among politicians, economists and others. Although these fears persist large-scale unemployment has led many governments to mute their criticism while wooing them for investment and jobs.

Despite their apparent power, the multinationals face enormous management and marketing problems. At the centre of these lies the problem of control, discussed earlier. For the multinational firm this issue looms large. Marketing planning has become a powerful element in ensuring optimum returns and minimum duplication and in establishing control. In some firms the process of centralisation has gone so far that totally standardised marketing plans are used throughout the corporation, from the group itself to the smallest operating unit. Other firms have placed considerable faith in building up shared ideas and values among corporate staff through recruitment, training and development.

The problem of standardisation has also emerged in product, distribution, pricing and promotional policies. Five basic strategies have been identified in marketing and communication:[9] same product, same message world-wide; same product, different communication; different product, same communication; dual adaptation (product and communication adapted to local needs but little questioning of basic proposition); and autonomy of foreign operations.

In the past the discussion of multinational corporations focused on the activities of US firms, e.g. IBM and Coca Cola, but recently British firms like BAT, Beechams and ICI, and even more recently European and Japanese companies like Philips, Nestlé, Toyota and Hitachi have become very powerful. The multinational company is increasingly becoming a worldwide phenomenon, and Third World multinationals are demonstrating very rapid growth (Table 12.5).

CONCLUSION

The export and international market-place is a complex and changing environment. It is made up of five basic types of firm:

1. Non-exporters: firms which, although they may have exported in the past or perhaps will export in the future, do not now.
2. Passive exporters: probably the largest group (in terms of numbers). Willing to service foreign business but do little to win it.
3. Active exporters: from a production base in one country these firms search out overseas business.
4. International marketing firms: production is spread over a small number of overseas plants.
5. Multinational corporations: giant firms operating throughout the world with an overlap between domestic and foreign business. Individual units of these corporations can fall into any of the above categories.

Although some firms progress from the first type through to being a multinational, the overwhelming majority operate for long periods in a specific category. Progress usually occurs because of a combination of the determination of a specific executive, effective marketing backed by mobilisation of all company resources and favourable demand conditions.

There are some constraints on the firm in international trade. One of the major disincentives to the newcomer is the complexity of documentation and payment systems, although bodies such as SITPRO (Simplification of International Trading Procedures Board) are attempting to solve some of these problems. However, while there are nations looking to protect their interests the problems will never entirely disappear. Care in these areas is vital in international trade.

Operating effectively in the international market-place is essential to the economic well-being of the United Kingdom. Over the past 500 years British businessmen have demonstrated their ability to compete successfully, and success in the future will depend on their ability to effectively adopt a marketing stance in overseas trade.

Notes

1. Cooper, A., 'An Economic Race with Population', *Marketing*, August, 1978.
2. Barclays Bank Report, *Factors for International Success*. London: Barclays Bank International, 1979.
3. 'Silentnight Wakes up to Exporting', *Marketing*, June, 1978.
4. Barclays Bank Report, *Factors for International Success*. London: Barclays Bank International Ltd, 1979.
5. BETRO Trust Committee, *Concentration on Key Markets*. London: Royal Society of Arts, 1977.
6. Both quotes from Hill, R., 'How Durco Europe went Direct', *Marketing*, March, 1977.
7. Business International Corporation, *Managing Global Marketing: A Headquarters Perspective*. New York: Business International, 1976.
8. Burkart, A. J. & Medlik, S., *Tourism: Past, Present and Future*. London: Heinemann, 1974.
9. Keegan, W. J., 'Five Strategies for Multinational Marketing'. In *International Marketing Strategy* (Ed.) Thoretti, H. B. Penguin Books, 1973.

Further reading

Barclays Bank, *Factors for International Success*. London: Barclays Bank International, 1979.
Day, A. J., *Exporting for Profit*. Gower Press. Authoritative and comprehensive review of the area.
Thorelli, H. B. (Ed.), *International Marketing Strategy*. Harmondsworth: Penguin Books, 1973. Excellent collection of articles referring to all facets of international and export marketing.
Tookey, D., *Export Marketing Decisions*. Harmondsworth: Penguin Books, 1975. Succinctly and clearly reviews the subject from a practical perspective.

Key organisations

British Overseas Trade Board,
Department of Trade,
1 Victoria Street,
London SW1H 0ET

Institute of Export,
World Trade Centre,
London E1/AA
A handbook listing all key export organisations is published by the British Overseas Trade Board.

CASE STUDY 10: KIRKBY CARPETS

The company

Kirkby Carpets have been established as carpet manufacturers in Kirkby, near Liverpool, since 1947. John Smith, the present managing director, is the son of the founder and, although it has been a public company since 1964, the family influence remains strong. The bulk of its production is medium–high quality Axminsters with wool being the primary material, reinforced by nylon. A wide range of designs is produced: 150 designs in 70 colours with ten alternative qualities. It was this range and variety of product which convinced the firm that real export opportunities existed. All its production is concentrated at its Kirkby site, which is well placed for Liverpool and its docks. The workforce of 180 is drawn largely from the surrounding towns. The current turnover of £3.5 million is divided into 70 per cent home market and 30 per cent exports. Their existing costing system does not permit them to separate the different markets to identify any differential experiences.

Export organisation

The firm operates primarily through appointed agents working on a percentage basis. Their agents vary considerably in size, from large firms with well established sales organisations to small firms depending to a considerable degree on Kirkby's Carpets' products. They prefer agents to have a range of complementary products. This flexible policy has enabled the firm to build up a very extensive network of national agents throughout the world.

Traditionally the white Commonwealth has been their largest market, with Canada and Australia as the leading markets (good sea links from Liverpool have assisted this process). The recent past has seen some decline in sales to both countries, with import restrictions making it difficult to build up trade. However, the growth of demand in Europe, the USA and the OPEC countries has more than compensated for the decline in the traditional markets. In Europe prior to EEC membership a healthy trade had developed with EFTA countries, of which Switzerland and Sweden provided the biggest sales volume. The links with these countries have continued since Britain joined the EEC, and in 1970 they made a serious attempt to tackle EEC markets. Agents were recruited in all member countries, France and Germany being given priority:

> The Germans were already importing similar quality products at much higher prices from Belgium and Holland, so we felt that we had a real chance of success.

The French are not large users of carpets but the comments in the press about the likely growth in national income during the 1970s stimulated this move. Holland, Belgium, Italy and Spain were also seen as potentially lucrative markets.

Even more recently a serious attempt has been made to establish a sales organisation in the Middle East. The oil price rises and comments about the oil-rich Arab states have prompted an initiative in that area. Two basic approaches had been taken: working through contractors in the UK, particularly those involved in major building projects, and building up a network of agents. A number of relatively small orders have been won, and the firm is currently tendering for a major order in a planned hotel complex. David Smith, the sales director, is planning to go to Saudi Arabia on a trade mission with the Liverpool Chamber of Commerce.

The most recent decisions have been to give considerable priority to developing the US and Japanese markets. David Smith, who is the managing director's younger brother, sees this search for new markets as clear evidence that 'it is from exports that we will be looking for growth'. He is very much the motivating force behind this search for market opportunities. His wife is Italian, and he believes this gives him a more international perspective than most of his rivals in the carpet industry.

The current sales set-up is based on David Smith as sales director and exports sales managers organised on a regional basis (Figure 12.6).

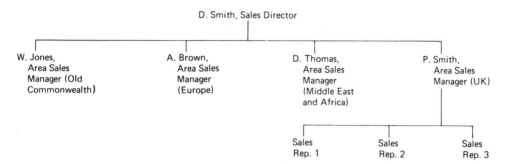

Fig. 12.6 Kirkby Carpets: sales division.

David Smith takes personal responsibility for the contracts side of the business and developing markets (Table 12.7). Co-ordination of their activities takes place through sales group meetings, the sales group reporting directly to the board.

Table 12.6 *Markets as a percentage share of Kirkby Carpets business*

Country	1970	1974	1975	1976
UK	80	74	70	70
Australia	7	6	5	4
Canada	5	3	2	2
New Zealand	2	2	2	2
Sweden	1	1	2	2
Switzerland	–	1	3	1
Germany	–	1	2	3
South Africa	2	1	–	1
Eire	2	–	–	1
USA	–	2	2	4
Netherlands	–	–	–	1
Iran	–	2	–	1
Saudi Arabia	–	1	3	2
Nigeria	1	1	1	1
Other Commonwealth countries	–	1	3	1
Other European countries	–	1	3	2
Other Opec countries	–	2	1	1
Others	–	1	1	1
Total	100	100	100	100

Task

John Smith has called for a review of current export activities and for proposals to improve sales and profitability. Put forward recommendations to increase the share of export sales over the next three years from 30 per cent to 40 per cent, with no overall decline in UK sales.

13

Managing the Marketing Mix

For many years one of the most successful firms in the instant coffee market was a company which few, if any, consumers could name. Sol Café built up a significant share of a market where branding and heavyweight advertising were the norm by adopting a diametrically opposite route. In establishing their position as a producer of own-label coffee, personal selling, prompt delivery and meeting customer product and price requirements dominated their marketing mix.

Avon cosmetics and Yardley present contrasting approaches to developing business in the cosmetics market. Avon concentrates on personal selling in the home, while Yardley backs its extensive dealer network with substantial advertising expenditure. However, they have one thing in common: success.

In setting up his business last year Dave Green faced the same basic problem as these firms had faced and, with varying degrees of success, had solved. He had decided on his market(s) and his offering: the rapidly increasing number of individuals and firms with video equipment and their need for blank cassette tapes.

In a new market such as this his options were wide open: should he concentrate on the commercial market, or perhaps on specific groups of the consumer market? Once he had made that decision he then had to decide what precisely his offering was. In raising that issue he was examining his marketing mix. The commercial and consumer markets differ significantly in composition and needs (Table 13.1):[1]

Table 13.1   *The marketing mix for different markets*

	Consumer	Commercial
Product	Good quality; preferably links with equipment manufacturer; robust technically for frequent erasures	Very high quality; compatible with existing systems; professional use reduces technical risks
Place	Links with rental or equipment sales firms very important; limited willingness to search; fears of direct mail or discount outlets	Willing to search; technical knowledge reduces direct mail worries; outlets providing other needs make buying easier
Price	Low enough to attract but not to undermine quality image; percentage discount for dealer may need to be high to persuade him to stock these instead of higher priced units	Low prices, especially if sold through direct mail; supplies shops may accept lower margin than TV shops as it is new line
Promotion	Main media plus point of sale for quality reassurance, perhaps allied to promoting different uses or storage to increase usage	Direct mail or personal selling to direct accounts

1. Consumer: affluent (A, B, C_1 socio-economic groups), using largely rented equipment; a newly developing market, thus experience low and equipment new; generally tapes erased after a fairly short time; (important sub-group building up libraries).

2. Commercial: often media-related (ad. agencies, marketing consultants) but growth in other sectors; mixture of bought and rented equipment; (in media) experienced with equipment and wide range held; tapes are often stored, hence volume is high.

Table 13.1 illustrates how managing the mix for different customers can produce very different offerings. The selection of mixes and the allocation of resources between the mix elements go far in determining the success of the firm and its customer proposition.

The marketing man is:

'a mixer of ingredients', one who is constantly engaged in fashioning creatively a mix of marketing procedures and policies to produce a profitable enterprise.

Neil H. Borden[2]

The essence of managing the marketing mix lies in providing each group of customers or segment of the market with the mix of product, price, place and promotion which most suits their needs. The product manager is in many ways turning his product or brand into a market in its own right.

THE MIX ELEMENTS

The marketing mix is the set of controllable variables that the firm can use to influence the buyer's response.

P. Kotler[3]

Although there are a number of different descriptions of the mix elements, probably the most popular is McCarthy's, the four P's: product, price, promotion and place.

Product

The product can be subdivided into quality levels, special features, styling, branding, product range or mix, service back-up, warranty, durability and packaging.

The product mix of these features can vary enormously. A firm might invest heavily in quality control and first-rate material to ensure a top-quality, durable product, which would keep its service and quality costs down. Another company might provide an array of products each with a different combination of these elements, e.g. a low-quality product backed by a high service element in combination with a masthead, high-quality product.[4]

Price

Price is the mechanism of exchange between firm and customer. It incorporates level(s), credit (terms and sources), discounts, margins, resources, financial services (e.g. advice), allowances or trade-ins and strategy and tactics. As in the case of products, considerable scope exists for establishing a different sub-mix of price elements. One firm might have a high premium price but offer generous credit terms, while another might have a far lower price but give virtually no credit. The mix can vary between levels of the market. The retailer might be encouraged through high discounts to buy low and sell high to end-users.

Promotion

This encompasses the two broad areas of *advertising* (including below-the-line) and *personal selling*: advertising (main media/display, main media/classified, below-the-line);

merchandising (promotional support for the retailer); personal selling (salesman's (special) discounts); and publicity (press and public relations).

There is a growing understanding of how these forces interact. The dangers of cold canvassing[5] are encouraging more and more firms to combine personal selling and media advertising.

Place

This makes the product physically available. It falls into two broad areas—channels and physical distribution—and covers channel strategy, intermediary systems, outlet, warehouse and factory location, service levels, documentation, coverage, stocks, freight and insurance.

Some writers have suggested that the sheer size of this area, allied to a number of other factors, takes it out of marketing altogether. However, the importance of intermediary policies and physical distribution in making the product or offering available demands a powerful marketing involvement.

Although there is a tendency to think in terms of a mix of four factors, in reality the offering is made up of a series of sub-mixes of the variables listed above. Decisions taken in one area have effects which go far beyond their immediate context. For example, a decision to adopt a penetration pricing stance[6] calls for extensive distribution, probably high stocks, high customer awareness (perhaps from media advertising) and high-volume production capacity. With a new product the large amount of trial sought by this strategy may call for a high degree of confidence in the organisation's ability to maintain quality levels.

Limitations to the four P's

The extent to which the notion of the four P's encapsulates the key areas of marketing action has disguised many of the problems of mix management that have emerged in practice. It is easy to become pre-occupied with the challenges of making decisions on individual parts of the mix or creating blends which fit the internal requirements of the enterprise. Successful mix management is not built on this. It depends on the fit between manageable resources (mix elements) and the needs of specific customer groups. A mix created without targeting or focusing on a market segment has no value.

This is closely related with the common failure to appreciate the importance of placing mix decisions in their competitive and environmental context. The elements are designed to:

1. Create a combination meeting customer needs.
2. Achieve competitive advantage.
3. Satisfy legal requirements.

Driver (1983) examined the importance of these and noted that:

> The prevailing conception of marketing in terms of the four P's, which largely excludes competitive and legal considerations, has tended to isolate marketing from a context which is a matter of practical and public importance.

DESIGNING THE OPTIMUM MIX

Most mix design is based on a mixture of intuition and research. As managers become more aware of the extent to which each variable is interdependent there is increasing interest in methods of designing the optimum mix.

The marketing mix depends on a clear vision of the *customer group* and target market and the *resources of the firm*. Marketing research, entrepreneurial insight and many other sources help to build the picture of the market or segment the firm wishes to satisfy, and the firm's resources include its personnel, history, current offering, and even the image currently held in the market of its offerings. Attempts by newspapers such as the *Daily Express* to reach new markets, e.g. to move from an older customer profile to a younger market, have often foundered on the clear vision the new target market has of the offering and their rejection of it. In many customer markets the phrase 'you can spin down but not up' holds true. It means that expensive products (or firms with high-quality images) can be a platform for cheaper derivatives but that cheap products cannot be a platform for expensive derivatives.

Borden suggests that designing the mix is a combination of arts and sciences, calling for a multi-step approach (Figure 13.1).

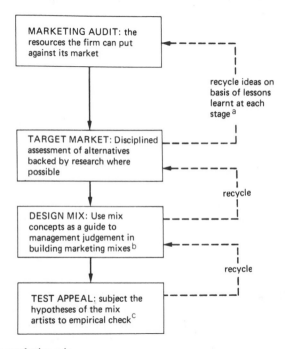

Fig. 13.1 Building the marketing mix.

[a] As decisions are made or information is gathered it may prove necessary to go back a step to rethink the ideas leading up to that point.

[b] Borden, N. H., 'The Concept of the Marketing Mix'. In *Readings in Basic Marketing* (Ed.) McCarthy, E. J., Grastief, J. R. & Brogowicz, A. A. Illinois: R. D. Irwin, 1975.

[c] Kotler, P., *Marketing Decision-Making: A Model-Building Approach*. New York: Holt, Rinehart and Winston, 1971.

It has been suggested by some writers that much more quantitative approaches can be adopted to set the optimum marketing mix for a particular firm at a given point in time. The aim of such analysis is to use estimates of pay-offs from specific combinations to arrive at an optimum mix.

In the discussion of this topic Kotler indicates how modern econometric techniques along with improved data-handling systems in firms can be of great help in coping with the problems involved in this type of study. His analysis does not set out to handle the very important subjective or corporate dimensions of these decisions.

Even within specific areas, e.g. setting the advertising appropriation, short-term economic circumstances may directly affect resource allocation. David Corkindale points out that one of the findings of a long-term research project at Cranfield is that subjectivity, interpersonal negotiations and external financial forces all have an impact on setting advertising budgets. In establishing both the overall mix investment and expenditure in specific areas a much more extensive network of interacting forces comes into play.

MIXES FOR LEVELS

Although a specific marketing mix may be targeted on a group of end-users, its impact on other parts of environment can be vital to its success. For example, in industrial markets, distributors frequently resist lower-priced substitute products. This derives from their recognition that they have no direct interest in supporting a product selling for £4 against another selling for £5 if the margin remains the same and the volume is constant. For a manufacturer with only one line this may be solved by adjusting the margin. A producer with a large number of other lines going through the same dealers might find the cost of this enormous.

Just as the mixes for the sub-groups of end-users have to be designed to meet their needs, the mixes for those involved in reaching these groups must similarly be considered. The interaction between these has an important role in determining the overall success of the policies.

CHANGE OVER TIME

The optimum combination of elements will change as the product passes through its life-cycle, as environmental forces change, as the consuming and intermediary groups adapt, and as competition responds. The design of the initial mix will therefore need to be able to respond to these circumstances. The ability to adapt can be seen in brands (Oxo, Guinness), manufacturers (Philips, Wedgewood), intermediaries (Sainsburys, W. H. Smith) and service organisations (Sotheby's, Barclays Bank).

The record companies have been very successful at building adaptations into the marketing mix. As the buying public for popular records has grown and key retail groups have increased in influence, they moved from the specialised record store, retailing at full price and using virtually no main media display advertising, to larger general stores, heavily discounted and with substantial promotion (Figure 13.2).

THE FUTURE

The next few years are likely to see increasing pressure on marketing management to demonstrate the optimal nature of their mix decisions, and quantitative approaches are likely to play an increasing part in providing the guidelines for these decisions. However, the rapid changes with which they will need to cope will also mean that intuition and creativity will have a continuing role to play in ultimate decision-making.

Notes

1. This was Dave's model of the market in the early days—subsequently modified as experience and information grew.

Up to £1.50 off albums you didn't think Woolworth sold.

FM (Featuring Steely Dan,
The Eagles and others.)
Original Sound Track
£1.50OFF
Man. Rec. Price

Out of the Blue
ELO
£1.50OFF
Man. Rec. Price

Moonflower
Santana
£1.00OFF
Man. Rec. Price

Saturday Night Fever
Original Sound Track
£1.50OFF
Man. Rec. Price

London Town
Wings
£1.00OFF
Man. Rec. Price

Natural Act
Kris Kristofferson
& Rita Coolidge
£1.00OFF
Man. Rec. Price

Once Upon a Time
Donna Summer
£1.50OFF
Man. Rec. Price

Footloose and
Fancy Free
Rod Stewart
£1.00OFF
Man. Rec. Price

Star Wars
London Symphony
Orchestra
£1.00OFF
Man. Rec. Price

The Album
Abba
£1.00OFF
Man. Rec. Price

And great savings on a stack of other albums too.

As well as the rock bottom prices on the ten top albums on this page, your nearest large Woolworth record department has savings of £1.00 and £1.50 off man. rec. price on many other great albums you may have missed.

(The only catch is that the offer closes on June 24th).

So if you want to save money on the albums you've always wanted, you'll have to hurry.

Great savings on cassettes too!

The life you want–at the prices you want

that's the value of
WOOLWORTH
Also at Woolco

Fig. 13.2 This advertisement demonstrates the effective combination of price, promotion and distribution. Reproduced with the permission of F. W. Woolworth and Co Ltd.

2. Borden, N. H., 'The Concept of the Marketing Mix'. In *Readings in Basic Marketing* (Ed.) McCarthy, E. J., Grastief, J. R. & Brogowicz, A. A. Illinois: R. D. Irwin, 1975.
3. Kotler, P., *Marketing Management*. Englewood Cliffs: Prentice-Hall, 1976.
4. A masthead product carries the firm's flag, i.e. establishes the highest standards for the range, e.g. Cadillac for General Motors.
5. Selling without any preparation of the ground with the particular prospect or group of potential buyers.
6. Pricing low for high volume (see Chapter 16).
7. Corkindale, D., 'A Practical Way to Set Advertising Budgets', *Marketing*, August, 1978.

Further reading

Borden, N. H., 'The Concept of the Marketing Mix'. In *Readings in Basic Marketing* (Ed.) McCarthy, E. J., Grastief, J. R. & Brogowicz, A. A. Illinois: R. D. Irwin, 1975. Effectively sets out the essential character of marketing mix management.

14

Product Policy and Innovation

The product is the most important element of the marketing mix, since it holds together promotion, distribution and pricing policies. Products are not necessarily tangible: the bank, travel agent, insurance company, consultant, architect and designer all have product offerings, but these offerings are largely intangible; and although the foundry, plastics moulder or aluminium processor deals in physical products, these are frequently made to the buyer's specification, and the firm's real offering is technical skills or production capacity. Even the finished products in the shops are made up of the components or semi-finished products of a large number of manufacturers. Raw material, chemical, commodity, food and other primary products markets all have their own special characteristics which the marketing managers in these areas have to understand. Planning, decisions and policies in all areas of marketing are directly affected by the product field in which the marketing manager operates (Figure 14.1).

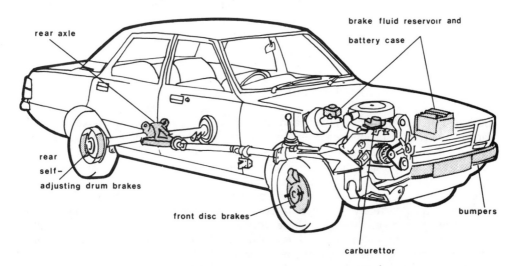

Fig. 14.1 Visual indicating components and car.

This immense variety is reflected in the American Marketing Association's definition of a product:

> Anything that can be offered to a market for attention, acquisition or consumption, including physical objects, services, personalities, organisations and desires.

Many firms owe their existence to an entrepreneur's determination to make a product. Often a market opportunity is recognised or there is a commitment to make something better or cheaper, but occasionally the simple desire to invent or to introduce a new service provides the spur to starting the firm. The commitment of Dr Land of Polaroid to his product breakthrough led him to build up his business in defiance of the prevailing wisdom and market power of the photographic industry. Henry Ford's genius at manufacture led to the creation of the Model T and laid the foundations of the Ford Corporation. In Europe, François Michelin of Michelin and David Brown of D. J. B. Engineering show the immense potential of inventiveness allied to a determination to succeed. In all these cases the product and its manufacturing process are the rocks upon which the firm's future stands. In the service sector, Charles Saatchi of Saatchi and Saatchi, Terence Conran of Habitat and Lord Grade of ATV demonstrate the continuing power of a commitment to a product offering in building up their firms in the service sector.

The importance of the product to the firm and its profits means that it lies at the centre of most managers' thinking about the company. In many cases the firm is identified in their minds and in the minds of the general public with the product or process. To them, Parker makes pens, and to prove it most of the workforce are directly involved in manufacturing pens. The British Gas Corporation supplies gas, and the majority of their management, staff and workers are involved in its storage or transmission, or associated services. This proximity and the resulting identification with the product go a long way towards explaining the product orientation, seen by Levitt as a source of potential danger to all firms:

> It is all too easy in this day and age for a company or industry to let its sense of purpose become dominated by the economies of full production and to develop a dangerously lopsided product orientation. In short, if management lets itself drift, it invariably drifts into the direction of thinking of itself as producing goods and services, not consumer satisfactions.

Recognition of this does not detract from the importance of the product, but does call upon management to see it in a number of different ways: the route to satisfying complex customer needs; a part of a selection of opportunities the buyer has to satisfy these needs; an aspect of the changing environment in which the buyer's needs and his methods of meeting them are constantly evolving.

THE COMPLEXITY OF CUSTOMER NEEDS

Increased understanding of buyers and their needs has highlighted the large number of factors involved in product choice. This goes far beyond the identifiable and relatively undifferentiated features of the *core product*. Commodity markets illustrate the characteristics of a core product market. It is almost impossible to separate the wheat produced by each of the independent growers in Britain from that produced by their competitors. The market may be akin to the 'perfect competition' described in Chapter 1, with each producer having virtually no power to control the market or his own business future. Many new products go through a phase when a large number of 'me too' brands almost create a commodity-market situation. Alfred P. Sloan, former president of General Motors, pointed out that during the period when the Model T Ford dominated the US motor industry the only real difference between it and the Chevrolet was the low price Ford could charge because of his massive economies of scale.

The homogeneity of need, implied by products showing virtually no difference, occurs very infrequently in the market place. This was recognised in the era of the tea clippers, when ships like the Cutty Sark would race from India or Ceylon to be the first to market, hence getting the best price. The modern concept of the *augmented product*, with its emphasis on quality, features, style, name, packaging, service, warranty, installation and instruction, and more recently environmental impact, plays a major part in effective product planning geared to winning real advantages in the market.

Effective control in these areas is as important as the core product's basic characteristics in winning sales and establishing customer loyalty. Overseas customers have often criticised the poor quality control of British goods, and the Advisory Council on Applied Research and Development note that:

> we believe that a major effort is due, indeed overdue, to place a greater emphasis in Britain on the sciences related to manufacture with special attention to the relation between production processes and the design, quality and reliability of products.

Special features meeting the buyer's particular needs can often sway the buyer more effectively than lower prices. The inclusion by Japanese car manufacturers of features such as number plates and radios in the basic car was a real product advantage in the eyes of many customers, even if the final price was actually higher. This is as important in service industries as in manufacturing. The core product of a bank may be its financial service, but special features such as outside money machines operating for much longer hours than the bank are important to many customers. Special services to manufacturers, ranging from advice and counselling to booklets on special topics, are also part of their augmented product.

In the tourist industry many areas of historic or leisure interest fail to fully realise their potential because of a lack of facilities, the wrong type of services or simply lack of thought about the total product requirements of the visitor. A research study compared the historic cities of York and Durham. Both share many core features of history, interest and reputation, but York had developed a wide range of catering and shopping facilities geared to the tourist and Durham had not. The effect was that the average visitor to York spent $2\frac{1}{2}$ times as long in York as his equivalent spent in Durham, with resulting pay-offs for the local tourist industry.

It is seldom fully realised how important aspects of the augmented product can be to the intermediary. He can be reassured by those features which are passed on to the customer, but some features can be designed specifically for the wholesalers and retailers, e.g. protective packaging, multipacks and specific pack sizes. In certain instances palletisation has made a dramatic difference to ease of handling, a feature equally important for industrial customers.

SELECTION OF OPPORTUNITIES

Until now the discussion has centred on the single product, although this may encompass many features. However, there are very few single-product firms. Most firms offer a range of products or *product line*, which is a broad group of products intended for basically similar uses and possessing similar physical characteristics. This tendency derives from a number of pressures. The internal economic logistics of products can create the opportunity to introduce related products, or the same capital plant may be able to produce a very wide range of goods. External distribution or sales economies can create similar opportunities. A representative visiting a contact can probably introduce additional product ideas or offerings to the buyer at relatively little extra cost.

In some cases an agent or intermediary may expect or demand complementary products, and it makes his purchasing more efficient and easier if valued suppliers provide additional related items. Analysis of the market-place may identify related items with market potential. Sometimes these are totally new sectors of the market, and at other times there may already be firms established there, but the sector shows signs of growth or appeals for other reasons.

The primary purposes are to achieve internal efficiencies and external *synergy*, which is achieved when the combined effect of a group of elements is greater than the sum of their individual impacts. The combination of separate products and product lines makes up the firm's *product mix*, 'the composite of products offered for sale by a firm or business unit'.

There is no need for a direct relationship between the items in a firm's product mix. In large firms a very wide spread of lines carried can be part of a deliberate policy of new venture development or may derive from a series of acquisitions. Imperial Group, Britain's sixth largest firm, illustrates this. Its spread of activities ranges from tobacco, through plastics and packaging, to food and brewing. Within a giant firm there may be specific units with a very wide product mix. The food division's mix includes motorway service stations, frozen chickens, potato crisps and pet foods. Successful management calls for control of the mix in terms of three variables: product width (the number of different lines), product depth (the number of items in each line) and product consistency (the closeness of the relationships between the products).

In smaller firms the mix tends to be much smaller. The major exceptions to this are firms in process industries, producing goods using a particular technology or material, and component manufacturers. These groups generally produce items to a customer's specification to be incorporated in his end product. In the case of process industries such as plastics, steel, rubber and aluminium, many firms have no product of their own, but have the skill to produce a massive array of items using their specific technology, e.g. plastics injection moulding or aluminium extrusion. Their offerings are their skills and capacity. The component manufacturer usually provides a wide range of goods but will often adapt, amend or even re-design particular items for a customer. Smallness can be a real advantage in this type of industry, as the commitment, flexibility, speed of response and low overheads of small firms can offer major benefits to customers.

BRANDS AND BRANDING

Product and brand management policies were introduced by some larger firms to build the qualities of the small firm into the advantages of the larger firm. A *brand* is a name, term, symbol, design or combination of these which is intended to identify the goods or services of one seller or group of sellers and to differentiate them from those of other sellers. Some brand names have become so powerful that they are now in everyday use, e.g. to Hoover a room rather than to vacuum clean it, and to do some Xeroxing rather than photocopying.

The development of brand- or product-management based marketing organisations has provided firms with the opportunity to establish internal profit centres. The brand manager is almost the 'managing director' for this specific product, with control over advertising, sales, distribution, price and even product development (usually within the range). In multi-brand firms, competition can emerge within the company, spurring each brand or product manager on to greater achievements.

The brand can provide the customer with a reassurance of quality and consistency. In some cases strong brand loyalty can emerge, with the buyer actively searching out his preferred brand. The identification of brand and symbol or trademark can give protection from price cutting and individuality, and is a powerful cue for potential purchasers, occasionally worldwide. In Britain and in some other countries with strong retailing groups the phenomenon of 'own-label' brands has emerged. Firms such as Tesco, Sainsbury's, Marks and Spencer and Woolworth have introduced products under their own labels. These are either the same name as the store, e.g. Tesco coffee, or the company brand, e.g. Marks and Spencer's St Michael label. In the past the tendency for these to cost less contributed to a lower-quality image, but today the quality demands of the stores and the reputation of the retailers have led to their being viewed as being equal to or better than manufacturers' brands.

All companies offering an array of products or brands can choose from a number of marketing strategies:

1. The entire output can be individually branded, with no obvious generic link, e.g. Procter and Gamble's Bold, Ariel, Daz, Tide and Fairy Snow.
2. There can be a series of family brands within a firm, e.g. the Sunsilk range of shampoos, hairsprays, conditioners and setting lotions within the Elida Gibbs division of Unilever.
3. A powerful brand symbol can link all the firm's offerings; e.g. the Kodak name and symbol are used to link the firm's films, cameras, photographic chemicals and other activities.

There are many permutations of these within the overall need to earn the maximum advantage from the corporate reputation while protecting the individual identity of specific items, and the choice is a problem which firms face every time a new brand or a new product is introduced onto the market.

For the overwhelming majority of firms, prosperity is based on a balance between skilful management of existing products and the search for and successful introduction of new products and developments. Competitive pressures, changes in customer attitudes and behaviour, and political and economic forces mean that no firm can assume that the product which successfully met an important need yesterday will continue to provide customer satisfaction and corporate profits tomorrow. In government markets, defence requirements and medical product needs change and adapt. In industrial markets, plastic mouldings may replace timber or metal. Pressure on the consumer-goods manufacturer to innovate will be felt through the chain of supply. Even markets such as agriculture, often seen as stable, face the demands of a changing environment.

This does not mean that change for change's sake is either necessary or advisable, particularly when related to specific brands, products or lines. Stephen King points out that the constant search for new brands can lead to the premature withdrawal of support for brands with continuing potential for projects and sales:

> One result can be a self-fulfilling prophecy. The company's major brand has a bad year ... funds are withdrawn from it ... the next year it does even worse, this confirms the original diagnosis and panic increases; new brands are hustled along faster and faster, and most fail: the company has talked itself into a decline.

When attempting to create a balance between supporting established products and brands and searching out innovations one must recognise that the firm must survive today to prosper and grow tomorrow.

THE CHANGING ENVIRONMENT AND EVOLVING NEEDS

In a modern industrial society such as Britain, changes are continually occurring in the market. They can be caused by technological developments, fashions, political pressures, economic circumstances and many other factors. The search for growth by companies, both in the home market and overseas, can itself be a major force in this process. This pattern of change and growth is probably the most important single factor distinguishing industrial from non-industrial societies, and as such it is something no firm can ignore, either in terms of pressures on the viability of its current offering or in terms of the opportunities it creates for projects and growth. No company can neglect it; nor can a country looking for national prosperity fail to recognise its importance or the vital role of marketing in this process. The first recommendation of the ACARD report was that:

> The Government should recognise the encouragement of industrial innovation as a major component of the industrial strategy.

There are four basic elements in the pattern of change and growth: technical change, invention, innovation and product development:

1. Technical change: the environment of adaptation, development and modification in technology surrounding the firm, its customers and the market.
2. Invention: the process of creativity and discovery, generally involving a specific addition to the sum of human knowledge, but although new, not necessarily useful or desired by any potential market.
3. Innovation: the technical, industrial and commercial steps which lead to the marketing of new manufactured products or commercial services and to the use of new technical processes, products or services.
4. Product development: the introduction of adaptations, changes or modifications into existing products, brands or services designed to extend their viable life, adapt to new markets or introduce new uses.

All these are capable of being viewed from or emerging out of the different perspectives of producers, intermediaries and customers.

WHAT BUSINESS AM I IN?

Even before 1960, when Theodore Levitt published *Marketing Myopia*, some businessmen had realised the dangers inherent in the close identification of the firm and the satisfaction of customer needs with specific products or offerings. Today the concept is at the centre of marketing thought. The firm which narrowly defines itself in terms of a particular form of product runs the risk of being overtaken by changes in the ways in which customers seek to satisfy their needs. 'They have always bought it' and 'everyone needs it' are phrases which have sounded the death-knell of or led to massive contraction in industries and companies ranging from cooperages to railways. Coopers saw themselves as being in the barrel-making rather than in the storage-container business, and railways identified themselves with trains rather than with transport. Even if outside factors lead to a revival, for example oil shortages leading to a railway revival, many firms will have failed to survive and many of the remaining will have paid a high price for this marketing myopia.

A recognition of the dangers inherent in this identification with specific offerings has led to a more critical examination of how products and brands develop over time. The notion of a life-cycle has emerged as a useful mechanism for analysing the process by which specific forms of meeting needs emerge, grow, stabilise and decline over time. Closely associated with this is the proposition that the marketing-orientated firm should closely study the needs which give rise to specific products, as well as studying the progress of its own products or services.

THE PRODUCT LIFE-CYCLE

The model suggests that all products go through a series of stages in their lives, as illustrated in Figure 14.2. At each stage the sales/profit relationship varies. Similarly, the relative importance of, appropriate form of, and interrelations between the marketing mix variables change. Product quality is vital during the introductory stage, as failures during trial of a product can lead to long-term buyer rejection, so advertising may be more informative or educational during this period. In later periods, widening distribution or cutting prices may become more important. Besides giving cues to the appropriate strategies for the existing product, the model can help the firm to better exploit the market position of the product by providing leads to the timing of new launches, the move to new markets and diversification. More general analysis may indicate general patterns of behaviour, e.g. whether product life-cycles are shortening. The model has provided a fertile source of ideas and developments both within firms and among marketing men.

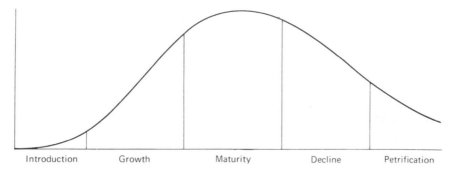

| Introduction | Growth | Maturity | Decline | Petrification |

Fig. 14.2   The product life-cycle.

A number of writers have highlighted limitations to the use of the product life-cycle model, and have even questioned the value of the approach. Stephen King points out that it can be applied effectively only to a specific form of product or service. Brands can incorporate dramatic changes in composition, sustaining long-term growth, and any attempt to apply the life-cycle model is likely to do more harm than good. Brand names like Oxo, Bovril, Hovis, Persil and Cortina in consumer markets and Dexion, Xerox and Formica in industrial markets have incorporated substantial changes apparently without following a life-cycle model. It has been agreed that failure to identify a clear life-cycle for such important products as steel, aluminium, glass and bread leaves the model with limited descriptive validity.

Despite these criticisms the model retains an important place as a guide to analysis and planning, giving direct cues to decision-making without being a scientific tool. The firm can try to exploit the life-cycle by looking for new product developments, innovations or new markets to extend the life-cycle (Figure 14.3).

The life-cycle concept places particular emphasis on the risks, for management in any firm, of failing to cultivate invention and innovation.

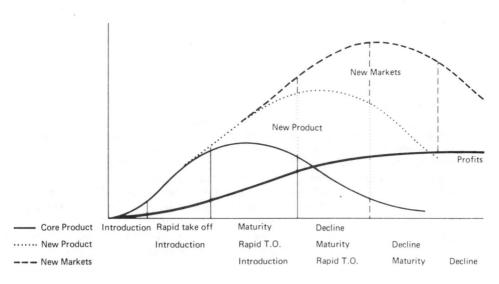

—— Core Product	Introduction	Rapid take off	Maturity	Decline		
······· New Product		Introduction	Rapid T.O.	Maturity	Decline	
– – – New Markets			Introduction	Rapid T.O.	Maturity	Decline

Fig. 14.3   Exploiting the product life-cycle.

INVENTION, RESEARCH AND CREATIVITY

Successful products derive from a stock of ideas, concepts and prototypes which firms can originate themselves or obtain from external sources. The fertility of firms in this area is largely dependent on the creative climate in the firm. The potential sources of new product or services are enormous. They range from the 'Eureka'-type invention to the marginal improvement of existing products. All have a role in sustaining the firm's competitive position if they are conducted with a view to meeting buyer needs more effectively. Among the sources of new ideas are:

1.   The firm's research and development department: this department may be working to a specific brief, e.g. to develop a drug capable of combating hay fever, but minimising side-effects and avoiding the use of anti-histamines, or it may have a much broader role, e.g. to explore new sources of energy or to spot new product opportunities. Generally there will be some relationship between the two, with ancillary roles such as reviewing related developments, e.g. by competitors.
2.   Outside organisations: these can provide a continuing source of inventions and developments. They range from major government projects, e.g. the NASA space programme which incorporated a dissemination project for new products, to private concerns or individuals offering opportunities to license or buy.
3.   The marketing department and other company units: these can produce leads through such activities as brainstorming, think-tanks, foreign search, market gap analysis, market research, activity analysis, long-range projections and segmentation analysis.

The establishment of an open, creative company environment stimulates a high degree of corporate inventiveness. It is important to overcome the resistance to change which can emerge in companies, where fear, vested interest and risk avoidance can produce internal barriers to needed change.

   The stock of high potential new product, process or service ideas is the vital base in the search for success. However, it is only the starting point in the development of offerings capable of making a real contribution to corporate performance. Successful innovation is the next crucial step.

INNOVATION

Innovation takes four basic directions:

1.   Improvement and development of existing forms: the manufacturer of a piece of earth-moving equipment can introduce features geared to make it operate more quickly or efficiently. An advertising agency may offer new client services.
2.   Improvement and development of existing processes: a printer may identify ways of printing a specific item to improve finish or reduce price, but calling for only minor modifications, if any, in a client's layout or presentation.
3.   Introduction of novel production process: this has been the basis of the growth of industrial society. Suppliers introduce new technologies to the production of basically similar products, often generating dramatic price cuts and improvements in product quality and consistency. From the Spinning Jenny to the silicon chip (Figure 14.4), it certainly offers new horizons for the adapting firm.
4.   The introduction of new products and services: in modern society, markets are in a constant state of flux, with modified, changed or revolutionary products or services being offered to potential customers. The craze for skateboards created massive but fleeting opportunities for those fast enough to adapt, and the digital watch threw the

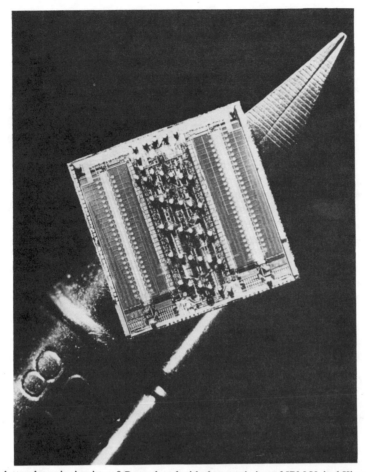

Fig. 14.4 A latter-day spinning-jenny? Reproduced with the permission of IBM United Kingdom Ltd.

Swiss watch industry into confusion, while revitalising the US industry. The emergence of media buying agencies is forcing many traditional advertising agencies to carefully evaluate their operations, while McDonald's Hamburger franchises are affecting the entire fast-food catering market.

The opportunities for innovation are matched by the risks. It has been estimated that between 50 and 90 per cent of new introductions on to the market fail. Disasters such as the Ford's Edsel, DuPont's Corfam and RCA's computers are the tip of an iceberg which also includes W. D. and H. O. Wills' Ambassador cigarettes and innumerable less well publicised failures. The mass of evidence that has been accumulated indicates that the root cause of much failure is commitment to a specific product, service or brand offering relatively little to the prospective buyer, but perhaps meeting some corporate need for representation in a sector of the market, meeting a specific launch date, or exploiting some internally developed technology.

SCREENING AND TESTING

Effective market-orientated screening and testing procedures are essential in order to cut down these high rates of failure. The firm can also use these processes to turn ideas, inventions or possibilities into a producible, marketable reality.

The first stage involves *evaluating* all developments against the firm's current or foreseeable production capabilities. Although many new-product proposals can be eliminated here, an open mind must be kept about those which do not fit into the firm's current technology. The market potential of some products or process may induce the firm to adapt their current capabilities to realise the opportunities in the market.

The remaining proposals then require careful *business analysis*. This involves exploring the market potential of the project, and 'concept research' makes a valuable contribution to this process. The underlying proposition is put before prospective purchasers, usually in a visual form, although mock-ups are sometimes used. These can be explored generally through in-depth interviews or group discussions. Occasionally there is sufficient data for more quantitative approaches, giving clearer insights into prospective pay-offs.

These approaches are particularly useful where the prospective buyers are already familiar with the underlying ideas, language or terminology involved in the product, but radical new ideas, so new that the bases for communication do not exist, cannot effectively use these systems. More complex, projective approaches such as delphic or futures analysis are being used increasingly. Traditionally there has been reluctance to use these approaches in industrial markets, and over the last few years there has been an increased use of empirical studies to analyse opportunities in these markets. A major goal of these initial screening stages is to minimise the costs involved in developing the idea, project or proposal to a finished stage.

Effective *development* is designed to ensure that the customer benefits underlying the initial proposal and providing the basis for business analysis are delivered by the final product. Some compromises may be necessary to arrive at an item capable of being produced efficiently or returning a reasonable level of returns for the firm, but these considerations should not be allowed to negate the primary buyer requirements. The smoker may want an absolutely safe cigarette, but does a merely safer cigarette have the same appeal? An aircraft capable of carrying passengers from London to New York in less than four hours has real appeal, but is that sustained when the payload is 115 passengers? Plastic-coated steel may have real advantages for the auto industry, but are these sustained if storage and handling problems dramatically increase wastage? The development programme must encompass manufacturing capabilities and efficient production: problems in this area were major factors in the eventual demise of Du Pont's Corfam.

The market-place is the final arbitrator of whether the final physical offering will deliver enough benefits to buyers to provide a long-term, profitable contribution to the firm. Test marketing has been developed to provide a situation in which the maximum information can be gleaned from the market-place at the lowest cost prior to final commercialisation. The aim is to replicate in miniature the complete market. There are two distinct approaches: *test markets* for forecasting and problem identification, using only one experimental area; and *matched-area tests* to obtain forecasts and identify potential problems but, equally important, to select the optimum marketing mix from a number of alternatives.

The value of test marketing is largely dependent on selection of the test area or areas and the process by which the experiment is conducted. Properly conducted, it invariably costs both time and money, but insights into the product's potential can be obtained. However, discipline must be exercised, particularly in the complex area of building up the forecasts. Simple extrapolation is dangerous: the complexity of the context must be built into the analysis. Equally important are experimental biases deriving from: concentration of effort behind the test, such as disproportionate promotional support or over-involvement by management or sales staff; poor choice of test areas, perhaps because areas are chosen for convenience rather than from a desire to model the market; and competitive response designed to maximise their information and sometimes muddying the water for the test. A Lever Bros executive described a test conducted by them when the competition 'came in so hard and heavy that as our sampling crews were going up one side of the block, the Procter (competition) men were coming down the other side'.

In Britain these problems have led to some reluctance to embark on large-scale test markets, particularly when the technological gap is so small that the competition can respond by introducing their own brands based at least in part on information obtained at the innovator's expense. In the USA the complexity of the market, its size and the costs involved have created an environment in which the savings usually outweigh the risks, and it appears that companies here which are introducing products, particularly in industrial markets, for a wide European market are adopting a mode of behaviour akin to the US model.

Although these disciplines help to reduce risk, it will never be totally eliminated. For this reason it has been argued that, as companies become larger, more centralised and more bureaucratic, there is a reduced willingness to take risks for radical new developments. In some instances this has led to the development of new-product management teams, product champions and venture management teams. At the centre of all these developments is the attempt to back small entrepreneurs with large-firm resources.

THE ENTREPRENEUR AND THE SMALL FIRM

The ability of the risk-taking entrepreneur to break out of the narrow bounds of the established situation and fan the flames of enterprise has been the basis of the growth of many of today's great industries. Ford, Durant, Kellogg, Singer, Krupp, Eastman, Courtauld, Daimler, Biro, Siemens and Dassault all created giant enterprises which are almost synonymous with the industries they built. The entrepreneur still plays a major part in the process of product management and development.

There is some evidence to suggest that in both new technology based firms (NTBFs) and in the majority of smaller firms the scope for and interest in effective product management and innovation are at their highest. At the same time their involvement in the product creates the dangers associated with a product orientation with a real need for a more powerful, structured and systematic marketing orientation. These policies must go beyond the product.

Effective product management calls for an approach incorporating current products, innovation and, where necessary, product abandonment strategies.

Further reading

Adler, L., 'Relating the Product Life-cycle to Market Needs and Wants'. In *Handbook of Modern Marketing* (Ed.) Buell, V. P. New York: McGraw-Hill, 1970. A thorough review of the issues involved in establishing a product line which successfully meets the firm's needs while providing an effective customer offering.

Advisory Council on Applied Research and Development, *Industrial Innovation*, HMSO, 1978. Report bringing out the importance of effective innovation to Britain's industrial future and the critical role of marketing in this process.

Brooks, J., 'Xerox, Xerox, Xerox, Xerox'. In Brooks, J., *Business Adventures*. Harmondsworth: Penguin Books, 1971. A perceptive and lucid account of the development of this major corporation.

Cannon, T., 'New Product Development'. In *European Journal of Marketing*, 12, No. 3, 1978.

Cannon, T., 'Test Marketing'. Anglia Television, 1982.

Key organisations

National Research and Development Corporation,
Kingsgate House,
66-74 Victoria St,
London SW1E 6SL

New Product Management Group,
Management House,
Parker St,
London WC2B 5PT

CASE STUDY 11: DEVELOPMENT AND LAUNCH OF THE NEXO PLASTICS COMPOUND HOPPER-FEEDER

For most of its history NEXO Plastics (Nottingham) Ltd has been firmly established as a good-quality injection moulder. In 1979 the firm had a turnover in the region of £2.5 million. Strong links exist with major firms in the locality (John Player and Sons, Raleigh Industries, Boots and Pedigree Petfoods) as well as with a large number of medium and small firms.

This array of blue chip accounts has led the firm to place considerable emphasis on increasing the efficiency of its production process. Jack Wills, the production director, has shown himself to be extremely talented at this, and his efforts are complemented by the small and enthusiastic technical staff he has built up.

One of their recurrent problems lay in filling the hoppers on their injection-moulding machinery with plastic compounds at an efficient and consistent rate. After a number of abortive attempts to solve the problem, sometimes with bought-in equipment and sometimes with units built themselves, they eventually developed a very effective piece of hopper-feeder equipment.

This home-made item seemed to do the job more efficiently and at a lower cost than any other equipment with which they were familiar, and the hopper-feeder was soon making a significant contribution to the smooth running of their production process.

About a year after the equipment became fully operational a 'productivity mission' from France, organised in association with the British Plastics Federation, visited the factory. Apart from making a number of more general comments, a number of the members of the mission expressed considerable interest in the hopper-feeder. A medium-sized moulder from Lyons was so keen that he offered to place an order for one immediately. A technical expert from RAPRA (the Rubber and Plastics Research Association) was also very complimentary about it.

This outside interest stimulated considerable discussion in the firm. The hopper-feeder had not been developed for sale, but was merely an aid to their current production. The low cost of producing it, along with its contribution to production efficiencies and the interest which had been shown in it, indicated that the firm had a highly marketable item. The only serious reservation they had about selling it lay in their reluctance to supply the fruits of their ingenuity to their competitors.

In spite of these reservations it was decided to place the hopper-feeder on the market. There was some discussion about licensing manufacture to an existing equipment supplier, but Jack Wills was keen to keep it in house, as this would provide them with ready access to any related developments. Alan Leith, the newly appointed sales director (he had been with the firm for many years), was confident that the company could handle the sales and marketing.

Funds were put aside for further development to make the hopper-feeder a more saleable item. The foreman in the technical department was given responsibility for setting up production facilities capable of earning £150 000 from sales in the first year, £250 000 in the second year and £500 000 by the fifth year.

It was decided to launch the product at the international plastics exhibition (INTER-PLAS) at the National Exhibition Centre, Birmingham, in ten months' time. The company was committed to having the equipment in a fully commercialised form by then. However, far more problems emerged than had been anticipated, and Jack Wills was very unhappy about the amount of time he ended up spending on the project. Eight weeks before the exhibition a fully operational unit was installed in their factory, and although there were minor teething troubles it was felt that it was now saleable.

To coincide with the exhibition, advertising space was taken in the exhibition catalogue, *Rubber and Plastics Weekly* and *Plastics and Rubber International*. Alan Leith invited journalists from these journals to the factory to see the hopper-feeder in action. In *Rubber and Plastics Weekly* a very favourable report was published ten days before the exhibition. (*Plastics and Rubber International* is a monthly, so their feature did not appear until later.)

It was decided that Jack Wills and his foreman would work with Alan Leith and his staff manning the stand. Peter Needham, the managing director, spent the first four days on the stand and was available in Nottingham at fairly short notice should any problems occur.

The exhibition was a tremendous success. Large numbers of firms visited the stand, a number of orders were taken, and there were far more inquiries than they had anticipated. When the results of the exhibition were reviewed it was found that the first year's output was almost taken up by orders received and those inquiries which Alan Leith felt confident would mature.

Because of this early breakthrough Alan Leith was keen to expand production more rapidly than originally intended. The overseas interest was particularly exciting, as the firm had never exported before. Within two months Alan had followed up a number of inquiries in Europe and these, combined with the firm orders taken at the exhibition, meant that orders worth £175 000 had been taken. Over 60 per cent of these were export orders.

The care taken in designing and testing the product now paid off handsomely, since there were very few problems or complaints. Despite this the sheer size of the demand placed the very limited resources devoted to this exercise under considerable pressure, and there was some tendency to drain resources from other areas of the firm's activities. It was well into the second half of the first operating year before equilibrium was established.

More worrying for the firm's sales management was the rapidly lengthening delivery times, which had stretched from two months to eight months.

Task

In the light of these factors review the firm's operations to date, bringing out any lessons for future introductions and making practical proposals for the future marketing of the hopper-feeder.

15

Test Marketing

No aspect of marketing poses more challenges than the effective management of change. This is true whether it is prompted by external forces or derives from internal initiatives. Both create uncertainty. This uncertainty involves risk for the individual and the firm. In marketing this can be seen in a wide range of areas. Demands for new products and services, pressure for increased product use, improved packaging, improved productivity and the constant drive for competitive success combine to create the need to adapt through innovation and change, with all the associated risks. Managing these risks is an integral part of effective marketing management. A major tool in this is 'Test Marketing'.

> Test marketing is a controlled experiment conducted in one or more limited, but carefully selected, parts of a market. These are chosen to be representative microcosms of the total market. The aim is to use the test to predict and explore the consequences of one or more proposed marketing actions, notably new product introductions.

The above definition of test marketing differs from some of those more commonly used, by broadening the term to include experiments on other aspects of marketing besides new product launches. Many firms are using the same techniques to explore the implications of change in other aspects of the marketing effort. The physical aspects of the product may remain the same but the total product proposition in the eyes of the consumer may be transformed. This may be akin to introducing a new offering.

Changes in the test market environment have influenced this. New technologies have emerged which enable firms to adopt novel approaches. At the same time the techniques are being employed in a wide range of circumstances. The decision by Tesco to join Lunn Poly in a test market to examine the scope for selling holidays through supermarkets took the techniques into two unusual areas: retailing and services. The same pressures which led manufacturers to employ this approach to gauging the market potential of their goods—expense and high risk—are encouraging other firms to follow this route. Despite the growing use of the technique, many questions persist about its role and value.

THE CONTROVERSY

Test Marketing is a subject on which many different and strongly held views exist. Philip Kotler in his classic marketing textbook[1] stated that:

> Test Marketing is rapidly approaching the state of a science.

This contrasts with Stephen King's comment[2] that:

> The delays of Test Marketing have often spoilt what might have been successful businesses.

These views are not necessarily contradictory, but they do focus attention on the two issues around which much of the test marketing debate revolves.

1. Is test marketing an important contribution to the scientific process of gathering useful information to aid marketing decisions?
2. Even if this is true, is the real price, in terms of money spent, delays, warnings to the competition, worth the effort?

In this chapter these topics, plus the issues which emerge from them, are studied.

THE SCIENTIFIC DIMENSION

The process of marketing research—gathering empirical evidence to assist in marketing decision making—owes a great deal to the scientific tradition. Anyone reading marketing research textbooks will continually come across the notion that market research aims to, or actually does, introduce science into marketing.

> 'Marketing research . . . the application of scientific method to Marketing.'
> P. E. Green & D. S. Tull[3]

Although this is less confidently asserted today than it was once, the link between the process of systematically gathering, recording and analysing marketing information and the empirical tradition of the natural sciences cannot be denied.

Experimentation is an almost essential part of that tradition.

> 'It is experimentation that expresses the basic empiricism of science.'
> Abraham Kaplan[4]

Test marketing is the attempt to apply the framework of the scientific experiment: constructing a situation in which certain developments and interrelationships of interest to the researcher can be observed and measured, with conclusions about relationships being drawn.

The laboratory experiment focuses attention on the questions under consideration, *excluding as far as possible all other influences*. The test market by its very nature cannot be as closed, as self-contained, as the laboratory experiment. Although this is a limiting factor, it is a mistake to assume that researchers in the natural sciences successfully exclude all possible sources of bias and every non-experimental influence. We are usually talking about matters of degree and the commitment to a research discipline. These qualifications accepted, test marketing provides access to a rich and powerful source of marketing intelligence.

The problems which faced Campbell's range of frozen food in 1980 highlight the variety of lessons that can be learned. Their objectives were clear and fitted neatly into an overall corporate commitment to growth and diversification. The range was targeted on the customer seeking new tastes and willing to pay a premium for quality and uniqueness. In the test, problems emerged which brought major features of the proposition into question.

Retail buyers challenged both the underlying proposition—'There is a limit to what customers would pay in this sector'—and the practicality of opening up this sector under the Campbell's label at this time—'The Campbell's name doesn't guarantee success. There are too many frozen food lines on the market'. The Campbell's test enabled the firm to assess these reactions in a limited experimental area. This was done at a far lower cost than a national introduction. It is estimated that the 'test' cost the firm around £750 000, including research costs but excluding product development. A national introduction into that market at the time would cost about £5 000 000 excluding stock. Clearly, the data above begs the question whether the same insights could be obtained from more conventional, lower cost research. Normally the test will only be conducted after a programme of market research has been completed. This is especially true in new product development.

THE CHALLENGE OF INNOVATION

Most discussion of test marketing centres upon its role in innovation. Until fairly recently, this was seen largely in terms of new consumer products. There is now a rapidly-growing awareness of the scope for using it effectively in a number of novel situations.

1. Improved performance in traditional areas: getting the best out of current brands, products and lines through optimising advertising, price, service display and other features of the marketing mix.
2. Use in areas such as services, retailing and industrial goods.

In all these areas, the act of innovation is acknowledged as probably posing more risks to management than any other area of marketing. It has been estimated that the failed 'Mr Burt' development by The Burton Group cost over £5 million during the mid-1970s. Test marketing is part of the battle to:

1. Limit these risks.
2. Help with the 'Go/No Go' decision.
3. Provide volume, profit and share predictions.
4. Eliminate bugs from the system.
5. Examine alternative approaches.
6. Bring out aspects of the product or service that can be improved for the firm's competitive advantage.
7. Supply data on as many aspects of the innovation and its performance in the market as possible.

Ansoff's framework[5] for exploring alternative growth paths demonstrates the strategic options open to firms. At the same time, evidence to date indicates that the likelihood of failure increases as the firm moves away from familiar markets and known products.

In each of the strategies in Table 15.1, a need exists to break free from the conventional notion that innovation can only be thought of in terms of the physical product. It is the total offering which matters, including image, cost, expectation, etc.

Table 15.1   *Alternative growth strategies*

		Products Existing	New
Markets	*Existing*	Market Penetration	Product Development
	New	Market Development	Diversification

Source: I. Ansoff, *Corporate Strategy*.[5]

The risks associated with new products and services and the associated costs are enormous. Most marketing men are familiar with new product failures, ranging from the almost apocryphal stories of the Ford Edsel and Du Pont's Corfam to the more routine failures of brands like Wills Ambassador. In very many cases, major contributory factors to their difficulties would have been spotted in test marketing.

The 1950s—Ford Edsel: serious difficulties made worse by the glare of publicity.

> Within a few weeks after the Edsel was introduced, its problems were the talk of the land. Edsels were delivered with oil leaks, sticking hoods, trunks that wouldn't open, and push buttons that couldn't be budged with a hammer.
>
> John Brooks, *Business Adventures*.[6]

The 1960s—Du Pont's Corfam: major problems with customer acceptance.

> Corfam shoes had to fit properly in order to be comfortable: they did not stretch and mould to one's feet even after prolonged wearing.[6]

The 1970s—New Smoking Material: proposition did not match up to customer expectations.

Customers wanted and expected a safer, cheaper product, not a safer, similarly-priced product.

A cautionary note should be made here. Test market success does not guarantee that the same pattern will emerge nationally. There are a number of examples of products performing well in a test market, but failing to make the grade nationally. Both Heinz Toast Toppers and 'Dine' Instant Mashed Potato performed sufficiently well in tests for large-scale, national launches to take place. Their failure highlights the importance of the market as arbiter of success and failure

SUCCESS, SURVIVAL AND FAILURE

Most contemporary studies put the rate of new product failures between 30 per cent and 60 per cent. Perhaps even more importantly, studies of truly successful brands put the chances of achieving this at less than one in ten. Although there has been relatively little research in the area, there is scant evidence that rates of failure are any lower in services, retailing or industrial goods. In the most comprehensive recent study, John Madell[7] found that only 4 per cent of new product launches in the British food market were truly successful.

Test marketing can help firms to:

1. Avoid expensive failure.
2. Identify the factors in the firm's offering which need to be changed in order to maximise the firm's chances of success.
3. Improve performance of existing products, services and brands.

Once the decision to test has been made, performing these tasks efficiently calls for the imposition of a rigorous discipline on the testing process. This discipline should be applied to all aspects of the test itself: opportunity, methodology, location, scheduling and duration, and besides the measurement and analysis of the research results.

Table 15.2 *The chances of success*

Year	1969	70	71	72	73	74	75	76	77	78	Total
Total Food Products Launched £4M+	53	76	94	92	64	81	55	70	73	72	730
Turnover	1	1	2	5	2	5	1	4	7	3	31
Per cent	2	2	2	5	3	6	2	6	10	4	4

Source: John Madell, 'Where Do New Products Come From?'.[7]

ARE TEST MARKETS WORTH DOING?

It would be foolish to deny that there are problems, risks and costs involved in test marketing. Some of these are, broadly speaking, controllable and linked to the research discipline and design itself: what to test, when to test, the controls to be imposed, choice of area, timing, measuring and assessing results, besides the techniques of projection, prediction and forecasting. These will be examined in depth later. Other difficulties are associated with the non-laboratory, competitive nature of this marketing action.

Placing the new product, service, other offering, or changed policy on the market exposes it to the public eye. Part of that public is the competition, so many of the advantages that might have been gained by surprise are forfeited. The benefits which could come from this are lost, and only lead times remain to offer the bonus of being first.

There are important areas in which this competitive dimension gives cause for serious concern. This is notably when the tester is entering a totally new market against well-established rivals. Faced with this dilemma when launching their Snack Soup, Cadbury, a firm usually convinced of the value of test marketing, decided to:

> 'Pre-empt the competition by introducing, distributing and promoting our brand nationally and being the first on the market.'

> N D Cadbury

TESTS: EXCEPTIONS AND OPPORTUNITIES

Earlier, Cadbury pointed out the risks for the newcomer conducting a test market in a field dominated by established producers. Although lead times can protect, the combination of established power and inherent risk is a strong argument against this experiment. Incidentally, the evidence on innovation to date suggests that simultaneously introducing new products onto new markets is the most dangerous launch policy. This is illustrated by the difficulties encountered by Wiggins Teape when moving into toys, Woolworth into durables and clothing, and even Marks and Spencer with their knitting wool.

At the other end of the spectrum, testing may be unnecessary where the costs and risks of national launch are low. Typically, this is the situation in which spare capacity on existing machinery can be employed for a minor product adaptation with low promotional costs. The firm's familiarity with the market can provide clear indications of the potential.

Other situations in which testing is probably impractical are:

1. *Fashion lines*, footwear or clothing, seasonal lines.
2. *Fads*, such as skateboards.
3. *Other short life-cycle items*, such as records and fiction books.

In each of these situations, their very nature is incompatible with the time needed for the process of constructing, performing and evaluating the experiment. It ought to be stressed that these criteria hold true for *risk avoidance* strategies.

It is possible that *opportunity maximising* can be at least as important. Therefore, test marketing alternative strategies may bring to the fore combinations offering significantly better prospects for sales and/or profits.

Until now, discussion has concentrated on the marketing costs and implications of testing. Often production, sourcing and delivery factors weigh more heavily with management. It has been suggested that consumer durables and other items calling for high pre-launch investment are not worth market testing, as there is so much 'up front' money spent that the launch has to proceed.

This reflects much of what is known about the psychology of innovation. It is very difficult for company management to accept that the item upon which so much time, money and effort has been spent can fail. Unfortunately failure is endemic. When marketing costs are likely to be high, it is usually worth testing to either *cut losses*, even if marketing costs are a small percentage of total investment, or *improve the total offering* through product testing, service levels, promotion or prices.

In the mid-1970s, BP introduced a low viscosity oil. The product had major technical merits which produced significant savings in petrol consumption. However, after two years, it had gained only 2 per cent of the market versus a target of 5 per cent. It became clear that many factors contributed to this: significant differences in results between new and older cars, doubts among customers about the product, and the low overall share of BP outlets in the total oil market.

The initial failure of BPVF7 in distribution and communication would probably have been identified in a test market. High development costs in this case were an argument for, not against, test marketing. In consumer durables, launches are regularly criticised for their poor quality, inadequate instructions, etc. If the firm is lucky, the product survives long enough to be debugged, albeit with national attention focused upon it and possibly a widespread body of resentment. The technical and distribution problems that plague the Waddington's Videomaster vividly illustrate the costs and risks that can occur with new consumer durables. These cost an estimated £2 million in 1979–80 alone.

To the question, 'Under what circumstances should I test?', the basic answer is *always*, unless certain specific and definable circumstances exist.

In general, the costs and risks of new product development are now so great that, assuming the product or services can be supplied in sufficient quantities, at an acceptable price, testing should take place.

More formal approaches for deciding when to test market include Bayesian and other decision analytic techniques where values can be put against the pay-offs from reduced risk because of improved information. Cost benefit analysis of test marketing has been used to further explore this key issue.[8]

WHAT CAN BE TESTED IN TEST MARKETS? (VARIABLES)

Although most British test marketing has been concentrated on new products or services, in other countries, notably the USA, a far wider array of factors has been subjected to tests. Overall increases in marketing costs, allied to recognition of the critical role played by these non-product features, has put the spotlight on their testability. At the same time, there has been growing research and media sophistication to make such research more practical and profitable. These developments enable test markets to explore most aspects of the marketing mix, notably:

Product: overall appeal and performance, quality, ranging, mix, presentation, packaging.
Price: appropriateness, levels, range, mix and their impact on sales.
Distribution: optimal combination of outlet choice, stock level, display, movements, trade terms, besides overall acceptance.
Promotion: advertising budgets, schedules and mix, creative approach, below-the-line merchandising and sales-force effort.

The importance of this was illustrated with the success of Dettol Deep Fresh, a new bath foam which combined the Dettol image with the characteristics of a luxury soap foam. David Beauchamp of Reckitt and Colman acknowledges that, once the concept emerged, 'developing advertising was difficult because we knew that if we missed the pinhead of acceptance it might not work'. Dettol Deep Fresh was tested in two areas.

Test markets enable the firm to monitor performance of these factors acting either in concert or (to some degree) separately. This can take two forms, as follows:

1. *Single test of the marketing package in the market.* Here overall performance is closely monitored to answer:
   (a) the Go/No Go question;
   (b) the performance question;
   (c) specific questions about aspects of the package.
2. *Multiple test of different combinations in the market.* Some features may be held constant, e.g. advertising copy, but others changed in various locations, e.g. Peterborough, Ipswich and Luton.

The Go/No Go decision focuses attention on avoiding failure. Overall acceptance can be measured and, equally important, the nature of the good or service appeal can be measured: who is buying it? how often? where from? under what conditions? in what volume? how often? The latter two questions are particularly important in gauging long-term market penetration and performance. Most brand share prediction techniques call for purchasing patterns over a period of time. Some success has been achieved using repeat purchased rates to predict ultimate market shares.

DEFINING INFORMATION NEEDS, DECISIONS AND CONTROLS

Even if the company is not intending to take its analysis as far as detailed forecasts, test marketing is a decision tool and the criteria for decisions should be established before introduction. These will include:

Targets

Sales: total and by target market. The target market should go right down the distribution chain, including distributors and retailers as well as consumers.

Shares: including not only introductions' performance, but impact on own and competitors' brands.

Advertising and Promotion Response: the gamut of goals from awareness and attitude to reaction.

Product Performance: this goes beyond technical evaluation to include match of consumer expectations and product delivery.

Distribution: the pattern of acceptance, in terms of individual stores, types and any regionalism which emerges. These might incorporate desired stock levels, even the amount of discounting.

All have to be linked to decisions which must be made and the criteria on which they will be based. The quality of the research facilities which the tester can use is vital to implementation.

In building the bases upon which this type of analysis is performed, the inherently dynamic nature of the market should be borne in mind constantly. This is clearly shown in one of the more successful food market innovations in the late 1970s; instant pot snacks. This grew from a relatively small base to over £30 million in a few years. Soon the novelty began to pall with Pot Noodle, Snack Pots, Quick Lunch and Knorr Knoodles competing vigorously for a stable market. Under these conditions, the chances of success for new offerings reduced rapidly.

The corollary to establishing targets is defining the conditions under which they will be achieved. These will include:

1. Advertising and promotional budgets.
2. Sales force activity.
3. Product availability.
4. Distribution.
5. Support services: technical, etc.
6. Competition: nature and activity.

SETTING UP THE TEST

Careful preparation is vital to experimental success. The more complex the situation being studied, the more critical the controls. This is clear in test marketing, as few areas are more prone to the accusation 'garbage-in, garbage-out'. Setting up the test calls for a clear definition of the research brief.

The research brief

This defines as clearly and as operationally as possible the problem under investigation and the material required from the study. The three simple rules for a brief are that it should be *actionable*, *communicable* and *internally consistent*.

Definition of the three types of variable

Dependent variables: those to be measured, on which performance will be judged.

Independent variables: those that are being examined or are the subject of the experiment.

Exogenous variables: those that are outside the test and, although they may have an impact, are not manipulated.

To illustrate, Scottish and Newcastle Breweries may have tested their new Kalback Lager. The *dependent* variables would be sales, the *independent* variables would be different advertising levels and creative treatment, whilst the weather would be an *exogenous* variable. It is within this framework that the controls mentioned earlier are established to:

1. Minimise personal or company involvement.
2. Establish performance norms.
3. Facilitate management.

Effectively combined, the brief, management and definition of variables and implementation of controls should ensure an effective marketing test or experiment, provided the appropriate practical disciplines are imposed.

ARE THERE ALTERNATIVES?

The costs and risks of test marketing, particularly the full-blown pre-launch test of a new product (sometimes called the experimental launch), have prompted a continuing search for more limited, lower cost alternatives. Two roles have been ascribed to these alternatives:

1. As substitute for the full test, i.e. if their ability to predict is as good, why incur the additional expenditure?
2. As a final pre-test research stage to screen out potential loss makers.

There is no general agreement that any of the methods so far tried provide a complete substitute for the full test. However, a number of alternatives have emerged which appear capable of giving some approximation of likely results in test and being valuable pre-test research steps. Among the most successful of these are:

1. *Limited area testing*, using small test towns or limited catchment areas.
2. *Outlet tests*, where one type of store (e.g. chemist shops) or main trade customer (say Asda) is used.

Mini area tests

Two factors have combined to heighten interest in the use of cities or more limited areas as test areas. These are:

1. Increasing costs of testing.
2. Desire to use tests to explore more detailed aspects of the marketing effort while certain factors, e.g. advertising, are held constant. These can include display material, differences in product or packaging for manufacturers, types of services offered, hours of opening, etc., for retailers and service firms.

Areas with the advantage of having a number of major cities (population over 100 000 = physically very separate, but no dominant conurbation, e.g. London, Birmingham, Southampton/Portsmouth, Liverpool/Manchester, Newcastle/ Sunderland) are invaluable.

When conducting these more limited area tests, it ought to be recognised that the smaller the area, the greater the likelihood of significant variation from the national average. This demands greater stringency in applying the controls previously mentioned.

Over the last decade micro-market testing (the mini test) has shown particular promise. The basic technique involves using panels of housewives from a 'Shoppers' Club'. Periodically each panel member receives a catalogue listing typical supermarket lines. At more frequent intervals, a 'promotions' bulletin is distributed, listing special offers and price changes.

Each week a van calls to collect the housewives' orders, meeting them from its stocks. This combination of catalogue, promotions bulletin and van provides a controllable, market-based environment in which new products can be tested, aspects of their marketing mix varied, while the entire process is closely monitored. Alternative formulations of the mini-test have mobile supermarkets or automarts as substitutes for the catalogue and van.

Evidence to date suggests that, for reformulations of existing products, the mini-test is a reasonably good predictor of likely response. In fact, the forecasts arrived at for new brands have been reasonably accurate. However, it is no substitute for the full test in highlighting the multitude of market place, logistical, physical or competitive variables which can:

1. Determine the likely success or failure of the product.
2. Determine the *best* available information for either a new or modified offering.

WHERE SHOULD I TEST? (THE EXTERNAL VARIABLES)

All experiments, and test markets are no exception, turn upon the appropriateness of the laboratory situation set up for them. In the natural sciences, it is probably fair to say that setting up the experiment is as important as the conduct of the test. In test marketing the costs, risks and demands are at least as great. A test conducted in an inappropriate location, perhaps unrepresentative of the total market, can result in, *at best*, valueless and, *at worst*, dangerously misleading information.

The first step in choosing the locale is to carefully review the total market in which the firm is interested. When the company seeks to extrapolate the results, the criteria upon which this will be done must be defined early in the planning process. The test market area ought to be typical or representative of the total market. This was central to the thinking when Heinz Coleslaw (tinned) was tested in Anglia, ATV and other areas in 1980. The product was breaking new ground, as the major competition was chilled cabinet coleslaw, while still compatible with brands in the Heinz salad range. The test provided an opportunity to evaluate overall acceptance and likely penetration. The promotional mix of TV, radio and 5p off coupons in *TV Times* was evaluated in terms of both consumer and retail appeal. The area chosen provided a bench mark for judging the brand's likely achievement throughout the marketing system. This test by Heinz contrasts sharply with the failure of Carlsen Lite (a low carbohydrate beer), despite initial success in the Southern test area.

Often the target market will be Britain itself. In this case, the company needs to carefully explore how Britain is really divided in terms relevant to their markets. The dynamic nature of today's environment adds a new dimension to this, as the composition of different areas, lines of communication and distribution, besides media mix, can vary rapidly over time.

> Television areas do not remain static. The introduction of a new booster signal—or the removal of an existing one—greatly affects the number of homes which can receive a particular channel.

For many consumer markets, the key variables in establishing the target markets and hence the sought-after features of the test area are:

1. Demographic characteristics.
2. Industrial and occupational structure.
3. Distribution patterns and retail structure.
4. Media pattern.
5. Company and brand strength.

Demographics: the age, sex and social class structure of the population.

Industrial and occupational structure: the balance of industrial, agricultural and other types of work and related work patterns, besides the general level of economic activity.

Distribution patterns and retail structure: these are the channels through which the goods must move to reach the ultimate buyers.

Media pattern: this includes factors such as the range of media available and the ITV media weighting.

Any special features related to product usage or consumption should be included in this analysis.

Seagrams recognised this in the test market for their sparkling wine, Crocodillo. The target was overwhelmingly young women 'who are experimenting with drinks'. This was reflected in both the choice of test area and the factors both producer and retailers were keen to measure: attitudes in target market and repeat buying among a group happy to experiment.

In reviewing these variables, extreme care ought to be taken that no major bias is inbuilt. A test area may appear attractive, but an occupation structure dominated by, say, the service sector, could distort results and give a misleading impression of the market potential. The test marketplace variables typically ought to be distinguished from experimental control factors and roll-out features.

The *control* features include:

Discreteness of the experimental situation. This includes both the extent to which the area as a whole can be handled separately from the total market, and the scope for treating specific parts as separate.

It is a harsh fact of life that no major test area can have a wall built around it. Some degree of overlap is inevitable in Britain, whether it is in TV transmission or large numbers of people moving in and out of the test area. When the extent of overlap is fully understood, greater control can be built into the situation.

Area structure. This is an important factor, if matched area experiments or other attempts to compare and contrast aspects of the test are sought. An area containing broadly comparable, but physically quite separate, areas is invaluable in tests geared to produce the best possible offering. Cambridge, Norwich and Ipswich, for example, are broadly comparable in size, but an average of 50 miles apart. Separate formulations of product, promotion, etc. could be tried with the vital element of the control in the third.

Location. This is critical if the offering is to be introduced initially into the next-door areas. It is desirable to ensure that a balanced move across to national launch, e.g. introduction to adjacent Southern, Midland and Northern areas simultaneously, is achieved. This helps to protect against regional competition or regional distortion in performance.

In the real world the *size/cost* factor plays a powerful role.

Assuming the points made earlier are applied, the area chosen should be large enough to increase the probability of its being representative, but small enough to make costs acceptable and effective management and control viable.

HOW LONG SHOULD THE TEST LAST?

Many pressures combine to encourage firms to cut test markets short: the relatively high cost, the desire to exploit any competitive lead, etc. It is a temptation which affects each stage in the process: pre-, during and post-test.

The pre-test. This is the base period in which the product, service or other change will be judged. It has to be long enough to allow the natural fluctuations which occur in every market to work their way through the experimental and control areas.

The test proper. This starts the moment the first sell-in starts. It has to be long enough to allow the experimental or test factors to pass right through the system as, at each stage, distortions can occur. The trade may be over-enthusiastic—for example, Cadbury's Chillo failed despite high trade ratings. Consumers may buy at high initial levels, but reject it subsequently. Key weaknesses in delivery and performance sometimes emerge late in the day. However, the reverse can occur quite easily—trade reservations can be overcome by consumer demand or new and potentially profitable uses may emerge later.

The key variables in this are the repeat purchase rate and the pattern of consumption. These are also important in allowing the tester to forecast long-term performance.

Post-test. This calls for a thorough review of the test and all the internal and external factors which can influence performance and judgements. A production problem, a strike, even things like the weather can distort results. The buyer for Laws stores in the North East highlighted the importance of weather on the test launch of Bovril Chicken—it simply was not 'chicken cube weather'. This point was endorsed by the buyer from Amos Hinton, 'Summer is not the best time anyway, so we'll hope for some improvement in the next few weeks'.

All data should be thoroughly reviewed and related to targets. This is particularly important, as there is a common tendency to fudge results by ignoring targets set initially in the hope that something would turn up.

THE TEST

The value of the test market depends upon the quality and range of information collected. Many aspects of this are devolved to the associated advertising and research agency, within the controls mentioned earlier. The main data sources are the following.

Factory sales. All goods despatched from factory or warehouse, preferably broken down by type of account or location. Extra controls are needed to assist both production and despatch, while ensuring no slippage in area definition occurs. When the firm is dealing with large direct accounts, care is needed so that their timing and distribution of orders does not distort results.

Store audits. These give a picture of the movement of goods through outlets, stockholding and purchase pattern. The importance of the major multiples in most fast-moving consumer goods markets puts special emphasis on this step.

Trade research. The support and involvement of the trade is vital for successful test marketing. Lack of information and the casual assumption that they will play a part causes considerable resentment in some quarters.

Consumer research. Panels, omnibus surveys, tracking studies and specially-commissioned surveys play a vital part in the on-going evaluation of the test. This research provides the framework for both revision as the experiment progresses and final evaluation in the key Go/No Go, Recycle and Abandon decisions. John Davis[9] points out:

> Too often, research in this area is merely confined to a single ad hoc survey some weeks or months after the launch which will show some single measure of awareness.

The performance of a brand, product or service emerges over time. A single snapshot can easily give a distorted picture. The recurrence of retail buyer comments like—'The tourist trade this summer hasn't provided a steady demand' (Cussons 'Only You' hand care) and 'The TV advertising definitely gave the product the boost it needed, but I don't think Polyripple would be selling as well without this support' (Polycell Products Polyripple) demonstrate how important continuing systematic study is in order to get a true picture of performance.

TEST AREA OVERLAP

One of the most striking differences between the regions defined by research organisations like A. C. Nielsen and those of the TV region is 'area overlap'. The nature of television transmission and the continual efforts by contractors to improve their range and quality has led to considerable and changing areas of overlap. There is an average of 10 per cent across the various regions. This means that it is virtually impossible to neatly define a test area and cut it off from all external media influences.

John Davis[9] highlights the advantages which can be taken of this by running two experiments side-by-side in the two adjacent areas. Different campaigns or approaches can be employed. Research in the overlap areas can be used to bring out key aspects of the different approaches, highlighting their relative effectiveness.

To be wholly effective, the overlap areas should be scrupulously examined. The firm must ensure that quality of transmission, patterns of usage and previous advertising are, broadly speaking, constant. The test in both areas can be very useful in advertising research and to explore competitive approaches to a key innovation.

HOW IS PERFORMANCE JUDGED?

Evaluation can be based on two separate, but inter-related criteria:

1. Did the tested product or service meet its targets?
2. Do our forecasts for national performance indicate a successful product or change in policy?

As indicated earlier, arriving at clearly worked-out objectives is an integral part of effective testing. These should incorporate such variables as penetration, repeat purchase rates, impact on competitor and own brands, distribution pattern, and returns on budgets. Performance should be carefully checked against these and other goals for the product or change in presentation. Alternative formulations being examined can be compared. It is largely in terms of relative performance that the innovation or change will be judged. At the same time, lessons learned in logistics, physical characteristics, promotion and competitiveness have to be explored in terms of the twin criteria of pay-offs and practicality.

The targets set for the test are the bench mark, but increasingly there is a desire to convert test market sales into longer-term forecasts. This area has been full of controversy. Gold[10] indicated the fallibility of test market results. A great deal of work has been conducted in the intervening period to produce major improvements in projection, production and forecasting from test markets. John Davis[9] developed a *projective technique* based on the proposition that differences between areas are reflected in existing (pre-test) brand shares. The extent to which existing brands lose share to the test brand in the test market indicates their overall vulnerability. The likely national brand share is likely to emerge from the combination of the test market's losses. Algebraically, estimated brand share nationally, T will be:

$$T_1 = 100 - \left\{ X_0 \frac{x_1}{x_0} + Y_0 \frac{y_1}{y_0} \cdots \right\}$$

hence if the pre-test market has four major brands, x, y, z and n:

	Test Area Shares (%)	National Shares (%)
X_0	40	X_0 45
Y_0	30	Y_0 25
Z_0	20	Z_0 15
n_0	10	N_0 15

x, y, z and n are the shares post-test. Test brand 'T' takes 10% from X_0, 5% from Y_0 and 3% from N_0.

Therefore:

$$T = 100 = \left\{ 45 \frac{30}{40} + 25 \frac{25}{30} + 15 \frac{15}{20} + \frac{7}{10} \right\}$$

Only equilibrium state market shares ought to be employed. Time lags, peaks and troughs in performance must be taken into account. This means that measurement of the entire market and the test is an on-going process.

It is possible to arrive at an early forecast of ultimate performance using a forecasting technique. The amount of work in this field means that it can only be dealt with in a cursory way here.

Three basic approaches can be used:

1. *Judgemental forecasts.* Test market performance can be a key part of the data on which the judgements can be made. Particularly interesting is the use of the Delphi Method. In this technique, a panel of 'experts' respond individually to questionnaires demanding a forecast and the assumptions behind them. Responses are anonymous and exchanged between the experts until a consensus is reached.

2. *Time series analysis.* A variety of methods have been used here. The availability of consumer panel data and recognition of the critical importance of repeat buying has heightened interest in this area. Rawlins and Sparks[8] highlighted the relative robustness of commonly-used models such as the Parfitt-Collins[11] and Fourt-Woodlock[12] approaches. At the same time, they put forward a model to predict the steady rate volume of the brand.

Thus,

Volume = Units per buyer × number of buyers

$$= \frac{\text{weight of purchase by repeat buyers}}{\text{relative purchasing of repeat buyers}}$$

multiplied by

$$\frac{\text{no. of repeat buyers}}{\text{proportion of repeat buyers}}$$

The later paper by Parfitt and McCloughlin[13] develops this further.

3. *Causal methods.* These involve the development and use of a forecasting model in which sales changes derive from changes in specified variables. Surveys of buyer intentions are perhaps the most commonly-used form. Chambers, Mullick and Smith[14] provide a very useful framework for choosing the most appropriate technique.

In most of these approaches, there is an assumption that effective management and control of the test has taken place and that sufficient time has been given to enable the test to properly develop and for equilibrium to have been reached.

FROM TEST TO LAUNCH

One of the most remarkable features of current research and writing on test marketing and innovations is the lack of attention paid to the process of moving from test to commercialisation. Even Philip Kotler, the US authority on marketing—quoted earlier as describing test marketing as rapidly approaching the state of a science—covers the problem in a few brief comments. A number of practical problems face the firm after the test has been completed. Hard decisions have to be made as to whether the offering has been a failure or a success.

An unsuccessful test product can be very de-motivating for all those involved, from field force through to retailers stocking the product. Debriefing them and revitalising their interest in the range of corporate activities is an investment in the firm's competitive future.

Often a generally unsuccessful product will not be rejected totally. Recycling aspects of the proposition will call for the maximum benefits to be gained from the test. This might lead to the modified offering or a new product incorporating certain features being due for test again. Faced with this issue, management must add broader, more subjective criteria to the objective criteria for area choice mentioned earlier. It may be unwise to test frequently in the same area, particularly if a specific pattern of response (failure or success) has occurred.

Following a successful test, a number of important questions face the firm, notably:

1. Do I roll out gradually?
2. Do I go national immediately?
3. How do I deal with the test area(s) in the post-test, but national launch, period?

Three factors determine the optimum course of action between progressive roll-out and national launch. These are:

1. The scale of the success.
2. The likely pattern of competitive response.
3. The practical considerations of producing, stocking, distributing, etc.

The greater the success, the shorter the competitive lead time, the more important an immediate shift to national production. Gearing up for this may take longer than the 'end of test/go national' schedule permits. This increases the importance of pre-launch research, notably of the mini-test type. Equally, forecasting techniques capable of giving early predictions of likely brand shares are essential to the continuing process of research.

Despite the urgency which can emerge in these circumstances, some caution is essential. Often the deteriorating product quality or reduced service which emerges during this early launch period provides competitors with their greatest chance to erode the brand's position or introduce alternatives. The opportunity for rivals is greatest during periods of stock-out or rationing. Among the most commonly reported reasons for failure following a successful test are poor product quality, irregular supplies and non-competitive pricing. Marketing managers responsible for this stage in the commercialisation process are generally better advised to roll out, rather than attempt a full national extension, if there is a real danger of these difficulties emerging.

In coping with the post-test but national launch period, two interrelated strands exist. Often it is to the firm's advantage to maintain a lag between activity here and national activity. For a period of time, this will enable the firm to contrast two different stages in a product's life span. It may be tempting to persist with this. However, it can seldom be maintained for long without undue investment of resources and distortions in behaviour pattern. These typically occur after a few trading periods. It is then in the firm's interest to restore the broad balance of area activity.

Notes

1. Kotler, P., *Marketing Management: Analysis, Planning and Control*. Englewood Cliffs: Prentice-Hall, 1980.
2. King, S., *Developing New Brands*. London: Pitman, 1973.
3. Green, P. E. & Tull, D. S., *Research for Marketing Decision*. Englewood Cliffs: Prentice-Hall Int., 1st ed., 1966.
4. Kaplan, A., *The Conduct of Enquiry*. New York: Chandler Publishing, 1964.
5. Ansoff, I., *Corporate Strategy*, Harmondsworth: Penguin, 1968.
6. Brooks, J., *Business Adventures*. London: Penguin, 1971.
7. Madell, J., 'Where Do Successful New Brands Come From?', New Product Development Seminar, Univas, Paris, 1979.
8. Rawlins, T. C. & Sparks, D. N., 'The Use of Repeat Buying Measures in Evaluating New Product Launches', MRS Eighteenth Annual Conference, 1975.
9. Davis, E. J., *Experimental Marketing*. London: Nelson, 1970.
10. Gold, J. A., 'Testing Test Market Predictions', *Journal of Marketing Research*, August 1964.
11. Parfitt, J. H. & Collins, B. J. K., 'The Use of Consumer Panels for Brand Share Prediction', *Journal of Marketing Research*, May 1968.
12. Fourt, L. A. & Woodlock, J. W., 'Early Prediction of Market Success for New Grocery Products', *Journal of Marketing*, 24 October 1960.
13. Parfitt, J. H. & Collins, B. J. K., 'The Use of Consumer Panels for Brand Share Prediction', *Journal of Marketing Research*, May 1967.
14. Chambers, J. C., Mullick, S. K. & Smith, D. D., 'How to Choose The Right Forecasting Technique', *Harvard Business Review*, July–August 1971.

Further reading

Blattberg, R. & Golanty, J., 'Tracker: An Early Test Market Forecasting and Diagnostic Model for New Product Planning', *Journal of Marketing Research XV*, May 1978.
Cannon, T., 'New Product Development', *European Journal of Marketing*, 21, No. 3, 1978.
Hirsrick, R. D. & Peters, M. P., *Marketing a New Product*. Benjamin/Cummins, 1978.
Wills, G., 'Cost Benefit Analysis of A Test Market', *Management Decision*, 1, No. 1, 1967.

16
Price

Few decisions that a firm makes create as much interest or stimulate as much external involvement as those concerning price. Customers, intermediaries and the firm's personnel, especially those in marketing and selling, are all directly involved. The prices themselves, particularly in aggregate, affect political and economic processes, and politicians, economists, civil servants, commentators and pundits study, comment and try to take action over prices (Figure 16.1). This interest derives from the pivotal role which price plays in the exchange process between buyers and sellers.

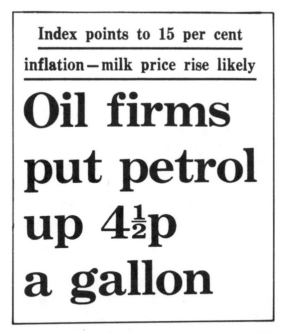

Index points to 15 per cent inflation – milk price rise likely

Oil firms put petrol up 4½p a gallon

Fig. 16.1 The newsworthiness of price. Lead story, *Guardian*, 25 May, 1979.

Price is the amount for which a product, service or idea is exchanged, or offered for sale, regardless of its worth or value to potential purchasers.[1] Although a monetary equivalent or value can be imputed, prices can incorporate goods exchanged, e.g. cars traded in or similar deals.

Within the framework of classical economic theory, prices are arrived at in a relatively deterministic manner, emerging from the interplay of supply and demand:

The quantity of a good that people will buy at any one time depends on price.

P. A. Samuelson[2]

In a perfectly competitive market the manufacturer has virtually no influence on his prices, which are determined by market forces created by competitive pressures and consumer buying patterns. The salient features of this perfectly competitive market—a homogeneous product, complete information among buyers, economically rational buying behaviour and large numbers of small competitive producers—are almost impossible to achieve in a complex modern industrial society. Even in an apparently homogeneous product field, such as wheat, differences exist, e.g. North American wheats tend to be harder, thus more easily milled.

Economic theory has incorporated these realities within the notion of pricing under imperfect competition:

All sellers in the oligopolistic industry[3] recognize a mutual inter-dependence of the price-output decisions, and therefore act interdependently rather than independently in adjusting their prices or outputs.

J. S. Bain[4]

Although terms such as oligopoly, imperfect markets and interdependence have accumulated certain pejorative associations, their true meaning should be considered. Simply, all that is being said is that in modern markets, industrial, consumer and service, a firm setting its prices must have one eye on its customers and another on its competition. Nowadays more eyes have to be grown to study government, pressure groups, the media, financial institutions and owners and shareholders.

Although price formation can be described within a framework of economic theory, for the practising manager it means simply hard work, assumptions, expectations, research and judgement in what is probably the most difficult area of marketing decision.[5]

THE JUST PRICE

Underlying much discussion about price is the notion of the 'fair' or 'just' price, the price that could be called correct on the basis of social considerations. A great deal of

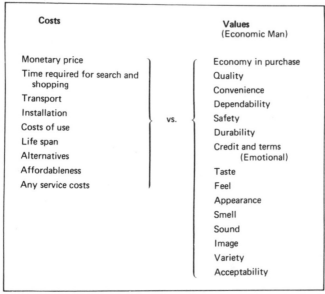

Costs	Values (Economic Man)
Monetary price	Economy in purchase
Time required for search and shopping	Quality
Transport	Convenience
Installation	Dependability
Costs of use	Safety
Life span	Durability
Alternatives	Credit and terms (Emotional)
Affordableness	Taste
Any service costs	Feel
	Appearance
	Smell
	Sound
	Image
	Variety
	Acceptability

vs.

Fig. 16.2 The exchange and interplay between costs and values. Adapted from J. L. Hesketh, *Marketing*. London: Collier-Macmillan, 1976.

government, pressure group and media action and discussion is geared towards achieving just prices, but it is seldom fully appreciated how sensitive this concept is to the point of view of those discussing it.

For the seller a fair price is probably the amount he or she needs for their offering in order to make a reasonable profit. The notion of a reasonable profit itself has to be discussed, as there are different approaches to this. To the customer a fair price probably refers to some general idea of affordability allied to some sense of intrinsic value, with previous experience a contributory factor.

In entering into the exchange both are seeking some degree of profit from it. The seller wants some excess of income over costs, while the buyer wants an excess of satisfaction from the goods or services over the satisfaction from holding on to his money or purchasing something else. In determining pricing policies the company needs to understand both the costs involved and alternatives open, and the responses of the different groups and the values they place on the goods or services (Figure 16.2).

THE POLITICAL DIMENSION

At a seminar at Durham University in 1979, a senior marketing executive from a nationalised industry asserted that price flexibility was a thing of the past. Prices were now so important to the political and economic management of the country that government was gradually eliminating any managerial discretion (Figure 16.3).

How Labour plans to keep prices down.

Fig. 16.3   Price: the political dimension.

Prices have dominated political discussion and each general election during the 1970s. Even the non-interventionist policies of the Conservative Government do not preclude some action on prices within specific areas or under the auspices of the Monopolies and Mergers Commission or the Office of Fair Trading.

Even within this framework it would be a mistake to take the marketing executive's comment at its face value. Price is likely to remain an area of some freedom of action, albeit limited, and the company's flexibility will depend to a considerable extent on specific circumstances.

THE PRICE DECISION

The need to make decisions about prices occurs under a number of specific circumstances for different types of products and services. For an existing brand or product the decision can incorporate increases, reductions and holding price. In the late 1960s Rothman's King Size cigarettes made significant inroads into the seemingly impregnable market share of Benson and Hedges King Size by simply holding prices when cigarette duty was increased.

The major circumstances in which pricing decisions need to be made are: new product introductions; changes in external circumstances, e.g. raw material, tax or duty changes; competitive action in raising or lowering prices; internal changes, from new products to new processes; promotions; and changes in market structure or size. In each of these the objectives, short or long term, of the firm must be clearly set before action is taken.

Although specific goals are set in initiating an action, more and more managers are recognising the need to adopt policies with medium- to long-term consequences in view. A market skimming price[6] might be seen as a mechanism for opening up a market with a view to penetrating new segments, with progressive lowerings of price.

New product pricing

This is the purest pricing situation the firm is likely to face, particularly if there are no existing, direct competitors. The firm is in a position to set its goals in terms of itself, its intermediaries and the end customer.[7] Dean [8] suggests that three factors determine the new product price: getting the product accepted; maintaining the market in the face of growing competition; and producing profits. To these should probably be added minimising government involvement.

To achieve the goals related to these Dean suggests two strategies lying at the extremes of a spectrum: skimming prices and penetration prices. *Skimming prices* are high prices, probably backed up by heavy promotion, which are used to open up the market. The manufacturer usually tries to position himself as the leading, highest-quality, most prestigious offering. The firm can steadily lower its prices to meet competition or open up new markets but generally holds on to a slight price advantage. A number of firms in the calculator market adopted this strategy. The most likely markets—education and business—were opened up first, and later other markets were penetrated by progressive price reductions. The success of this strategy has now created a significant defence reaction among customers: they are reluctant to buy new products 'because the price is bound to come down'.

Penetration prices are the opposite end of the spectrum. Everything is done—promotion, discounts, publicity, high stocks, etc.—to open up the market as quickly as possible.

Until recently it was very difficult to escape from a pricing policy adopted at launch. An overpriced product could not easily be brought into a different price bracket without questions about quality and reliability being raised, and an underpriced product could not easily be corrected because of the buyer's pricing assumption. However, inflation has done much to alter this. Change is now expected and customers accept frequent modifications.

A major exception to the concept of penetration prices being difficult to increase is introductory offers. In consumer markets at least,[9] this type of promotional action appears to have virtually no effect on perceptions of quality unless it is held over indefinitely without any explanation. However, the scope for this is limited by price legislation.

Briscoe,[10] in a substantial study of the interaction between price and the product life-cycle, highlights the importance of linking pricing policies with the stage in the life-cycle. He suggests that even when it is undesirable to overtly vary monetary price, 'by using these disguised price variables (credit, discounts, rebates) which can be more readily varied over the product life-cycle, price can be made a more effective marketing tool'.

Changing external factors

During an inflationary period such as the late 1970s, perhaps the most significant factors influencing firms to modify their prices are changes affecting them. Price increases by suppliers must be met through internal economies, the use of alternative materials or price increases. The overwhelming majority of firms review the first two alternatives thoroughly before embarking on the third, potentially dangerous, step. A number of industries have been rocked by price increases in materials during the late 1970s. Plastics and other petroleum-based industries have been particularly severely hit. After a long history of growth, the plastics industry's competitiveness has been weakened by increases which were running at 50 to 60 per cent at times. The ramifications spread to boat-building, caravans, toys, construction, automobiles, electronics and many other high plastics-consumption industries.

Most firms are reluctant to modify their prices frequently, and this poses a major forecasting problem during an inflationary period (Figure 16.4). The scale of the price increases and their timings are based on estimates of inflation. Failure to get either right can mean the firm trading at a loss for long periods of time. The problem is made more difficult by two recent developments: materials shortages, perhaps requiring the purchase of more expensive stocks, and the tendency for inflation to be non-linear, accelerating over time.

In retail markets the scheduling of buying can influence the firm's profitability dramatically. Warnings of imminent price increases are a common ploy by salesmen to increase volume of sales and establish stronger rapport with customers. The real impact of this on their own firm may be extra sales of money-losing lines, but most companies recognise this and build it into their costings.

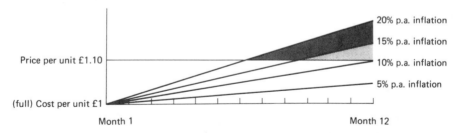

Fig. 16.4 The impact of inflation.

Competitive action

The concentrated nature of most consumer and industrial, and some service, industries means that few firms can ignore the pricing policies of their rivals.

None of the manufacturers mentioned in Table 16.1 can ignore the pricing policies adopted by their major competitors. Increases, reductions and stability create new opportunities and problems. For example, Unilever (Birds Eye) might announce a price increase. Faced with probably the same basic cost position Imperial (Ross) can respond either by increasing in time, knowing volume losses will be slight, or by holding or reducing prices to search out extra volume.

There is a common assumption among economists that the only real means of appraising these options is through holding or reducing prices. Hence markets in which this does occur indicate some degree of collusion or excess market power. In fact, most firms and managers have experimented at some time with both these policies and when faced with an increase they apply the knowledge acquired in these situations. However, there is a sense in which the circumstances have changed and past experience may be a

Table 16.1   *Concentration: a perspective*

Product field	Major manufacturers	Share of three largest firms (%)
Ready-to-eat breakfast cereals	Kelloggs Nabisco Quaker	95
Frozen foods	Unilever Imperial Group Findus	86
Soups (canned)	Heinz Cross and Blackwell Campbells	95

Source: Cannon, T., *Advertising: The Economic Implications*. London: Intertext, 1975.

poor guide. Against this is the risk and cost involved in holding or cutting price. Most firms manage this balance by occasionally holding to gauge the opportunity but generally keeping in line.

Internal change

It may sometimes be convenient to think of pricing in terms of single-product, single-market situations, but the dominant pattern for companies is multiple products and multiple markets. The responsibility of corporate marketing management is to balance the different pricing policies and structures to gain the best returns for the firm.

Product line pricing occurs in a number of different situations. Sometimes the price of one product or brand affects the price of another. This can be a deliberate part of company policy:

> The special committee ... recommended that the policy of the corporation should be to produce and market only six models, and that as soon as practicable the following grades should constitute the entire line of cars:
> (a) $450-600
> (b) $600-900
> (c) $900-1200
> (d) $1200-1700
> (e) $1700-2500
>
> Alfred P. Sloan, Jnr[11]

Here, in a relatively simple situation, the network of prices has been established and, perhaps more importantly, the relationships are set. These relationships provide a guide for product, promotion and distribution policies.

These interrelationships exist in many situations. For example, petrol sales, car repairs, and new and used vehicle sales are all part of the motor trader's interrelated product range. Petrol sales might dominate the business at a major service station, with repairs merely as a service, or new car sales may be the main business, with used car sales being merely a method of disposing of trade-ins. Over time, however, these priorities will change, e.g. shortages of supply might lead to a re-examination of the returns from the used-car operations and a realignment of priorities.

In many situations of this type of interaction the notion of the loss leader plays a part. A *loss leader* is a product or service sold at lower-than-normal margins for the purpose of attracting customers who might then purchase other items at normal margins. Traditionally it has been associated with supermarkets, where staple products such as sugar and butter are often sold cheaply to attract trade. It occurs in many other situations, however. Industrial suppliers might price the initial project for a major customer below cost merely to become an accredited supplier, and management consultants will often perform a small limited project at a low price with a view to longer-term, more substantial contracts. The special offers made by many banks to students might even be described as loss leaders.

Interrelated prices take a very different form in those industries where costs of raw materials, production and labour are tied together. A tannery might specialise in high-quality suedes but use all its waste to make garden or industrial gloves, or a manufacturer of sheepskin gloves might use his offcuts to make belts. At any point in time one line may appear dominant, but the contribution of the other lines may be significant in real profit terms if the marginal cost is borne in mind.

Promotional prices

A glance at any newspaper or a walk through any shopping area will show the importance of the price cut or special offer (Figure 16.5).

Fig. 16.5 Promotional pricing.

There are dangers in promotional pricing: it builds short-term volume but no loyalty, and the customer's image of the product can deteriorate.

In consumer-goods markets, trade discounts and volume bonus (dealer loading) can be an important part of key-account management. The supermarket group will share the cost of the price reduction in order to increase turnover.

NON CORE-PRICE POLICIES

So far much of the discussion has centred on the cash or monetary price of the product, but in industrial markets credit terms play a major part. A supplier may give 7, 30, 90, even 120 days to pay as a major part of his offering. Some firms adopting this policy balance long terms to some clients with shorter terms to others, while other companies offer prompt payment discounts to minimise the costs of credit.

Moving into international trade or exporting to a new country is very similar in pricing terms to launching a new product. The firm may be facing a new demand situation, perhaps with very little or no competition, and tariff barriers and government attempts to restrain imports may limit the firm's freedom of action. However, although a new and perhaps very different demand situation may exist, it is clear from the research into the area that careful study of the market plays only a minor part in price setting for most firms.

SETTING PRICES

The majority of firms follow policies which can be broadly described as 'cost plus' pricing. In a large-scale study in the USA, Lanzillotti[12] recorded the responses of a sample of major corporations (Table 16.2).

Table 16.2 *Pricing goals of major companies*

Company	Major pricing goal
General Foods	$33\frac{1}{3}$% gross margin
US Steel	8% on investment (after taxes)
International Harvester	10% on investment (after taxes)

If the same questions were asked in Britain today there would probably be broadly the same type of response from both large and small firms. In the retail business it would probably be defined as a combination of gross margin and stock-turn.

These answers reflect the desire of most managers to achieve what they would define as reasonable profits, perhaps a combination of funds for reinvestment, income for wages, salaries and other overheads, material and processing costs, resources for promotion, distribution and product development, returns to shareholders, enough to keep the financial institutions supportive, and taxes. For the company to survive the money for all or most of these must come from what it earns from its product array. Individual products may be following routes which do not directly contribute to this, but overall the price mix has to be viewed in this light.

Competitors cannot be ignored, so the firm might adopt a competitive pricing stance. Here the company will try to find itself a niche in the market. Using the prices of other companies as cues it can try to charge the going rate, seek to undercut or keep a good 'price advantage'.

Gabor,[13] in an important series of studies on prices, highlighted the importance of customer-orientated pricing:

> There is no uniform formula by which a price could be judged. It will be a good price or a bad price according to how well it serves the aims of the firm.

The response of the customer is the key to effective pricing within this frame. Systematic research should be conducted by a firm to establish the price which most closely meets the customer's needs. This involves building up estimates of both the returns on specific prices and the shape of the demand curve under different circumstances. One company might find that its demand increases with price (to a point), while another might find that the way to satisfy its customers is by combining high-priced prestige brands with low-priced bread and butter brands. The optimum policies will depend on the estimated response.

BREAKEVEN ANALYSIS

This is a straightforward device for enabling a manager to estimate the minimum sales required in a given period or in the launch of a product to ensure that his product does not

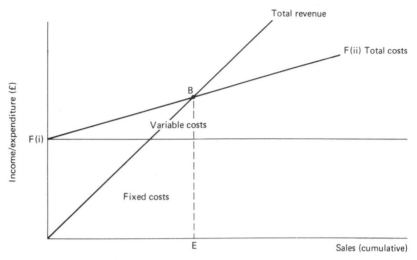

Fig. 16.6 Breakeven chart.

make a loss. It consists of three basic elements: fixed overheads (or fixed costs), marginal costs, i.e. those that change with sales, and income. In Figure 16.6, at each given price the sales volume required to break even (B) can be established from the point where total costs (F(i) and F(ii)) intersect with income (Total revenue).

Although it has some value, breakeven analysis is based on three major assumptions:

1. A fixed relation between sales volume and returns.
2. The firm can accurately forecast the demand curve.
3. A true picture of the cost situation can be established.

MARGINAL PRICING

There has been a growing interest in industry in marginal pricing. This is based on the proposition that many of the firm's costs are fixed, and whether the company sells 100 or 1000 items will not affect rent, rates, interest on loans or depreciation on machinery, and once these fixed costs have been met the returns are on each extra unit sold under the average pricing method assumed in the breakeven chart.[14]

The firm bases its prices on the cost of each extra unit of output sold after the fixed overheads have been met. It has been suggested that the ability of the Japanese to undercut European firms is derived from their widespread adoption of marginal pricing policies.

PRICING IN THE REAL WORLD

In developing pricing policies in the firm there is seldom complete freedom for any one area or manager. Corporate management may provide an overall framework such as that described earlier by Sloan, or perhaps even a more general one, e.g. 'Seek growth in high-technology fields'.

Invariably there is a sales and marketing dimension. The sales force may report back about fierce overseas competition, and to ignore this can cause production disruptions and erosion of the competitive position. Marketing may advise the 'milking' of existing brands to finance new developments.

The finance department has the responsibility for ensuring effective cash flows and maintaining the financial stability of the firm, so it will set targets for returns and impose constraints on action. Effectively balancing these corporate, financial, competitive and marketing forces is the essence of successful pricing. It should not be assumed that these are incompatible. Gabor mentions the importance of the relationship between price and quality, pointing out that many buyers use price as an indicator of quality.

Notes

1. Adapted from the definition of the Definitions Committee of the American Marketing Association.
2. Samuelson, P. A., *Economics*. New York: McGraw-Hill.
3. Oligopoly is where a small number of manufacturers control a large part of the market.
4. Bain, J. S., *Industrial Organization*. New York: John Wiley and Sons, 1968.
5. There is not scope here for a full discussion of pricing under imperfect competition from the economist's perspective. The reader is directed to Bain, J. S., *Industrial Organization*. New York: John Wiley and Sons, 1968.
6. These are high prices probably backed by extensive promotion.
7. This slightly exaggerates the situation as few innovations are totally new and the probability of competitive introductions in response influences thinking.
8. Dean, J., 'Pricing a New Product'. In *Fundamentals of Marketing* (Ed.) Taylor, J. L. & Robb, J. F. New York: McGraw-Hill, 1979.
9. There is some limited evidence that a similar pattern exists for supplies, components and end products in industrial markets.
10. Briscoe, G. & Lewis, A. L., *The Marketing of Steel Products and the Role of Innovation*. London: British Steel Corporation Fellowship.
11. Sloan, A. P. Jnr, *My Years with General Motors*. London: Pan Books, 1963.
12. Lanzillotti, R. F., 'Pricing Objectives in Large Companies', *American Economic Review*, December, 1958.
13. Gabor, A., 'Pricing in Theory and Practice'. In *Modern Marketing Management* (Ed.) Lawrence, R. J. & Thomas, M. J. Harmondsworth: Penguin Books, 1971.
14. Simply stated, the average pricing would be: total costs, £10 000; mark-up, 20 per cent; volume sold, 5000; price, $12 000 \div 5000 = £2.40$ per unit.

Further reading

Gabor, A. & Granger, C. W., 'A Systematic Approach to Effective Pricing'. In *Marketing Concepts and Strategies in the Next Decade* (Ed.) Rodger, L. W. London: Associated Business Programmes, 1973. Clearly describes both the economic framework for pricing decisions and the practical realities of pricing in the market.

Hague, D. C., *Pricing in Business*. London: Allen and Unwin, 1971. A useful and thoughtful study, particularly strong on the interplay between corporate objectives and pricing policies.

CASE STUDY 12: A MINI PRICING PROBLEM

Few cars have achieved either the volume sales or the eclectic appeal of the Leyland Mini. In the twenty years from its introduction in 1959 to 1979 over 4.5 million Minis were sold. It was consistently among the top five best-selling cars in the UK. However, serious reservations were expressed about its financial contribution to the British Motor Company (BMC), British Leyland (BL) or Leyland Motors.

When introduced, the car was targeted on first-time car buyers primarily in the C_1 and C_2 socio-economic groups. Employing tremendous technical and design skills, Sir Alec Issingonis produced a car with a low petrol consumption and capable of carrying four adults, for less than £500. A policy broadly akin to penetration pricing was adopted to achieve maximum penetration in this sector.

John Barber, then with Ford, recalls that:

> Ford was amazed that BMC priced the Mini down to compete with the very old and very basic Ford Popular.

The low price was very much a double-edged sword. It made the car more accessible to the target market but drastically reduced the dealer's freedom of action, as well as causing the customer to have some doubts about the car's quality.

Despite this pricing policy the car was slow to move into high-volume sales (Table 16.3). A number of other factors eventually combined to stimulate substantial sales volume, notably fashion changes in the 1960s and rally successes.

Table 16.3 *Price and market shares of the Mini*

Date	Total Mini price (£)	Market share	Indexed Mini price Oct. 59 = 100	Oct. Retail Price Index	Total Mini price in 1959 prices
Oct. 1959	496.95	NA	100.0	100.0	496.96
Oct. 1960	496.95	NA	100.0	102.0	487.21
Oct. 1961	496.95	NA	100.0	106.0	468.82
Oct. 1962	526.25	NA	105.9	109.1	482.35
Oct. 1963	447.65	14.0%	90.1	111.5	401.48
Oct. 1964	469.80	10.8%	94.5	116.0	405.00
Oct. 1965	469.80	9.5%	94.5	121.6	386.35
Oct. 1966	478.00	8.7%	96.2	126.2	378.76
Oct. 1967	508.75	7.4%	102.4	128.7	395.30
Oct. 1968	561.10	7.8%	112.9	135.9	412.88
Oct. 1969	595.50	7.0%	119.8	143.2	415.85
Oct. 1970	638.50	7.5%	128.5	153.8	415.15
Oct. 1971	640.63	7.9%	128.9	168.1	381.10
Oct. 1972	695.15	5.9%	139.9	181.4	383.21
Oct. 1973	738.84	5.8%	148.7	199.3	370.71
Oct. 1974	1003.26	7.1%	201.9	233.4	429.85
Oct. 1975	1299.00	7.1%	261.4	293.8	442.14
Oct. 1976	1496.00	6.4% (to end Oct.)	301.0	324.6	460.87

Reproduced with permission. Sharman, H. & Rines, M., 'The Maxi Task of Marketing the Mini', *Marketing*, January, 1977

By the mid-1970s the market for the Mini bore only limited resemblance to its initial target.It was far more classless, its major customer groups being AB women and first time buyers among ABC_1C_2 men.

During the period of its success the fortunes of Leyland Motors (formerly BMC and BL) waned considerably. It has been suggested that a factor in this decline was the poor returns earned from the Mini, its best seller. This coincided with a long period (for most of the 1960s) of underinvestment by BMC.

Task

Explore the issues affecting the pricing policies adopted to the Mini and consider the wisdom of the choices made.

17

Channel Management

In Chapter 9, intermediaries and intermediary systems were examined from the point of view of the middlemen themselves and the problems they face in developing their markets were explored. Manufacturers are dependent to a considerable degree on the effectiveness of their intermediaries in this area if their channels of distribution are to meet their marketing goals.

Channels are the networks of intermediaries linking or capable of linking the producer to his market (Figure 17.1). The term 'channel' is used to symbolise the flow of goods and services around the network. This movement is not merely physical, i.e. of the goods, but includes title (ownership), payment, information and promotion.

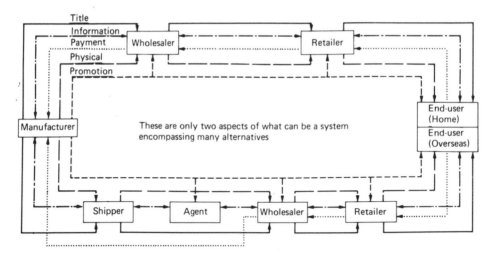

Fig. 17.1 Channel flows.

In building up an effective channel system or managing a current one, the firm is faced with a number of decisions:

1. The levels (different stages in the system between producer and user) and numbers (the width of distribution at each level) of intermediaries.
2. The roles the different channel members will play in the flows.
3. The support that will be offered (level and type).
4. The extent of channel leadership that will be sought.
5. The level of integration between the middlemen in the marketing of the firm's offerings.

This may imply a degree of manufacturer dominance that may not exist, since these decisions are also faced by other channel members. For example, the giant retailer buying a wide selection of own-label goods might decide either to buy in supplies or to use only wholly owned suppliers. He can decide on the availability of these goods to other traders (perhaps overseas). His promotion might feature the store or particular private-label goods.

THE ROLE OF INTERMEDIARIES

Channel intermediaries have many roles. One is to perform the distribution at a lower cost per unit than the manufacturer could, and to balance the production efficiencies of the supplier with the purchasing needs of the customer. For example, a cigarette machine might produce ten million cigarettes of a fixed size per day, but if sizes and specifications were changed to match the needs of small-volume buyers this could drop to one or perhaps two million. The wholesaler or retailer, through his volume buying, gives the producer the opportunity to maximise his production efficiencies while keeping prices down for customers.

Another intermediary role is to break down the large volumes produced into the small quantities bought. For example, a retail furniture company might place an order for 100 suites of furniture but the individual customer buys only one suite.

Intermediaries can minimise the number of transactions involved in the selling process, as Figure 17.2 shows.

They may also assist in cash management by producers, e.g. small craft and clothing firms may provide the small producer with the income needed to increase his production.

Providing information and insight into markets is another role of the intermediary. Small firms entering into exports often benefit enormously from the practical insight and

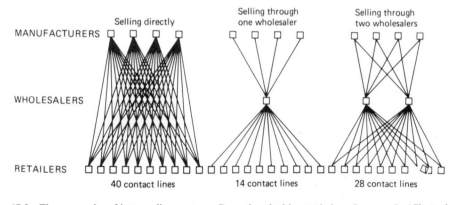

Fig. 17.2 The economies of intermediary systems. Reproduced with permission. Gattona, J., 'Channels of Distribution', *European Journal of Marketing*, **12**, No. 7, 1978.

guidance provided by buyers from such stores as Macy's or Gimbel and Saks.

Some intermediaries provide limited processing services, e.g. timber merchants or steel stockholders may cut to length or do some finishing work.

In some markets channel members may lead the marketing and promotional effort.

Intermediaries bring together a range of similar or related items into a large stock, thus facilitating the buying process. For example, the supermarket buys in 6000 to 10 000 lines to provide the shopper with choice, and the builders' merchant will provide everything (from sand to light fittings) that the builder can use, on occasion even assembling some parts.

After-sales service and some filtering and management of warranty are also provided by intermediaries.

These are some, though not all, of the tasks performed by intermediary channel members. The manufacturer is faced with a range of different types of intermediary and an array of possible services when determining his channel policies. His decisions gain added significance when the relatively long-term character of these decisions are considered.

CHANNEL CHOICES ARE LONG TERM

The company adopting a specific channel strategy usually cannot extract itself easily if difficulties arise. It is the practice in many markets to invest significant sums in supporting middlemen, providing them with anything from relatively small point-of-sale items to substantial kiosks or gantry units, and promotional investment may be used to support this effort. Customer loyalty is frequently shared between the outlet and the product. For example, a retailer may regularly purchase a specific branded product from his local cash and carry, and unless his customers' demand for that line is substantial he will not visit another cash and carry if that line is dropped. The individual consumer can often be persuaded by the retailer to switch to a substitute if his original choice is not available.

The agent or intermediary in many countries is afforded legal protection if the producer wishes to transfer his trade, and contractual agreements are sometimes used in Britain to achieve the same effect.

CHANNEL NETWORKS

The construction or modification of the channel requires careful and thorough review from a marketing perspective, in which the number of intermediaries sought is a fundamental consideration. Four basic options exist:

Intensive Distribution

This involves seeking every possible outlet for the firm's product. It is characteristic of fast-moving consumer goods, e.g. cigarettes, soft drinks, sweets, where every exposure to the customer is an opportunity to buy. The outlet has relatively little impact on the customer's impression of the product.

Selective Distribution

The manufacturer limits the search for outlets to a limited number of fairly broad categories. These can be related to type (e.g. only pharmacists for the firm's toothpastes) or style (e.g. only large, clean outlets with adequate display area for the firm's products). Selective distribution is employed when there is some limited interaction between product and outlet.

Exclusive distribution

The producer selects the intermediary very carefully and then provides him with exclusive rights to a particular area. Certain cosmetics firms demand some customer advisory service, and car manufacturers insist on repair, service and warranty handling facilities.

Which of these summer shoes does your child's feet most harm?

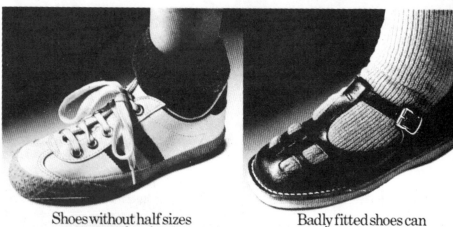

Shoes without half sizes can cause bunions.

Badly fitted shoes can cause hammer toes.

Loose fitting shoes can cause callosities.

Have we worried you?

Good.

In a survey of 50,000 schoolchildren, over half were found to have at least one form of foot deformity.

You can avoid this happening to your child by insisting on Clarks summer shoes and sandals. All are designed to allow natural growth with no unnatural side effects.

The trained fitter at any Clarks specialist shop will measure the size <u>and</u> width of your child's feet with a Clarks footgauge.

She'll measure <u>both</u> feet to be absolutely sure.

Then she'll bring the correct fitting shoes for your child to try on.

If she doesn't, do the only sensible thing. Walk out.

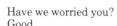

Nobody takes more care of their feet.

Fig. 17.3 The success of Clarks shows the power of a strong product intermediary link. Reproduced with the permission of Clarks Ltd.

This characterises markets where the interplay between product and outlet is considerable (Figure 17.3). Part of the basic customer proposition may involve close links with the retailer.

Vertical integration

Under certain circumstances the producer might need to become directly involved with its intermediaries. It may buy itself into them or start its own wholly owned outlets; e.g. Finlay's tobacco retailers are owned by Imperial Group (Players and Wills). The firm is then faced with a major problem of integration; whether or not the intermediary should buy on the open market, i.e. be an independent profit centre. Closely related to this problem is the horizontal competition (i.e. wholesaler v. wholesaler, retailer v. retailer) that can emerge. Vertical integration can quickly alienate the firm's existing customers since the firm will then be in direct competition with them.

CHANNEL DESIGN

This calls for the firm to conduct a thorough review of the objectives of the system and the constraints under which it will operate. The channel must match the capabilities of the firm, a point shown to be very important in the case of a small Scottish golf club manufacturer seeking a US distributor. A major group was interested in the product, but expected back-up promotion expenditure of about $200 000, more than the firm had spent in its entire existence.

The marketing-orientated firm focuses its attention on the needs of the different customer groups it is trying to interest. This may mean other intermediaries as well as end-users.

The amount of search time the customer is willing to invest can directly affect the extent of distribution sought.[1] Perishable goods require intermediaries willing to invest in special storage equipment. Bulky or heavy goods need investment in handling equipment.

Once the goods are out of the manufacturer's hands he has relatively little control over their display and merchandising, although some firms have their own merchandising or display teams. For complex or technical products adequate customer service can be vital. Interest in the retail-selling process itself may be critical, since there is belief among some middlemen that they are merely stockists, and therefore have little need to try to build in any customer service or systematic selling effort. In most builders' merchants and hardware stores, and even in some appliance or department stores, this is clearly demonstrated. Sales staff use incomprehensible technical jargon and provide limited advice and assistance, if they are found at all. Anthony Jay once commented, 'The problem in Britain isn't selling, but buying'.

PUSH AND PULL

Effectively moving a product through the channels and managing the various flows of information, title etc. is a combination of push and pull. The push is the manufacturer's or first-level intermediaries' efforts to persuade other channel members to stock or promote the product. The pull is the pressure exercised by customers on the trader to stock the item. Balance here is essential, as Figure 17.4 illustrates. Excess push may lead to the middleman overstocking the line.[2] In the short term this disrupts demand, as the trader holds back orders to achieve a more balanced position. Excess demand may lead the dealers to seek new sources of supply.

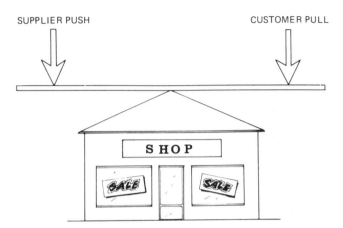

Fig. 17.4   The balance between supplier push and customer pull.

Achieving effective distribution is a mixture of pull and push. Pull is placed first simply because the trader's basic interest is in lines which effectively meet buyer needs, and which move through their outlet:

> There is no point in their offering me a 50 pence per case bonus if the goods never move out of my shop.
>
> Supermarket owner's comment

Insights into future promotional activities play a part in this.

Trade prices and discount structure are the basis of the relationship between producer and intermediary. The increased concentrated buying power and purchasing skills of dealers have created severe strains on traditional regional sales structures. Key-account management has emerged to play a major part in handling the special needs of and to cope with the massive power of major retail groups.

Originally this was concerned with price negotiations, including special discounts, volume bonuses and even agreements to develop own labels. At a conference in 1979, Andrew McDonald of Robinson, McDonald Marketing suggested that the major retailers were now so significant that products and brands could be designed to meet the special needs of their target customers, e.g. the Sainsbury's or the Tesco customer.

INTERMEDIARY RESPONSIBILITIES

The producer seeking to fully realise the potential of his dealers starts with a clear idea of the degree of responsibility he is transferring to them. This can encompass freedom over pricing. In some situations, e.g. where the agent or distributor is the principal (has title to the goods), the producer's power is limited once the sale is completed. Giving the intermediary responsibility for price is a major step which the producer should never take without careful consideration.

The pricing policies adopted by the dealer can have a major effect on the image and viability of the product. For example, Hathaway shirts were forced to invest heavily to rectify problems created by the pricing policies adopted by its US distributors. In a number of instances, notably industrial markets overseas, the degree of ignorance about the prices being charged for the firm's products is alarming.

The amount of service back-up provided by the dealer must be established at a very early date. This can encompass both repair and warranty as well as information and advisory services.

Responsibility for business development and meeting targets is particularly important in opening up new middlemen accounts. The firm should always spell these out even to the point of defining the manufacturer's rights of access to clients. Many small firms face particular problems here, as intermediaries can control all the flows in the system.

CONFLICT AND CO-OPERATION

The idea of a channel may leave readers with the impression that movement downwards is smooth and even. Although this may be the case, there are areas in which conflicts can and do emerge. The root of this lies in the attempts of the independent channel members to maximise their profits. The intermediary is both a customer involved in an exchange and a partner in distribution.

Some forms of conflict are beneficial to the system. They can create better balances of resources, skills and abilities can be improved, and inefficient, even dangerous or dishonest traders or manufacturers can be eliminated from the system.

Particular problems can emerge when specific channel members have too much power or act negatively. The desire of some retailers or wholesalers to restrict their lines, limit the numbers of new products, or demand promotional bonuses can stifle competition and innovation. At the same time, the policies of some manufacturers to restrict supplies or even refuse to supply certain traders may seriously reduce the end-customer's freedom to buy.

CONCLUSION

The growing complexity of modern industrial societies has pushed the producer further and further away from the prospective or actual buyer. However, channels of distribution have emerged to provide links, and many manufacturers are increasingly dependent on intermediaries to manage the flows that link them with their customers. Effective channel management calls for a determination to fully realise the opportunities available. Change has long characterised channel systems, so the marketing-orientated manager must build up his system with the expectation that changes will create new opportunities for or real threats to his firm.

Notes

1. Economists have suggested that to the customer real price (P) is actually a function of search time cost (c) and monetary price (p). Thus $P = c + p$.
2. The concept of 'stock push' has been developed to describe the practice of supplying excess stock to force the retailer to work hard setting the product out, sometimes called 'dealer loading'.

Further reading

Gattona, J., 'Channels of Distribution', *European Journal of Marketing*, **12**, No. 7, 1978. An excellent overview of the concepts and knowledge accumulated.

Hill, R., 'How Durco Europe went Direct', *Marketing*, March, 1977.

Lewis, E. H., *Marketing Channels*. New York: McGraw Hill, 1968. Although written from a US perspective, provides a comprehensive treatment of the area.

Seydel, J. & Jacobs, G., 'How Unigate Redirected its Sales Effort', *Marketing*, February, 1978. This case and the one mentioned above, 'How Durco Europe went Direct', (one industrial and the other consumer) provide valuable insights into channel management.

Key organisation

Distributive Industries EDC,
Millbank Tower,
London

18

Physical Distribution Management

Few management concepts have excited more interest over the last decade than physical distribution management:

> Physical distribution is the broad range of activities within a company (or other type of organization) concerned with the efficient movement of goods and raw materials—both inwards to the point of manufacture and outwards from the production line to the customer.

> Physical distribution management (PDM) is that part of management which is responsible for the design, administration and operation of systems to control the movement of raw materials and processed goods.

Both quotes from the Centre for
Physical Distribution
Management

Crucial to the physical distribution concept is the belief that management in this area calls for the integration of all parts of the organisation involved in the movement and storage of goods, the need to view in terms of the efficiency of the total organisation, and recognition that this efficiency is defined in terms of effectively and profitably meeting customers' needs, and that the goals of management in this area are the creation of time, place and form utility.

'Time, place and form utility' means getting the goods and any associated documentation and services to the right place, at the right time, and in the form required by the recipient. For example, a production manager may need 15 tonnes of zinc-coated steel (zintec) on a certain date. If he gets it too soon the firm pays interest on the capital involved, storage space is taken up unnecessarily, handling costs are involved and pilferage and wastage can occur. If he gets it too late production lines are disrupted, delivery schedules can be affected and customer dissatisfaction can be caused.

A HISTORICAL PERSPECTIVE

Given these dimensions of physical distribution management, it is perhaps surprising that the concept did not emerge earlier. It is now estimated that about 20 per cent of the Gross National Product, i.e. about £25 000 million, is involved in this area of business. It is little wonder that Peter Drucker[1] described it as 'the economy's dark continent'.

The last decade has seen many moves towards redressing the balance. These have been spurred partly by a combination of inflation and technical change. Inflation has hit particularly hard those companies whose stocking and warehousing policies were inefficiently managed. The technical changes affecting physical distribution management have been extensive, and include containerisation, roll-on/roll-off ship, wide body jets, palletisation, and computerisation of warehousing and stocking.

The EEC, with its interest in direct transport methods (equipment, operating methods, axle weights, drivers' hours etc.) and increasing involvement in other areas, has accelerated the process, and the changing documentation and legal requirements and the work of bodies such as SITPRO (Simplification of International Trade Procedures Board) have also played an important role.

Although these environmental pressures have helped to stimulate interest, a number of organisations and bodies have played a major part. The National Council of Physical Distribution Management (US) has played a major part in refining and developing the area, and the Centre for Physical Distribution Management, although a very young organisation, has already become a focal point for discussion, research and the dissemination of ideas. The staff at Cranfield School of Management have also played a major part in expanding knowledge in this area, and the *International Journal of Physical Distribution Management* is playing an increasingly important role in disseminating ideas.

The combination of these factors makes physical distribution management one of the most dynamic areas of opportunity for the student or young business-man. Companies like Boots, GKN, ICI, Johnson and Johnson, RHM Foods, and United Biscuits have developed or are in the process of developing fully integrated PDM systems.

THE PHYSICAL DISTRIBUTION SYSTEM

As indicated earlier, PDM encompasses all functions directly involved in the movement of goods. The primary areas are transportation, materials handling, packaging, warehousing, inventory, location and processing (orders and associated communications and documentation).

A research project conducted by the CPDM Research Liaison Committee broke this down even further when examining the main areas of work by management in these areas:

Transportation: vehicle utilisation, selection of model, vehicle schedules and routes, vehicle design specifications, vehicle selection, use of third-party contractors, direct v. indirect deliveries, load planning, vehicle rent, purchase and lease and carriage of specialised products, e.g. glass and dangerous materials.

Materials handling: in-plant movement, order picking techniques, sorting systems, pallet movement, unit loads and handling systems.

Packaging: packaging warranty.

Warehousing: warehouse space, facilities utilisation and warehouse layout.

Inventory: stockholding policy, stock-level requirement forecasts and control procedures.

Location: best methods of achieving national distribution coverage and location of field warehouses and depots.

Processing: order processing, administrative systems and drop size/cost analysis.

Costs: audit procedures, refusals, transport and handling, customer account profitability, cost allocation, backhaul waste capacity and labour incentives.

Strategic and general issues: service level offerings, service levels and their cost/revenue sensitivity, policy formulation, legislation, policy towards shared transport and other facilities, incentives, motivation of distribution staff and balance of own fleet versus use of third-party contractors.

It is clear from this not only that the range of activities is enormous,[2] but also that there are significant areas of overlap, particularly in marketing.

MARKETING AND PDM

Bowersox, Smykey and Lalonde,[3] in their authoritative book on the subject, place PDM firmly as part of the marketing mix, not as a separate function. Physical distribution can be 'a positive force in obtaining a competitive advantage in the market-place' through: achieving a balance of customer service and efficiency capable of meeting real customer time, place and space needs profitability; building up optimisation policies which can identify internal and external efficiencies, helping to protect the firm from the worst effects of inflation; providing an approach which views the channel and physical distribution system as a whole, thinking it through and maximising benefits for the entirety rather than for the parts. The overall purpose is synergy through integration and efficiency.

The scale of physical distribution has led some commentators to view PDM as related to but separate from marketing, and a number of firms have established independent (of marketing) units to reinforce this autonomy. Regardless of the perspective taken in this debate, the interdependencies are extensive, and effective company management calls for these areas to work together, whether formally independent or not.

THE GOALS OF PHYSICAL DISTRIBUTION MANAGEMENT

Although the overall objective of an efficient physical distribution system was described earlier in terms of creating time, place and form utility, this can be usefully divided into two sub-goals. Physical distribution management is concerned with both internal efficiencies and external services.

The success of PDM is dependent on its contribution to the more efficient operation of the elements listed earlier within some identifiable objective of a certain level or type of customer service. Traditionally the various parts of the physical distribution system (transport, materials handling, packaging etc.) have operated independently of each other, and their interactions with other parts of the firm have tended to be individual. This has created massive system inefficiencies.

The freight manager may cut back on his fleet to reduce his costs, and this in turn may place extra pressure on the warehousing or parts departments to hold extra stocks. If both decide to cut back or not adapt, the end customer will suffer, and perhaps extra marketing costs will be required to recruit new buyers. A number of gas regions faced this problem recently. Under pressure to reduce overhead costs, parts departments were running down their stocks. The immediate result was that service engineers were forced to reduce the amount they carried with them, and thus were often unable to effect a repair on their first visit, so there were sometimes long delays before appliances were repaired. Eventually consumer complaints departments had to expand to cope with the greater numbers of dissatisfied customers.

Customer service is difficult to define. To the customer it probably means the effort made by the manufacturer to ensure that the product is made available to him at the time, in the place, and in the condition he requested it. Companies, however, tend to use specific measures when considering customer service.

Order lead time is the period from the moment the customer first places the order or request (including repairs) until he receives it. This may be measured in terms of days (same-day delivery, repairs within 48 hours) or by some other objective criteria.

Percentage of orders satisfied provides an objective measure of the stock levels required to supply a fixed proportion of requests from stock. The cost of trying to satisfy all customers will be prohibitively high, so most firms target on an 'achievable' proportion.

The efficient operation of the physical distribution system calls for the various parts to work efficiently internally but, more important, also to work effectively as a whole. System inefficiencies are caused by the desire of each part to achieve its own goals (Figure 18.1).

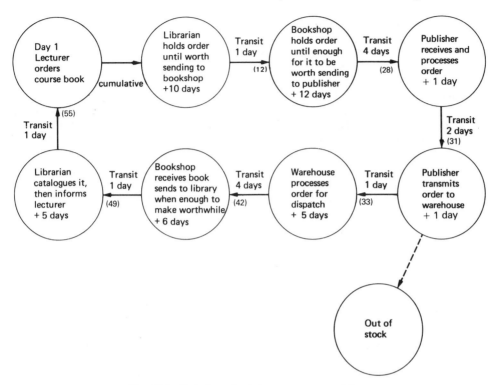

Fig. 18.1 Ordering a book (an extreme example).

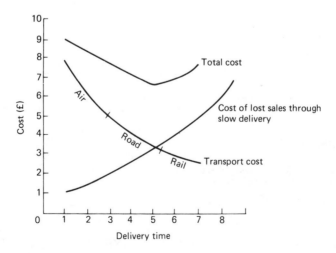

Fig. 18.2 The full cost of transport alternatives.

THE TOTAL COST APPROACH TO DISTRIBUTION

This focuses on the interrelationships that exist within the parts of the system. Tradeoffs are sought between the different elements, and there is scope for both direct savings and improved customer service.

Savings may be achieved in areas outside the scope of specific managers. For example, the cost of holding production stocks may not lie with either purchasing or production, and as a result these stocks may creep up until they are a drain on corporate resources. The total cost approach highlights these areas.

More importantly, the total cost approach focuses on the effect on the total system. This approach demands that the effects of changes in each item are reviewed in terms of their overall impact. This can be seen in terms of the effect of increasing or reducing the expenditure on quicker delivery through transport and communication. As a result, the total cost graph differs dramatically from the graph of the individual area (Figure 18.2).

PHYSICAL DISTRIBUTION: THE FUTURE

In 1979 James Morrel of the Henley Centre for Forecasting reviewed some of the factors likely to affect PDM in the 1980s. He found that transport costs will rise faster than other costs, packaging costs will increase, warehousing and material handling will increase in importance to compensate, and high interest rates will increase stockholding costs.

This will force management to look increasingly to distribution to contribute both to keeping costs down and to making an increasing contribution to overall corporate effectiveness. The development of physical distribution management will play an increasingly important part in this.

Notes

1. Drucker, P., *The Economy's Dark Continent*. Edinburgh: Fortune Press, 1962.
2. One could identify a number of other areas of activity that could reasonably be included, such as documentation, forecasting and purchasing.
3. Bowersox, D. J., Smykey, E. W. & Lalonde, B. J., *Physical Distribution Management*. New York: Macmillan, 1965.

Further reading

Bowersox, D. J., Smykey, E. W. & Lalonde, B. J., *Physical Distribution Management*. New York: Macmillan, 1965. A powerful and comprehensive review of the topic.
Wentworth, F., *Handbook of Physical Distribution Management*. London: Gower Press, 1976. A practical approach including a number of excellent specific articles. Note especially Chapters 1 and 3.

Key organisation

Centre for Physical Distribution Management,
Management House,
Parker Street,
London WC2B 5PT

CASE STUDY 13: THE NO HANDS FOOD MIXERS DIVISION OF HOPEFUL DURABLES LTD

The No Hands Food Mixers division of Hopeful Durables Ltd has been in existence for eight years (since 1978) and was originally set up as an organisational entity to exploit the growing demand for kitchen gadgetry in the UK. Hopeful Durables is currently turning over £6 million a year, of which No Hands contributes about a third.

Recently a number of problems have emerged which have resulted in a decline in net margin of the No Hands business even though turnover has steadily risen. It is felt within Hopeful Durables that a number of major decisions have to be taken.

The market

The market for food mixers is small and is dependent upon imported products. As can be seen from Table 18.1 no real growth has been evident in recent years but Hopeful Durables, a large durables manufacturer, is optimistic about long-term growth and has formed No Hands to develop sales and distribution, within the UK, of its existing lines. The managing director, Mr Ian Moody, has been given this task.

Table 18.1   *UK sales (including imports)*

	Units (000)
1982	979
1983	667
1984	980
1985	736

The relatively low sales in 1985 are due to lower imports from the Netherlands and France. Preliminary estimates for 1986 showed an increase and it was hoped that they would be back to the 1984 level. The value of the market (1985) at retail was estimated at about £10 million.

In the past ten years imported mixers have become the most important source of supply. In 1985 imports accounted for about 60 per cent of supplies compared with 40 per cent from home sources, a reversal of the situation prevailing six years previously.

Products and prices

There are many different kinds of food mixers and a wide range of attachments. The largest are table mixers, retailing at between £50 and £75. The smallest, hand mixers, sell at between £15 and £20. No Hands have products throughout the entire price range. (These are typical 'realised' retail prices, i.e. after all manner of discounting activities. Hopeful, on average, gets 75 per cent as its NSV).

Companies in the market

Whiskers Limited has the dominant market share, with three others, No Hands, Kordless and No Fuss, as main competitors. Market shares are estimated in Table 18.2.

Whiskers' position has been eroded by increased competitive activity from No Hands and Kordless.

Mixer ownership is extremely low when compared with other European countries. Hopeful considers that there is a lot of room for expansion in the British market. It is felt that it is unlikely that the low UK ownership is caused by price, as the cheaper mixers are well within the housewife's reach, but rather is due to cooking habits. Many British housewives only occasionally prepare elaborate meals and even when they have a mixer it is used infrequently.

Table 18.2 *Market shares*

	%
Whiskers	35
No Hands	25
Kordless	25
No Fuss	5
Others	10
Total	100

Distribution

Most purchases are made at independent electrical dealers. Multiples have been growing increasingly important and now account for over 10 per cent of mixer sales. Electricity Board showrooms are believed to have about 12 per cent of sales. A further 12 per cent of sales are made through department stores and a similar percentage through mail order. Some 7 per cent of consumer sales are directly accounted for by wholesalers. This is summarised in Table 18.2

Table 18.3 *The pattern of sales by outlet types*

	%
Independent electrical dealers	47
Multiples	10
Electricity Board showrooms	12
Department stores	12
Mail order	12
Wholesalers—direct sales	7

The normal channel flow is for manufacturers to deal through electrical wholesalers and, because of the high proportion of imports, the importance of such wholesalers is likely to continue.

Although many retailers are prepared to stock more than one brand, it is nevertheless very difficult for the smaller companies to obtain distribution.

Within No Hands, the managing director, Mr Moody, thought that the future development of his company's logistics function should be the responsibility of an expert. He appointed a director to be responsible, Mr R. Suppards.

Mr Suppards immediately commenced an appraisal of No Hands' existing capabilities and the specific physical distribution service requirements of retailers. A review of the situation is presented below.

Sales force

Until recently No Hands food mixers were sold by all Hopeful salesmen. However, this policy has just been changed and a specialist sales force recruited. At present it numbers 20, based on regional sales offices as shown in Table 18.4.

Salesmen perform varied functions, i.e. taking orders, checking inventory, arranging displays, dealing with customer complaints and other general selling activities as directed from time to time. A breakdown of the time used by salesmen shows that on average each salesman makes eight calls per day and each call takes some 40 minutes. Of this time the various functions accounted for are as shown in Table 18.5.

No Hands sales had increased slowly but steadily over the past five years and it was this slow and steady growth that had prompted the company's re-organisations.

Table 18.4 *Regional sales*

	Percent sales		No. of No Hands salesmen
	All Hopeful products	No Hands	
South East, London	30	50	8
West and South West, Bristol	15	15	3
Midlands, Birmingham	25	20	3
North West, Manchester	10	5	2
North East, Newcastle	10	5	2
Scotland, Glasgow	10	5	2
	100	100	20

Table 18.5 *Breakdown of time used by salesmen*

	%
Checking inventory	50
Arranging displays	10
Customer complaints	10
Selling	10
General chat	20
	100

Facilities locations

Hopeful has warehousing facilities close to each of the regional sales offices. These have each been fed from production sources in Birmingham and from Holland. Each is at capacity loading and a decision is required on whether to extend the warehouses or to review the service policy.

Inventory

Inventory levels are currently based on sales forecasts. For each location and item maximum sales levels are forecast. In recent years inventory holding has increased due basically to two factors, an ever-widening product range with increases in model types, colours etc. and the need to carry higher safety stocks of those items imported from Holland. A further source of concern is that, in order to achieve possible production economies, senior management in Hopeful are considering concentrating production in Holland and in France. Such a change is becoming even more likely in the face of present UK industrial relations problems.

Management has always considered that the cost of holding inventory (valued on an NSV basis) should be most carefully and stringently examined. Recent estimates have been of the order of 24 per cent p.a., a significant increase from the mid-1970s, when it was just less than 20 per cent p.a. Much of the difference can perhaps be accounted for by the higher cost of capital, but obsolescence is playing a significant role.

Transportation

Hopeful's distribution manager, N. N. Kelley, was for many years the company's transport manager. In 1985 he was awarded the Gold Medal of the Institute of Transport. He was considered by many as the best freight rate negotiator in the business and was proud of the low rates obtained from carriers. These low rates invariably necessitated maximum cube use on all carriers and vehicles, both for trunking and for deliveries to retail and trade outlets. Kelley's policy had always excluded any own-transport fleet.

Order processing

Orders are received in a number of ways, i.e. phone, mail, teleprinter and from representatives by mail or phone at the regional offices. Dispatch notes are prepared and forwarded to the warehouse staff. Invoices are all raised by head office in Birmingham.

Order cycle times vary because Kelley's policy is to accumulate orders until such time as full vehicle loads can be dispatched, and thus lowest unit transport cost obtained.

Trade relations

In the past Hopeful has enjoyed good relations with the trade. However, in the past year some murmurs of discontent have been apparent. The trade appears to be satisfied with discounts but feels that inventory investment is growing too high. Paradoxically, lost sales due to stock-outs are beginning to occur on some lines which to them seems illogical when total investment in inventory is increasing.

This case study is reproduced with the permission of Dr David Walters of Cranfield School of Management.

19

Advertising and Sales Promotion

Advertising and sales promotion are the most obvious aspects of the marketing effort. To many people, they are synonymous with marketing itself. Media advertising stares down from posters, enters the home through television, radio and newspapers and is in the workplace through the industrial, trade and technical press. Promotional activity is frequently related to the act of purchase, meeting the shopper in the outlet or geared to influence the middleman's buying behaviour. When asked to describe marketing, most consumers would start off with specific advertisements they have seen and offers they have taken up or rejected. This awareness reflects the success of advertising and sales promotion in establishing their presence. It is this access to the buyer or prospective buyer that the firm seeks when considering an investment in advertising or sales promotion.

Advertising is purposive communication. The firm spends its money to communicate with groups in the market-place and achieve certain results. The objectives can vary enormously and the means of reaching customer groups have evolved over time to service these needs. The simplest form is the individual trying to sell his car through classified ads, and the most complex form is corporate advertising for a giant multinational trying to create a favourable climate for the firm's operations, improve the image of its product offerings, boost company morale and establish specific links with the market.

Although advertising has established a high level of awareness, the proportion of the UK Gross National Product invested in media advertising is small—1.39 per cent in 1983. Even if the most generous estimates of the scale of sales promotional activity are incorporated, it is still below 2 per cent.

MEDIA ADVERTISING

The American Marketing Association defined advertising as:

> Any paid form of non-personal presentation and promotion of ideas, goods or services by an identifiable sponsor.

The overwhelming majority of the expenditure is directed through press and television (Table 19.1).

Advertising as an industry has emerged partly in response to the needs of firms to communicate with their customers during a period in which markets have become larger, more diffuse and more competitive, and partly as a reflection of the media owners' ability to provide the means of effective, purposive communication.

The revolution in thinking about newspaper financing brought about by Lord Northcliff in the *Daily Mail* in 1896 brought together the need of manufacturers to reach their customers and that of newspaper proprietors to keep their cover prices down through the sale of advertising space, and this is still an important part of the current advertising

Table 19.1   *Total advertising expenditure by media*

Media	£m 1974	1975	1976	1977	1978	1979	1980	1981	1982	1983
National newspapers	161	162	197	251	295	347	426	467	515	584
Regional newspapers	273	283	331	396	483	593	640	684	737	817
Magazines and periodicals	71	79	92	116	143	180	192	200	209	224
Trade and technical	80	86	103	133	169	203	214	222	247	276
Directories[a]	16	20	31	43	50	62	82	97	124	154
Press production costs	48	49	58	73	96	119	130	146	154	181
Total press	649	679	812	1012	1236	1504	1684	1816	1986	2236
Television	203	236	307	398	482	471	692	809	928	1109
Poster and transport	34	35	43	54	68	87	107	115	124	137
Cinema	8	7	8	9	13	17	18	18	18	16
Radio	6	10	18	26	35	52	54	60	70	81
Total	900	967	1188	1499	1834	2131	2555	2818	3126	3579

Media	Percentage of total 1974	1975	1976	1977	1978	1979	1980	1981	1982	1983
National newspapers	17.9	16.7	16.6	16.7	16.1	16.3	16.7	16.6	16.5	16.3
Regional newspapers	30.3	29.3	27.9	26.4	26.3	27.8	25.0	24.3	23.6	22.8
Magazines and periodicals	7.9	8.2	7.7	7.7	7.8	8.5	7.5	7.1	6.7	6.3
Trade and technical	8.9	8.9	8.7	8.9	9.2	9.5	8.4	7.9	7.9	7.7
Directories[a]	1.8	2.1	2.6	2.9	2.7	2.9	3.2	3.4	3.9	4.3
Press production costs	5.3	5.1	4.9	4.9	5.2	5.6	5.1	5.2	4.9	5.1
Total press	72.1	70.3	68.4	67.5	67.4	70.6	65.9	64.5	63.5	62.5
Television	22.6	24.4	25.8	26.6	26.3	22.1	27.1	28.7	29.7	31.0
Poster and transport	3.8	3.6	3.6	3.6	3.7	4.1	4.2	4.1	4.0	3.8
Cinema	0.9	0.7	0.7	0.6	0.7	0.8	0.7	0.6	0.6	0.4
Radio	0.7	1.0	1.5	1.7	1.9	2.4	2.1	2.1	2.2	2.3
Total	100	100	100	100	100	100	100	100	100	100

[a]Including Yellow Pages
Reproduced with the permission of the Advertising Association

industry. New media have emerged, with the balance of relationships, the skills and the techniques changing over time, but the mutually supportive relationship persists.

There are now three parties involved in the advertising process: the advertiser, who supplies products or services; the advertising agency, who translate the advertiser's message into a form appropriate to the media and relevant to the prospective customer, place the advertisements and are legally responsible for the space bought;[1] and the media owner who provides the vehicle for reaching the specific target groups or audiences.

Originally the agencies were literally the agents of the media, paid a commission on their sales of space. Although the character of the relationship has changed over the years, with agencies focusing their talents and developing skills to meet the needs of advertisers, the form of payment, by commission from the media, has remained basically constant.[2] In a sense this meets the needs of all parties: the agent has increased independence, the media owner has a secure relationship with a body of experts in communication, and the advertiser has access to a wide and varied group of autonomous specialists.

The complexity of the media, their interplay, the varied goals of firms and the different responses of consuming groups all call for highly developed talents in communication. The agency may be called upon to devise a campaign to put across varied and subtle ideas to an audience which may not be particularly interested in them and may be unaware of the transmission of the message, in the space of a 15-second commercial or in a newspaper advertisement. At the same time, the scope for a particular form of expression is limited by the regulations of the British Code of Advertising Practice.

Advertising media

The media have played a major part in the evolution of advertising through the provision of access to consuming and decision-making groups, by supplying an environment for specific forms and styles of advertisement, by developing a cost structure and research into audience characteristics, and through a recognition of the interplay of specific media, advertisements and campaigns.

Access

The media provide advertisers with access to prospective purchasers both in general and in specialist groups.[3] Before the advent of television, the national newspapers were the sole means (in the UK) of reaching the mass market quickly and effectively. The huge circulations of the 'popular' daily and Sunday papers were the major incentive for firms to use them. However, the growth of television has led to a revision of thinking about newspaper audiences, and it has been recognised that the selective character of readership is as important as the sheer size of the market. This has coincided with a progressive change in the relative market share of the 'quality' compared to the 'popular' press.

The regional press has for many years been the largest single area of advertising expenditure. Their firm basis in the local community has given them real strength in specific areas, particularly classified advertisements. These dominate the advertising expenditure in the regional press, accounting for 58 per cent of all expenditure compared to 12 per cent in the nationals (1983).[4]

This reveals how important the local press can be to advertisers. Messages directly relevant to the community served, perhaps geared to action in the near future, can have great impact. Retail advertising, local event promotions and producers attempting to build a strong regional base for their output provide the majority of non-classified regional advertising, and the low absolute cost of space allows these small advertisers to use the medium. Under certain circumstances local press has been used in national campaigns, e.g. to boost coverage in areas of special interest or to bring out regional aspects of the message.

Achieving access to the many specialist-interest groups is made relatively easy for the advertiser through magazines catering for specific market segments and the trade press. These range from the huge-circulation women's magazines to relatively small-volume technical and trade publications. The advertiser can define his target group with a high degree of accuracy and can focus all his media expenditure on them. The detailed interest which the reader has in the subject matter of specialist magazines usually means that he carefully reads all the content, including advertisements. Many non-regular readers purchase such magazines when considering purchases, partly to search the advertisements. A clear definition of the target market should be compared with the readership profiles of the magazines, and much background information about their readers is available from the publishers themselves.

Industrial and commercial advertising has grown dramatically during the 1970s and 80s partly because of the five-fold increase in retail advertising. During the same period industrial advertising has increased two and a half times. A great deal of expenditure has been directed towards the trade and technical press and magazines, which provide the advertiser with the opportunity to direct his message towards the experts in his field of interest. The purchasing and influencing power of relatively few people can determine the success of his efforts, and the interest in the product offerings often leads to follow-up of advertisements. British industrial advertisers have the advantage of being able to advertise in leading UK and US journals, which often reach overseas markets and provide valuable exports leads.

Magazines such as *The Engineer, Design* and *Nuclear News* have a worldwide readership and reputation which the advertiser can turn to his own advantage. In the context of industrial media it is worth noting the growth of trade directories, buyers' guides, annuals and, a more recent development, controlled circulation papers. Trade directories have long been invaluable to the professional buyer, who knows that a careful search of his ABC directory will identify a number of prospective suppliers. More recently, specialist-interest groups have published guides to their industry, e.g. *The European Plastics Guide*, or even to their region, e.g. *North East Buyers' Guide*. There is some evidence that purchasing officers are increasingly using these as the starting point in their search for supplies.

So far our attention has been focused on the variety of the press media, but interest in the selectivity of these media has been stimulated by the growth of television as the dominant mass medium. Only the Sunday papers can effectively compete with the top TV programmes.

Fig. 19.1 The IBA companies and their potential audiences. Reproduced with the permission of the Independent Broadcasting Authority.

The overwhelming majority of homes in the UK have television receivers capable of receiving ITV programmes from the regional contractors (Figure 19.1).

Using this network it is possible to reach an enormous national audience simultaneously with a single message. However, only the largest advertisers would beam their transmission out in this way. Most advertisers use the regions selectively, attempting to combine number of 'impressions' with a degree of targeting. Major regional advertisers will direct their efforts solely towards their particular areas. Some organisations combine national campaigns devised centrally with regional messages; e.g. the Gas Corporation's 'Cookability Road Show' runs nationally, while Northern Gas promotes on Tyne Tees Television the range of cookers in its shops. Some smaller television regions obtain a significant proportion of their income from test marketing in their region, with local advertising often earning significant media discounts.

> New products or services, or products or services not advertised on television before and which are advertised either exclusively in Scotland, or in Scotland and one television area within the UK, will qualify for a 25 per cent reduction.
>
> British Rate and Data

Major changes have been taking place over the past few years, notably Breakfast Television, Channel 4, and the emergence of networks of cable television.

In 1973 the first commercial radio stations based on the mainland of Britain started broadcasting, the way having been paved by Radio Luxemburg and the off-shore 'pirate' radio stations. Although many of the pioneer stations suffered teething troubles, commercial radio is now established as an important and rapidly growing medium. Only Radio Luxemburg provides national coverage. Most of the forty-nine British stations are confined to specific urban areas (Capital and London Broadcasting Co. in London, BMRB in Birmingham, Radio Clyde in Glasgow, Radio City in Liverpool). Their specific audience profiles vary considerably, with overall strengths among housewives, young people and commuting motorists. Leading national advertisers are finding that radio provides an access to specific groups that are difficult to reach by other media, e.g. the young, or provides access in particularly favourable circumstances, e.g. housewives planning their shopping.

Poster and transport advertising has traditionally been faced with severe access problems. The most important of these for the poster industry have been the lack of detailed audience data (JICPAS has been set up to provide this) and the overwhelming dominance of the best sites by relatively few industries, which hold them on long-term contracts.

The overwhelming majority of the population have the *opportunity to see* (OTS) posters every day, and certain specific sites have very high OTS scores for their area. The cigarette and liquor industries have built up massive portfolios of such sites in order to keep their products visible to customers,[6] and until recently this prevented the generally fragmented poster industry from offering meaningful coverage to prospective clients.[7] The 1970s and 80s have seen progressive rationalisation and a greater willingness to co-operate in the poster industry, which in turn is encouraging more advertisers to use posters. However, any dramatic broadening of the industry's base is dependent on the policies adopted towards and by the cigarette and liquor advertisers.

Transport advertising, with its similar dependence on these advertisers plus a few specific groups, e.g. cinemas and 'own' advertising (BR, London Regional Transport), has long been the Cinderella of the outdoor media. It offers a large number of access points to the travelling public on road and rail and in airports and ports. Transport authorities, particularly London Regional Transport, are now adopting a much more aggressive approach to marketing their product, but there is still the major problem that the lack of data leads the advertiser to view the poster or transport media audience as relatively undifferentiated other than by area. The emphasis on selectivity of audience by advertisers has created problems for the industry.

This interest in selectivity has helped the cinema advertising industry to maintain its share of media advertising despite the rapidly escalating costs of producing films suitable for cinema broadcast. The audience profile is dominated by the young (under 24) and unmarried. This powerful consumer group, with its high discretionary income and little reluctance to spend it on acquiring material possessions, is of tremendous importance to producers of leisure goods, clothing, cosmetics and specific consumer durables (cars, motor bikes, watches etc.). Although these factors are important to the national advertiser, local advertisers use cinema to reach specific local-interest groups. The cinema audience has shown itself to be extremely changeable, news of cinema closures contrasting with the box-office booms of films such as *E T*, the *Star Wars* films and *Chariots of Fire*. These are important considerations for any prospective cinema advertiser. His returns on a major investment in a commercial are partly dependent on the success of specific films.

Environment

Although the access to an audience provided by a medium is a critical factor, very few advertising media are thought of by their audience as merely a source of advertising information, or by the advertiser as a blank sheet of paper to be managed to the advertiser's specific advantage. All the media and the specific advertising vehicles impart their own characteristics to the advertisements appearing in them. These may be structural (newspapers are static and generally black and white, while television commercials are mobile and often in colour) or they may be determined by specific contexts (the *Mirror* and the *Sun* have a specific style and method of presentation which can make an advertisement designed for the *Financial Times* totally ineffective). These environmental factors provide the canvas for the creativity of the advertiser and determine the effectiveness of the copy placed in front of specific customer groups.

The complexity of the press media almost defies any global categorisation. Even the conventional notion of the static nature of the media can be confounded by the near genius of some creative teams. Creativity in the face of the variety of the media is capable of refuting almost any of the general points made below.

The static character of newspapers is a constraint on advertising. However, the impact of effective copy can be tremendous. The reader makes a conscious effort to purchase his newspaper, searching for news, interest and stimulation. This provides the opportunity to relate the advertisements to his search. However, those who really satisfy these needs are the paper's own journalists and editorial staff. Advertisements are competing for impact against the immediacy of the news itself. Two positive[8] approaches to this problem have been adopted. The advertisements can compete for impact (Figure 19.2):

> Out of 4850 (newspaper ads) I managed to find nine.
> John Webster, Creative Director of BMP, *Advent*, June, 1978

Or they can recognise their difference (Figure 19.3):

> An advertisement either has to set out to do what the editorial does or it has to do the opposite ... Most of the eight (ads) I have picked are opposites.
> E. McCabe, Senior Vice President,
> Scali, McCabe Sloves Inc,
> *Advent*, August, 1976

Magazines add another dimension to the environment of the advertisements that appear. Many offer colour, which brings a vitality and impact achievable in only the very best black and white copy. The interest and involvement of the readers provide the ideal

Fig. 19.2 *Bike* magazine's ad. competes for impact with the headlines. Reproduced with the permission of Mirror Group Newspapers Ltd.

focus on leisure, the traditional women's magazines (*Woman's Own, Woman's Realm*), with their emphasis on the home, the modern women's magazines (*Vogue, Cosmopolitan, Honey, 21, Spare Rib*), catering for very diffuse groups, and the special-interest magazines (*Custom Car, Popular Photography*) are only a few of the vehicles offering opportunities to weld a specific offering to the acknowledged interest of the reader. These often have the great advantage of gaining longer and repeated exposure: a newspaper is normally finished within a day, while the *TV Times* boasts that it is 'the nine day magazine'. Regular contributors to specialist magazines may keep them indefinitely.

The use of magazines as reference sources is an important characteristic of much of the trade and technical press. Company libraries and individuals will keep specific periodicals for many years, referring back again and again to specific issues and occasionally even individual advertisements. This information element has led David Ogilvy to recommend advertisers to use case histories and testimonials, demonstrate and use long copy. The reader is a specialist and will be selective. When he refers to an advertisement it will be for a purpose, and information will help him to recognise the value of your offering in solving his problems.

> Print is the purest form of advertising. It puts the creative mind one-on-one against a blank sheet of paper. With no outside influences. No tricks. No gimmicks. No hiding behind actors or music or jokes or props. When it comes to print, it's just you, that blank sheet of paper—and the moment of truth for the creative person.
>
> Hank Seiden, Executive Vice President,
> Hacks and Greist[9]

Fig. 19.3   The Marina advertisement contrasts with surrounding copy. Reproduced with permission of Mirror Group Newspapers Ltd.

Marshall McLuhan, the media expert, contrasts the 'hot' medium of paper with the 'cool' medium of television. The emergence of television, entering the audience's homes with vision, sound, movement and, most recently, colour added a new dimension to the media environment. The home environment is both a blessing and a curse. The well designed advertisement is like a welcome visitor, achieving an impact and audience unrivalled by other media. The structural characteristics of the medium are creatively combined with the specific context of the transmission to achieve a rapport with the target audience. The poor advertisement, however, is an unwelcome intrusion into the evening's enjoyment and can alienate prospective purchasers. It must be recognised that these advertisements are directed towards specific audiences and objectives, and it is their contribution in those directions which determines their value, not winning awards or praise from non-target groups. The medium does have operational constraints. In 15 to 30 seconds a message which may have taken months to develop must be delivered in such a way as to elicit the required response from the audience without unnecessarily alienating other groups and at the same time comply with the regulatory requirements of the

Government and other agencies. The following simple rules appear to contribute to more effective commercials:[10]

1. The picture must tell a story.
2. Provide a 'key visual'.
3. Grab the viewer's attention.
4. Be single-minded.
5. Register the name of your product.
6. Show people, not objects.
7. Have a pay-off.
8. Reflect your product personality.
9. Avoid 'talky' commercials.
10. Build campaigns, not individual commercials.

This recognition of the environment in which the message is received is particularly important for the minor media, i.e. posters and transport, radio and cinema. Much of their value is derived from the specific circumstances in which messages are received and the attitude of the audience towards them.

Posters are seldom studied carefully. They are geared towards the passer-by, who may even be isolated from the media in a car or on a bus, so the copy or visual must break into the audience's consciousness to deliver its message. A great deal of poster advertising is effective in providing supportive, reminder impacts behind a campaign being carried on through other media. Smaller sites are used in shopping centres to trigger off purchase-linked behaviour. Different effects can be achieved by different poster sizes and locations. Sizes are usually in multiples of 30 by 20 inches (Figure 19.4).

The last four years have seen the emergence of radio as an important medium, with its own distinctive style and environment. Most of its content is popular music. Most of the stations, apart from Luxemburg,[11] are based in urban centres, drawing their audiences from the locality and rapidly establishing powerful links with the immediate community. The music of local radio has rapidly become the continuous background sound in houses while the housework is being done and in the car while travelling. The nature of the content has led to local radio being particularly popular among the young, who are both difficult to reach by other media and often fiercely loyal to the local station and specific DJs. During the day local radio creates an environment in which shopping-linked, local messages can be transmitted, e.g. 'visit Savacentre now for bargains in the food department'. Directed at both the housewife and the motorist, these messages can establish a strong purchase link. However, messages which fail to recognise the impact on their advertisements of the context of 'music background' can easily be lost in that background. The message must instantly establish a memorable impression on the target audience. It appears that listeners are willing to stretch their imaginations in interpreting messages, and this has allowed some advertisers to be extremely imaginative and evocative. Other advertisers have effectively translated campaigns from other media to radio. Problems do exist, however, particularly in adapting for radio advertisements which normally have powerful visual images.

As indicated above, involvement is an important aspect of any medium. It is difficult to achieve this in the home, where many distractions surround the commercials. It has been estimated that over half the audience are engaged in some other activity during commercial breaks—leaving the room, doing domestic chores, switching channels etc. However, this is not a problem for cinema advertisers. The cinema is blacked out and attention is focused on the screen, so the opportunity exists to establish a powerful link with the audience. However, the audience is generally young and expects to be enter-tained, so the entertainment value of any cinema advertisement must be extremely high, competing as it does with the multi-million-dollar movie offering which follows. Effectively produced commercials can thrive on the atmosphere, but poor advertisements quickly die.

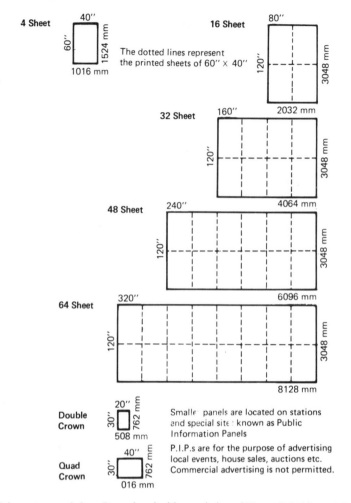

Fig. 19.4 Main poster panel sizes. Reproduced with permission of Young & Rubicam Advertising Ltd.

Costs

Advertising costs are made up of two distinct but interrelated elements: exposure costs for space and time, and production costs. A rough rule of thumb puts production costs at 10 per cent of exposure costs, although specific circumstances can distort that balance.

British Rate and Data is the bible of the UK media planner. It appears every month and provides details of the costs of all media for specific spaces and timings. These costs must be viewed in terms of both absolute cost, e.g. £12 500 for an unspecified[1] page in *The Mirror*, and cost to reach a specific audience. The concept of cost per thousand is used to highlight the real costs per thousand of the audience using specific media. For example, the absolute cost of a full page in the *News of the World* is far higher than a full page in the *Newcastle Sunday Sun*, but the readerships are so different in size that the cost per thousand is far higher in the *Newcastle Sunday Sun* than in the *News of the World*. It is therefore better for an advertiser who can afford the absolute cost to invest his funds in the medium offering the lowest cost per thousand for his target audience. This point is very important. There is generally little point in investing funds in getting the lowest absolute cost if the cost of reaching the target audience is higher.

Research into audiences and their characteristics is a continuing process. The basic source of newspaper-audience data is the National Readership Survey, which annually samples 30 000 individuals aged 15 and over. The survey measures readership of over 100 publications, including all major newspapers and magazines. A similar function is performed for television by JICTAR, which is a national panel of 2700 homes containing 7000 individuals aged four and over. Minute-by-minute home ratings for all channels are produced by a meter on the TV set. Similar information on poster audiences is collected by JICPAS, and on radio audiences by JICRAR. The Screen Advertisers' Association performs a roughly similar service for cinema. These surveys are only the tip of a massive iceberg of continuing study: advertising agencies, large advertisers and the media owners themselves perform regular studies of their audiences and their characteristics.

Interplay

It is dangerous to think of advertising in terms of single advertisements in individual media. Even the smallest advertiser should plan his activities in terms of bringing all his sales promotion together in a promotional campaign. The classified advertisement provides the information to stimulate contacts, and the selling process relates to the classified advertisement to ensure that the best sales prospects are seen, with neither seller nor prospective purchaser wasting his time. In planning substantial advertising efforts a campaign approach is central. The overall plan is identified, and each advertisement and all the media are reviewed in terms of their contribution to the plan. The target audience can be as specific as 'all readers of the *Manchester Evening News*', but a significant proportion of *News* readers will not buy the paper on a specific night, and a large number will not notice the advertisement. Thus even defining the market in terms of a specific newspaper will involve repeats, which pose their own creative problems, e.g. what is the advertisement's effect on those seeing it for the third or fourth time?

Very seldom is the specific audience of an individual medium anything better than an approximation of the firm's target audience. Even the million buyers of *The Mirror* are only a small part of the C_2DE population of the UK, although it is true that repeats in *The Mirror* will gradually increase the coverage of the newspaper[13] (Figure 19.5). Using other newspapers and additional media may mean better returns (in terms of market penetration) for additional expenditure (Figure 19.6). This pattern occurs in both one-medium and multi-media advertising: repeated exposures in a single medium lead to diminishing returns for money spent in terms of audience reached, and adding further media, even with smaller audiences, may improve penetration of the target audience. It is worth remembering that people employ a number of media in their lives (an estimated 40

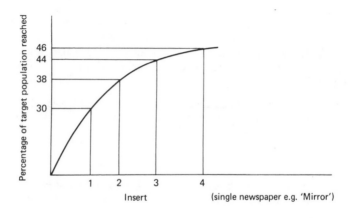

Fig. 19.5 Diminishing returns from concentrating on a single newspaper.

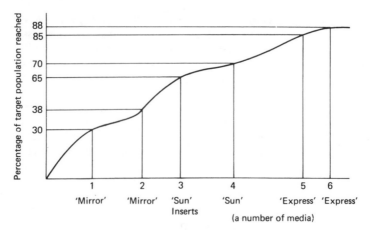

Fig. 19.6   Increasing returns from spreading coverage.

per cent of *Mirror* readers also read the *Sun*, and the majority of TV viewers will also see posters), so a scheduling decision must take this into account. This interplay can also be effectively used to add further dimensions to the campaign, e.g. to build up images using TV and colour magazines, to remind and heighten brandname consciousness through posters, to suggest action in the press and on the radio, and to trigger purchase at point of sale. The concepts of campaigning and interplay are central to any decision on budgets and schedules.

Setting the advertising budget

The firm's advertising budget sets the limits within which the media planner must operate and is thus a major factor in determining the extent to which the firm's advertising objectives can be achieved. A certain minimum level of exposure is necessary before even the best advertising can have any effect. There are a number of basic approaches to setting the total budget.

Affordability

This is probably the most fundamental approach. The company decides (probably subjectively) how much it can afford, and these funds are then allocated to the different media. Although this approach is very common, particularly among small and industrial firms, it derives from a total misconception of advertising by which advertising is treated as a luxury to be indulged in when times are good and dropped when times are bad. In fact, advertising is vital for building links with customers, the basis of every strong firm. Research has indicated that:

> (increased) advertising during depression generally resulted in an increase in sales relative to the sales of competitors who did not make such increases.
>
> R. S. Vaile[14]

Percentage of sales method

This method sets the advertising budget as a simple percentage of either sales during last full year or forecast sales of the budget year. This avoids the severe fluctuations in expenditure which often occur with the 'affordable' approach. At the same time, it is a simple method of solving the problem of different opinions about what the firm can afford, e.g. the sales manager may say £100 000 and the finance director £1 000. However, this approach treats advertising almost as a tax on sales, implying that advertising results from sales, not vice versa.

The competitive parity approach

This looks beyond the firm to the competitive environment. The company locates itself in terms of its perceived competitors and invests the amount appropriate to its position in the market. This method almost totally ignores the firm's customers and its own needs, assuming that its goals and objectives are the same as its competitors'. Equally important, it presupposes that the competition know what they are doing and are adopting a planned approach to setting their budgets.

The objective and task method

This involves the firm establishing its advertising goals and making available funds sufficient to achieve them. It is usually seen as the optimum method of exploiting the purposive character of advertising. The resources are made available to perform the task set.

Combining the approaches

In fact the majority of firms adopt some combination of these methods. Setting the budget is not a once-and-for-all task. Appropriations are proposed (by line managers), discussed and reviewed (by managers, agencies and directors) and determined (by the board). When circumstances change the sensible firm modifies its position. In this process all four approaches described above play a part.

1. Advertising objectives are set by top management for all brands. The brand managers (probably after discussions with the agencies) indicate the budgets required.
2. Top management relate these to hard criteria such as current sales of brands, perhaps indicating a percentage of sales which might be available. Some firms will even distinguish between types of sale, e.g. 5 per cent of historic sales, 15 per cent on new sales.
3. Considerable discussion usually ensues, particularly in firms with a number of products and brands attempting to achieve their objectives with limited resources. Competitive advertising levels play a major part in establishing the realistic nature of budgets and objectives.
4. Assuming that the budgets finally agreed can be 'afforded', given the many other demands on company resources, the firm determines its advertising budget. The agency is then officially notified of the sums it can spend to achieve agreed objectives.

Throughout this process the lessons that the firm has learned in previous years provide the backcloth to discussions and decisions. Information about responses in the market-place to company expenditure is a vital element in budgeting, and in the USA larger firms conduct market experiments to help determine advertising expenditure.

Scheduling

Once a budget is set the media scheduling task is to achieve the most efficient allocation of the funds among alternative media and over time. These two decisions, where and when, constitute the basic task of the media planner. A good brief is vital to the planner as his proposed schedule in terms of number of media and alternatives within media, number of insertions and balance of types of insertion, and timing is a function of the type of audience wanted, target number of exposures and desired response. Scheduling is an area which involves both sophisticated computer-based models, based on linear programming, simulation and other techniques, and individual media-buying skills where the buyer's negotiating ability is critical.

The role of an advertising agency

Throughout this discussion advertising agencies and specific tasks identified with them—media buying and scheduling, creative development, communications development—have been mentioned. This reflects the development of the agency from the days when its brokerage task dominated to today, when an awareness of the total communication is vital. Through this process two key features have been important:

1. Agencies are outside the advertiser's firm. The independent perspective they can provide is necessary for the firm wanting a realistic judgement of its work. This independence allows a degree of honest appraisal not always possible within the producer's firm.
2. Agencies work for many clients. This enables them to feed into the companies' policies an extremely wide range of ideas and experiences. It is particularly important for creative workers to avoid the staleness which can occur when handling only one product or a narrow range of products.

Although this implies that all advertising agencies are very similar, in fact they operate as very individual entities. Powerful and creative personalities dominate the agency world to a degree unusual in industry. The character of the industry provides the talented with almost unrivalled opportunities to stamp their own personalities both on their firms and on advertising in general. The industry's role today is very much the creation of people like Charles Saatchi (Saatchi & Saatchi Garland-Compton Ltd), Ronnie Kirkwood (Kirkwoods), Peter Marsh and Rod Allen (Allen, Brady and Marsh), David Ogilvy (Ogilvy, Benson and Mather) and Martin Boase (BMP).

The structure of an agency

Agencies differ enormously in size, structure and range of services. There are creative 'hot shops' whose sole activity is creative development, with very few ancillary activities. Media-buying agencies have emerged over the last few years to provide centralised space-buying services. Their expertise is in media, in which they offer special discounts, but they offer little support in other areas. However, the majority of agencies retain a full service capability, attempting to match the complete range of client needs with the services they offer, i.e. creative services, media services, marketing services, account planning and handling and occasionally PR and below-the-line promotions. An example of the structure of an advertising agency is shown in Figure 19.7.

The recruitment, selection, management motivation and control of agencies is a continuing concern of most firms. An outsider looking at the advertising press would get the impression that accounts are constantly on the move from agency to agency, but in fact many of the most successful agency/client relationships endure for decades. Some degree of mobility is probably an advantage, as it introduces new ideas and keeps agencies alert, but although it may be a good thing in general, it is not necessarily so for specific accounts. This is one reason why the largest advertisers employ a number of agencies.

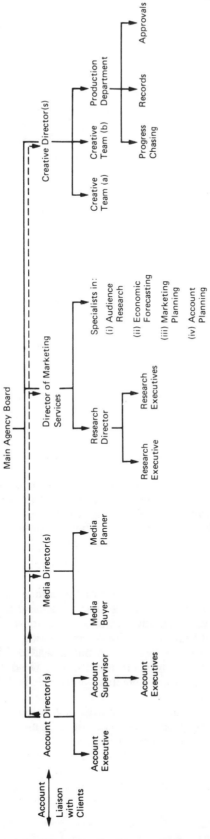

Fig. 19.7 Advertising agency structure.

They are often involved in new product launches, and a successful launch may mean long-term good billings for the agency.

Objectives in advertising

The clear communication of objectives is essential to a strong client/agency relationship. In this discussion two distinct areas are examined: how advertising works—the overall ways in which advertising can contribute to company objectives; and the definitions of specific tasks for individual campaigns or advertisements.

How advertising works

A number of models which attempt to describe the way advertising affects the customer have been suggested. The majority assume that the task of advertising is to help the consumer move through a series of states of mind, usually starting with 'unawareness' and ending with 'action' (Table 19.3).

Table 19.3   *Advertising task and consumer's state of mind*

	Models		
DAGMAR	The Lavidge and Steiner Model	AIDA	Advertising Task
1. Unaware	1. Awareness	1. Awareness	Moving the customer through the early
2. Aware	2. Knowledge	2. Interest	stages is usually seen as the information task
3. Comprehension	3. Liking	3. Desire	of advertising. Ultimately the consumer
4. Conviction	4. Preference	4. Action	must be persuaded to take action to
5. Action	5. Conviction		purchase the product. Starch argues that an
	6. Purchase		advertisement must be seen, read, believed and then acted upon.

Although these models provide a useful way of thinking about the way consumers respond to advertising and the consequent tasks of advertisements or campaigns, there is no evidence that consumers move through the stages in the manner described or that any specific advertisements propel the prospective buyers along in the way suggested. However, advertising does appear to be important in:

1. Information communication: in terms of absolute expenditure this is probably the single most important task set.
2. Highlighting specific features: the concept of the unique selling proposition (USP) suggested that by bringing out a single unique element in the product offering, directly related to a buyer need, advertising could establish a link between prospect and product that would lead to purchase-directed action.
3. Building up an overall 'brand image': image-building advertising contrasts with USP advertising by emphasising the total product offering. The different characteristics of the brand are brought together in a creative whole which relates to the overall needs of groups of buyers of the product category.
4. Reinforcing behaviour: research has indicated that attitudes are very dependent on previous behaviour. The positive attitudes of existing buyers can be effectively reinforced enhancing brand or product loyalty.
5. Influencing intermediaries: much advertising is geared to winning shelf space in retail outlets for the company's offerings. Even when this is not a primary task of advertisements it is still an important function.

In achieving all these goals it must be stressed that it is the product or service offered which is important and the consumer's positive responses must be in that direction, not towards the advertisement or slogan.

Defining specific tasks for individual campaigns or advertisements

Clear and actionable objectives and goals are very important in advertising, with the advertisers' need to operate through intermediaries, their distance from the point of purchase and long response time scales. Objectives must be set, openly discussed with the agency and clearly communicated to all those involved in achieving them. The primary objectives set by a firm may be:

1. To inform: on its own 'to inform' is meaningless. The target group and the time scale within which it will be informed must be identified, e.g. 'to inform all C$_2$DE housewives currently using electric cookers over ten years old that the SE Electricity Board is offering £25 on their cookers with new cooker purchases'. The information can be directed to many groups and focuses on many marketing areas, e.g. price offers available in new outlets, new forms, at new terms or in new markets.

2. To build up an image of the brand or highlight certain features: this must be stated much more clearly. The statement or objective should be clearly reviewed so that the firm can measure its effectiveness, e.g. 'To establish X as the most prestigious brand in the market-place, it should be clearly preferred by all buyers to whom price is relatively unimportant. It should be aspired to by all other buyers'. Images can be defined in many ways and in many circumstances: a common image-building objective in fast-moving consumer-goods markets is to clearly distinguish the brand from own-label products.

3. To reinforce behaviour: this can be restated to highlight the specific behaviour patterns that are to be reinforced, e.g. 'To increase the usage of the drink among AB customers who currently only purchase it at Christmas. The overall special image is to be maintained by focusing on other family festivals: birthdays, weddings, Easter etc.' This reinforcement can even involve persuading buyers to act now; e.g. reducing the period between furniture changes will dramatically improve the furniture industry's profits.

Although the definition of advertising goals lies at the core of effective advertising, often rigour is neglected in favour of detailed discussion of specific creative presentations, artwork quality or even the appropriateness of particular models.

Evaluating advertising

It is perhaps characteristic of the advertising industry that one of the most popular quotes about the effectiveness of advertising is 'we know that 50 per cent of our advertising is effective but we don't know which 50 per cent'. This reflects the difficulty of making any universal comments about attempts to measure the effectiveness of advertising, particularly in increasing sales.

A number of large-scale studies have been sponsored by research institutes, government departments and firms themselves. Some have shown considerable promise in specific product fields and under particular circumstances, but none has been universally applicable. This is not surprising in the light of the relatively small amount of marketing expenditure accounted for by advertising, the diffuse objectives set by advertising, the heterogeneous nature of markets and the very complex nature of consumer behaviour. For the individual firm at a specific point in time these studies are not important. The key is still the firm's objectives and the contribution of advertising to achieving these objectives.

A carefully planned, implemented and sustained process of monitoring the performances of advertising in the market-place is essential. This can be directed towards the broad advertising tasks identified earlier:

1. Task: to inform. Evaluation: recall – the extent to which the advertising message is read, noted and remembered (spontaneously and prompted). 'Reading and noting scores' are regularly collected for the main press media and advertisements carried. Spontaneous and prompted recollection of the advertisements and specific features is measured by a number of market research agencies.
2. Task: image-building. Evaluation: awareness—overall awareness of the firm, its specific product offering and the message of specific advertisements can be studied through structured questionnaires.
3. Task: behaviour reinforcement. Evaluation: attitude research—this is a critical area of modern research. However, there are problems of effective measurement and interpretation of results. In-depth interviews and group discussions are often used to study this area.
4. Task: action. Evaluation: sales reasearch—a regular appraisal of sent-out sales, retail ordering, stocks and consumer purchases geared to both the immediate and lagged effects of advertising.

Most of this discussion has been directed towards mainstream media advertising. Direct-mail advertisers to both industrial and consumer groups have coupon returns, product purchases and the number of sales visits stimulated as a basis for measurement.

NON-MEDIA ADVERTISING

Non-media or below-the-line advertising[15] is one of the fastest-growing areas of activity in modern marketing. Much of this growth has been stimulated by the direct-purchase link which often occurs with a sales promotion: the promotion can be taken up only if the product is bought (sometimes repeatedly). This is important in building up short-term sales volume and provides an effective means of directly tracing the pay-offs from any promotional activity. Growth in this area over the last decade has been considerable, in both the absolute amount of activity and the areas in which non-media advertising is used.

Typology of non-media advertising

Consumer

On-pack offers: free flowers with detergents are the classic example; they are often used by magazines, e.g. motoring magazines giving away simple tools.

Free sample: small packings pushed through letter-box or invitations to be sent in to manufacturer for samples.

Free gifts: these are frequently linked with loyalty-building activity requiring a number of packet tops, coupons or trading stamps.

Coupon offers: distributed through retailers and door to door, they often involve money off the purchase of specific products or in particular outlets.

Competitions: this activity, although still popular, faces the problems of the ingenuity of professional entrants and the complexity of the law.

Exhibitions and demonstrations: these range from giants such as the Ideal Homes Exhibition and the Motor Show to small in-store demonstrations.

Mail-in offers: these include reduced prices and premium gifts, e.g. sets of glasses, requiring the customer to send off to the manufacturer or his agent some evidence of purchase and, often, money.

Catalogues, leaflets and brochures: usually distributed at the point of purchase but include the giant mail-order catalogues.

Personality offers: these experienced a boom in the 1960s, with White Tide Men, Egg Chicks and many others visiting customers and outlets. Activity in this area is now relatively limited.

Price cuts: these involve short-term price cutting in store. The normal pattern is for both a retailer and manufacturer to finance the offer in order to increase store throughput in a specific line.

Trade

Point-of-sale material: usually distributed by salesmen to establish maximum in-store impact. It ranges from the substantial in-store sales units of the cigarette firms to shelf strips, wobblers and many other items.

Merchandising support: manufacturers introduce their own merchandising staff into outlets, including wholesalers. They will exhibit, demonstrate and sell the product in support of the retailer.

Exhibitions: these provide the backbone of the attempt of many firms, particularly in consumer-durable markets, to place their products in front of the middlemen.

Catalogues: these are widely distributed throughout the retail trade.

Special discounts: usually short-lived and often allied to other promotions.

Industrial

Exhibitions and trade fairs: the diffuse locations of large buyers make exhibitions a critical part of industrial sales promotion. They range from domestic exhibitions (Inter-build, the British Medical Equipment Exhibition) to major international exhibitions (International Leatherweek (Semaine de Cuire), Paris, Nuclex (International Nuclear Exhibition), Basle).

Catalogues: showing the range of products and production capability of firms.

Mail-in offers: usually associated with advertisements in the trade and technical press.

Price-off deals and trade-in allowances: these are given to dealers, distributors and end-users.

Premiums and inducements: usually of the desk-top or executive-gift type, including diaries, calendars etc.

Systems and installation support: the concept of systems selling has already been discussed; systems or installation support is a facet of this. It is the free provision of services necessary for the effective use of a product or service.

Dangers of non-media advertising

The enormous range and scope of non-media advertising have led many firms to employ it in many situations, and in volume-sensitive markets its appeal is enormous. However, dangers do exist. A product or brand's long-term future depends on the attitudes and behaviour of the purchasers. Cutting back on media advertising to build up short-term sales may mean that the customer's overall impression of the product deteriorates. A strong individual product may end up being seen as the product that is always on offer. Very seldom can short-term increases in volume fully compensate for the promotion costs. An effective balance of media and non-media advertising will sustain the overall consumer image of the brand while building long-term volume.

ECONOMICS AND ETHICS IN ADVERTISING

The growth of advertising as a substantial industry has been marked by the emergence of two interrelated debates on the role of advertising in society. The first centres around the role of advertising in the competitive process, and the second focuses its attention on the impact of advertising on the moral fabric of our society. Both are legitimate areas of concern, assuming a responsible and rigorous approach is adopted by all parties. Unfortunately, much of the debate has consisted of argument between two parties holding specific polarized views:

1. Advertising is anti-competitive, building barriers to entry into markets and preventing smaller firms from making any headway against the power of major manufacturers. At the same time, it encourages consumption for its own sake, allied to a hedonism which undermines our moral codes.
2. Advertising is competitive. The media are open to all, with the success of the larger firms merely reflecting the efficiency with which they meet consumer needs. Any impact on the values of society is primarily reflective. Advertising is such a small part of our total communication that it cannot determine values. In fact, it is most effective when operating within existing norms and values.

The past twenty-five years have seen a large number of studies of the economics of advertising, and certain key themes have been identified.

The competitive process

Much of the debate centres around different views of the competitive process. To the traditional economist the notion of 'perfect competition' is an ideal at which to aim. However, the underlying assumptions of product homogeneity and perfect information are difficult to achieve in the majority of markets in modern industrial economies, since product differences are introduced to satisfy the varying needs of different consumers. A great deal of evidence has now been accumulated to indicate that advertising is particularly effective when real product differences exist.

A more recent feature of the argument focuses on the idea of spurious product differentiation. It is suggested that advertising acts to create differences between products which have no basis in the product's physical characteristics, e.g. 'Daz whiteness' and the 'little perforations' in tea bags. However, these points may merely reflect the different values of specific commentators. The majority of these concepts emerge from pre-testing of advertisements and are sustained because they have some meaning to buying groups. The real danger is if the power of certain manufacturers is so great that consumer rejection of these implied qualities could be ignored by firms whose market position enables them to prop up:

> inferior products . . . enabling them to survive longer than would otherwise be the case.
>
> Rt Hon. Roy Hattersley

Empirical investigation indicates that the capital costs of entry and other non-marketing costs are normally more important in building barriers to entry than is advertising. In many consumer markets, as well as among manufacturers, there is also competition among stores, which often offer the same brand at different prices and have own-label brands. Intermediaries are thus a major force in preventing any abuse of market power by manufacturers. In some markets abuses may exist, but the problems probably have more to do with the infrastructure of the market than the promotional superstructure. The claim that there are too few manufacturers is complemented by an alleged information problem, and this is at the core of the marketing process. The notion of perfect competition solves the problem by proposing that all product offerings in a market are the same, e.g. Canadian wheat is more or less the same as US, Soviet or British wheat. In highly differentiated markets the buyer faces problems of gathering, understanding and organising information. Brand images can play a major role in identifying a totality with which the purchaser can identify, particularly when backed by previous purchasing experience. At the same time the manufacturer investing £3 million in advertising should maintain product quality to ensure repeat purchase.

It is possible for major manufacturers to use the information power of large budgets to direct product-selection criteria along the lines most favourable to them, e.g. appearance more important than safety in cars, and to swamp the advertising of the competitive products of smaller firms or counter-advertising, e.g. the £12 million spent by cigarette companies against the £2 million spent on anti-smoking advertising.[16]

There is some evidence to suggest that even regular purchasers of products are ignorant of many key product features, including price, competitive offerings, and size. However, it is important to recognise that most consumers are unable to handle the amount of information which even relatively limited weekly shopping would need if full price/quality buying were carried out. The purchase of forty items under these conditions might involve awareness of perhaps six brands with different prices in four shops and encompassing four meaningful product differentiations for each brand: a total of 4240 pieces of information.

Access to media and communications skills presents a much more serious problem. The demise of newspapers, increasing advertising rates and discount structures constitute real problems for the small manufacturer trying to place his product before his potential audience. The tendency of some advertising agencies to cut back on their smaller accounts may prevent small firms from gaining access to the best talents. However, the highly competitive nature of the advertising industry does operate as a constraint on this.

The ethics of advertising

Comment in this area has been directed at false and misleading advertising and immoral and amoral advertising. False advertising is all advertising which is demonstrably untrue. It is the side of advertising which all responsible persons involved in the industry work hard to stamp out. Misleading copy is a grey area open to a considerable amount of debate, as what is misleading to some is clear to others. Puffs, blandishments and emphases often fall into this area. For example, the Royal National Institute of the Deaf criticised advertisements for hearing aids which included phrases such as 'like having new ears' on the grounds that hearing aids do not restore hearing, but merely amplify sound. The RNID felt that false hopes were being raised by misleading copy.

Any view of immorality or amorality in advertising depends very much on the standpoint of the commentator. Some writers argue that the harm done by certain advertised products, e.g. cigarettes and alcohol, is so great that a total advertising ban is necessary to discourage consumption and progressively erode demand. Ultimately the responsibility for decisions in this area lies with the country's political leaders, who must gauge the evidence and be willing to pay at least part of the price in lost tax revenues and any industry support necessary to ensure employment for workers and compensation for others involved in the industry.

The most common moral criticism of advertising is that it encourages materialistic values. In a society such as ours, with complex and constantly changing values, any attempt by advertising to promote specific values would most certainly be resisted by many, and it does appear that advertising is most effective when it reflects values rather than teaching them. It is possible that this may lead to the amplification of certain trends in society, and in this area socially responsible executives must act to impose controls. The British Code of Advertising Practice, as revised in 1974, is important in this:

The Advertising Standards Authority . . . discharges its duty to keep advertising legal, decent, honest and truthful with speed and success.

Rt Hon. Roy Hattersley

It is inevitable that society will take a keen interest in the impact of advertising on the economic and moral structure of society, and the British Code of Advertising Practice is an important source of information and guidance to advertising and marketing executives whose commitment to specific messages and themes may lead to some neglect of broader issues. In the past the response of the industry has been positive: there has been a willingness to listen which would be welcomed in other industrial, political and academic communities.

PUBLIC RELATIONS

Awareness of the need to draw together the range of corporate activities and present them to the public has led many firms to identify clear public relations (PR) policies. Industry and commerce are central features in modern society and the specific communities in which they are based, and public relations policies are designed to bring out that role. At the same time the responsible PR executive feeds back to the firm the likely overall impact of its broader range of industrial and commercial policies.

Many firms, particularly smaller firms, fail to realise the contribution an intelligently designed PR policy can make to supporting general promotional policies. Trade press, local press and even the national media will respond positively to approaches featuring company achievements. The Central Office of Information will assist firms wishing to place their major accomplishments before a large audience.

CONCLUSION

Advertising and sales promotion provide a diffuse and exciting range of opportunities for the marketing man. Effectively used and integrated with other aspects of the marketing mix, the scope for the effective presentation of the firm's offering to the market is almost unlimited. Costs, with their associated need for control, are involved, but these costs are directed towards building business in both the short and the long term. Successful advertising and promotion emphasises pay-offs rather than payments, within a socially responsible perspective. Few aspects of marketing are likely to see more changes than advertising with the video revolution, Breakfast Television, Cable TV, Channel 4 and the possibility of advertising being introduced to BBC television and radio.

Notes

1. Not all agencies perform all functions: media buying agencies and creative shops have emerged over the last decade as major forces.
2. Commissions provide approximately 60 per cent of total agency income, although the importance of fees has gradually increased. Recently the NPA (Newspaper Publishers Association) has indicated its interest in revising the system.
3. Large-scale audience research is conducted under the auspices of the Joint Industry Research Committee: JICTAR (Joint Industry Committee for Television Audience Research), JICNAR (Joint Industry Committee for Newspaper Audience Research), JICPAS (Joint Industry Committee for Poster Audience Surveys) and JICRAR (Joint Industry Committee for Radio Audience Research).
4. Watson, M. J., *Advertising Expenditure in the UK: 1983 Survey*. International Journal of Advertising, 1984, Vol. 3.
5. It should be noted, however, that there has been a steady expansion of coverage out of major cities.

6. Another factor has no doubt been the threats to advertising by these industries in other media and the ban on TV advertising of cigarettes.
7. The number and location of sites is regulated by the Town and Country Planning Acts.
8. There is little doubt that some advertisers give up the struggle and look merely to gain access to the customer.
9. Seiden, H., *Advertising Pure and Simple*. New York: American Management Association, 1976.
10. Roman, K. & Mass, J., *How to Advertise*. New York: St Martin's Press, 1976.
11. There has been a tendency among some writers to play down the importance of Radio Luxemburg, but it still has an audience of over three million listeners per week.
12. Particular pages and spots are 'specified' and carry a premium charge.
13. Only part of the readership buys it every day. The audience is constantly changing, with new readers joining and old readers leaving each day.
14. Vaile, R. S., The use of advertising during depressions. *Harvard Business Review*, April, 1927.
15. Called 'below-the-line' as no media commission can be charged on it by agencies.
16. These sums are purely illustrative.

Further reading

Broadbent, S. R., *Spending Advertising Money*. London: Business Books, 1975.
Broadbent, S. R. (Ed.) *20 Advertising Case Histories*. London: Holt, Rinehart and Winston, 1984.
Cannon, T., *Advertising Research*. London: Intertext Marketing Research Series, 1973.
Cannon, T., *Advertising: the Economic Implications*. London: Intertext, 1975.
Chiplin, B. and Sturgess, B., *Economics of Advertising* 2E. London: Holt, Rinehart and Winston, 1981.
Driver, J. C. & Foxall, G. R., *Advertising: Policy and Practice*. London: Holt, Rinehart and Winston, 1984.
Fulop, C., *Advertising, Competition and Consumer Behaviour*. London: Holt, Rinehart and Winston, 1981.
Jefkins, F., *Advertising Today*. London: Intertext, 1971.
Ogilvy, D., *Confessions of an Advertising Man*. New York: Athenium, 1963.
The range of informative booklets and pamphlets of the *Institute of Practitioners in Advertising* give insights into many organisations. *International Journal of Advertising*, published quarterly by Holt, Rinehart and Winston, includes many interesting articles related to all aspects of advertising.

Key organisations

Advertising Association,
15 Wilton Road,
London SW1V 1NJ

Advertising Standards Authority,
15-17 Ridgemount Street,
London WC1E 7AW

Institute of Practitioners in Marketing,
44 Belgrave Square,
London SW1X 8QS

CASE STUDY 14: VW GOLF

Marketing conditions

For twenty years Volkswagen's production programme centred on the Beetle, which accounted for the major share of its turnover. By the beginning of the 1970s the Beetle no longer fulfilled the consumer's expectations as to what a modern automobile should be, and VW was therefore forced to switch as quickly as possible to a new, modern, progressive and comprehensive model programme.

In 1973 and 1974 VW incurred losses of 950 million marks as a result of the problems caused by a difficult international economic situation and by the oil crisis, which led to a worldwide recession and a shift in consumer attitudes towards economy and energy-awareness. Not only in Germany, but to a comparable extent all over the world, there were

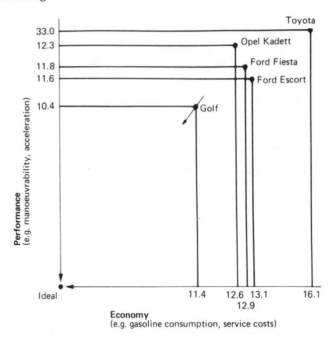

Fig. 19.8   A graphical representation of the results of a Volkswagen image analysis regarding the product characteristics, performance and economy. (*Source*: Volkswagen).

the first concrete signs of a downward trend in the automobile market since the Second World War.

After various market studies had been analysed, several new aspects of domestic automative demand in particular were revealed: the development of motorisation by no means always runs parallel to overall economic conditions but according to its own laws of growth towards a total market saturation which is estimated to be approximately 800 cars per 1000 adults and is expected to be reached at the end of the century; demand depends on the amount of disposable income in private households, on levels of private consumption and the accumulation of wealth by these households. Within these development parameters, the market for cars in the 1 litre to 1.5 litre class grew during the crisis by 40 per cent, to be superseded two years later by a renewed increase in demand for larger automobiles.

In West Germany the automobile market plays a fundamental role; consumer behaviour regarding the automobile is determined by life-style, standard of living and by a sense of status. The automobile provides a feeling of personal freedom and of belonging to a certain stratum of society; at the same time factors which influence purchasing change as time goes by, so that in periods of economic difficulty initial and replacement buying are often postponed.

This insight was partly responsible for VW modifying its rather production-oriented attitudes which it had adhered to in the past to a more market-oriented mode of operating, which was based on the customers and their wishes.

The most important marketing instrument in this revised company philosophy was the new range of Volkswagen models, which was introduced successively in the period 1974/1975 and consisted of the Golf, as focal point, accompanied by the Passat and the Scirocco. (These models are sold in the United States under the names Rabbit, Dasher and Scirocco respectively.)

Particularly the Golf met the purchasers' demands for functional styling, high utility value, high chassis, engine and engineering standards and outstanding economic performance. It formed the focal point for a range of VW models, upon which the recovery of the company ultimately depended. These models encompassed a broad range from the smaller to the larger class of automobile but with the main emphasis on the middle-class vehicle. Within each class VW offered a basic version with a wide selection of decor, styling, performance and comfort extras.

An after-sales service policy, which was particularly important for VW and was based on the maximum quality service for customers as well as automobiles, was successfully established through a comprehensive series of measures.

The network of service outlets and dealers was more tightly organised, and VW assured itself of marketing control by acquiring direct holdings in wholesaling companies. At the retail level, VW operated with independent firms by means of franchising arrangements. As a whole, the service network was more tightly organised and the mechanics trained so as to secure optimal market coverage.

The pricing policy placed VW's various new models just above the competitors' comparable models without, however, crossing the threshold of the consumers' price-sensitivity; VW wanted to be presented in all of the most popular price categories.

The Golf was positioned in terms of its major rivals as shown in Figure 19.8.

In view of the hoped-for market position as well as VW's other marketing objectives (consolidation and expansion through a modern range of automobiles in a variety of classes, all tailored to consumer demand and incorporating the very latest technology), it was quite evident that considerable importance would have to be placed on communication as a marketing instrument if success were to be achieved.

Communications strategy

Communication policy was VW's most important tool for realising its marketing-strategy decisions. Volkswagen here made the distinction between dealer- and consumer-oriented communications

Dealer-oriented communications strategy

In the context of a dealer-oriented communication policy, three instruments were especially important:

1. The company's information and training activities.
2. The company's advertising activities aimed at the dealers.
3. The dealer's advertising activities aimed at the consumers.

When the Golf was launched, these three instruments formed the core of all of the company's communication activities vis-à-vis the VW dealers.

Before, and also during the launch period, the VW company above all had to generate enthusiasm for its new product and keep it constantly alive. In order to achieve this, VW used information and training events, as well as dealer meetings, both at a regional and at a national level, in order to stay in constant communications contact with retailers and wholesalers.

In 1974, for example, a dealers' congress was held just shortly before the launch of the Golf. This congress was attended by more than 10 000 people from the VW and Audi sales organisation from all over Europe.

They were divided into various groups, e.g. directors and executives, salesmen, service department employees, supervisors, parts managers, as well as other employees with primarily technically-oriented jobs. The main purpose of these activities (including training courses) was to provide these various groups of employees with information on the new car, to familiarise them with it and to motivate them.

Futhermore, these activities were intended to provide the dealers with a standard set of sales arguments of their customers and to prepare the ground for effective post-sales service. In addition, communications with the dealers were to ensure uniform and effective conduct of the dealers towards their customers.

In co-ordination with the dealers, VW had developed an advertising concept which had the crucial task during the launch period of familiarising the public with the new model and making it popular. The main idea was to talk about the new car as often as possible and make it sound as interesting as possible, to show pictures of it and also have it appear 'in person'.

The dealers' advertising activities, which were mainly aimed at establishing a connection between dealer and product performance, were characterised by a common colour. As a result, all advertising media used by the dealers had a high recognition value, which was particularly important in view of the large number of various activities carried out.

The dealers' launch strategy consisted of three elements:

1. Preparations: a number of particularly impressive media were employed before production of the new car was started in order to draw the public's attention to the coming event. The media used for this purpose were: large 18/1 sheet posters; joint ads commissioned by several dealers; ads by individual dealers; and the 'Golf Post', consisting of a letter with the Golf journal (mass circulation pamphlet) and a bumper sticker for potential Golf buyers taken from the dealers' customer files, as well as for people who sent in ad coupons.
2. Product description: a description of the new car and its main technical data was provided by means of outdoor advertising (18/1 large size and Fries posters), ads commissioned jointly by several dealers and ads by individual dealers. These primary advertising media were supplemented by display materials such as large-size transparent PVC stickers for showroom windows, rear window car stickers, advertising racks for holding pamphlets and showroom design.
3. Merchandising activities: the public's interest in the new model was aroused through a large number of activities that simultaneously helped the Golf to become a popular, well-known and prominent car.

Consumer-oriented communications strategy

Objectives. The communication objectives were partly derived from the problem of substituting the Golf or the Beetle, and were partly determined by the general marketing idea.

The short-term objective during the launch period of the Golf was to convince the buyers that the Golf was not the successor to the Beetle, but rather a partner model, in order to avoid an abrupt loss of all the old, loyal Beetle drivers.

In addition, the public, and especially the fans of the traditional VW concept, had to be convinced of the Golf concept. The attention of potential buyers had to be drawn to the fact that VW, too, was now offering a modern, pace-setting product concept in the lower middle-class range, a product which furthermore could be 'smoothly' integrated into VW's product family.

VW wanted to make potential buyers familiar with their new top-of-line product, the Golf, in a very short period of time. In fact, they wanted to make the Golf known to 80 per cent of the population within only two months!

A major long-term objective was to achieve a high-level image. In this context, two aspects had to be taken into consideration simultaneously. First, the traditional VW image with its characteristics 'quality, reliability, and good service' had to be transferred to the Golf, which additionally was described as being 'practical, trouble-free, fun to drive'.

And secondly, the modern concept of the Golf, in combination with the existing company image, was intended to add the aspects of progressiveness and modernness to VW's image.

Secondly, VW's advertising style consisted of several material guidelines to be followed:

1. As a general rule, the advertising message must be consumer-oriented, realistic and credible, with the major emphasis on product-related information.
2. The presentation of the product should be perceived as something quite natural.
3. There should be a smooth transition from the advertising style for the Beetle to the advertising campaign for the Golf, with a strong emphasis on the particular product characteristics.
4. Adjustments to short-lived fashion trends should be avoided when this affects the basic concept.

These guidelines were applied both to the Golf's launch campaign and to the period following the launch. But in this later stage, more emphasis was placed on an adaption to the buyers' objectives and their experiences with the Golf. The typical character of VW's advertising style, which can be accurately described as 'product-oriented advertising', was, however, maintained.

This indicates that the Golf campaign was to be built on a clear presentation of the most essential facts (not following the motto: 'something for everybody'). The arguments presented were to have a very strong reference to the product's practical uses, i.e. they had to be mainly rational. The key idea around which the advertising concept was built was the following promise:

VW is offering a practical, trouble-free car that the whole family can enjoy because it suits all their various needs as a result of its product concept.

Furthermore, the Golf's compact design had to be popularised. The consumers had to be made aware of the fact that despite its small outer appearance, the Golf was a full-fledged middle-class car that was in line with current automotive trends.

VW wanted to prevent the consumers from confusing a compact with a sub-compact car. At any rate, VW had to prevent the Golf from being regarded as a small car or as a sober, functional 'mini station-wagon', when compared with Opel's Kadett and Ford's Escort.

Another long-term objective of VW was that Golf buyers should be characterised as having 'neutral status' in order to prevent the Golf from being associated with a very specific, closely defined market segment.

The advertising concept for the Golf was in principle a continuation of VW's advertising strategy, which is characterised by consistent advertising style. The most important elements of this style are partly of a purely formal nature. The standard VW advertising layout, which had been built up in the course of the years, was to be maintained in order to obtain a high recognition value for VW's advertising activities.

Basically, every Volkswagen ad had to be composed of three elements: picture, headline and text with possible variations of these three fixed elements to allow for interesting advertising layout and message suggestions.

The presentation's central theme was therefore the product's versatile uses, such as a family car, a shopping car, a city car, a travel car, and the family using it in these various situations.

One of the VW's strategy principles has always been a uniform European communications policy. The communications concept was therefore regarded as a concept for the whole of Europe.

Target groups. The Golf's main function as VW's major source of revenue in the future made it necessary to take into consideration specific buyer wishes when planning the new automobile, but also to make sure that the Golf would appeal to a quantitatively large segment of automobile buyers. Socio-demographic and psychological analyses of the

potential buyers of the Golf led to the following results:
Demographic profile:

1. Sex: 70 per cent men, 30 per cent women.
2. Professional status: self-employed, 5 per cent; white-collar workers, 43 per cent; blue-collar workers, 32 per cent; civil servants, 10 per cent; others, 10 per cent.
3. Age: 20 to 49 years (average 34).
4. Income: net household income: minimum, DM 1000; average, DM 1700.

Psychological profile:

1. They are individuals who have a pronounced tendency to follow society's norms and conventions, and who tend to have a rather timid personality and therefore try to avoid being conspicuous in any way.
2. When buying cars, they prefer touble-free and practical models to streamlined bodywork, rapid acceleration and high speed.
3. The importance of the car and emotional attachment result from the high investment value that the car represents for this type of person. They do not regard their cars primarily as status symbols, but they expect their cars to meet certain standards and look after them and treat them with care.

As far as the owner structure was concerned, the two groups that VW's campaign was supposed to appeal to were first of all people currently owning Beetles, and secondly, people who had driven Beetles in the past, but had switched over to competitors' models (both German and foreign) in them meantime. VW hoped to be quite successful with the Golf in attracting owners of competitor models. Studies had shown that people who had been driving cars like the Opel Kadett, the Fiat 127/128, Ford Escort, Simca 1100 and Peugeot 102/104 for the last two to four years would be particularly susceptible to the Golf.

Strategy. The advertising objectives and the size of the target group led to the following strategy considerations.

The Golf must be optically presented in such a way that the consumers rate it one class above most of the smaller models with a similar concept. The Golf must acquire an unmistakable character of its own.

The Golf with its product characteristics must be shown in an explanatory environment because VW must convince the consumers of its ability to offer and manufacture genuinely compact cars.

The Golf must become a popular and attractive car that everybody likes. VW has to be credible in describing the car's benefits to the consumer. Therefore, Volkswagen expressed the entire concept of the Golf in a simple, straightforward motto:

> Golf, der Kompakt-VW:
> Auto, Motor und Spass.
> (Golf, the compact from VW:
> Auto, Motor and Fun)

All expectations that are nowadays associated with a car in this class are communicated by this slogan.

The 'compact from VW' stands for a full-fledged middle-class car that is small in size and as reliable as all VW products. 'Auto' represents the company's claim of having developed an adequate and superior overall concept. 'Motor' stands for sophisticated engineering, value and dynamic performance. A car promising manoeuvrability and liveliness. 'Fun' to drive, fun in everyday life, but also enjoying more serious things such as economy, roominess and reliability.

With these statements, the Golf's image profile was given the widest scope possible. As a result, the market segment was not artificially limited and the product's expected benefits were communicated in a way that was credible to everybody.

The advertising media to be selected had to measure up to the following requirements which were based primarily on the advertising strategy considerations mentioned above:

1. The Golf's overall concept must be communicated to a large group of the population.
2. Advertising messages that deal with the Golf must become predominant in this market segment, i.e. the media strategy has to be aimed at quantitative predominance.
3. The Golf must be present in the potential buyers' awareness; the potential buyer has to be constantly confronted with various types of advertising messages that are related to the Golf.

Other major factors that influenced the selection of advertising media were the main advertising messages, the division of the campaign into a launch period and follow-up period, the specific advertising objectives and the cost factor (finding the most cost-efficient way of reaching the desired target group).

Print media, i.e. newspapers and magazines, and television were chosen as basic media. In the print media group, consumer magazines were of primary importance because they fulfilled the necessary prerequisites for realising an optimum advertising effect. The relevant target group could be reached accurately and extensively, and the creative possibilities that magazines offered facilitated an optimal translation of the advertising message into a visual image and a written text as required by the basic concept.

The launch campaign was primarily aimed at achieving the greatest possible coverage and the highest possible contact frequency. In order to reach this objective, identical ads were placed in several magazines at the same time, and in individual publications different ads were not inserted one after the other, but several at a time. In these advertising activities, VW concentrated mainly on the publications with the highest circulations in the German magazine market, i.e. general-interest and programme magazines.

The follow-up campaign was dominated by consumer magazines to an even greater extent. After reaching the objectives of the launch campaign, i.e. familiarising a large percentage of the population with the Golf, this medium was particularly suitable for emphasising or playing down specific product characteristics perceived by consumers as positive or negative. But at the same time, it was the most suitable medium for realising product or experience-oriented advertising concepts during the follow-up period.

Television was used mainly to familiarise as many people as possible with the new product as quickly as possible. In the follow-up campaign, the relevance of this medium diminished. However, VW continued to make use of it in accordance with its position in the German media scene.

Daily newspapers also played a certain role in the campaign, but they were a medium which was used primarily by the dealers (see section on dealer-oriented communications policy). Especially during the launch campaign, the information character of this medium corresponded to the topical and innovative nature of the advertising message about the Golf. After the launch, dealers advertised in dailies only sporadically.

Radio and special-interest publications, such as automobile and sport magazines, did not initially play a very important role. Radio was used only during the launch campaign, and this only in a few isolated cases, and there were also relatively few ads in special-interest publications. However, this must be seen against the background that the primary function of these journals in the automobile industry is not that of an advertising medium, but rather that of a medium for forming opinions or for objective reporting and evaluating.

As the Golf's primary task was to avoid losing VW's customers—especially Beetle drivers—in the future, a direct mail campaign aimed at 425 000 VW owners was carried out during the launch period.

A supplementary medium that VW used during the launch period was outdoor. Impressive poster designs updated and emphasised the information that the observer had already been given on the Golf by other media and added to the impression that the Golf's presence on the road was quite natural. During the launch period, outdoor advertising reached a level of 6 per cent of the total advertising budget, but played no role in the follow-up period.

Advertising message. The central theme of the launch campaign was the car's suitability for the family, as manifested by the product concept, as well as the versatility and the roominess of the Golf. The key features of the advertising message were: practical, trouble-free, fun to drive (lively).

These key features were rounded off by the following supplementary features, which could in turn be associated with the key features: economical (trouble-free), versatile use (practical), suitable for shopping, suitable for city driving and easy to park, suitable for long-distance travelling, safe handling characteristics (fun to drive).

In those export markets that closely resemble the German market's demographic and psychological buyer structure (Austria, Switzerland, Netherlands, Denmark, United Kingdom), the advertising message basically consisted of the same elements as in Germany.

Apart from this, the VW Company shifted the emphasis between the various key elements of the advertising message in different domestic markets. Depending on the particular target group that VW primarily wanted to reach within the Golf market segment (e.g. sporty drivers, drivers with an interest in the car's engineering, women), different elements of the advertising message were stressed.

The major theme that was chosen for the Golf's ad campaign was the Golf's positive characteristics that its drivers experienced, e.g. the car's excellent cornering ability, the comfortable and hard-wearing seats, the good mileage, its 'suitability' for women. At the same time, the continuous checks on the Golf's ranking as compared to its competitors, based on a large number of criteria, provided some useful clues for the advertising message, e.g. the themes 'reasonable price' and 'comfort'.

The Golf's styling, which was unconventional for its price category and was also rather sober, had to be made attractive to the conservative tastes of the above-mentioned psychological segment to be reached. Thus the aim was to interpret the car's sober, clear design in combination with its distinct overall concept as being technically aesthetic.

Seen from this perspective, it would have been conceivable to present the vehicle 'as such' in its 'pure' form. But on the other hand, such a confrontation with the new product appeared inappropriate in view of the psychological characteristics of the main target group.

Instead, the process of getting to know the new car had to be emotionally supported by a familiar, general setting, i.e. a context in which the new product would look quite natural: the versatile car and various situations in which it can be used by the entire family.

The technical product characteristics were explained in the context of a given use; the novel product concept was much more convincing when shown directly in a practical situation. Despite its technical soberness, the Golf had to be, and could be, presented in a personified, emotional environment.

In this way, undesirable defence reactions which might have been provoked by the association with the unexpected and the new were diverted to produce positive associations about the car's versatile use for the whole family so the new product concept could gradually become the accepted standard, as planned.

Communication budget. The Volkswagen Company fixes its communication budget

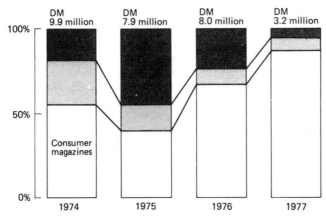

Fig. 19.9   Development of the advertising budget distribution for VW's Golf shown as percentages. (*Source*: Schmidt-Pohlmann.) On this graphical representation an 'ideal' automobile would have the performance and economy ratings of zero. The further an automobile's scores lie from zero, the less 'ideal' it is considered by the respondents.

annually. Plans for concrete measures are drawn up on the basis of the marketing and advertising objectives. This then automatically leads to the required budgets for the various communication instruments. If the required budget exceeds the funds available, a feedback process sets in to modify the measures planned. As regards the absolute size of the budget, only figures on expenditures in the major advertising mass media are available. Table 19.4 shows that over a period of three years, VW's advertising budget for the Golf stayed at a rather high level and then receded to a lower level from 1977 onwards.

Table 19.4   *Total advertising expenditures for the Golf in West Germany in DM 1000s*

1974	1975	1976	1977
9890	7912	8036	3236

Source: Schmidt + Pohlmann.

The development of the budget distribution for the Golf was a direct consequence of advertising strategy considerations on the one hand, and VW's experience with media on the other. The budget distribution in Figure 19.9 shows that the statements made above about media selection or reasons for choosing particular media have consistently been put into practice.

During the launch campaigns (1974), VW's main emphasis in media advertising was clearly placed on ads in consumer magazines (approximately 60 per cent of the budget). In 1975, the two major advertising media used were television (about 45 per cent) and consumer magazines (about 40 per cent). In the following years, consumer magazines played the predominant role (at times exceeding 90 per cent of the advertising budget).

These figures again show that media such as special-interest publications, radio and cinema advertising were of little or no importance in the realisation of the Golf advertising objectives. Outdoor advertising and direct mail played a minor role during the launch campaign when their shares in the Golf's total budget amounted to 6 per cent and 9 per cent respectively.

A comparison of this budget distribution with that of the Golf's main competitors (Opel Kadett, Ford Escort) shows that VW's activities lay within the industry's usual range. VW's most important competitors also concentrate their advertising activities on consumer magazines.

The realisation of the communication strategy and the desired advertising objectives required exact timing of all activities aimed at the 'outside world'.

In August 1974, the first Golf came off the line. Catalogue sales started as early as June 1974 in order not to surrender the time between the popularisation of the new car and the first deliveries without a defection to competitors. Local and national advertising activities for the Golf started in July 1974. The actual launch campaign lasted till the end of 1974 and was then succeeded by slightly modified follow-up advertising.

An analysis of the seasonal distribution of VW's communication activities shows that VW concentrated its consumer-oriented media advertising on the periods from February to May and from mid-September to mid-December. The resulting advertising gaps were filled with special campaigns (e.g. discontinued models, new models) and with stronger regional orientation. Regional particularities (e.g. school holiday dates) were given special consideration in the dealers' advertising activities, which as a result were less uniform in their timing, especially since special campaigns played the main role in the dealers' advertising.

Examples of advertisements. The balanced and consistently pursued advertising strategy can be easily illustrated by means of a few examples. During the launch campaign, ads with the following slogans were used: 'Golf, the compact from VW: Auto, motor and fun'; 'The new popular sport: Golf'; 'A new car, hot off the press'; 'Here you can stretch out on long stretches'; 'Easy open, easy close'; '3.75 metres short, 1 family large'.

Examples taken from the follow-up advertising period used the following slogans: 'Golf. It helps you around the corner'; 'Ace acceleration'; 'A star with curves'; 'The key to success'; 'It's a sure thing—the Golf'.

Marketing success

Overall objectives reached

The precarious development of the entire VW group, which started at the beginning of the 1970s and reached its peak in 1974/75, was warded off by means of the Golf's striking success in the market, and the company's development subsequently took an extremely positive turn.

Car sales rose to 2.14 million vehicles in 1976 and reached another record peak in 1977 when 2.28 million cars were sold.

The sales volume reached 21.4 billion marks in 1976 and about 24 billion marks in 1977.

Profits (annual balance sheet surplus) amounted to roughly 1 billion marks in 1976 and ranged in the same order of magnitude in 1977.

The Golf's market success is documented by the following sales data. From the Golf's launch in July 1974 till June 1978, about 1 950 000 cars were delivered worldwide to the VW organisation. This figure can be broken down as follows: West Germany, 775 000 units; USA, 460 000 units; European volume markets, 550 000 units.

When the data was broken down to individual markets, the Golf turns out to be a 'best seller' in several countries (see also Table 19.6).

In Switzerland and in West Germany, the Golf has been, since its launch, the most frequently sold automobile ever. In the twelve most important European volume markets the Golf was number two in 1976 and 1977 behind the Ford Taunus and followed by the Fiat 127 (Ford Taunus: 397 000; VW Golf: 364 000; Fiat 127: 335 000).

If all European automobile markets are considered as a whole, the Golf ranks fourth.

In 1977, the Golf was number four worldwide (Table 19.5).

Table 19.5   *Development of Golf sales (worldwide and in selected markets) in units*

	1974	1975	1976	1977	Jan.–May 1978
Worldwide	110 000	426 400	496 000	602 000	260 000
W. Germany	71 000	168 000	206 000	216 000	93 000
Europe	37 000	140 000	132 000	156 500	67 000
USA	58	98 000	112 000	165 000	59 000
Canada	—	10 600	17 900	23 000	10 000
Mexico	—	—	—	10 200	11 000

Source: Volkswagen

Golf's market success is also clearly reflected in the development of its share in the market. Looking at the class relevant to the Golf (comprising a segment of roughly 35 per cent of the total market), the data listed in Table 19.6 give clear evidence of VW's very positive development. Not only was the company successful at an early point in stopping and neutralising any fading of its share in the market which might have been caused by the Beetle's collapse, but it even succeeded in increasing its market share in this class with the help of the Golf.

Communication success

The criteria applied by VW to determine the communication success of the campaign were media efficiency, level of familiarity, image and brand preference.

Table 19.6   *Market shares of new car registrations in West Germany (in the Golf's class) as percentages*

	1970	1971	1972	1973	1975	1976
VW Group	44	42	38	38	40	45
Ford	5	6	6	6	12	11
Opel	24	19	20	20	17	17
Foreign manufacturers[a]	27	33	36	36	31	27
	100	100	100	100	100	100

[a]Mainly Simca, Renault, Fiat.
Source: Volkswagen

The media efficiency, particularly during the launch campaign, is impressively demonstrated by the following data: the chosen media combination resulted in a coverage of 96 per cent of the total adult population (14 years and over); and the average number of contacts per person reached amounted to 17 for the total population.

The Golf's level of familiarity among the population was determined by means of an initial market research survey carried out six weeks after the beginning of the launch campaign. Even after this brief period, it had already reached 90 per cent (normally 60 per cent after six weeks).

The first check on the Golf's image was also made six weeks after the launch, and the result was compared with the desired image. This then provided an important basis for adjusting the image by modifying the contents of the advertising messages.

After the launch period, annual image analyses were carried out, mainly concentrating on the image that the Golf had for non-buyers when compared to the Golf's competitors. These brand preference analyses were a useful source of information for determining the various product-oriented components of the advertising message.

All in all, the image objectives envisaged for the Golf were reached to a large extent. The Golf was primarily considered a modern, progressive and sporty car which the buyers regarded as being extremely manoeuvrable and fuel-saving.

In general, the Golf was rated as a car for younger people, while some important competitors had images associated more with older members of the population.

Undesirable impressions existed mainly with regard to the statements 'reasonable price' and 'easy to get in and out of'.

Non-owners of the Golf rated the car as being relatively expensive—despite its other economic benefits, which were widely recognised (e.g. fuel consumption, insurance cost, maintenance)—and, due to the car's compact outer appearance, they were also rather sceptical with regard to the ease of getting in and out.

As far as Golf owners were concerned, a survey by the 'mot'-magazine ('Testen Sie Ihr Auto Selbst' (Test your car yourself), *Motor-Presse*, Stuttgart, 1977) by and large confirmed the impression held by the Volkswagen Company. 940 Golf drivers rated their cars as 'very good' or 'good', particularly for the criteria 'top speed', 'acceleration', 'oil consumption', 'cornering ability', 'cross-wind sensitivity', 'room in front'. Poorer ratings were given for the Golf with regard to the bumpers, room in the back, standard equipment and shelf space.

An important indicator of the economic and communicative success of a car is its 'capture rate', i.e. the number of buyers who had previously driven competitors' models. The Golf confirmed—as expected—that it is very capable of attracting drivers of competitors' models. In 1976, 29 per cent of the Golf buyers had driven other brands before and in 1977, 40 per cent of the buyers had switched to the Golf from competitors' models.

An analysis of the structure of models formerly owned by Golf buyers shows that in 1976 and 1977, for instance, it was mainly former Beetle drivers (48 and 30 per cent respectively), Opel Kadett drivers (4 and 3 per cent respectively), Ford drivers (5 and 3 per cent respectively), Fiat drivers (3 and 5 per cent respectively) and Renault drivers (4 and 5 per cent respectively) who were attracted to the Golf.

The Golf's success in terms of sales and communication, as described above, shows that the strategy pursued by the VW Company (i.e. drawing the buyers' attention to the Golf by means of product-oriented advertising which emphasised the Golf's specific product advantages and using magazines as the main medium for communication, as well as creating a clear product image distinguishing the Golf from its direct competitors) was right and still is.

The case study is reproduced with the permission of Gruner and Jahr Advertising.

20

Sales and Sales Force Management

In his book *The Rise and Fall of the British Manager*, Alistair Mant places a special emphasis on the role and responsibility of the salesman:

> The salesman's job is shot through with technical skill, leadership and trusteeship—he goes into the environment and, so to speak, takes the skin of the organisation with him when he goes—he *is* the organisation so far as his prospects and clients experience it.[1]

This is something which any well run organisation recognises, and something which is given special emphasis by some of our trading rivals. In West Germany, for example, the salesman, particularly the engineering or technical respresentative, is part of the corporate elite, and his skills in establishing links with customers, building up relationships and closing and following up orders are an essential part of the success of many German companies.[2] It is a pattern reflected in France, Italy, the USA, Scandinavia, Japan and the better UK firms. Even in Eastern Europe the export salesman holds a special place.

For many companies this pattern is natural. The salesman is the key intermediary, the presenter of company offerings and the interpreter of customer needs. Closing a sale is the tangible sign that all the efforts of development, promotion and pricing have been worth while, and the salesman is in the fortunate position of being 'in at the end'.

Despite these factors there has been a tendency to play down the salesman in modern British society. To a considerable degree this derives from a failure to appreciate the nature of the salesman's job, the many different types of salesman, the skills required and their central role in corporate effectiveness.

Selling is a rapidly evolving discipline. Changes are being forced by new understanding of the nature of the relationship between customer and client, awareness of the factors which influence the individual spending so much of his time (up to 90 per cent) out of the firm, with no direct contact with other company staff, technological developments, recruitment problems and the changing structure of the market. Although these are changing the form of selling, they have not changed the basic tasks that the people involved in sales and merchandising perform.

SELLING

No other function which involves so many highly skilled individuals operating in so many different environments can be as neatly compartmentalised into one simple task as can selling. McMurray identifies seven selling tasks:

1. Product delivery: sales are secondary to the milk or bread salesman. He may be able to produce some increases in sales, but orders generally have been placed earlier. There may be some scope for selling in extra volume, notably new products[3] or those on offer.

2. Inside order taking: perhaps the largest group of sales staff is those in stores, car showrooms, parts departments and at the end of telephones waiting for the potential buyer to arrive. Although their role is sometimes played down, any Boots or Marks and Spencer's executive will explain the important role their shop staff have played in their success. The car manufacturers invest considerable time and effort in attempting to stimulate positive selling attitudes in auto salesmen.

3. Outside order taking: the field forces of many large consumer-goods fields are actively involved in this area. It ranges from regular calls to small outlets, where the salesman almost does the ordering for the owners, to visits to the branches of large outlets, where lists of suppliers are carefully defined but the value of giving the local manager some discretion is recognised.

4. Goodwill building: often staff whose job is goodwill building are given no freedom to solicit orders. They educate customers, assist with display and have many other roles. They are often tied in with the firm's merchandising force, and some operate in specialised areas such as pharmaceuticals.

5. Technical or engineering representation: here the emphasis is placed firmly on the technical and product knowledge of the salesman. He will give advice and guidance even to the point of helping to draft specifications.

6. Creative selling of tangibles: this encompasses every sphere from the door-to-door encyclopedia salesman to the Ministry of Defence salesman negotiating £ billion contracts for aircraft or tanks.

7. Creative selling of intangibles: this is the selling of services, including insurance, banking, credit, advertising and consultancy.

Although it is useful to present these as different types of selling, in fact many salesmen will perform all or most of these tasks. For example, the car salesman will usually have responsibility for: delivery, or at least handing over the key; inside order taking, when the client is in the showroom; outside order taking, generally with fleet or company buyers; goodwill building, including in-store display, advice to former buyers, reassurance about faults; technical representation, providing insight into the vehicle's specification and performance; creative selling of tangibles, i.e. the vehicle and accessories; creative selling of intangibles, perhaps a hire-purchase agreement, insurance or even AA membership. In many cases his freedom to negotiate trade-ins and discounts also adds a pricing dimension to his role.[4]

THE SALESMAN'S TASK

To perform in these very different situations the salesman performs a number of distinct tasks:

1. Develop product and market knowledge: the salesman should be knowledgeable about both his offering and the firm's objectives for each segment of the market.

2. Prospect for potential clients: within the framework or territory given to the salesman it is his task to identify prospective clients, e.g. through the Yellow Pages, buyers' guides etc.

3. Prepare the sale: each potential buyer or group of buyers should be studied as closely as possible, e.g. by examining company reports, and a sales plan prepared.

4. Sales pitch: the potential buyer should be approached in the way and with the offer most likely to succeed with him. This may take place in one visit or over many, e.g. in a capital project two, four, six or more visits may be necessary.

5. Close: the ultimate purpose of most sales contacts is to close the sale effectively. This should be carefully considered and the optimum time and form determined.

6.   Follow up: there are two elements in this: to avoid loss of the contract and to be in a good position to win future contracts.

To successfully follow this system the salesman must perform a number of related tasks as well as calling on more general corporate resources.

Related tasks

These will include careful monitoring of the environment in his territory, e.g. a local newspaper might feature a local firm winning a major contract, and this can provide opportunity. Communication is a major part of the salesman's job. This goes far beyond merely setting up meetings: an important aspect may be effectively transmitting the customer's comments and complaints to head office. Planning is often neglected by salesmen who prefer 'to be getting on with the job', but properly conducted it can make a major contribution to effective resource and time allocation. Administration plays a major part in any sales operation. Many firms are now giving salesmen a major customer-information gathering role.[5]

Linking with other corporate resources

Theodore Levitt,[6] in an excellent paper on the subject, highlighted the important part that advertising can play in preparing the ground for effective selling. The salesman must be fully integrated in the firm's marketing effort.

Integration is an important part of the management of any sales force. Most salesmen spend the majority of their time 'out in the field', and this can lead to a situation in which they start to identify with those they spend most of their time with—customers—rather than with the firm.

Some firms who have attempted to maximise eye-contact time, i.e. the time the salesman spends in front of the customer, have actually found that performance deteriorates. This does not mean that there is no value in 'eye-contact time': it merely highlights the importance of planning it carefully and recognising that it is merely one of many variables influencing performance.

SALES MANAGEMENT

In making the types of decision mentioned above a clearly thought-out approach to sales force management is necessary. Effectiveness here is built up through recruitment of the right staff, allocation in the optimum manner, management of the staff and other resources for maximum returns, motivation to ensure consistently high performance, and control to maintain the sales force's continuing contribution to effective company performance.

Recruiting

Recruiting the right kind of salesmen is a recurrent problem for most firms. The company will have its own individuality, the customers will be of a particular type, and the current staff will do much to create the environment in which the sales person must operate. The problem is finding the right person for the job. Some writers have suggested that the firm should seek out 'good salesman types', and there are a number of suggestions about what are the traits to be sought in the good salesman:

1. McMurray's traits[7]: high level of energy; abundance of self-confidence; chronic hunger for money, status and other rewards; well-established industriousness; perseverance; competitiveness.
2. Mayer and Greenberg's traits[8]: empathy (ability to identify with prospects, customers and their needs); ego drive (the determination to succeed).

Whether one of these models is adopted or a specific company approach is used, a number of good-quality recruits will be a major first step. A well thought-out and clear job description allied to a carefully designed recruitment campaign is necessary. It is now estimated that the cost of keeping one salesman on the road is over £15 000 per annum. Investment in this valuable resource needs careful planning.

Allocation

Allocation of the sales force plays a major part in ensuring that the optimum returns are earned. Three basic approaches have been adopted to the allocation of field forces:

1. Geographical: here the salesman represents the entire offering of the firm in a specific geographical area or patch. These areas can range in size from a part of Central London to 'Africa and the Middle East'. The essential feature of this system is that it combines local knowledge with organisational simplicity.
2. Product: each representative is given responsibility for a part of the company's offering. It might be a particular product line in which he has special knowledge, e.g. cooker clocks and timers, or a particular service, e.g. marketing consultancy. In-depth knowledge of the offering and an ability to respond authoritatively to specific queries are the strengths of this approach.
3. Customer: in situations in which the firm is dealing with a heterogeneous group of clients, e.g. footwear manufacturers, car makers, furniture producers, knowledge of their special needs and awareness of any particular strength of the company's offerings in this area can provide a real asset to sales development.

Key account handling has emerged over the last decade as a major aspect of sales force organisation. Although it can be linked with the customer approach (differentiation by customer size is still customer-based), its significance goes beyond this.

Key accounts can be so substantial that individual approaches, treating each account almost as a market segment, can be devised. A major grocery account could be worth 10 to 15 per cent of turnover for specific lines. Handling these customers calls for special skills, and the high investment of the retailers in their buyers is a good meaure of the investment the producer should make in his key account team.

Before embarking on a key account development programme, six questions should be asked:[9]

1. What is the maximum share of our business that these top customers should account for?
2. How can we organise ourselves to best deal with them?
3. What information do we need?
4. How should our relationships with them develop?
5. What sales and marketing policies should we adopt?
6. What sales and marketing staff and what skills are needed to most effectively work in this area?

A number of developments are directly affecting the role of the salesman in this area. Key account staff need highly developed negotiating skills and considerable awareness of business development, and it is normal to give staff in this area considerable negotiating discretion and even some responsibility for product development, advertising, promotion and price. This has led to increasing involvement by corporate marketing management—marketing directors and product and brand management—in key account work, and it is to be hoped that this type of interaction will improve their understanding of one another's roles.

Management

Management of the sales force goes far beyond recruitment and allocation. It calls for clear insight into the different selling situations faced by sales staff. Newton[10] suggests that four basic situations face the salesman: trade selling (volume building through intermediaries); missionary selling (assisting intermediaries to sell); technical selling (providing the array of support needed in industrial markets); and new business selling (opening up new accounts, making new contacts).

An important part of the sales manager's job is to instil:

1. A sense of identification between the salesman and company goals, i.e. overcoming some of the barriers that can be built up from factors such as spending so much time outside.
2. An effective operational balance. This often means ensuring that a constant search for new accounts is weighed against ensuring good service for existing clients.
3. A commitment to enable the company to fully capitalise on the store of knowledge and awareness of customers held by the salesman. More and more companies are recognising the value of sales force and marketing think-tanks in establishing a good cross-fertilisation of knowledge and ideas.

Motivating

Motivating the sales force calls for a clear understanding of the forces that influence performance. The very high turnover in many sales forces and sales departments suggests that a combination of the personalities of the staff involved and the policies adopted are not preventing demotivation and the desire to leave. Replacing top-quality staff is expensive and the costs incurred during transfer can sometimes be enormous. The recurrent problem in advertising is that those staff closest to being sales staff, account executives, leave, taking their major accounts with them. Despite this, management often seem to be unwilling to invest time or effort in trying to understand the forces that affect sales-force motivation. Communication and involvement in decision-making appear to be very important, and close contact with a clearly communicated sense of belonging are often needed by sales staff to sustain their commitment.

A recurrent complaint of sales staff in both small and large firms is the apparent lack of response to their comments and suggestions:

> We are told we are the main point of contact with the customer but no-one appears to listen when we report what the customer is saying.
> Comment by experienced salesman with large firm

The normal approach to motivation is defined in terms of sales force incentive payments and bonuses, but there is some evidence[11] to suggest that remuneration is best seen as a control mechanism rather than a motivator:

> Payment systems are best thought of in terms of their ability to demotivate rather than motivate.

Control

Control is generally exercised through three vehicles: payment and supervision, promotion and targets. Remuneration can be seen in terms of both level and form. Payment is usually in terms of a fixed salary, salary plus commission, or straight commission. The individuality of salesmen and the varied nature of marketing conditions suggest that any general analysis of strengths and weaknesses should be handled with care in any specific situation, but it does appear that overall these appear to be as shown in Table 20.1.

Table 20.1   *Alternative payment systems for sales staff*

	Strengths	Weaknesses
Salary only	Provides security for opening up new territories. Minimises internal tensions. Achieves effective balances when lengthy negotiations can be followed by long-term repeat orders. Easy to administer.	No incentives for extra efforts. Does not fit in with achievement and reward needs of many salesmen.
Salary plus commission	Achieves balance between incentive and security. Stimulates marginal opportunity spotting. Makes salesmen more likely to be creative in pushing for new developments.	Incentives for efforts still limited. Difficult to administer, particularly if target-related.
Straight commission	Maximises effort. Provides powerful reward-stimulus learning pattern. Leads to attempts to fully exploit major accounts. All costs tied to returns.	May cause jealousy and antagonism among staff. Danger of short-term pay-offs with accounts rather than long-term relationship being emphasised. Little incentive for missionary work. May deter some applicants. Can create some financial distress when performance is poor.

Sales-force targets are infrequently associated with these payment systems. Targeting has been the cause of fierce debate among marketing and sales staff, the arguments of each being: 'If the man's doing his job properly, targets are expensive and cumbersome methods of restating the inevitable' and 'Targets provide salesmen and managers with clear ideas about expected performance and added incentives for achievement'. The move towards tailoring sales-force compensation to specific management objectives has done much to sustain interest in targeting.

It appears that many of the criticisms are related to systems of arbitrary targeting. Management may decide on the basis of some evidence or analysis that specific targets should be set, and these are then set to the sales force. Although the response may be short-term uplifts in sales, in the medium to long term it appears that sales-force turnover increases, sales in some accounts decline in the medium term as orders, brought forward to meet targets, lead to increased stocks and sales costs increase dramatically.

Mutual targeting appears to overcome many of these problems. The salesman, his immediate superior and perhaps the relevant manager work together to establish agreed targets and the best means of achieving them. It is essential that the firm has a clear idea of its priorities in this area. Multi-brand or multi-product firms sometimes adopt the dangerous stance of changing or modifying targets, e.g. for each journey cycle.[12]

Evaluating performance may be related to these targets or defined in terms of some other criteria. Although there is much discussion about evaluating individual salesmen, relatively little research has been carried out into measuring the overall effectiveness of the sales force.

Some analyses have implied that evaluation of the sales force is perhaps best seen in terms of measuring the impact of increasing (or reducing) the sales-force size. The sales force can thus be increased or reduced until the maximum returns, as defined by the firm, have been earned.[13]

Evaluation of the individual salesman is usually conducted in terms of two parallel sets of criteria:

1. Quantitative: meeting targets; sales volume and profitability; visits, usually split between established and new accounts; promotional or display work, i.e. placing display material; customer comments.

2. Qualitative: assessed contribution to company achievements; satisfying superiors' expectations; attitude and contribution to development of sales force and his colleagues; organisational skills; longer-term potential; customer relationships; appearance.

THE CURRENT CLIMATE

> As a positive reaction to the energy crisis and the resulting material shortages, a significant majority of manufacturers are developing marketing plans to deal directly with shortages. Although marketing theories of how to do this vary, the key element in all is the salesman.
>
> *Industry Week*, 18 March, 1974

This situation is posing particular problems for the salesman. Even when his own firm is not directly affected, its supplies may be limited, so he may have to modify his operations to incorporate the skills to effectively allocate, perhaps even ration, supplies. In some industries this has even led to salesmen taking a positive role in the reallocation of stocks from one outlet to another.

The high interest rates of today mean that sales staff in many companies also have to become actively involved in debt collection. This has created severe problems of behaviour modification for some staff, who may be forced to restrict supplies to well established clients whose payment record is poor, thus affecting the overall profitability of the account.

This broader role, with sales staff acting almost as account managers in some instances, is leading to an increasing information and communication need among sales staff. In the short term this has led to a pattern of feeding increasing amounts of market intelligence to the field sales force, and it is possible that in the foreseeable future this will be followed by on-link link-up through computer or video systems.

As communication systems between the firm and its sales force improve many of the traditional problems of sales-force management—geographical dispersion and lack of immediate control, notably of the consistency of messages—are likely to be reduced. It is quite likely that this, along with environmental changes, will lead to a revitalisation of the role of the salesman. This is already occurring in industrial markets,[14] and may soon happen in consumer markets. The importance of salesmen, already great, may steadily increase, as will the demand for high-quality recruits.

One factor of growing importance in sales-force management today is the increasing degree of trade unionism in the sales force. Scott and Jeffrey[15] suggest a number of practical steps to help sales and marketing cope more effectively with this situation. In particular, it is emphasised that management will need to consciously develop the 'delicate art' of trade union negotiation.

Notes

1. Mant, A., *The Rise and Fall of the British Manager*. London: Macmillan, 1977.
2. Barclays Bank Report, *Factors for International Success*. London: Barclays Bank International, 1979.

3. New products here would include new to the firm, e.g. milkmen selling fruit juice or eggs.
4. Given the range of skills required, it is perhaps surprising that research has shown that car salesmen hold their job in very low esteem.
5. Although this can prove useful it can also be dangerous. The firm must be clear about the primary task of its sales force, since all too often salesmen are given so many ancillary tasks—information gathering, display, stock checks, allocation—that they have almost no time left for selling.
6. Levitt, T., 'Communications and Industrial Selling'. In *Readings in Marketing Management* (Ed.) Kotler, P. & Cox, K. K. Englewood Cliffs: Prentice-Hall, 1972.
7. McMurray, R. N. & Arnold, J. S., *How to Build a Dynamic Sales Organization*. New York: McGraw-Hill, 1968.
8. Mayer, D. & Greenberg, H. M., 'What Makes a Good Salesman', *Harvard Business Review*, July–August, 1964.
9. From an article on the subject by Lidstone, J. & Melkman, A. 'Make Marketing Plans for Major Customers', *Marketing*, October, 1977.
10. Newton, D., 'Get the Most out of your Salesforce'. Harvard Business School, September–October, 1969.
11. Zachariades, C. Z., *The Management Motivation and Control of Salesmen*. Durham: Unpublished MSc dissertation, 1976.
12. The time taken by the firm's sales force to complete a regular tour of its accounts.
13. Salmon, W. J., 'How Many Salesmen Do you Need?' In *Analytical Marketing Management* (Ed.) Doyle, P., Law, P., Weinberg, C. & Simmons, K. London: Harper and Row, 1974.
14. This has probably been more fully realised in Britain's trading rivals than in Britain itself.
15. Scott, R. & Jeffrey, R., 'What to Do about Unions and the Sales Force', *Marketing*, February, 1978.

Further reading

Lidstone, J., 'How to Get the Salesforce Right', *Marketing*, August, 1978. A succinct and relevant paper on the processes involved in building up a picture of sales force motivation and morale.
Smallbone, D., *An Introduction to Sales Management*. London: Staples Press, 1971. A thorough and comprehensive study of the entire process.

CASE STUDY 15: ROYALE MOTORS LTD

Geoff Brown had recently been appointed sales director of Royale Motors of King's Lynn. In his first two months in his new job he had conducted a thorough review of the firm's operations, and this filled him with foreboding about the future.

The company consisted of four garages and showrooms, all holding British Leyland franchises, in the King's Lynn area. For the last three years the firm had suffered badly from stock shortages. Popular models such as the Austin Princess, the Mini, the Rover and the Jaguar had been very difficult to obtain. Now, although stock was available in all the showrooms, sales were very sluggish.

Much of this could be blamed on Leyland's poor overall performance, but Geoff was not content to use this as an excuse. He felt that the company could not afford to simply wait for Leyland to solve their problems:

That will take years, if it happens at all.

His sense of disquiet was made worse by a number of unhealthy behaviour patterns which he observed among his sales staff: sales-force turnover was steadily increasing, notably among younger men: and a passive attitude to winning business existed (on one day alone he noted seventeen visitors to one showroom: of these, only three were spontaneously approached by a salesman; six called into the sales office for attention, and the rest left). Also, trade-in values and price discounts were increasing as a proportion of the purchase value of new and used vehicles sold, and increasing numbers of old and difficult-to-sell foreign cars were being accepted. In contrast to this, fewer cars from the 'majors' (Ford, Fiat, VW and the leading Japanese manufacturers) were being traded in for new Leyland cars: 'The only major manufacturer whose cars are traded in is Leyland,

and often the impression is that Leyland dealers were the only ones offering acceptable trade-in.' The major bright spot was the relative strength of second-hand sales.

Geoff put these points to the board at the first board meeting after completing his review. There was some discussion of the scope for seeking out a new franchise. Geoff, along with his fellow board members, rejected this on the grounds that they had for over forty years 'invested in Leyland', and besides, the better producers (Ford, VW, Honda, Fiat etc.) were well represented in the area. It was generally agreed that revitalised sales and marketing would go a long way to resolving their problems, at least in the short to medium term.

Geoff decided upon a number of immediate steps:

1. He reorganised the sales force, giving each outlet far more freedom and responsibility for turnover and profitability. He then looked for a method to generate a spirit of constructive competition between outlets.
2. He restructured the payment system. In the past the commission element had been very small ('Leyland cars sell themselves' was almost the message). Now commissions allied to agreed sales targets would constitute a significant part of the salesman's income.
3. Layout of the showrooms was drastically changed. The sales offices were eliminated and a more open-plan format adopted: 'they must not hide behind glass walls'.
4. Stricter controls over trade-ins and discounts were introduced. These were linked to the commission system.
5. The sales manager in each outlet was given special responsibility for 'fleet' business. The type of 'fleet' sought was closely defined, i.e. small firms with seven to ten company cars. The managers and their staff were required to go out and actively seek this business.
6. Advertising and sales expenditure were boosted, primarily through local radio.
7. Links were established with the East Anglia Regional Management Centre for a continuing counselling relationship.
8. Leyland inspectors were actively involved in future developments.

These were put before the board at the next board meeting. Some of the board members were already aware of complaints among the sales force about the scale of these developments.

Task

Review the developments.

21

Marketing Communications

Much of marketing activity centres around the communication process. Despite this, there has until recently been relatively little attention paid to the total communication process. Writers have preferred to concentrate on the more specific areas of communication such as advertising, press relations, selling and personal contact. Failure to understand the underlying communication process can undermine the dialogue the firm is seeking to establish with its client groups.

Communication has been defined by Delozier[1] as:

> The process of establishing a commonness or oneness of thought between a sender and a receiver.

This places emphasis on two vital but often neglected features of communication.

1. It involves a number of partners.
2. The reception of the message is as important as its transmission.

The 'classic' communications error assumes virtually the opposite: that the needs of the receiver and the sender are the same, and that all receivers of information are the same.

THE COMMUNICATION PROCESS

All communication processes have certain features in common, whether they involve a salesman speaking to a client or an advertising campaign using a number of media. In Figure 21.1 a model of this process is presented.

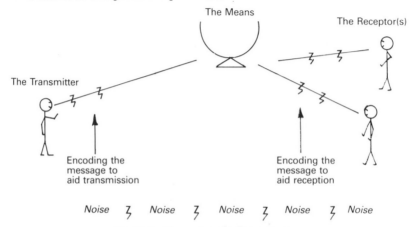

Fig. 21.1 The communication process.

Transmission

Although it is useful to describe the communication process as starting with the 'transmitter's' rather than the 'receiver's' data, most of the time it is difficult to draw the line between the two, as the interactions in healthy communication are on-going with the dialogue being the most important feature. At the same time it is necessary to recognise that communication is not necessarily a conscious process. We are continually taking in or giving out impressions through our appearance, manner and attitudes, as well as the words we say and the images we project. Anyone seeking a career in marketing needs to be as conscious of the unintended impressions as of the thought-out and designed campaigns. This can include the appearance of the salesman, the frontage of the shop and the appearance of the factory or workplace. The company is constantly transmitting messages even if it does not know it. Marketing's function in this area is to ensure that the message transmitted is the one the firm seeks to send. Figure 21.2 illustrates how the sender and receiver are in constant interaction with roles continually changing.

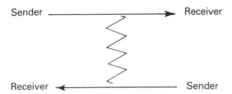

Fig. 21.2   The simple two-way communications model.

Encoding

Sending any message involves choices about the best way of sending it and then converting the message to the form required by that means. In the personal sales situation it involves choosing the right terms to use, the language best suited to get across the message and providing supportive cues. This is most obvious in international trade where the sales staff is dealing in a foreign language. It is equally true in the home market where the sales staff need to phrase their message in ways which relate to the understanding and information needs of the client.

> In certain international markets there is increasing reluctance to deal always in English with British salesmen. The story is told of the Managing Director of the West German firm who arrived in his office to find the salesman from a US company waiting to see him. He took him into his office, sat him down and asked:
>
> 'Are you selling to me or am I selling to you?'
>
> When the salesman replied that he was selling to the Managing Director, the German replied:
>
> 'Well, now we speak in German.'

This was a perfectly proper and suitable response.

Often the process of encoding calls for more obvious marketing skills and disciplines, such as:

1. Phrasing market research questions so that the respondent understands and can respond to them.
2. Designing a TV commercial in a way which gets across a complex message, reflecting a challenging marketing strategy to a largely indifferent audience in 15 seconds.
3. Building an exhibition stand which attracts customers, allows the firm to display its products and meets safety standards . . . comfortably.

The process of encoding involves converting the message the firm wishes to send into terms which meet the needs of the medium in which it is being transmitted.

Noise

The sender has another all-pervasive factor to deal with in any encoding process—noise. This is the general term used to describe the variety of external and potentially distracting influences or stimuli which affect the transmission. It can be very basic, such as background noise from the factory making it hard for the salesman to be heard. It can be totally negative, such as the loud complaining previous customer distracting current buyers. It can be intangible and positive, such as the delicious smells from the kitchen of a restaurant, or tangible and negative, such as black smoke from the next-door café.

Certain forms of noise can be unavoidable. Many messages are converted into forms which cannot communicate the full nature and character of the product and service. Often the firm can avoid the negative effects with care and attention to detail. The Marketing Director of the Scottish Development Agency describes how she is frequently addressed in letters from overseas as 'Mrs Scottish Development Agency' in letters which then proceed to say 'Dear Sir'. There is no doubt that British firms are as guilty as anyone in this process of failing to appreciate the impact that noise can have on any process of turning an idea into a tangibly expressed concept.

Terpstra[2] identifies many of these 'noise' communication barriers. He indicates how they can both distort messages and produce very different results from those sought.

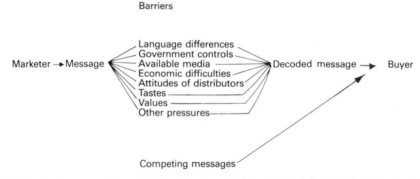

Fig. 21.3 Communication barriers in international marketing. Adapted from V. Terpstra, *International Dimensions of Marketing*.[3]

THE MEANS

The range of opportunities for transmitting messages is virtually endless, from the direct mail letter to the beer mat. The options are enormous, especially when the scope for combined means is included. Despite that, until some form of telepathy is available, all have limitations. Each has its strengths and weaknesses under different conditions and in getting various messages across. The options open are discussed at length in Chapter 19. However, it must be recognised that all have their impact on:

1.   The nature of the message
2.   The process of transmission
3.   Reception

Preparing a message for transmission, sending it and organising for its reception involves a series of transformations. Each of these creates an opportunity for noise and distortion. These problems are made worse when the firm fails to keep clearly in mind the objectives of the exercise and the needs of the receiver.

THE RECEIVER

Both the transmission and reception of information and communication are personal processes. The individuals who are expected to 'take in', 'understand' and 'act on' the message are diverse and subject to many other influences and pressures.

As receivers of information, human beings are relatively imperfect. They are not standardised or specialised like TV sets or computers. It is surprising that so many firms act as if this were the case. Companies seldom take into account the physical limitations of individuals.

> The 'Friends of the Earth' in Durham was one of the earliest organisations to recognise the importance of good household insulation to protect the elderly from the worst aspects of cold Northern winters. With the help of the Manpower Services Commission, Friends of the Earth embarked on a campaign to persuade pensioners to let them insulate their homes *at no cost*.
>
> They undertook an extensive poster campaign to reach the elderly. However, in the first month they had virtually no takers. They stood back and looked at their advertising with the help of a marketing lecturer from the University. It soon became apparent that the size of the writing on the posters was so small that it was virtually invisible to most old people, especially when stuck on the inside of a post office window.

Problems of hearing and sight are seldom taken into account by marketing staff, although it is estimated that over 70 per cent of the population over the age of 30 have problems in these areas.

A number of models have been developed to describe the process by which information is taken in, organised and acted upon. In applying these or other approaches, firms seldom take into account the double loop which is involved in converting learning to action. The loops in Figure 21.4 describe how developing the means to ensure the reception of a

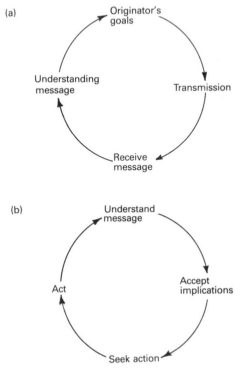

Fig. 21.4(a) Loop 1: The learning process. **(b)** Loop 2: The action process.

message is intimately associated with the mechanism for ensuring that routes to action are included.

Problems of communication

These can be summarised as:

1. Bias by the receiver—*we only hear or see what we want to.*
2. Omission or distortion by the sender—the dangers of gaps and misleading messages.
3. Lack of trust.
4. Non-verbal forces always obliterate verbal.
5. Overload.
6. Hidden sources and data.
7. Distance.
8. Fear.
9. Immediacy—the present always obscures the future.
10. Conflict—pulling people in many ways usually means they go somewhere else.
11. Obscurity.

Overcoming these problems is partly a function of the means being used to transmit the message. However, certain basic rules should be applied:

1. Recognise the problem.
2. Use a variety of means to get messages across.
3. Build campaigns, not individual actions.
4. Encourage two-way communication.
5. Keep the links in the chain of communication as few as possible.

These steps, allied to a programme of research to understand the needs of the receptor group, provide the best promise of getting the desired message across.

Notes

1. Delozier, M. W., *The Marketing Communications Process*. New York: McGraw Hill, 1976.
2. Terpstra, V., *The Cultural Environment of International Business*. Southwestern Publishing Co., 1978.
3. Terpstra, V., *International Dimensions of Marketing*. Boston, Massachusetts: Kent Publishing, 1981.

VICTORIA HOUSE, SOUTHAMPTON ROW, LONDON WC1B 4DB.

Fig. 21.5 Images.

22

Strategic Marketing

The economic recession of the last decade has prompted a range of responses from marketing staff. Initially there was a sense of almost 'suspended animation', as managers and academics struggled to accept that the conditions of growth and prosperity which had been experienced since the end of World War II had come to an end. Many of the policies adopted in the early to mid-1970s were based on the belief (hope) that the drop in demand, the new, harsher levels of competition, were temporary setbacks which 'more of before' could overcome. A great deal of the advice in the textbooks appeared to be designed to sustain this belief with little re-examination of ideas and approaches. In the mid- to late 1970s, a different mood seemed to develop. This was a sense of near despair as firms found that following established routes often meant losing way. Many of the textbooks shared this despondency. Attention was focused on shortages and difficulties. How to cope with a permanent energy crisis or continuing high levels of inflation were the pre-occupations of many writers. This extreme view was as dangerous as the complacency which preceded it.

At the same time as these 'reactive' approaches to marketing and business policy were being adopted and preached, a very different phenomenon could be discerned. This was a recognition that out of difficulty can be built challenge—and competitive challenge has always been the driving force behind creativity in marketing. The re-examination of ideas which followed led to a re-examination of the central role of marketing, giving the firm a sense of direction. From this came recognition that the formulation of strategies to manage and take advantage of all the challenges posed by the market was a vital task for marketing management.

Strategic management is seen by many firms as a critical element in helping them:

1. Cope with the increasing complexity of business operations today, especially in large organisations.
2. Provide a sense of direction and basis for co-ordinating corporate activities.
3. Help the firm to identify and capitalise on development in the marketplace.

This notion of the role of strategy provides the framework within which a definition of strategy can be developed. A number of approaches to identifying the features that distinguish strategy and strategic decisions from operational and tactical issues have been developed. Luck and O'Ferrel suggest a relatively simple definition of strategy:

> The fundamental schemes or means for reaching objectives.

Weitz and Wensley[1] place their emphasis on:

> (the process by which) a company determines where to 'place its efforts, which markets and market segments it chooses to participate in, and what product it attempts to sell in those markets'.

In sum, it encompasses those activities which:

1. Give the firm its sense of purpose.
2. Provide a measure against which proposed actions can be assessed.
3. Supply the firm's differential advantage in the market.

THE NATURE OF STRATEGIC DECISIONS

A number of writers have suggested that the distinctive nature of strategy lies in the types of decisions encompassed by this area. These enable the executive to distinguish between the tactical and strategic in his work. Two approaches to this are presented:

The characteristics of strategic decisions (These are concerned with):

Johnson and Scholes	Steiner and Miller (quoted in Weitz and Wensley)
1. Importance	1. Importance
2. Long time horizons	2. Long time horizons
3. Matching the firm to its environment	3. Top level decision makers
4. Matching activities to resources	4. Level of detail
5. Allocation of major resources	5. Regular formulation
6. The values of policy makers	6. Unstructured and unique problems
7. The scope of the firm's operations	7. Largely subjective information
8. Complexity	8. Difficulty of evaluation

Sources: G. Johnson and K. Scholes[2]
B. Weitz and R. Wensley[1]

The placing of emphasis by the different authors reflects the rather different nature of their pre-occupations. Johnson and Scholes focus on the strategic decision as it affects the organisation, while Steiner and Miller[3] give their attention to the challenges this type of decision poses to the manager. However, the consistency of their emphasis on the relative importance of strategic decision, its long time horizon and its complexity, gives some flavour of the nature of the task faced by the marketing strategist. In this context, his/her skills in strategic analysis are the major determinants of success.

STRATEGIC ANALYSIS

In Chapter 7, 'Marketing Analysis', many of the major issues in this area were introduced. Effectiveness in this field calls for an ability to wed the skills introduced in that section with an ability to place the strategy into a wider context. Figure 22.1 highlights the multi-faceted nature of strategic decision-making. It brings out the three basic elements: analysis, choice and implementation.

The analysis calls for a clear understanding of the environment in which the firm operates. The extent of change, allied to the complex and sometimes conflicting signals from the environment, calls for the detailed analysis in terms of the key market conditions. This form of analysis was introduced earlier. It is possible for the firm to review the market in which it operates in terms of a 'turbulence matrix' (see Fig. 22.2). The firm can locate its various offerings within this framework to explore the nature of the strategic planning tasks it will face.

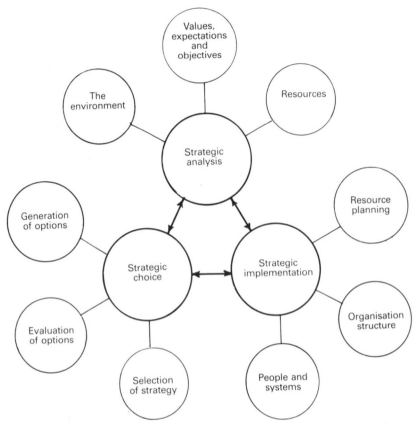

Fig. 22.1   The context for formulation of marketing strategy: a summary model of the elements of strategic management. (*Source*: G. Johnston and K. Scholes).[2]

Understanding the environment represents only one aspect of the process of successful strategic management. The internal organisation and resources of the organisation need to be in tune with the strategies being pursued if they are to be achieved. This is a two stage process:

1.   Understanding the needs and capabilities of the firm (the internal, marketing audit).
2.   Communicating strategies and overcoming internal resistance.

SWOT analysis and other related techniques are regularly used by firms seeking the maximum fit between strategies and capabilities. However, there has been far less attention paid to the tasks of communicating strategies, building support and overcoming resistance. This area has received increased attention following evidence that in many situations, internal resistance posed the biggest problems to effectiveness.

> Real live businessmen have learned that the big challenge is not in concocting strategy but making it work.
>
> *Fortune*, December 27, 1982

Ansoff[3] identifies a number of forms and explanations for the resistance to the introduction of marketing strategies, notably:

1.   Delays and procrastination as those involved express their fears and lack of confidence in both the policies and the management's commitment to the changes.
2.   'Sabotage' or 'absorption' by those who see their current activities placed at risk in the proposed changes.

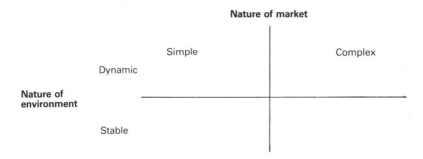

Fig. 22.2   The environmental turbulence matrix.

3. 'Deflection', as those with alternative approaches attempt to bend strategies to their ends.

These barriers are situations which senior management must tackle if their policies are to be effective. The first stage of this lies in the process of developing strategies. The greater the degree of pre-involvement, the greater the later commitment. At the same time, once the programme has been established and communicated it is the responsibility of top management to ensure compliance.

TIGHT–LOOSE STRATEGY

Peters and Waterman[5] highlight the effectiveness of a particular form of strategy in the most successful firms. They call it the tight–loose approach. It has two distinct characteristics:

1. Strategies are 'tightly defined' but kept to critical and fundamental areas.
2. Management are 'loosely directed', i.e. given considerable discretion in the ways they work to achieve the strategy.

The underlying philosophy of the approach is that, provided the marketing manager is committed to the direction the firm is going in and understands his role in this, he/she is the person best able to choose the directions and make the operational decisions.

STRATEGIES AND PORTFOLIOS

The appeal of this approach lies in its ability to wed the underlying strength of strategic planning to the real world limitations on management control in marketing today. The problems should not let us lose sight of the importance of strategy in allowing the firm to locate itself and its product in the marketplace. In this work, 'portfolio analysis' has emerged to play a central and important role. This approach has developed in a number of forms, but these have certain characteristics in common. The most critical of these is the notion that the products of the firm should be reviewed as if they represented a 'portfolio' of investment opportunities. A number of criteria can then be used to explore the nature of the investment opportunity, and the likely benefits and risks of expending additional funds and efforts to support the product to penetrate the market.

The best known of the approaches to portfolio analysis is that employed by The Boston Consulting Group.

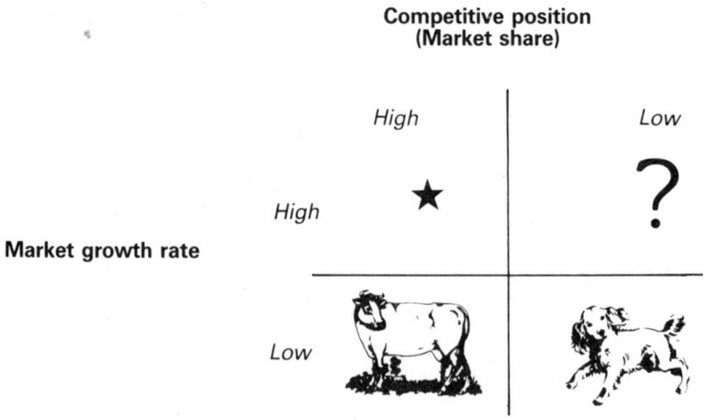

Fig. 22.3   The business portfolio or growth share matrix.

Examination of the firm's position, allied to knowledge of the general characteristics of these markets, prompts consideration of a number of approaches to these situations.

The two determining variables are growth and share. It is suggested by Headley[6] that these are the two single most important criteria on which investment decisions should be based. There is a close relationship between the returns a firm earns from a brand or product in a market, and its strength in and experience of a market. Both these factors are associated with larger market shares. At the same time:

> The growth of a business (market) is a major factor influencing the likely ease . . . and hence cost . . . of gaining market share.[6]

Each of the following categories will place particular demands on marketing resources, have differential potential and call for different strategic responses.

1. *Stars*. These absorb considerable resources but have considerable potential for growth and profitability.
2. *Cash Cows*. These were probably 'stars' once, but there is now little growth in the market. They offer good returns now, but may have reached their peak.
3. *Question Marks*. 'High growth, low share—have the worst characteristics of all'. They consume major resources but offer little prospect of good returns.
4. *Dogs*. These consume relatively little in the way of resources but offer little prospect of returns to the firm.

A number of other approaches, such as the Shell Directional Mix, provide a similar framework but within the same overall method.

STRATEGIC BUSINESS UNITS

The analysis of markets in this type of strategic framework has led to the identification of these areas of activity as 'Strategic Business Areas' (SBAs).

> 'This is a distinctive area of business in which the firm does (or may want to do) business.'[7]

Recognition of these SBAs has led firms to seek ways of matching these with 'Strategic Business Units'. These may be defined as:

> 'A unit of a firm which has the responsibility for developing the firm's strategic position in one or more SBAs'.[7]

The SBUs focused managers' attention on the areas for development without imposing the types of operational constraints typically associated with brand and product management. The market could be developed as an integrated totality rather than in a piecemeal way through specific offerings. At the same time, management were forced to look at markets in terms of benefits and costs. Attention was redirected towards the returns being earned. At the same time it allowed senior corporate management the freedom to rigorously appraise the different areas of activity within an internally consistent framework.

Despite these claims, it is clear that SBUs have not lived up to their early promise. It would appear that simply devising alternative organisational structures cannot compensate for a lack of strategic insight.

THE MIND OF THE STRATEGIST

In his examination of business policy in Japan, Ohmae[8] places considerable emphasis on the thought processes and mental disciplines associated with success in this field.

> What marks the mind of the strategist is an intellectual elasticity, or flexibility of response, that enables him to come up with realistic responses to changing situations, not simply to discriminate with great precision among different shapes.[8]

It is the ability to integrate this creative insight with the effective use of the disciplines of marketing strategy that will mark the effective marketing man of the future.

Notes

1. Weitz, B. & Wensley, R., *Strategic Marketing*. Boston, Massachusetts: Kent Publishing, 1984.
2. Johnson, G. & Scholes, K., *Exploring Corporate Strategy*. London: Prentice Hall International, 1984.
3. Steiner, K. and Miller, R., *Making Management Decisions*. London: Prentice Hall International, 1984.
4. Ansoff, I., *Corporate Strategy*. New York: McGraw Hill, 1967.
5. Peters, T. J. & Waterman, R. H., *In Search of Excellence*. London: Harper and Row, 1982.
6. Hedley, B., 'Strategy and The Business Portfolio', *Long Range Planning*, February 1977.
7. Ansoff, I., *Implanting Strategic Management*. R. D. Irwin, 1984.
8. Ohmae, I., *The Mind of the Strategist*. London: Pan Books, 1984.

CASE STUDY 16: THE MACPHERSON CARR GROUP

Macpherson Carr is a medium-sized corporation trading across a number of areas with a significant income from exports and overseas earnings.

It is based on two old established companies, Macpherson Engineering and HA Carr Engineering. Most of the manufacturing is done in the Midlands or the South of England. Macphersons was originally a Midlands company, founded in the early 1920s and steadily expanded through the 1930s, 1940s and 1950s. It took over Anderson and Thompson in 1952. HA Carr Office Furniture was founded somewhat later (mid-1930s). Their fabrication company was the original point of contact between the two firms. Their joint wish to move into plastics and other materials provided much of the spur to merge the cash-rich Carr's with the capital-intensive Macpherson company.

1979	Sales	Net Assets	Pre-Tax Profit	Net Current Assets	UK Employees
	(£000's)	(£000's)	(£000's)	(£000's)	
	218 275	96 528	14 787	55 452	7 280

Group activities include engineering, plastics, packaging and office equipment. In 1979 approximately 18 per cent of sales were exported, primarily by three firms, Anderson and

Thompson (manufacturers of special purpose vehicles), HA Carr (Office equipment) and B.I.G. Precision Ltd (manufacturer of mechanical power transmission equipment). These firms account for 50 per cent of total sales and 80 per cent of exports. However, only B.I.G. Precision export a large proportion of their turnover. The group has some holdings overseas: HA Carr have manufacturing and sales subsidiaries in Germany, South Africa and Australia; Anderson and Thompson have an assembly plant in India and joint ventures in Nigeria and Iran. Both the joint ventures are largely assembly plants. Effective control of the overseas operations rests with the UK manufacturing units rather than the group.

The group has traditionally been highly devolved, with the trading companies (manufacturing units) exercising considerable discretion. The main group Board has consisted of the Chairmen of the five divisions—engineering, vehicles, plastics, office equipment and chemicals—with some limited service support. These vary enormously in size and structure (Table 22.1). The group has grown largely through a series of mergers, primarily during the 1960s. Throughout the early 1970s the high degree of de-centralisation produced a number of new formations—Arnold Hydraulics, Macpherson Systems, Synthetic Rubber Inc.—but most notably the growth of the chemicals division.

Table 22.1

Division	Sales (at 1979 prices) £000	
	1969	*1979*
Vehicles	65,210	71,125
Engineering	24,700	27,150
Plastics	10,850	20,910
Office Equipment	49,140	59,030
Chemicals	10,710	40,060
	160,610	218,275

During the two years since 1979, virtually no growth (by value) took place with some units, notably those tied to the automotive industry: Arnold Hydraulics and Bilson Mouldings were hit badly by cut-backs. It is strongly felt that the devolved nature of the group, allied to the relatively poor exports of most firms and weak overseas representation, has played a major part in making the company vulnerable to the decline in the market.

These sentiments are supported by the continuing success of the chemicals sector, which has been closely involved in setting up partly-owned manufacturing units in Venezuela, Peru, Mexico and is in negotiations for projects in Indonesia and Malaysia. The relative prosperity of B.I.G. Precision adds extra weight. The enormously successful introduction of the B.I.G. Torque Limiter into the US is held up as showing just what can be done, even in difficult times.

The B.I.G. Torque Limiter

B.I.G. Precision had traditionally conducted a great deal of its business with the steel industry in North America. One particular customer, Crucible Steel, was having recurrent problems with one of the strands of its 80-inch hot-strip mill. The rolls were jamming frequently. This resulted in broken couplings and extensive down-time. They needed either to improve the process and do away with jams, or find a means of eliminating the resulting damage and lost time, or both.

Their close links with B.I.G. led them to approach the B.I.G. sales engineer in Pittsburgh. Together the firms identified the possibility of employing a torque-limiting coupling to overcome the problem. The unit operates as a 'weakest link', or circuit breaker, in the drive. It disengages, in the event of a jam, before damage can be done. The unit could then be reset to resume operations with a minimum loss of time.

Identifying and solving this problem opened up a major new market for the firm. Although it took three years to get it right, within a year 150 units were sold (50 UK, 100 US). By the end of the 1979-80 financial year, sales of this one line and spin-offs were over £6 millions, with 80 per cent exported.

Corporate perspective

At the annual Chairman's Conference, the Chairman used the comparison of this success and failure elsewhere to focus attention on the poor transfer of internal skills, expertise and contacts. The Chairman felt that the moment had come for the group to be reorganised with a high degree of de-centralisation.

He identified three key steps in this:

1. Re-organisation of main board with functional responsibility.
2. Production of standardised marketing plans by the company, the divisions and each operating unit.
3. The determined effort to improve skills in certain key areas, notably marketing, innovation and international trade.

Implementing the proposals

As indicated above, the Chairman's first proposal was for a major expansion in group functions and responsibilities. Main board directors would hold responsibilities for *Marketing, Finance, Personnel, Engineering, R & D* and *International*. This last director was to be responsible for the newly-formed International Division. In future it would be responsible for *all* overseas manufacturing or sales subsidiaries, besides servicing and co-ordinating export development for group companies. In the future the functional specialists, plus the chief executive based at Carr House, would have a working majority on the Board.

Using a famous firm of management consultants, the firm had arrived at a standardised business plan format. The purpose was to simplify the submission of strategic planning, business and marketing data, while additionally providing a standardised format for presentation. A 'plan' was to be produced for each country being developed by the firm. It was split into three sections:

1. *Country Summary*. Standard 'guidelines for growth' were produced for completion by the Managing Director.
2. *Business Development by Product or Service*. This was to explore the different aspects of performance and special problems or opportunities.
3. *Business Plan Schedules*. This was to include detailed financial budget forms for the different areas of business development.

Co-ordination of planning was to be the responsibility of the Group Marketing director.

The first stage in implementing this programme and improving key skills was to be a series of corporate planning and business policy workshops organised through a major University Business School.

Reaction

The proposals on first presentation to the Board generated fierce resistance from many quarters. This turned on three key issues:

1. *The cost*: particularly in terms of extra group overheads for the operating units.
2. *The home market implications*: this degree of standardisation would stifle initiative.
3. *The overseas market implications*: the economic, cultural, technical and general trading conditions of the overseas units were so different that centralisation would be totally dysfunctional.

The challenge was led by Jack Hodson, Chairman of the Vehicle Division and Managing Director of Anderson and Thompson. He argued that the group was reasonably efficient with a range of products they could be generally proud of. The central problem to him was that his firm in particular was badly hit by market conditions over which they had no control. Most of their vehicles went to municipal (airports, port authorities) or government (defence, health) consumers. The cut-backs there had knocked a massive hole in their market. They had not been able to build up exports because their product 'was better than most countries wanted', 'they just aren't willing to pay'. In his eyes, adding further overheads would make him even less competitive.

His views were endorsed by Ian Carr of the Office Furniture division. He suggested that the reasonable performance of his subsidiaries overseas owed a great deal to their historic association with HA Carr. 'They depend on us for design and development—without us they'd be lost.'

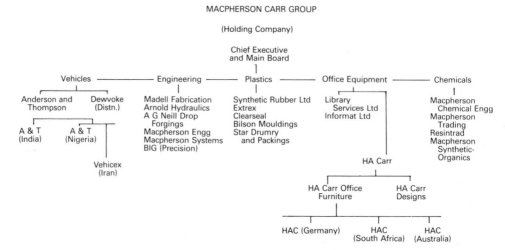

Fig. 22.4   Outline of the Macpherson Carr group.

23

Marketing Planning

Marketing is essentially an operational and purposive pursuit. The firm adopting a marketing perspective is building its business around the particular concept 'success is based on effectively meeting customer needs'. In implementing this concept the forces outside the firm and the resources at the company's disposal must be wedded to an idea of how these are going to be made operational and the direction the organisation is taking.

The marketing plan provides both the vision and the direction. Winkler,[1] in what is probably the best practical UK book on this subject,[2] states:

> The planning process does two supremely important things. First, it identifies corporate problems and searches for alternative solutions. Then it provides the corporate body with a focus and a direction.

In coping with the environmental pressures on the company and managing the resources at its disposal and their complex interplay, a clear sense of direction is invaluable.

In discussing the planning process two terms drawn from military usage are frequently used: strategy and tactic. Here they will mean:[3]

1. Marketing strategy: the art or science of projecting and directing the larger movements and operations of the firm,[4] in the market-place, to the company's advantage.
2. Marketing tactic: the art or science of managing or manoeuvring the specific resources of the firm, usually within a framework defined in the overall strategy.

Kotler[5] encompasses both these notions within his concept of strategic marketing:

> The process of analysing opportunities, choosing objectives, defining strategies, formulating plans and carrying out implementation and control.

The process of analysing opportunities to define the direction in which the firm wishes to move is central to strategic marketing. It is made up of two distinct but interrelated elements, which have already been discussed:

1. Identification of the options open to the firm, i.e. what business the firm is in and what the customer needs which underpin this business are.
2. The resources at the firm's disposal that can help identify these options, bringing out those most capable of being met by the firm, and the differential advantages that the company may have in this process.

In these terms planning is best seen in terms of a continuous feedback loop with the options and resources interacting (Figure 23.1). This interplay is managed by the marketing or corporate staff, whose understanding, determination and ability can influence both options and resources.

Strategic marketing and the plans which emerge are dynamic. The plan is not written on tablets of stone: it is an operational document in the real world.

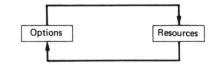

Fig. 23.1   Interplay between options and resources.

MARKETING AUDIT

Successful planning is based on an understanding of reality. Objectives which can neither be achieved nor evaluated play no part in practical marketing, and tactics or strategies which are beyond the firm's resources can be an impediment to action. The marketing planner must start his planning process with a thorough review of the firm's current position.

Seeking this understanding takes time. It means that the marketing staff must start with an awareness that few plans of any real value can be prepared quickly. In some firms the planning process is a year-long activity. This may be necessary when one is:

> drawing on the past, to decide in the present what to do in the future.[6]

The marketing audit calls for an investigation of the demand variables in the immediate market network, including intermediaries and more general economic forces.

This picture of the current and historical situation facing the firm provides the background for all other action. The company is not locked into its current environment but it is very difficult to separate completely the situation in the firm and how the firm is seen in the marketplace. The shortage of firms and industries which have repositioned themselves in time for a major shift in demand is not simply a matter of 'marketing myopia', but is because this is very difficult. It calls for a very rare vision of the future:

> It may not be generally known that at the turn of the century Mr Durant . . . was the leading wagon and carriage producer in the United States . . . Mr Durant incorporated General Motors Company on 16 September, 1908.
>
> A. P. Sloan, Jnr[8]

The marketing audit should be conducted on a regular basis. Some firms prefer to use outside consultants, while others employ their own staff. Out of the audit should emerge a diagnosis of the current situation facing the firm and an evaluation of the situation, across its different areas. These should provide a picture of the likely futures for the firm, perhaps through a prognosis (extrapolating trends) or through a series of hypotheses about development under certain clearly definable circumstances.

FORECASTING

In defining the future of either the firm or its specific products or offerings, forecasting plays a major part. Managers have always built up pictures of the future of their firms and the likely response to their actions, and recently there has been a more systematic search for methods of prediction or forecasting.

> World economic growth will be lower over the next ten years than the rates seen in the 1960s.
>
> J. Morrell[9]

> Junior executives with good career prospects are increasingly reluctant to invest time and money in an MBA programme, particularly in today's difficult job situation.
>
> Anonymous director of Masters
> Programme

Marketing decision variables

Marketing decision variables are those factors capable of affecting demand under the firm's direct control:

> I can decide on the number of vans, their communication tie-ups, the advertising, their location and hours of work, but I can do nothing about the numbers of windscreens shattered.
>
> Managing director of windscreen
> repair service company

Marketing mix and sub-mixes

The marketing effort includes both the level and any awareness of effectiveness.

The marketing allocation is the deployment of the firm's resources between products and markets, even internal investment against external:

> In the first year we found that the bulk of our investments were in staff mortgages.
>
> Director of major foreign bank
> in Britain

The marketing response is how the market will react or how it is believed the market will react to particular actions.

Marketing procedures are the methods by which decisions are made and implemented.

In some firms advertising and market research agencies are actively involved in the entire decision-making process, including planning; in others they are outsiders, brought in for their specialist skills.

The organisation is the structure, responsibilities and procedures adopted by the firm in order to manage its marketing.

Estimates from informed opinion

Informed opinion still plays a major part in forecasting. This may come from within the firm. For example, the agreed sales targets discussed in Chapter 20 can provide guidance, or the sales staff can be asked for estimates, or other staff and management can give estimates of future demand based on their expectations.

Forecasts may also be built on estimates from outside opinion. Expert comment can play a part here. This usually derives from general economic or market projections such as those published in the media, or industry-specific estimates, often produced by trade associations or the industry research association. Some firms also approach specialist experts for their opinions.

The Delphi method is also being used by a number of companies. This provides estimates from experts in a systematic and structured way. Considerable success has been reported with this approach in novel situations, e.g. it was used very effectively to forecast visitors to the Stockton–Darlington Railway Festival and Cavalcade of Steam in 1976.

Consumer marketing research can be used to provide a picture of customer intentions, but care must be taken in projecting from this.

There has been a dramatic growth in the use of quantitative methods of forecasting in marketing.[10] These have encompassed most areas of marketing activity: estimating effects of changes in advertising, promotion, distribution and price; predicting the future of a new product; determining the potential of possible retail or catering outlets; etc.

Time series projections

Time series projections depend on the analysis of past behaviour to determine the future. It may be a trend projection, where the pattern is expected to be repeated in the future (Figure 23.2). The basic assumption is that past patterns reflect an underlying causality which will recur in the future.

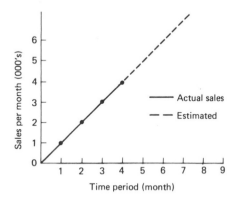

Fig. 23.2 The simple linear projection.

Unfortunately, the simple projection shown in Figure 23.2 seldom occurs in reality: erratic events, business cycles, seasons and marketing action by the firm, its competitors and its intermediaries all combine to produce a much more obscure situation (Figure 23.3).

It is in these situations that the firm must answer questions about the future viability of the product, the effect of promotional activity and the returns from further investments. Statistical demand analysis can be used providing there are sufficient observations to make projections, the variables examined are fully independent, a normal distribution exists, causality is one-way, and no more factors emerge on the market to distort the results. In the situation described above the firm can attempt to smooth out the variation in a number of ways.

One of these ways is by simple moving averages. As each new observation becomes available the average is updated and used to modify the forecast (Table 23.1).

The more observations that are included the greater the smoothing effect is. In a stable situation this improves accuracy but, as can be seen here, the more erratic the figures the greater the discrepancy.

Table 23.1 *Simple moving averages[a]*

Month	1	2	3	4	5	6	7	8	9	10	11	12
Sales (000)	3	4	2	3	1.5	2	2.5	3	3	5	6	
Three months' moving average				3	3	2	2	2	2.5	3	3.5	
Five months' moving average						2.5	2.5	2	2	2	3	

[a]All numbers are rounded to the nearest 0.5.

Although this approach has proved useful, interest in forecasting has led to a number of other developments. Exponential smoothing (Table 23.2) overcomes some of the data-handling problems of the moving average, as well as giving extra weight to the most recent period, thus, $S_{t+1} = S_t + \alpha (X_t - 5_t)$, where S_{t+1} is the forecast sales for the next month, S_t is the forecast for this month, X_t is the actual sales for this month and α is a smoothing constant.

Table 23.2 *Exponential smoothing*[a]

Month	1	2	3	4	5	6	7	8	9	10	11	12
Sales (000)	3	4	2	3	1.5	2	2.5	3	3	5	6	
Smoothing values ($\alpha = 0.3$)		3	3	3	3	2.5	2.5	2.5	2.5	2.5	3.5	4.5

[a]All numbers are rounded to the nearest 0.5.

Among the other approaches that have been used (with varying degrees of success) to forecast aggregate sales and the response to specific actions are simple and multiple regression, correlation, simultaneous equations and many other methods.[11] The use of quantitative techniques is likely to grow in importance in modern marketing.

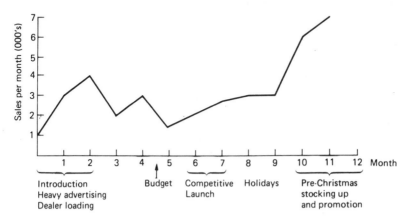

Fig. 23.3 An erratic market situation.

OBJECTIVES

The marketing audit and a picture of the type of futures that face a firm provide the framework in which the firm's objectives can be set. Setting objectives is a critical part of planning, since objectives can originate from any part of the organisation and can be short, medium or long term. Their essential features are that they are:

1. Quantitative: wherever possible, numerical, measurable values are imposed, e.g. a market share of 12 per cent, a reading and noting score of x, 400 extra outlets.
2. Actionable: discernible actions can be taken to achieve them.
3. Realistic: targets set should be within the conceivable range of the firm. There

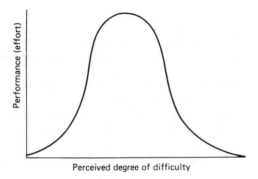

Fig. 23.4 The relationship between performance and difficulty.

appears to be a relationship between performance and perceived degree of difficulty in achievement, as illustrated in Figure 23.4.

4. Consistent: most firms will have a number of goals and these must be internally consistent.

RESEARCH

At this stage, or even earlier, the firm might find it necessary to gather further market intelligence. These information needs should be defined early in the plan. The research may be needed to establish the relative priorities of goals.

STRATEGY

As indicated earlier, the strategy shows the overall direction that the firm will adopt to achieve its purposes or objectives. A clear and communicable strategy statement can play a major part in facilitating the evaluation of tactics.

The strategy statement should be capable of being measured against the objectives and the tactics defined later. For example, a medium-sized engineering firm might set itself the strategy of developing overseas business through networks of strong relationships with customers designed to establish the firm in their eyes as a producer of high-quality, precision-engineered goods. This type of strategy can be measured against the firm's objectives: 20 per cent of business from overseas; improved profile of work, i.e. x per cent of work to technically advanced fields; and access to innovative technologies. At the same time specific tactics can be judged in terms of the strategy, for example the sales manager's suggestion that they appoint a commission agent in Holland, with responsibility for Benelux and West Germany.

TACTICS

The tactics define precisely the actions to be taken, e.g. investment in different mix elements, planned interplay, besides giving specific responsibilities for their implementation. They should be carefully drawn up to provide a consistent presentation of the organisation to the market. They must fit in with the strategy. Their contribution to achieving the stated objectives should at least be able to be described if not quantified.

CONTROLS

The measures described above for ensuring that the elements in the plan hang together are only a part of the control system. This requires clear patterns of responsibility and authority.

Control procedures need to be built in to monitor the overall performance of the actions laid out in the plan. Over time a series of reference points in the marketing system can be established to provide an early warning of potential problems, e.g. sales-force resistance to new display material may lead to poor distribution, with serious consequences for business developments.

An important part of the planning process is that over time the firm monitors its performance in certain key areas. The lessons learnt may be capable of incorporation into the system of controls.

CONTINGENCIES

In the real world, few plans, no matter how carefully detailed and researched, can be expected to run smoothly, with no competition, environmental or organisational problems. Sets of contingencies should be drafted to cope with specific situations.

COSTS AND TIMINGS

These should be described in considerable detail. The effect of time in certain areas can be critical. It may be especially important when corporate management are reviewing the interplay between certain discrete areas, e.g. should two independent units introduce major new brands simultaneously?

EVALUATION

There are elements of both art and science in the drafting of plans, and learning is important in building up the knowledge of those involved in drafting and implementing plans. A systematic approach to evaluation is needed to ensure that all the lessons learned during one period are built into succeeding periods.

DIFFERENT APPROACHES TO PLANS

Although the framework provided above generalises about the experiences of many firms, there is a wide scatter of practice in industry. In some multinational corporations, headquarters management are so distant from local management that the plan is their only mechanism of management and control. In such organisations the plan has taken on a major corporate role. Some firms have developed a consistent planning format which is employed through the organisation from the corporation itself to the smallest national firm, product or brand.

In many small firms planning as a formal or written-down activity scarcely exists. This is due partly to the entrepreneurial nature of managers themselves and partly to a certain mystique about planning itself. Instead of a plan being a simple, practical and disciplined guide to action, far more complex notions have been built in. In specific circumstances these can play a part, but only when they add to rather than detract from understanding and action.

CONCLUSION

Planning is playing an increasing part in corporate activity, and plans and controls in specific areas of marketing—innovation, pricing, communication, sales and many others—are being subjected to rigorous scrutiny. There is a danger that poorly introduced (perhaps in an over-rigid or negative manner) plans can stifle the creativity that is crucial to these areas, but this is not a weakness of planning itself. Plans can provide a solid base for creative development.

Notes

1. Winkler, J., *Winkler on Marketing Planning*. London: Associated Business Programmes, 1972.
2. This area is reasonably well served for good books. Another particularly useful one is: Stapleton, J., *How to Prepare a Marketing Plan*. London: Gower Press, 1971.
3. Adapted from the definitions used in the Shorter Oxford English Dictionary, 1973.
4. Although the term 'firm' is used, it can incorporate all types of organisation.
5. Kotler, P., *Marketing Management*. Englewood Cliffs: Prentice-Hall, 1973.
6. Stanton, W. J., *Fundamentals of Marketing*. New York: McGraw-Hill, 1978.
7. Most of this discussion is based on Winkler, J., *Winkler on Marketing Planning*. London: Associated Business Programmes, 1972.
8. Sloan, A. P., *My Years with General Motors*. London: Pan Books, 1969.
9. Morrell, J., *The Transfleet Lecture*. London: Centre for Physical Distribution Management, 1979.
10. For a thorough review of the subject see Briscoe, G. & Hirst, M. *An Appreciation of Alternative Sales Forecasting Models: Recent Techniques Based on Historical Data*. Warwick: Centre for Industrial, Economic and Business Studies, December, 1972.
11. For a review of the different approaches, see Samuels, J., 'The Effect of Advertising on Sales and Brand Shares', *British Journal of Marketing*, winter, 1970.

Further reading

Stapleton, J., *How to Prepare a Marketing Plan*. London: Gower Press, 1971. Gives a detailed picture of the fundamental processes involved in effective planning.
Winkler, J., *Winkler on Marketing Planning*. London: Associated Business Programmes, 1972. An invaluable guide to the manager or student who is serious about building practical plans.

24

Marketing: The Social Dimensions

Perhaps the clearest illustrations of the dynamic nature of marketing have emerged from the discussions on, and research into, the various social dimensions of marketing. No area of business activity as strongly defined in terms of its interaction with the environment as marketing is can afford to stand back from the fierce discussion taking place in the countries of the West about the future direction of modern industrial society.

> Consumerism, environmentalism, re-ordering of national priorities, urban renewal, price controls, education, welfare, shortages of natural resources, economic development, social costs of products and services and a host of additional quality of life factors are among the challenges now facing marketing.
>
> William Lazer[1]

Each of these areas poses a challenge to aspects of modern business and the environment in which the marketer operates. In response to them, a number of different avenues of development have been opened up:

1. Consumerism: this has posed in the most forthright way a challenge to certain aspects of the marketing concept. The most fundamental question that can be asked is how, when marketing is at least tacitly accepted as the basic business approach by many firms, consumerism can emerge and gain such growth. Marketing is about meeting customer needs, so why do some customers demand protection from marketers?
2. Social responsibility: this takes the debate about consumerism on to a much broader level. It raises questions about whether marketing management should adopt particular stances in the firm about a wider range of 'social issues'.
3. Marketing and non-profit-making organisations: although not strictly linked with these earlier concepts, this issue is often raised in this context. At its most basic the question here is the degree to which marketing is context linked or implies a more general approach to organisation, group or industrial links. Some authors argue that marketing is essentially a business discipline.[2] Others suggest that it is about the broader 'exchange' process and has merely developed in a business context.[3]
4. Economic development: linked to this notion of the transferability of the marketing concept to different social and economic circumstances has been a limited discussion on the contribution marketing, its underlying ideas and application make to probably the most intractable economic problem of today: economic development.[4]

Although many of the ideas which underlie these discussions emanate from the USA, the issues themselves are worldwide. The subject is not new: there have been discussion and action in both Europe and Britain for many years. In the middle of the last century Charles Dickens was writing about 'advertising traps', and at the turn of the century Sweden was passing consumer-protection legislation. Also, the formation of the Co-operative movement was part political and part consumerist. An essential feature of the responses of different societies to the questions posed has been the individual or culturally related nature of these responses.

A major tenet of marketing is that the marketing system is affected by and in turn affects the broader environment. This interrelation will determine the nature of responses in Britain and Europe to the issues raised in this worldwide debate.

CONSUMERISM

Consumerism has been defined as:

> a social movement seeking to augment the rights and powers of buyers in relation to sellers up to the point where the consumer is able to defend his interests.[5]

As such, it has a history which stretches back at least to the nineteenth century, when there were protests against company shops.[6] The consumer movement today differs from most earlier similar movements in two ways:

1. Adoption of an apolitical stance: in the past similar movements linked themselves with formal political groups, generally Populist, Liberal or Socialist. Most modern groups, however, adopt a firm policy of avoiding such links. This does not preclude links with government, local authorities or quasi-government bodies.
2. Interaction with marketing: although it is an exaggeration to suggest that business-men in the last century and the first half of this century were ruthless in their approach to customers, there was far more general acceptance of ideas such as 'never give a sucker an even break', 'buyer beware' and 'any profit we can make is a fair profit'. The advent of marketing has changed this. The customer and his needs have supposedly become the firm's primary interest.

In the development of consumerism from the 1960s to the present day a number of overall trends can be distinguished. The first of these is that its penetration of the international environment has generally followed a path of affluence. The United States and Sweden were at the forefront of this penetration, followed more recently by Western Europe and Japan. Although there are consumer groups in many parts of the Third World, consumerism is relatively unimportant when set against the crushing economic problems many of these countries face.

This path of affluence appears to recur in the franchise of the consumer groups in individual countries:

> At the beginning members (of the Consumers Association) were recruited almost entirely from the AB and C_1 social classes ... Nor has the CA succeeded in widening its membership to embrace a more representative cross-section of the population.
>
> C. Fulop[7]

In their study of the economic determinants of complaints, Morris and Reeson[8] found that:

> Complaint rates (complaints recorded per 1000 population) are closely related to the level of expenditure on consumer advisory services.

This suggests that access to a mechanism for complaint, allied to awareness of the freedom to complain, is a significant factor in generating action. This has now gone so far that Crozier[9] suggests:

> Some commercial firms are at last treating 'consumerism' as an unsolicited market research feedback from a highly significant segment of the total consumer population.

In these groups and probably also in the broader population the growth of consumerism and its related stages is a function of:

1. The dangerous product: actual or apparent physical danger related to certain products gave rise to many consumer groups, e.g. Nader's 'Unsafe at Any Speed'.
2. The dishonest producer or seller: examples of dishonesty provide a constant spur to the growth of consumerism.
3. The abuse of power: a great deal of discussion now centres on the actual or alleged ability of some firms to control the market by manipulating supplies, make excess profits and generally act with little external restraint.
4. Inequality: in the majority of areas there persists a sense of inequality which needs to be resolved through various means, from trust breaking to product information.

The consumer movement[10] has taken a number of different stances in these situations, but these can be broadly divided into responsible and liable stances.

Responsible stance

This is based on the proposition that the overwhelming majority of manufacturers generally accept that there is a mutual interest between them and their markets. Decisions may have been made in the past which do not agree with this notion but these are neither irrevocable nor malicious.

Within this framework a continuing dialogue (with inevitable highs and lows) will provide the optimum mechanism for change. Kotler[11] brings this view out clearly when he asserts that: consumerism was inevitable; consumerism will be enduring; consumerism will be beneficial; consumerism is pro-marketing; and consumerism can be profitable.

Liable stance

This is based on a much more conflict-based view of the relationship between producer and consumer. Within this framework the producer is held liable in law for his product's shortcomings. In the USA the special character of their legal system has led to a certain punitive element in this area.

Although there are some fears that a similar punitive aspect could emerge in the UK, it is probable that even if 'product-liability' legislation was enacted the very difficult legal customs would not lead to the same situation.

SELLER'S RESPONSE

Management's response to the challenges posed by consumerism has varied enormously in terms of specific management groups, the approach to the consumer groups and the consumerist issue.

In general, there is broad recognition by American[12] and European[13] executives that consumer pressure has been generally beneficial to the buyer. There are some, however, who suggest that the price paid in some circumstances was not fully appreciated:

> I merely ask whether the people of Europe—or indeed, the people of America—have been asked whether they really want this state of affairs.
>
> Sir J. Methven[14]

In general there is little dispute about the need for and value of restraint on dangerous goods and dishonesty. Far more open to dispute, however, is the question of whether outside pressure groups, often drawn from specific sub-groups in the population, play any significant part, given the existing competitive pressure of the market, in dealing with alleged abuse of power and inequalities.

Overall, it appears likely that consumerism will remain part of the marketing environment for the foreseeable future. Marketing management and consumerists generally share an overall interest in improving standards and offerings. Where disputes are likely to arise is over the recognition by marketing management that requirements differ significantly between groups. At the same time, these standards are related to cost, and communicating this to certain consumer-interest groups can play a part in the true dialogue from which both are likely to benefit.

MARKETING AND NON-PROFIT-MAKING ORGANISATIONS

Developing this view of the market-place in terms of the complex networks of needs facing any organisation and the impact of the environment on them is perhaps the greatest single contribution that marketing can make to non-profit-making organisations, and it is a view that is being increasingly recognised by this type of body.

Simmons[15] brings out the rapid rate of growth in the use of market research by these organisations (Table 24.1).

Table 24.1　*Users of market research*

	1966	1974	1976
	1100	1400	1400
Total user members	(%)	(%)	(%)
Food, drink and tobacco	19	19	22
Other manufacturing	32	28	28
Service	3	7	6
Advertising	30	19	15
Media	8	9	8
Academic institutions	4	9	10
Public sector	4	9	11

This probably under-represents the non-profit-making sector as some voluntary bodies conduct the research themselves and others, e.g. charities, may have access to expert but free assistance.

The argument for the introduction or acceptance of marketing in non-profit-making organisations is based on the proposition that they:

> face a host of problems that would be analysed as straightforward marketing problems if found in the profit sector.

Just like any business trying to manage its relationships or its exchanges with a franchise the non-profit-making organisation seeks to manage its demand, needs to understand its market and franchise, operates within a system and is influenced by its environment, and has at its disposal a marketing mix.

The understanding that is called for can operate at many levels, as the following example shows. In a Northern city the local Friends of the Earth group were actively involved in insulating the homes of the elderly. Unfortunately they were facing serious recruitment problems, so they decided to produce a poster. A number of activists drew it up, had it printed and placed copies in friendly shops. There was no reaction. They then examined the problem in greater detail with some residents of a nearby old people's home. Problems emerged immediately: typefaces that were legible to students were difficult for old people to see and 'friendly' record shops, clothes shops and craft shops were seldom visited by old people.

In a situation like the one in The Friends of the Earth example the parallel between profit-making and non-profit-making organisations is fairly close, but the problems become far more serious when the body has multiple goals. A sense of direction is essential to effective marketing. In many commercial concerns this derives from the stated goals, probably co-ordinated or established by a clearly defined executive structure. In some non-profit-making organisations, however, the scope for this does not exist. This is particularly true when inner directed goals clash with outer directed goals, as can often be seen in historical sites, academic institutions, and government departments.

Using the historical site illustration, the inner directed goal might be the historical studies of the research staff, the excavations etc. The income from visitors may contribute towards the funding of this but interfere with the real work. Resolving the clashes between these internal goals and an external 'bring more visitors' goal puts serious strains on the setting of objectives.

Ideology or strongly held attitudes can play a significant part in this. The director of the historical site might be a committed historian who is unwilling to invest time and effort worrying about the marketing infrastructure. In some instances the product may be the sole reason for involvement in the institution, and an activist for a pressure group or political party may totally reject the notion of 'modifying the product' to suit the needs of specific target groups.

In the case of the historical site it may be argued that a high-level marketing officer should be employed or that they ought to buy marketing services. Unfortunately, the narrowness of vision of some organisations will make them recruit another subject specialist, e.g. an archaeologist, rather than a marketing man. The overwhelming majority of non-profit-making organisations lack the resources to adopt either policy, and in these organisations the production of a simple marketing plan is probably the most important first step. Agreeing to invest resources in this is a necessary preamble.

Government

The state is by far the largest single non-profit-making organisation. In managing its exchanges with the environment an increasingly positive attitude to marketing is being adopted at senior levels.

Investment in research into such critical areas as energy conservation, family planning and allocation of social services is now beginning to contribute to policy formulation.[16] However, as was noted in the section on service marketing, the impact of this will be restricted until methods of communicating this notion throughout the organisation are established.

CONCLUSION

Throughout this text the need to develop a broader perspective on marketing and the different contexts in which managers operate has been emphasised. This broader social dimension to marketing both poses a challenge and gives an opportunity. The challenge lies in the failure to recognise that many of the complaints contain an element of truth. The challenge to the concept itself is whether the emergence of consumerism is derived from a weakness in marketing or from flaws in its application.

The opportunity is provided for marketing men to contribute to some of the areas of social, environmental and economic difficulty facing the world. At the same time the horizons of marketing men can be widened by their attempting to understand and adapt to the needs of non-profit-making organisations.

Notes

1. Foreword to *Marketing and Social Priorities* (Ed.) Fisk, G. New York: American Marketing Association, 1974.
2. Luck, D. J., 'Broadening the Concept of Marketing—Too Far', *Journal of Marketing*, July, 1960.
3. Kotler, P. & Levy, S. J., 'Broadening the Concept of Marketing', *Journal of Marketing*, January, 1969.
4. Drucker, P. F., 'Marketing and Economic Development', *Journal of Marketing*, January, 1958.
5. Mann, J. & Thompson, P., 'Consumerism in Perspective', *European Journal of Marketing,* 12, No. 4, 1974.
6. These protests were about the activities of some employers, who paid workers in tokens which could be traded only for goods, usually of poor quality, from company shops.
7. Fulop, C., 'Twenty Years of Which?', *European Journal of Marketing*, 12, No. 4, 1978.
8. Morris, D. & Reeson, D. I., 'The Economic Determinants of Consumer Complaints', *European Journal of Marketing*, 12, No. 4, 1978.
9. Crozier, K., 'The Contribution of Market Research to Social Marketing', *Journal of the Market Research Society*, 21, No. 1, January, 1979.
10. The notion of a consumer movement should not hide the true heterogeneous nature of consumerism.
11. Kotler, P., 'What Consumerism Means for Marketers', *Harvard Business Review*, May–June, 1972.
12. Greyser, S. A. & Diamond, S. L., 'Business is Adapting to Consumerism', *Harvard Business Review*, September–October, 1974.
13. Straver, W., 'The International Consumerist Movement', *European Journal of Marketing*, 11, No. 2, 1977.
14. Methven, Sir J., 'Market Research in Business and Industry', *Journal of the Market Research Society*, July, 1968.
15. Simmons, M., 'The British Market Research Industry', *Journal of the Market Research Society*, July, 1978.
16. Phillips, N. & Nelson, E., 'Energy Savings in Private Households', *Journal of the Market Research Society*, October, 1976.

Further reading

Kotler, P., *Marketing for Non-Profit Organizations*. Englewood Cliffs: Prentice-Hall, 1975. A wide-ranging and pioneering examination of the topic. Note particularly Chapters 1 and 3.
'Consumerism' (Ed.) Mann, J. *European Journal of Marketing*, 4, 1978. A series of papers of direct relevance to anyone wishing to explore this topic further. Note particularly the contributions by Mann himself (with P Thornton and G. Foxall).

CASE STUDY 17: KNOXBRIDGE: A SUITABLE CASE FOR TREATMENT?

Introduction

The closure by British Rail of the Knoxbridge Engineering works brought the problems of this once-prosperous town in the central belt of Scotland to national attention. The loss of five hundred jobs was a severe blow to a community which had seen its major industries and leading firms steadily decline for a number of years, and with increasing speed during the recent recession.

Knoxbridge has an industrial history dating back as far as that of Scotland itself. Although links with the railways have always been strong, the industrial base was much wider. Coal and fireclay were mined for much of the last century. The last pit closed as recently as 1962. Although there was a steady rundown in the mining industry, jobs emerged in new industries such as papermaking, refractory brickmaking, iron castings, general engineering and more recently plastics processing and some chemicals manufacture. As recently as the late 1960s, Knoxbridge was sufficiently prosperous to offer most of the youngsters leaving its schools a good chance of an apprenticeship or a job.

Aside from being a manufacturing base, Knoxbridge has been an important commercial centre for the nearby rural community. The shopping centre is large and contains a number of major retail outlets, such as Marks and Spencers and House of Fraser. However, trade has been lost to nearby Silvertown. The new indoor shopping centre in that town has drawn some trade from Knoxbridge.

Although Knoxbridge is within 30 miles of both Edinburgh and Glasgow, access to the motorway network could be improved. Rail links are good, but the closure of the engineering works has raised some questions about this.

Recent decline

There are now about 46 000 people living in the Knoxbridge area. The conurbation is bounded by the motorway to the west. With the exception of some more recent housing developments, the town is skirted by good 'A' roads to the east and south. The newer developments mentioned above were primarily developed to accommodate overspill from Glasgow—almost 90 per cent of the houses there are Council houses. An industrial and commercial estate was developed nearby; unfortunately, this has been especially hard hit by the recession. Unemployment in this area is very high.

The rest of the township is less well defined and concentrated. Home ownership is low, with 77 per cent of all houses Council-owned. There are a number of relatively isolated communities in outlying areas, such as the old mining community of Kintry. Here there are major social problems, especially with the aging population.

These particular problems have to be seen in the context of the area's progressive decline. Unemployment has grown rapidly. At the same time there is low demand for existing skills. The College of Technology has recently opened an Information Technology Centre. The College of Commerce has a well-established programme of work, but there has been a dramatic increase in youth unemployment. These have to be seen in the national context of long-term decline in industrial output, rising unemployment of surviving firms, and a number of major closures, such as that experienced in Knoxbridge recently.

Figures from the Knoxbridge Employment Office show that it is proportionately one of the worst-affected areas in Scotland. Although relatively small and with significant numbers of employed people in the community in relation to other areas, it is now estimated that the workforce has contracted to just over 7500 in 1982 from just under 14 000 in 1971.

The general picture is dismal, with:

1. A number of recent closures.
2. Negligible growth in existing firms.
3. Low rate of new company formation.
4. Poor prospects of inward investment.

Between 1974 and 1980 there was a 35 per cent decline in total employment in the area. At least 34 companies have closed and job losses of at least 1400 people have occurred between the beginning of 1978 and March 1983. Twenty-five of these closures were in manufacturing and construction, accounting for over 1000 of the jobs lost.

Overall employment changes (Knoxbridge Employment Office)

Sector	1973	(%)	1978	(%)	Change
Primary	386	(2.7)	222	(2.0)	− 164
Manufacturing	7226	(51.5)	5424	(54.0)	− 1802
Construction	1484	(10.6)	1404	(14.0)	− 80
Services	4946	(35.2)	3084	(30.0)	− 1842
Total	14042	(100.0)	10134	(100.0)	− 3908

Although the last few years have seen some new developments, notably a new hypermarket and a major DIY superstore, these have done little to arrest the overall decline.

Community action

The announcement of the closure of the railway engineering works prompted a number of people from different parts of the community to come together to explore ways of tackling their problems. The Regional and District Councils, along with the Chamber of Commerce and a number of other employers, met with the Scottish Development Agency. The latter strongly advised them to set up an Enterprise Trust. This has now been done with the Regional Council, the District Council providing 'pump-priming' financial support and ABL distilleries providing a secondee as director.

The challenge: 'What part can marketing play in reviving this community?'

Name Index

Subject Index

Page references in italics refer to illustrations. '(T)' after a page number indicates a table, '(F)' a figure.